A D. H. LAWRENCE
COMPANION

A D. H. LAWRENCE COMPANION

Life, Thought, and Works

F. B. PINION

First edition 1978
Reprinted 1980

Published by
THE MACMILLAN PRESS LTD
London and Basingstoke
Companies and representatives
throughout the world

Printed and bound in Great Britain by
Redwood Burn Limited
Trowbridge & Esher

British Library Cataloguing in Publication Data

Pinion, Francis Bertram
   A D. H. Lawrence companion
   1. Lawrence, David Herbert – Criticism and
   interpretation
   I. Title
   823'.9'12   PR6023.A93Z/
   ISBN 0–333–17983–8

Contents

Contents

Maps and Illustrations

MAPS

ILLUSTRATIONS

between pages 148 and 149

1 (*left*)   the Lawrence family. Children, left to right: Ada, Emily,
       George, David Herbert, Ernest
    (*right*)   Mrs Lawrence, a few months before her death

2 Eastwood:
    (*above left*)   Lawrence's birthplace, Victoria Street
    (*above right*)   the British School, Albert Street, below the Con-
       gregational Chapel
    (*below*)   the Lawrences' home in the Breach

3 (*above*)   the colliery at Brinsley where Lawrence's father worked
    (*below*)   Lamb Close

4 (*above*)   Beauvale School
    (*below*)   Beauvale Priory

vi

Illustrations

14 Kiowa Ranch:
  (*above left*) the kitchen
  (*above right*) the adobe oven at the back
  (*below left*) Lawrence with two of the ranch horses
  (*below right*) with Susan, the black cow, Frieda's nephew assisting

15 (*above left*) Villa Bernarda, Spotorno
  (*above right*) with Ada Lawrence at Mablethorpe in 1926
  (*below*) in the sun near Villa Mirenda, Scandicci; under this tree
    part of *Lady Chatterley's Lover* was written

16 (*above*) Lawrence's grave at Vence
  (*below*) his memorial chapel, with Frieda's tomb in front (left),
    at Kiowa Ranch

Reference Abbreviations

Novels

AR	*Aaron's Rod*	*R*	*The Rainbow*
K	*Kangaroo*	*SL*	*Sons and Lovers*
LC	*Lady Chatterley's Lover*	*T*	*The Trespasser*
LG	*The Lost Girl*	*WL*	*Women in Love*
PS	*The Plumed Serpent*	*WP*	*The White Peacock*

Travel and Miscellanea

EP	*Etruscan Places*	*SS*	*Sea and Sardinia*
MM	*Mornings in Mexico*	*TI*	*Twilight in Italy*

Ap   *Apocalypse*

Fan   *Fantasia of the Unconscious*

St.Am.   *Studies in Classic American Literature*

Collections

CP   *The Complete Poems of D. H. Lawrence* (two volumes, ed. V. de Sola Pinto and W. Roberts), London, 1972

P   *Phoenix, The Posthumous Papers of D. H. Lawrence* (ed. E. D. McDonald), London, 1970

P2   *Phoenix II, Uncollected, Unpublished and Other Prose Works by D. H. Lawrence* (ed. W. Roberts and H. T. Moore), London, 1968

Letters

References are given by dates (e.g. 1.ii.15, ?26.i.25) as in *The Collected Letters of D. H. Lawrence* (two volumes, ed. H. T. Moore), London, 1962

CL   Used for the above when dates are very uncertain

HL   Aldous Huxley (ed.), *The Letters of D. H. Lawrence*, London, 1932

Acknowledgments

More than forty years have passed since a visit to Beauvale Priory and recognition of 'Nethermere' led me to Felley Mill and Haggs Farm. Inevitably, when pursuing Lawrence investigations in Eastwood, I was directed to Mr William Hopkin's shop, almost opposite the premises which had once been London House, the original of Manchester House in *The Lost Girl*. Mr Hopkin could not have been more helpful. He not only answered my inquiries; he showed me a number of places connected with the Lawrence family, took me into the Congregational Chapel, and invited me to his home. His generosity and stimulating conversation then and on subsequent occasions have not been forgotten; nor the unfailing hospitality of his wife Olive, to whom I am most grateful for assistance in recent years, especially on topographical questions relative to Lawrence's fiction.

My greatest literary indebtedness is to Professor H. T. Moore. The value of his biographical study *The Priest of Love* as a reference book has been exceeded only by that of his two-volume edition of Lawrence's letters.

For assisting my research at various biographical points I am particularly indebted to Mrs J. Drury of the County Library, Nottingham; Mrs Ellen S. Dunlap, Research Librarian of the University of Texas; and Miss Lucy I. Edwards, M.B.E., formerly head of the Department of Local Studies at the Nottingham City Library.

Obligations are cordially acknowledged to Miss R. Wells and Mr D. Jones of the University Library, Sheffield; Mr P. R. Morley, Mr W. Thornhill, and Mr B. E. Coates of the University of Sheffield; Michael Bennett, Librarian, Eastwood; James A. Stone, Director of Education, Nottinghamshire, and Miss Christine H. Shinn, administrative assistant in the University of Nottingham School of Education; Charles Dunbar,

Acknowledgments

F.C.I.T., and Mrs Phyllis Humpidge; Michael Hudson of the Sheffield City Libraries; Miss Challice B. Reed of the B.B.C., and Peter Seward of the British Film Institute; Professor H. Orel of the University of Kansas; Professor David Farmer, Assistant Director, Humanities Research Center, the University of Texas; and Professor David De Laura for kindly examining and recommending suitable illustrations from the Lawrence collection at that university.

For permission to reproduce illustrations I gratefully acknowledge obligations to a member of the Lawrence family who prefers to remain anonymous (no. 1 right); to Professor J. T. Boulton (7 right); the Walker Art Gallery, Liverpool (7 middle); Laurence Pollinger Ltd (10 above right); the University of Texas (13 left and right, 14 above left and right, 14 below left, 15 above left; and, with the approval of Professor H. T. Moore, 11 below left, 14 below right, 15 below, and 16 above). 11 above left and right are taken from Francis Bond, *The Cathedrals of England and Wales*, London, 1912. With the exception of 16 below (the author's), all the remaining photographs have been supplied, with generous permission to reproduce them, by the Nottinghamshire County Library.

Special acknowledgments are made to T. M. Farmiloe and Allan Aslett for their co-operation on behalf of the publishers, and to my wife for assistance with proof-checking, and much more for critical attention to the text at various stages in its development.

The author and publisher wish to thank the following who have kindly given permission for the use of copyright material from the works of D. H. Lawrence:

Laurence Pollinger Limited, on behalf of the Estate of the late Mrs Frieda Lawrence Ravagli, for extracts from *Lady Chatterley's Lover* and 'The Flying Fish';

Laurence Pollinger Limited, on behalf of the Estate of the late Mrs Frieda Lawrence Ravagli, and Alfred A. Knopf, Inc., for extracts from *The Plumed Serpent*;

Laurence Pollinger Limited, on behalf of the Estate of the late Mrs Frieda Lawrence Ravagli, and the Viking Press, Inc., for extracts from *Apocalypse, Studies in Classic American Literature, Sea and Sardinia, Kangaroo, The Captain's Doll, Twilight in Italy*, and *The Collected Letters of D. H. Lawrence*.

Lawrence's Life

The hills of Annesley, 'bleak and barren' to Byron after the marriage of Mary Chaworth in 1805, are now pleasantly wooded. The traveller on the M1 may notice them on one side, and on the other, to the south-west, catch glimpses of the country with which Lawrence was more familiar. From Annesley Hall, the home of Byron's lost love, to Eastwood, the mining village where Lawrence was born on 11 September 1885, lie the principal settings for *The White Peacock* and *Sons and Lovers*. In December 1926 Lawrence described this landscape as the country of his heart. He associated it with happy farming activities and walks; less pleasurably, in retrospect, with his earliest love. Mary Chaworth rejected a young and oversensitive aristocrat; Lawrence, a miner's son, caught in a tangle of feeling, complicated it further, and in the end renounced Jessie Chambers with little apparent compunction. With her he had experienced deep friendship, probably the greatest of his life.

The main street of Eastwood runs along a hill eight miles to the north-west of Nottingham and above the valley of the Erewash, which forms a boundary between Nottinghamshire and Derbyshire. On the western side coal used to be transported south by barge along the Erewash canal to the River Trent, and two railway lines served the neighbourhood. One became part of the London North-Eastern Railway, linking villages with Nottingham; the other was the main Midland line which ran south from Sheffield to Derby and Leicester. Most of this second railway was inaugurated in consequence of a meeting of local colliery owners at the Sun Inn, Eastwood, in 1832, when £32,000 was subscribed for its development. As Lawrence records at the opening of *Sons and Lovers*, small-scale coal-mining had been common in the area from the time of Charles II, but it was the development of collieries by Barber, Walker & Co. in the nineteenth century which led to the rapid expansion

1

of Eastwood village. It became the market and shopping-centre for the neighbourhood, and at the time of Lawrence's birth had a population of more than three and a half thousand.

Some of the new houses for miners were built in hollow squares on the northern side of the main shopping-street (Nottingham Road); they were 'little four-room houses with the "front" looking outward into the grim, blank street, and the "back", with a tiny square brick yard, a low wall, and a w.c. and ash-pit, looking into the desert of the square', which consisted of hard, uneven, black earth 'tilting rather steeply down', with 'little back yards all round, and openings at the corners'. The squares were big, like barrack enclosures, and 'absolutely desert, save for the posts for clothes lines, and people passing, children playing on the hard earth' (P.134). Near one of these stood the Wesleyan Chapel and, just above it, in Victoria Street, Lawrence was born, above the small front-room shop his mother kept for the sale of haberdashery (lace caps, aprons, linen). He was the fourth child in a family of five.

When they married in Nottingham, at St Stephen's, Sneinton, on 27 December 1875, Lawrence's parents, Arthur John Lawrence and his wife (née Lydia Beardsall) were twenty-nine and twenty-three respectively. Before settling at Brinsley near Eastwood, Arthur's father had acquired considerable fame in and around Nottingham, for his boxing and rowing feats; he was a man of great physical strength and a tailor by trade. Lawrence remembered boyhood visits to his old cottage 'in the quarry hole just by Brinsley level-crossing' and the strange old machine 'like nothing on earth' which his grandfather used mainly for making miners' working-clothes. He had married the daughter of a Nottingham lace and silk manufacturer. Little seems to have been spent on Arthur's education (cf. P2.580), for he was employed at Brinsley colliery from an early age. He was a chorister at Brinsley, and Lawrence states (3.xii.26) that he sang in the Newstead Abbey choir. When he met Lydia Beardsall at Basford, Nottingham (at the home of his aunt, who had married Lydia's uncle), he was, in Lawrence's words (*SL*.i), 'well set-up, erect, and very smart'; he had black shining wavy hair and a full beard which had never been shaved. Genial, 'full of colour and animation', gallant and humorous, he danced gracefully and had a musical voice. Lydia had not known such zest for life. It was the attraction of opposites, felt all the more keenly by one who had recently been jilted.

Lydia was descended from a Beardsall who moved to Nottingham from

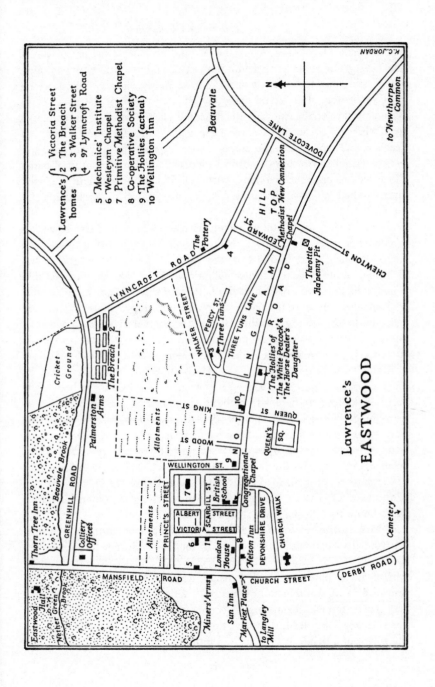

Lawrence's { 1 Victoria Street
homes { 2 The Breach
{ 3 3 Walker Street
{ 4 97 Lynncroft Road

5 Mechanics' Institute
6 Wesleyan Chapel
7 Primitive Methodist Chapel
8 Co-operative Society
9 The Hollies (actual)
10 Wellington Inn

Lawrence's
EASTWOOD

K.C.JORDAN

Wirksworth, Derbyshire, when the lace industry promised prosperity. A market collapse led to her grandfather's ruin, and her father, an engineer, left Nottingham to become a dock foreman at Sheerness, after marrying Lydia Newton, the grand-daughter of a prominent Nonconformist hymn-writer. At Sheerness, Lydia Beardsall's father was long remembered as a Wesleyan preacher. She was a great reader, found employment as a teacher, and wrote verse. *Sons and Lovers* suggests that she rejoined her retired father in Nottingham after suffering in health as a result of being discarded by an educated man with religious leanings. The man she married had no time for books (*St.Am.*vii) and little inclination for chapel.

Before living in Victoria Street, Eastwood, where Mrs Lawrence opened her small shop, the Lawrences had lived at Sutton-in-Ashfield near Mansfield, Old Radford on the western side of Nottingham, and Brinsley, where Arthur resumed colliery work. In 1887 they moved into a larger house in the Breach at the bottom of the hill, on the north side of Eastwood. Here eight blocks of tenements in two rows of four had been built for mining families. For an additional sixpence a week in rent, the Lawrences occupied an end house with an extra strip of garden at the side. There were five children: George, born in 1876; William Ernest, 1878; Emily, 1882; David Herbert, 1885; and Ada, 1887. In 1891 the family moved to a new, higher-class, bay-windowed house, the third of the first six houses to be built at the end of Walker Street. Now number 8, it overlooked open land (a natural playground) above the Breach, the country beyond between Brinsley and Moorgreen colliery, and the more wooded uplands towards Annesley and the Misk Hills. Immediately opposite the house stood an ash which reminded Lawrence of his parents' discord, for he had often been awakened by the howling of the west wind in the tree and heard their wrangling when his father came home the worse for drink (CP.36, *SL*.iv).

If Mrs Lawrence soon found that she had little in common with her husband, he discovered just as quickly that he could not live up to the standards of the lady he had admired. Small and slight but intrepid, with fearless blue eyes and a ready tongue, 'she was certainly not prepared to be humble to her husband' (*Ap*.ii). She could be haughty and contemptuous, dismissing objections with a sniff and a toss of her head. Increasingly Arthur sought the company of his miner friends and the solace of a drink or two in local public houses. Lydia Lawrence was puritanical; she rated her husband, and grew to despise him. She lived for her children; she would save the boys from mining and drunkenness, and ensure that they were all as well educated as possible. They 'idolized' her, and did not realize their father's humiliation and good-heartedness until long afterwards. He loved animals and early morning cross-country walks on his way home from Brinsley pit. Lawrence had happy memories of him, sitting tailor-wise on the rug, hammering away and singing at the top of his voice as he mended boots, shoes, kettles, and pans. He was convinced that his mother learned to regret having made 'a tragedy out of what was only a nuisance' (P.168).

Mrs Lawrence had to be thrifty, for her husband was not always generous in his allowance, and his share of the weekly wages (as a 'butty' in charge of a small group of miners on a 'stall' or coal-face section) varied according to joint output. Strikes resulted in severe domestic economies and hardship. She succeeded nevertheless in furnishing her home much according to her taste, and in a style, her daughter Ada tells us, unlike her neighbours'. The kitchen was comfortable, with father's chair on one side of the fireplace and mother's small rocking-chair on the other; the sofa with its shake-up bed was covered with pretty chintz cushions to match; and the bookcase held rows of books of which the children were proud. Mrs Lawrence took a special pride in the furniture of her front room, with its chiffonier, its oval table covered with a fawn and green tapestry cloth to match the Brussels carpet, and its oleographs framed in gilt. It was the 'cosy parlour' where Lawrence remembered sitting when he was very young, under the keyboard of his mother's little brown piano as she played on Sunday evenings in the winter, leading the hymn-singing while he pressed her 'small, poised feet', in 'the boom of the tingling strings' (CP.148,958).

Industrial depression and a proposed reduction of wages led to ugly scenes at Watnall colliery in September 1893, when a mob, organized at Bulwell and swollen by local supporters, set fire to waggons and buildings. A company of the Royal Dublin Fusiliers was called in to assist contingents of police that had been drafted in from several centres, and Lawrence heard much on the subject in his boyhood. He refers to the violence and the redcoats in one of his novels (*WL*.xvii) and two of his plays.

All the Lawrence children attended Beauvale Board School, but whereas the others began at the age of five, Lawrence, who was frail from birth, did not start until he was seven. On his first day he wept to think that he had been captured and roped in, a common feeling among the first generation of compulsory school attenders. The headmaster W. W. Whitehead was 'an excellent, irascible old man with a white beard', a martinet who flew into a rage when he discovered that Lawrence did not wish to be called David (P2.581). Boys tended to make fun of Bert Lawrence because (unlike his brother Ernest, who was large-limbed like his grandfather and an excellent athlete and swimmer) he took no part in school games and preferred the company of girls on his way to and from school. Nor did he shine scholastically as Ernest had done, and his ultimate success owed much to his mother's persistent encouragement and attention.

Not surprisingly Mrs Lawrence disliked having animals about the house, but the children insisted on having pets. They even had white rats, and hid the young ones in their hair or clothing, much to the horror of an old Irish woman, Mrs May, their neighbour at 2 Walker Street. Mr Lawrence, returning from night-shift on his customary route past Coneygrey Farm, found a mother rabbit and three little ones all dead, and beside them another young one motionless but still alive which he brought home. The children would have it kept in the house, and readers of 'Adolf' (P.7–13) will remember its antics on the tea-table and among the lace curtains in the parlour. He had to go. Then there was the pup which Mrs Lawrence's brother, a Sneinton publican, persuaded them to rear. Lawrence brought it home by train from Nottingham, and hearing it whimper the first night took it to bed with him. His mother sarcastically called it 'Rex – the King'. Rex proved to be a demon, utterly ferocious, but loved by the children. The sequel showed that he loved them. When their uncle came to claim him, and saw Rex gambolling with the children, he complained that they had made him 'softer than grease'. Rex had brought in large dead bleeding rats and laid them on the hearthrug; he had killed ducks and attacked sheep. News came that he had to be shot, and after him the Lawrences kept no more pets (P.14–21).

Mrs Lawrence must have rejoiced that her children joined the Band of Hope (which met one evening a week), signed the pledge, and sang 'There's a serpent in the glass, dash it down'; they were members also of the Young People's Society of Christian Endeavour. She worshipped at the Congregational Chapel, at the corner of Albert Street and Nottingham Road. Built of stone, with a tall neo-gothic spire, it was an impressive feature of Eastwood. Behind it stood the British School, where Lawrence attended Sunday School. He learned to love the Congregational hymns, and liked the chapel interior for its light, its 'colour-washed pale green and blue, with a bit of lotus pattern', and the large-lettered text round the pointed arch framing the organ-loft: 'O worship the Lord in the beauty of holiness' (P2.600). He inherited a religious strain from his mother, was steeped in the Bible and religion, and at one time thought of becoming a minister. 'I was brought up on the Bible, and seem to have it in my bones', he wrote. 'From early childhood I have been familiar with Apocalyptic language and Apocalyptic image: not because I spent my time reading Revelation, but because I was sent to Sunday School and to Chapel, to Band of Hope and to Christian Endeavour, and was always having the Bible read to me' (P.301–2). Biblical rhythms and references, prophetic utterances, and Apocalyptic imagery are frequently found in his writings.

Ada Lawrence recalls Saturday morning walks past the gates of Eastwood Hall park on the Mansfield Road, under the railway bridge and on, beyond a row of straggling cottages, to grandfather's house at Brinsley. The front room was a shop where his wife sold oddments of drapery, bought in Nottingham; he was deaf, invariably powdered with snuff, but generous, especially with his apples. Further on, in a country lane near the church which served Brinsley and New Brinsley, the children would visit two of their father's sisters. Aunt Sally, the sexton's wife, did not always welcome them, but Aunt Emma, who kept an old donkey, received them warmly when they had hurried to her door, past the madonna lilies, red-hot pokers, and golden rod. The widow of their father's brother James, who had been killed in a mining accident, also lived in the Brinsley area; and Lawrence had her in mind when he wrote 'Odour of Chrysanthemums' and *The Widowing of Mrs Holroyd*.

Most of the social life of the Lawrence children was centred in chapel activities. They were encouraged to attend the 'penny readings' at the British School, where local enthusiasts recited from their favourite authors after the fashion set by Dickens; programmes often included musical items. Annual diversions came with the September and November fairs, the first outside the Three Tuns, and the second (the Statutes Fair) in Church Street and the market-place by the Sun Inn. A Christmas treat was given to miners' children at Lamb Close, the home of the

7

Barbers of Barber, Walker & Co. in the country beyond Moorgreen colliery; Band of Hope 'treats' were held in the park of Eastwood Hall, the home of the Walkers. Entertainment was also provided by travelling theatrical groups; it varied from the most popular sensationalism of *Sweeney Todd* and *Maria Marten* to Shakespeare. In 'The Theatre' (*TI*) Lawrence recalls visiting 'the twopenny travelling theatre' to see *Hamlet* when he was a child, and how, as he sat 'in pale transport' while the Ghost recited 'Amblet, Amblet, I *am* thy father's ghost', a voice came from the audience 'like a cynical knife' to his 'fond soul': 'Why tha arena, I can tell thy voice.'

One of Lawrence's most humiliating experiences was the collection of his father's 'butty' wages after school on Friday afternoons from the colliery offices at the junction of Greenhill Road and Mansfield Road. There he suffered 'the tortures of the damned' (*SL*.iv), being too nervous to count the money deducted for rent and tools, afraid of taunts about his schooling, and always on edge lest the cashier (a reformed drunkard) should provoke laughter by asking loudly if his father was too drunk to collect the money himself.

George, the eldest and most handsome of the Lawrence boys, had been apprenticed to picture-framing with an uncle in Nottingham from 1887; he became a textile engineer. Ernest, the life of the home and the pride of his mother's heart, became a clerk, first at Shipley colliery, then nearer home with the Co-operative Society at Langley Mill; he learned shorthand and typewriting at evening school. For a short time he worked in Coventry, cycling home at week-ends; then, at the age of twenty-one, he became a clerk in a London shipping-office, furthering his qualifications with correspondence courses in French and German. Meanwhile Bert had made good progress at Beauvale School; in the summer of 1898 he had the honour of being the first of its scholars to win one of the newly instituted County scholarships to Nottingham High School. The award barely covered his tuition fees and travelling expenses, but his mother was happy to economize for his sake. The railway journeys between Newthorpe and Nottingham, with long walks at each end, proved to be tiring; he left home at seven in the morning and did not return until seven in the evening, after which there was homework to be done. George Neville, a Beauvale School boy who won a scholarship to the High School the year after Lawrence, and travelled with him, noticed the 'hacking cough' that brought Lawrence's left

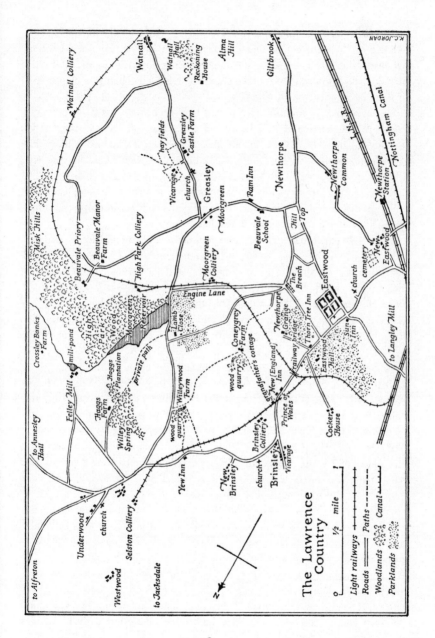

The Lawrence Country

Light railways	+—+—+	
Roads	═══	
Paths	-------	
Woodlands		
Canal		
Parklands		

0   ½   mile   1

K.C.JORDAN

hand 'so sharply to his mouth'. He stayed three years at the school, leaving in the summer of 1901, when he was fifteen. His school record suggests that his routine was too exhausting for him to maintain his initial success. He made few friends, scholarship boys being 'a class apart' in this 'bourgeois' school (P2.300).

His mother was undoubtedly pleased to see him in his Eton coat and collar. When Ernest visited Eastwood from London, and walked down the main street with her in his silk hat, frock coat, and yellow kid gloves, the feathers in her bonnet seemed to nod with triumph. She was a staunch supporter of Robert Reid, the Congregational minister. He had formed a literary society, which met in the British School, and they enjoyed discussions, particularly in religion and philosophy; she frequently invited him to tea at 3 Walker Street.

Over the years a friendship had grown between her and Mrs Chambers. It began when they both lived in the Breach and Mrs Lawrence confided her domestic troubles one evening after chapel service. Mr Chambers had a milk-round. In 1898 he moved to Haggs Farm, but it was not until the early summer of 1901 that Mrs Lawrence accepted the invitation to visit it, after Lawrence had been told the shortest route. Beyond the Breach and Moorgreen colliery with its white waving plumes of steam (*SL*.vi), they followed Engine Lane, turned left by the reservoir, and took a private path on its western side (almost opposite the entrance to Lamb Close). After crossing meadowland, they skirted Willey Spring wood, with 'The Warren' (two fields of young firs and spruce) on the right, to emerge with the red farm buildings straight ahead by the side of the wood. Not far to the east, above Moorgreen Reservoir, stood Felley Mill; above it lay the large mill-pond, and a track ascended to Annesley Kennels. Across the reservoir, High Park Wood extended towards the Misk Hills and above the ruins of Beauvale Priory. It was 'still the old England of the forest and agricultural past'; 'the mines were, in a sense, an accident in the landscape, and Robin Hood and his merry men were not very far away' (P.133). Lawrence in his school outfit was tall, fair, and pale; he was very shy, but delighted with the farm and its surroundings, and attracted by Jessie Chambers, more than a year his junior. For the remainder of the term he rarely failed to renew his visit on his midweek half-holiday.

Ernest had become engaged to a London stenographer whom he brought home that summer. Mrs Lawrence's devotion to her son was intense; she would have looked critically at any girl-friend he chose. With the vain and affected Gypsy Dennis she could feel little affinity. Ernest helped Bert to compose a successful application for the post of junior clerk at J. H. Haywood's of 9 Castle Gate, Nottingham, a firm which had manufactured surgical appliances and sold 'druggists' sundries' since 1830. Lawrence worked there for only three months. For six days a week he caught the early train from Newthorpe; work rarely finished until late in the evening, even on Saturdays, and he had to walk from Kimberley station, reaching home about twenty past nine (*SL*.v). Ernest came home for a few days at the beginning of October, staying with his brother George (now married) in Nottingham during Goose Fair. Realizing that he was very ill, George urged him to see a doctor on his return to London. His landlady found him unconscious, and telegraphed his mother. She travelled with Arthur Lawrence, who seemed dazed and helpless; Ernest was too far gone to recognize his parents, and died of pneumonia and erysipelas. Mrs Lawrence had to handle all business with the officials and undertaker; the coffin was conveyed to Eastwood at the end of the week, and laid on chairs in the Walker Street parlour. On Monday, 14 October 1901, Ernest was buried in New Eastwood cemetery.

A few weeks later Lawrence himself was stricken with pneumonia. He was nursed by his mother, and it seemed a long time before his life was out of danger. However much she loved Ernest, she told Mrs Chambers, it was nothing to what she now felt for her youngest son. On mild days he sat in the garden, wrapped in blankets. Early in the spring Mr Chambers took him to Haggs Farm in his milk-float. The Chambers were delighted to see him again, and he was invited to come whenever he wished. Soon he became almost one of the family, and his mother told him 'he might as well pack his things' and live with them. After a convalescence with an aunt at Skegness on the Lincolnshire coast, he was much stronger. At Haggs Farm he helped Mrs Chambers in the kitchen, taught the family whist, and entertained them with his mimicry; he was full of vitality. Some of his happiest days were spent hay-making with Jessie's elder brothers in the two fields which Mr Chambers rented opposite Greasley Church, in open country on the Nottingham side of Moorgreen, the main part of Greasley parish. 'Work goes like fun when Bert's there', he said; 'it's no trouble at all to keep them going.'

Yet, however happy Lawrence was with the Chambers, Jessie was reluctant to enter 'Bleak House', as Lawrence christened 3 Walker Street from its exposure to northerly winds. There was tension there which she attributed at first to Ernest's death and Mrs Lawrence's fight for the life of her youngest son. Perhaps, she decided later, the atmosphere was charged with tension between mother and son, if not between husband and wife, and father and son. Jessie was frustrated with life at home and on the farm. She shared Lawrence's literary interests, and spent much time reading and discussing the books they borrowed from the Mechanics' Institute, Eastwood.

The indelible association of Ernest's death with 'Bleak House' and the approach of another winter threat to her youngest son were much in Mrs Lawrence's mind when she decided in 1902 to move to 97 Lynncroft Road. Mr Cooper, the owner, lived next door, and it was his flute-playing which suggested the central character in *Aaron's Rod*. At the end of the summer, on the invitation of the Congregational minister, Lawrence began pupil-teaching at the British School, receiving lesson-instructions from the head teacher, George Holderness. Lacking experience and attempting to cope with a large class in a place where he was too well known to command professional respect, he encountered great difficulties, and was relieved at the end of his first year to have the opportunity of attending the course (normally two years) for pupil teachers at Ilkeston. At first it was held in rooms at the British School (off Wilmot Street) which was founded in connection with the Wesleyan Chapel in Bath Street; then, from August 1905 (by which time Lawrence had left) in rooms over the Carnegie Library by the church. Students attended two and a half days a week, first year alternating with the second; they received tuition in academic subjects, and hoped to qualify for full-time teacher-training. Admissions for the following year (1904) included Jessie Chambers, who taught at the Church school in Under-wood; she found herself in the same class as Ada Lawrence (Beauvale School), George Neville, and Louisa Burrows, who taught in the school near her home at Cossall. With Francis and Gertrude Cooper (Lawrence's neighbours) and Alice Hall, they became members of a Lawrence circle called 'the Pagans'. Jessie Chambers thought the two years of her attendance at the pupil-teacher centre the 'most completely happy' period of her life.

Lawrence loved excursions. When he heard that the elder Chambers children had never seen the sea, he prevailed upon their mother to

allow them to accompany him and Ada to Skegness; she refused, how-
ever, to let Jessie join his party for a jaunt round Goose Fair. Mrs
Lawrence, as secretary of the Women's Co-operative Guild, organized
parties to Matlock, and members of the 'Pagan' group had memorable
outings during the next few years. Jessie remembered the walk from
Alfreton to South Wingfield Manor, Crich Stand, Holloway, Lea,
Whatstandwell, and Ambergate, where they caught the train to Langley
Mill; and another via Ilkeston to the Hemlock Stone at New Stapleford
(*SL*.vii). It was on their return from the latter that she turned and saw
Lawrence bending in anguish over Ernest's damaged umbrella; his
wish to spare his mother's feelings brought home to Jessie the strength
of her own feelings towards him.

'Christmas was a wonderful time', she wrote. 'There were parties at
one house or another during the holidays, and always thrilling charades
at our house, with Lawrence directing things, and father joining in the
play like one of us. Then towards midnight, to escort our friends through
the Warren and over the dim field path, singing, with the stars flashing
above the silent woods, and the pale light over the water, was perhaps
the most wonderful bit of all. We seemed to be living in a world within a
world, created out of the energy of the imagination. Life in those days
was full to the brim, pressed down, and running over.'

After attending church at Underwood, the more devotional members of
the Chambers family had returned to the more active and fervent
Congregational Chapel they had attended at Eastwood. On Sunday
evenings they would call at the Lawrences'. Lawrence did the entertaining, while his mother sat in black, and Ada played the piano. Jessie felt an
undercurrent of hostility, noticed Mrs Lawrence's air of disapproval,
and was glad when they were on their way home with Lawrence as
companion.

In December 1904 he sat for his King's Scholarship examination to
qualify for a free place at a teacher-training college. A local newspaper
reported that he came out top in the whole of England and Wales.
T. A. Beacroft, the principal of the Ilkeston centre, then helped him to
prepare for the London Matriculation examination, which he took in
June 1905. His passing made him eligible for admission to University
College, Nottingham, but, as he could not afford the admission fees, he
decided to teach a further year and save.

Lawrence helped Jessie with the King's Scholarship examination she was due to take the following Easter. Until Christmas they met at Lynncroft Road on Friday evenings, when she was on her way home from Ilkeston and Mrs Lawrence shopped in the market-place. He helped her particularly with French and mathematics. They discussed religion and writing, and Lawrence said he would be a poet. At Christmas a shadow fell when, on inviting her to a party, he said he would call for her but for jealousy at home. During the holidays he insisted on their reading *Coriolanus* together, commenting at the end, 'You see, it's the mother who counts, the wife hardly at all. The mother is everything to him.' Lessons were continued at Haggs Farm on Saturday afternoons. On the Easter Monday after Jessie's examination, Lawrence arrived unexpectedly late on his bicycle. After they had read French together for some time, he suggested in a strained voice that their friendship was getting out of balance. Then he explained that his mother thought they should be engaged or else less friendly; he had considered the matter and found that he could not love her 'as a husband should his wife'. If she thought she loved him, they would become engaged, he said. Jessie, trying to maintain her self-control, told him she had not thought about love, and couldn't become engaged in such circumstances. She knew that her life with Lawrence could never be the same. A strained relationship continued between them for some years before it was broken. In the spring of 1911 Lawrence wrote to her: 'You say you died a death of me, but the death you died of me I must have died also, or you wouldn't have gone on caring about me. . . . They tore me from you, the love of my life. . . . It was the slaughter of the foetus in the womb.'

For four years they had discussed books which they borrowed from the Mechanics' Institute. No list can evoke the range and quality of Lawrence's reading. Their discussions ranged from novels to poetry and philosophy. In 1902 they read so much imaginative literature they seemed to be living in another world. Scott's novels became more familiar than their actual surroundings. Dickens followed, with Fenimore Cooper, R. L. Stevenson, *The Cloister and the Hearth*, *Lorna Doone*, and *Cranford*. George Eliot aroused great adolescent interest, and Lawrence was fascinated by *Jane Eyre*. Thackeray led to Swift, and *The Golden Treasury* became 'a kind of Bible'. At some time or other, Lawrence read all the poems in this anthology to her, Jessie thought. He made her promise not to read *Wuthering Heights* lest it upset her. He loved Lamb's essays, and was 'wildly enthusiastic' over Thoreau's

Walden. In the spring of 1906 he read Carlyle studiously; 'I have a feeling I have something to say', he uttered weightily, adding, 'I think it will be didactic.'

A year earlier he had written his first two poems, but it was during the year before college that his 'demon' shook poems out of him which were 'more real' (CP.27). He was already thinking of *The White Peacock*. 'The usual plan is to take two couples and develop their relationships', he said. 'Most of George Eliot's are on that plan. Anyhow, I don't want a plot, I should be bored with it. I shall try two couples for a start.' Lawrence began the novel at Easter (cf. 4.v.08), brought Jessie the opening pages at Whitsuntide, and further pages almost every time he came.

One evening in the spring of 1906 Ada Lawrence cycled to Haggs Farm with the news that George Neville had 'got a girl into trouble'. The following evening Lawrence arrived, white and upset, and startled Jessie by thanking God that he had been 'saved from that . . . so far'. The King's Scholarship examination results showed that she and Louie Burrows had been very successful; they were placed in the upper division of First Class, George Neville in the Second Class, and Ada Lawrence in the Third. During August Jessie was one of a Lawrence holiday party at Mablethorpe. It was windy on Sunday morning, and she tied her hat on with a broad silk scarf. Invited by Lawrence to admire her, his mother gave her a bitter glance, and the light died out of his face. That evening, as he and Jessie wandered along the beach, his preoccupation intensified until, with the sudden appearance of the low red moon, something seemed to explode within him; 'his words were wild, and he appeared to be in great distress of mind, and possibly also of body', she wrote, influenced by his own description of this experience (end of *SL*.vii). This scene was repeated with increasing, almost frightening, intensity at Robin Hood's Bay in 1907, and at Flamborough in 1908.

In September 1906, at the time of his coming of age, Lawrence entered Nottingham University College, a grey stone building of neo-gothic design in Shakespeare Street, near the centre of the city. Although he was too interested in creative writing to have academic ambition, he was persuaded by the head of the Normal (teacher-training) Department to work for a London degree in Arts. Unable to obtain sufficient tuition in Latin, despite assistance by the minister of the Eastwood Congregational Chapel, he gave it up, and reverted to the two-year training course for teachers. His originality as a writer was not encouraged, and gradually he became disillusioned with his studies. He thought the staff treated the students like 'school-kids', and advised Mr Chambers not to let Jessie go to college and waste her time. He loved singing, and therefore preferred the music course. His school-practice in Nottingham gave him little pleasure. The teacher whose classes he took destroyed spontaneity in writing, and Lawrence was critical of the general curriculum. He saw the value of education for leisure, of attaching importance to singing, dancing, the enjoyment of art and crafts, for example, especially in evening schools. One of his college contemporaries was the attractive Louisa Burrows of Cossall. Unlike him, she was an outstanding student, earning distinction at the end of her first year. By this time Lawrence had completed the first version of *The White Peacock*.

In the summer he visited Cossall to have tea with Louie Burrows and discover whether he felt he could marry her 'from the purely animal side', as he told Jessie Chambers he could do. A few days later he handed Jessie the poem 'Snap-Dragon'. On her twenty-first birthday the following January, she received a letter in which he said that he saw not 'the kissable and embraceable part' of her (although it was 'so fine to look at, with the silken toss of hair' curling over her ears) but 'the deep spirit' within her. She was a nun, he continued, and 'I give you what I would give a holy nun. So you must let me marry a woman I can kiss and embrace and make the mother of my children.' Louie did not respond to the 'animal' in Lawrence, but the dichotomy which he first conceived in relation to her and Jessie Chambers dictated the unfolding design of *Sons and Lovers* (cf. end of ix).

He still read widely, and shared much of his reading with Jessie. In French they advanced beyond the simpler tales and *Lettres de Mon Moulin* to Balzac (for whom Lawrence had a great admiration). He was interested in Maupassant's tales, and gave her a translation to read, telling her not to let her mother see them. They made her wretched, but she could see that he was thrilled by them; 'it's the technique that matters', he assured her.

In the hope of easing his financial difficulties at the beginning of his second year at college, Lawrence decided to compete for three prizes of three pounds each, offered by *The Nottinghamshire Guardian* for the best original Christmas stories. He persuaded Jessie and Louie to submit two for him, and won one of the prizes with 'A Prelude', which appeared in the Christmas number as the work of Jessie Chambers. It was Lawrence's first appearance in print. The story he submitted was rewritten, and appeared in *The English Review* as 'A Fragment of Stained Glass'; the third story developed into 'The White Stocking'.

Lawrence's private reading continued apace. He studied much philosophy, including Locke, Spencer, J. S. Mill, Darwin, Huxley, Haeckel, and William James. He and Jessie read and discussed 'The Metaphysics of Love' from Schopenhauer's *The World as Will and Idea*, and its influence may be detected in Lawrence's first novel. With Renan's *Vie de Jésus*, she was 'the threshing-floor on which he threshed out all his beliefs' (*SL*.ix). He was absorbed by Cellini's memoirs, the life of Borrow and his *Lavengro*, admired Mark Rutherford's *Autobiography* and *Clara Hapgood* with reservations, and introduced the plays of J. M. Synge to the Chambers in addition to Gissing's *The Private Papers of Henry Ryecroft*. With Hardy they had been familiar for some time. They read Meredith, both prose and poetry; 'Love in the Valley' had a special appeal for Lawrence. On Saturday evenings at Haggs Farm he often read dramatic lyrics and monologues to Jessie from a Browning selection; he knew *Paracelsus* and *The Ring and the Book*. Tolstoy's *Anna Karenina* was the greatest book in the world to him; the Chambers were fascinated by the farming experiments of Levin and Kitty, but Lawrence was more interested in the problem of Anna.

He had organized play-readings at the farm, including *Macbeth* and plays by Ibsen, whom he ranked far above Shaw; he admired *Rosmersholm* but disliked *Hedda Gabler*. With Jessie, he saw *Hamlet*, Galsworthy's *Strife*, D'Oyley Carte opera, and Gilbert and Sullivan in Nottingham. Sarah Bernhardt in *La Dame aux Camélias* was 'wonderful and terrible', 'a wild creature, a gazelle with a beautiful panther's fascination and fury'; he felt he could love such a creature to madness (25.vi.08); but the power of the performance and the realization that he too might become 'enslaved to a woman' upset him so much that 'at the end he rushed from the place and found himself battering at the doors until an attendant came and let him out'. He ran to the station and, finding the last train gone, had to walk home. This happened at the end of his college career.

During his second year at college, Lawrence found time to revise *The White Peacock*. Academic work came easily to him, and he was informed that he had reached distinction level in all subjects except

English. His teaching certificate simply records, however, that French and Biology were his optional subjects, and that his final grades were A for Reading, B for Drawing and Music, and B for Teaching. The report on his teaching practice shows great discernment. 'Well-read, scholarly, and refined, Mr L. will make an excellent teacher if he gets into the right place', it begins. Rather surprisingly, it emphasizes weaknesses arising from 'lack of experience of the elementary school boy and his management', and 'a want of that persistent driving home and recapitulation which are necessary'. He tended to teach the best pupils 'exclusively'. Mr Lawrence, it concludes, 'is fastidious in taste, and while working splendidly at anything that interests him would perhaps easily tire amid the tedium and discouragements of the average classroom. With an upper class in a good school or in a higher school he could do work quite unusually good, especially if allowed a very free hand.'

Lawrence made up his mind that he would not accept any teaching post at less than £90 a year; he had to wait until October until he found one. In July he helped with the farming at Greasley, as he had done the previous year, when he translated from Virgil's *Georgics* to Alan Chambers, Jessie's eldest brother, as they thatched the stacks. This year, while he was camping there one night with George Neville and Alan, a tramp arrived and mistook them for fellow-tramps – an incident which merged with the general situation to create the story 'Love Among the Haystacks'. Jessie was still regarded as a useful literary adviser, and he brought her much in manuscript for her consideration. He had been some time in correspondence with Blanche Jennings, a friend of Mrs Dax and Sallie Hopkin, two prominent members of the Socialist group in Eastwood; its leader was William Hopkin, Sallie's husband, manager of the bootshop he had inherited from his father. In the course of his effusive high-horsed letters to Blanche Jennings, Lawrence states that the girl who is in love with him, but whom he does not love, cares deeply for his writing but is a poor critic because she approves too much (4.v.08). On Bank Holiday Alice Hall, Jessie and Alan Chambers, and Louie Burrows (who was staying at Haggs Farm) would join him and his mother for a picnic at Beauvale Priory; the next day it would be fun when Louie and Jessie came to Greasley, where the haystacks were to be finished. On Wednesday, after a walk to Codnor Castle with them, he would read Verlaine and perhaps Whitman to the girls (including Louie, the 'big, dark, laughing girl' he was fond of) at Haggs Farm. On Thursday a party was to be held at the Lawrences', where they would play bridge and be jolly, after singing Schumann, Giordani, Schubert, and the song classics. On Friday they would pack and escort Louie to the station. On Saturday they were off to Flamborough for a fortnight. There Jessie found his behaviour terrifying on the shore by moonlight. Alice Hall was one of the Lawrences' holiday party; 'she sits on my knee and makes mocking love . . . she is a delightful little devil', Lawrence writes (1.ix.08). While he was at Flamborough, Louie Burrows stayed at Scarborough, and they met. Later he cycled from Eastwood to stay with his maternal aunt (wife of the Orientalist Fritz Krenkow) in Leicester; chiefly to see Louie, now living at Quorn. When he left for Croydon, where he had been appointed to teach at £95 per annum, Jessie Chambers thought 'he looked like a man under sentence of exile'. 'What shall *I* do when he's gone?' his mother moaned.

*   *   *

The Davidson Road School to which Lawrence was appointed had been opened in 1906; it was spacious and well-lighted, but set in drab surroundings of undeveloped building land close to railways and marshalling-yards. On the Norwood hills to the north, the 'round blue curves' of the Crystal Palace often caught the eye. Lawrence's main teaching subjects were art, English, and biology. His interest in flowers and natural life was always intense; it is evident in his first novel and earliest poems, and remained keen to the end. Sometimes he enjoyed his teaching; he felt sorry for the poorer boys, but discipline was difficult, and the tension often too much for him. There were fifty boys in his class; he said he could instruct a hundred, but doubted whether he could educate a dozen. Fortunately he was given a relatively free hand by Philip Smith, the headmaster. He undertook a number of voluntary duties, including the management of the school library; and was able to develop the interests of many of his pupils, often in accordance with the best educational methods and principles. Yet he was never robust, and often his heart was not in his work; his ambition was to be a writer, and some of his verses were written in the classroom.

His relations with the staff, the men especially, were not very close. At first he appeared lonely and unhappy; his later air of 'confident amusement' screened anxieties. Miss Agnes Mason invited him to her home, and he and Arthur McLeod found a common interest in literature. He lodged happily in Colworth Road, off Lower Addiscombe Road, at the home of J. W. Jones, a school attendance officer. The Joneses had two children, of whom Lawrence was fond. When his mother heard that one of them was a baby, she was pleased, for she was certain it would keep him 'pure'. As his homesickness wore off, he settled down to writing. He corresponded with Jessie Chambers, sent her poems and (after receiving Blanche Jennings' comments on the previous manuscript) further instalments of *The White Peacock*.

The first number of *The English Review* appeared in December 1908, and Lawrence took a copy to Haggs Farm at Christmas. Mr Chambers was impressed and became a subscriber. Jessie later suggested that Lawrence should send some of his work to the editor. He refused, then left the decision and choice to her. In June she submitted some of his poems. When Jessie reminded Lawrence of his promise to take her to Nottingham, Mrs Lawrence made her hostility felt. At the end of their visit, he gave her the copy of 'Amor et Psyche' he had bought, saying 'You are Psyche, you are the soul, and I leave you, as I *must*.' The next evening, after persuading her to walk most of the way with him towards his home, he left her, after declaring that he would marry on the morrow if only he could find someone he *could* marry. In July he had spent a day in London with Louie Burrows, now headmistress of a Leicestershire village school. The following term he thought of marrying Agnes Holt, a Croydon teacher, but changed his mind when he found she sought romantic worship rather than physical love.

While the Lawrences were on holiday in the Isle of Wight, Jessie received a letter from Ford Madox Hueffer, editor of *The English Review*, recommending Lawrence to visit him. He did so in September, and three of his poems, 'Dreams Old and Nascent', 'Discipline', and 'Baby-Movements', appeared in the November number. About the same time Jessie went to London at Lawrence's request, and stayed at his lodgings. He showed her more of his poems and the manuscript of his play *A Collier's Friday Night*. After telling her that he could not afford to marry, he hinted that he might ask the girl he thought of marrying if she would give him sexual intercourse without marriage. They visited her (Agnes Holt) the following morning before walking with Hueffer to lunch at Violet Hunt's, where Jessie thought the loquacious Ezra Pound by whom she sat 'an amiable buffoon'. She was tired and glad to catch the train home, glad also to think that her family was moving in the New Year to Arno Vale Farm near Daybrook, on the northern side of Nottingham, and that she was to teach at West Bridgford on the other side of the Trent. At Christmas the 'old fire burned up afresh' in Lawrence. He told Jessie he had loved her for years without knowing it, and 'mad little scenes' took place now and again between them. It seemed 'so strange, after ten years, and I had hardly kissed her all that time. She has black hair, and wonderful eyes, big and very dark, and very vulnerable; she lifts up her face to me and clings to me, and the time goes like a falling star' (28.i.10).

Whatever his views on the subject later, it is clear that about this time Lawrence thought that sexual attraction was the most important thing in woman, so much so it did not matter very much whom one married. George Neville told Harry Moore that a married woman in Eastwood was responsible for Lawrence's sexual initiation, and William Hopkin overheard Mrs Dax say to his wife 'Sallie, I gave Bert sex.' She felt she had to when she saw him struggling at her house with a poem he couldn't finish. The story does not seem wholly convincing, and Lawrence's widow thought it very odd and unlikely when she first read it, even though Mrs Dax had written her a letter, claiming to have been in love with Lawrence until she realized she was 'never *meet* for him'. Perhaps he was writing of her to Louie Burrows (20.xii.10): 'One is a little bitch, & I hate her: and she plucked me, like Potiphar's wife.'

In the autumn of 1909 another Croydon teacher, Helen Corke, a friend of Agnes Mason, excited Lawrence's interest. They had walked together in the spring on Wimbledon Common and Putney Heath; their talk had turned to Swinburne, who once lived on the edge of the Common. That summer she also had spent a holiday in the Isle of Wight, with her violin teacher, a married man, who had committed suicide after returning home. The poetical prose of the diary she had kept was the inspiration for the main part of Lawrence's second novel *The Trespasser*. Lawrence discussed it with Helen, and his sympathetic interest, and help in the reading of German poetry, earned her gratitude and regard. During weekend walks on the Downs, she began to realize that his feelings towards her were quite other than her affection for him. At first she attributed this to his absorption in the novel. When it was finished, he told her about Jessie Chambers, the 'Emily' she knew from reading *Nethermere*, the manuscript of *The White Peacock*. The two

21

young women met, took to each other readily, and remained great
friends for a few years. Lawrence told Helen Corke that he and Jessie
were tacitly engaged but that his mother would never consent to their
marriage. More mature than either, Helen wrote:

> Their conflict was inevitable: social principle and the inheritance
> of a sternly Puritan code obliged her to dismiss as intolerable the
> suggestion of a physical intimacy less binding than that of marriage;
> nor did she lack the desire of the normal woman for a unique right
> in the man to whom she would devote her life.

Helen was less drawn to Lawrence than Jessie had been, and his poems
make it thoroughly clear that, when he realized that she would not
respond to him physically, he tired of her.

In the summer of 1910 he had arranged to stay with the Chambers,
but he went home and a few days later renounced his engagement to
Jessie. She stood, she says, for 'complete union or a complete break';
'then I am afraid it must be nothing', Lawrence answered. Jessie's
kisses moved his 'sex fire', he wrote to Helen Corke; 'Mein Gott, it is
hideous', he declared, feeling he was despicable. Soon afterwards Mrs
Lawrence's fatal illness began while she was staying with her sister at
Leicester. Lawrence was on holiday with George Neville in Lancashire,
and when he reached his aunt's he learned that his mother was suffering
from cancer. The next term he came home to spend alternate weekends
with her.

He had met eminent Socialist and Labour leaders at the Hopkins',
and read his paper 'Art and the Individual' (P2.221–6) to Croydon and
Eastwood groups. Mrs Dax was one of the most advanced and relentless
workers for social causes and women's rights, but Lawrence was becoming
disillusioned with the movement. In Croydon he found the Socialists 'so
stupid' and the Fabians 'so flat'. He was preparing to lecture on the
poetry of Mrs Rachel Annand Taylor (P2.217–20) to the Croydon
English Association. Writing to her, he said he had just broken his
betrothal of six years' standing 'rather disgracefully', and muddled his
love affairs 'most ridiculously and most maddeningly'. On 3 December,
when he was at Eastwood to attend his dying mother, he informed the
same correspondent that he had been to Leicester that very day and
quite unpremeditatedly proposed to a girl in the train between Rothley
and Quorn. She had accepted him, and he had wronged Jessie ('Muriel'),

he added. The girl was Louie Burrows. He recorded his happiness in 'Kisses in the Train', told Jessie that he had not intended to propose to Louie, but that she had accepted and he would 'stick to it'. When Jessie remonstrated after his mother's death, he told her he had nothing to do with 'ought' and 'should', and that he could not love her because he had loved his mother 'like a lover'. With that he gave her a draft of the poems he had just written: 'The End', 'The Bride', 'The Virgin Mother'. Early the next year he told her that the 'best man' in him belonged to her, and that he had 'great faith' that things would come right in the end.

Lawrence's reading was immensely widened during his Croydon years. He sent Jessie Chambers copies of Charles Doughty's *Adam Cast Forth*, Francis Thompson's essay on Shelley, Swinburne's *Atalanta in Calydon*, W. H. Hudson's *South American Sketches*, and Sterne's *Sentimental Journey*. He disliked *A Shropshire Lad* but was enthusiastic over Butler's *Erewhon*, read Nietzsche's philosophy, and became familiar with the fiction of Pushkin, Gorky, Turgenev, George Sand, Anatole France, H. G. Wells, Galsworthy, Bennett (he loved *The Old Wives' Tale*), and Conrad. He could not agree that Dostoevsky's *Crime and Punishment* was a great book, and thought it 'a pamphlet' compared with *Anna Karenina* or *War and Peace*. He admired George Moore, and sent Jessie copies of *Evelyn Innes* and *Esther Waters*; he told her that Olive Schreiner's *The Story of an African Farm* would wring her heart. He read Alfred de Musset, but his favourite French poets were Verlaine and Baudelaire. Gilbert Murray's translations of Euripides gave him great delight, especially *The Trojan Women*; and Whitman's *Leaves of Grass* became one of his favourite books.

Before his mother's death in December 1910, Lawrence had begun *Sons and Lovers*. Thinking it would please her to see *The White Peacock*, he had requested that an advance copy be specially expedited. She glanced at the title-page, then at him; the book was put down, and she never saw it again. Reluctantly she had agreed to his prospective marriage with Louie Burrows, but her opposition to Jessie Chambers was undiminished. She would have risen from the grave to prevent his marrying her, Lawrence told Louie. He hoped they would find a school in Cornwall, but the plan did not appeal to her. After a holiday with his sister Ada at Hove, he went to Quorn in the New Year. His health was declining; the break with Jessie, the poor reception of his first novel, and

23

lack of the financial resources necessary to solve his complication with Louie, combined with the loss of his mother to depress him. Blanche Jennings had sent him a reproduction of 'An Idyll' by Greiffenhagen from Liverpool at Christmas, and he had felt intoxicated with it, as though he were falling in love. In March he made a large copy of it for Louie. He recommended Meredith's 'Love in the Valley', read Stendhal's *Le Rouge et le Noir*, continued *Sons and Lovers*, revised several of his short stories, and wrote 'Daughters of the Vicar'. Helen Corke was amazed that he could think of marrying Louie, a girl whose quality of mind he appeared to despise; she regarded him and Jessie Chambers as 'complementary'. In the summer of 1911 Helen was even more amazed when Lawrence proposed that he should marry her, the words coming with a tentativeness that seemed to surprise even him.

After the summer holiday with Louie and Ada at Prestatyn in North Wales, he visited Southwell, staying subsequently with George Holderness (formerly head of the British School, Eastwood) and his daughter Kitty at Eakring, then with the Daxes at Shirebrook; he then went on to Lincoln and Quorn. Back at Croydon, he found he could make no further headway with *Sons and Lovers*, and sent the entire manuscript to Jessie Chambers for her opinion. He visited Edward Garnett, reader for Duckworth, hoping to publish some of his short stories; he had also three plays and enough for a volume of poetry. At the end of November he fell a victim to pneumonia; Jessie, who was with Helen Corke at Christmas, went to see him; and before the year was out he informed Garnett that Louie, 'big, swarthy, and passionate as a gipsy', was with him, and that he would begin to rewrite *The Trespasser*, which he had sent for Garnett's consideration three weeks earlier.

Lawrence seems to have excited his landlord's jealousy, and continued his convalescence at Bournemouth. After staying there four weeks, during which he learned that Hannah Krenkow, the sister-in-law of his aunt at Leicester, would like him to stay with her in Germany during the spring, he asked Louie Burrows to dissolve their engagement. Meeting her a week later in Nottingham, he thought her 'aggressively superior' and treated her rather heartlessly (12.ii.12). He had discovered that she was too 'churchy' to be the passionate girl of his dreams, and her parents had never accepted her engagement with any enthusiasm. Months later, he wrote apologetically for being 'such a rotter', saying that the wrong was all on his side.

After a short stay with Edward Garnett, he returned to Eastwood early in February; Ada and her father had moved to 13 Queen's Square. At the end of a dance at Jacksdale, she was indignant to find Lawrence kissing one of her friends 'like nuts'. A few days later he sent his resignation in to Croydon; he hoped to make his living as a writer. He had finished *The Trespasser*, accepted Jessie Chambers' recommendations on *Sons and Lovers*, started rewriting it, and hoped to finish it before he went to Germany. She saw him several times, but he was not the same. He told her he could not write poetry when he was away from her, but she thought that, though they were together again, his mother's ban was more powerful than ever. It probably was, for he was in the grip of his novel, which he finished in about six weeks. He sent 'Love Among the Haystacks' to Austin Harrison, the new editor of *The English Review*, before visiting George Neville, now banished to 'a little headship' at Bradnop near Leek, Staffordshire, after his enforced marriage had come to light (8.iii.12). Writing from Bradnop on 28 March to Mrs Holbrook, Jessie's elder sister, who lived at Moorgreen and whom he often visited, he mentions Mrs Weekley; he had promised to meet Jessie at her sister's and discuss the manuscript of *Sons and Lovers*. He arrived late, tired, and in a cynical mood. Nothing was said about the novel until the next day, when he walked with Jessie past Greasley Church, and along the footpath on one side of the fields where he and her brothers had worked at hay-harvest. He was looking for violets; she was in no mood to discuss the novel when the subject was raised, and told him he would find her notes with the manuscript. After tea she left him at the top of Watnall hill, and began cycling home while he walked back with her sister. He expected to finish his 'colliery novel' early in April. He had written some short stories on the miners' strike which was still in progress, and the proofs of *The Trespasser* had arrived. When Mr Chambers drove with Jessie to Moorgreen towards the end of the month, they found Lawrence spending the weekend with the Holbrooks. The look of despair had gone, but he was tongue-tied. Later he talked 'with forced brightness' about going to Germany. On their way home he accompanied the Chambers beyond the main ascent of Watnall hill, where he descended from the trap to return to Moorgreen by the fieldpath. Before turning the bend in the road, Jessie looked back and saw him standing where he had alighted. She raised her hand, and 'he raised his hat with the familiar gesture'. She never saw him again. On Friday, 3 May 1912, Lawrence left England with Frieda Weekley.

Most probably Lawrence first met her when he called to see her husband at Cowley, Private Road, Mapperley, the newest residential area of Nottingham, to discuss the possibility of becoming a *lektor*, a teacher of English, at a German university. Weekley had been a *lektor* at Freiburg, and it was there that he married Frieda von Richthofen, a German girl fifteen years his junior. The von Richthofens had been a titled family since the seventeenth century; one had recently been Secretary of the Foreign Office and Secretary of State; a distant cousin became one of the most famous air aces in the 1914–18 war. Frieda's father had served in the Franco–German war and become a civil servant at Metz. His three daughters were beautiful. The eldest, Else, was married to Dr Edgar Jaffe, Professor of Political Economy at Munich. Frieda and Johanna ('Nusch') had attended school together, enjoyed military parties at Metz, and participated in society life and gaiety in Berlin. After her marriage to Ernest Weekley at the age of twenty, Frieda found life in Nottingham rather dull. First they lived at 9 Goldswong Terrace, Cranmer Street, where Charles Montague Weekley and Elsa Agnes were born in June 1900 and September 1902. The third child Barbara Joy was born at Vickers Street in October 1904. Frieda was often lonely, her husband being engaged in extra-mural evening work, and lecturing in London, as well as at Nottingham University College. He did not realize the frustration of his emancipated wife. She had one extramarital affair with a lace manufacturer who used to take her in his car to Sherwood Forest; then, on the Continent, she became involved with Otto Gross, a disciple of Freud and a member of a revolutionary, Bohemian cultural group in Munich. He wished Frieda to join him with her children, and encouraged her to think of woman as the Magna Mater, an idea which Lawrence was to resist (?21.xi.18). Gross rejoiced that Frieda did not believe in chastity, Christianity, democracy, 'and all those heaps of nonsense'; he believed in sexual freedom, and maintained that the 'great future' could be born only out of decadence. This was not quite Lawrence's belief in later years, but many of the ideas which Frieda had absorbed were to influence his outlook and writing.

When Lawrence arrived at Professor Weekley's in Nottingham, Frieda received him, and he excited her interest by brashly declaring that he was through with women. They talked in the drawing-room about Oedipus while her children played on the lawn. At lunch he noticed that she paid her husband scant attention. He was so captivated by his hostess that he thought it worth while to stay until the evening and walk back to Eastwood. He wrote, telling her that she was the most wonderful woman in England. The second time they met, he told her she was quite unaware of her husband. Frieda took her two little girls by train to meet Lawrence in Derbyshire, and it was while he was absorbed in playing with them by a brook that she realized she loved him. One Sunday evening, while her husband was away, she invited him to stay for the night, but Lawrence refused and insisted that they should go away together. Her plans to attend the celebration of her father's fifty years' service in May facilitated their arrangements, which he disclosed to his literary adviser Edward Garnett, taking Frieda to his farmhouse home, the Cearne, near Edenbridge, Kent. Finally, without having told Weekley the truth, as she had promised to do (29.iv.12), she left Montague at home and took her two daughters to their grandparents' at Hampstead. Lawrence joined her in London; he set off with eleven pounds to cover their expenses to Metz, and Frieda remembered crossing the Channel 'full of hope and agony'.

In Metz they had separate rooms at a hotel, and Frieda spent much time with her parents. Lawrence preferred the French to the Germans (P.71–81), particularly after being arrested as a British spy near some fortifications. Baron von Richthofen made his acquaintance by securing his release; he was upset at his daughter's precipitancy. Lawrence had tea with Frieda's family, and was immensely impressed despite parental hostility. He moved on to Trier above the Mosel, where he loved the apple blossom that seemed to explode in pink puffs, and the vinesticks that made the hills bristle like angry hedgehogs. The poem 'Bei Hennef' was written while he was waiting for a train connection on his way to his aunt's sister-in-law Hannah Krenkow at Waldbröl near Bonn, where he continued his revision of *Sons and Lovers*, and insisted in letters to Frieda that their marriage must not be 'clumsily handled', and that he was prepared to wait until he was more secure financially and knew Weekley's decision about a divorce. He met Frieda at her sister Else's in Munich, and they then had an eight-day 'honeymoon' at Beuerberg, by the Isar river in the Oberammergau country, with the blue, snow-streaked mountains of the Tyrol to the south. At Icking they stayed in a flat belonging to Else's lover, Professor Alfred Weber of Heidelberg

University. Lawrence had begun to feel that life can be great and 'god-like'; he had discovered how 'barbaric' one could be in love, and thought what fools the English were, 'fencing off the big wild scope of their natures' (11.vi.12). Frieda had 'a genius for living'; but it was he, she insisted, who had 'brought it out'.

Lawrence suffered despite his love, as he wrote at Hennef, and as is illustrated in other poems (CP.207,213) and in a letter to Edward Garnett where the violence of his rage spills over uncontrollably. Although he had heard that reviews of *The Trespasser* were encouraging, nothing else was right: Weekley would not agree to a divorce, his children were unhappy, Frieda pined for them, and, worse still, she was away at Wolfratshausen, looking after Else's children (3.vii.12). Lawrence could not bear to be separated, and he would 'fight tooth and claw to keep her'. Fortunately David Garnett arrived from Munich, at his father Edward's suggestion, and the two walked along the Isar to see Frieda at Wolfratshausen. Garnett was charmed by each of them, contrasting the gaiety of Lawrence's blue eyes, his weak narrow chest, and plebeian, odd-man-out appearance with the fearless gaze of Frieda's tawny-green eyes, her magnificent shoulders, and the noble carriage of her sturdy frame. Shortly before she and Lawrence began their adventurous walk into Italy, her mother appeared at Icking, and berated him soundly for expecting the daughter of a baroness and wife of a professor to clean up for him and live like a barmaid, and he not able to keep her in shoes.

The journey Frieda and Lawrence made to Italy, mostly on foot, bears witness to their love and zest for life. They had, he wrote to Sallie Hopkin (19.viii.12), 'struggled through some bad times into a wonderful naked intimacy'. They sent their trunk in advance, and left via the Isar valley, carrying what they needed in rucksacks. Late one evening, crossing the mountains, they found they were lost. Lawrence entered a wooden chapel, where he lit candles, and continued inspecting numerous devotional pictures offered in propitiation by women of many generations, while Frieda discovered a hut full of hay where they could sleep for the night (P2.29–43). At Mayrhofen they stayed at a farmhouse, making it their centre for more than two weeks until the end of August. They took long walks in the valleys, and occasionally drank with the peasants and danced in the Gasthaus. Lawrence wrote a good deal and continued his revision of *Sons and Lovers*. David Garnett and, later, his friend Harold Hobson joined them, and they had great fun. Lawrence's mimicry of himself and others was masterly; 'he told you that he had once seen Yeats or Pound for half an hour in a drawing-room, and straightway Yeats or Pound appeared before you'. In the village he pointed out everything and seemed to know everybody and their love affairs, though he had been there only a week. Though the Lawrences had only one reception room for their guests, company and conversation did not upset him when he wanted to write; he scribbled away in the corner, jumping up at intervals to attend to the cooking.

Continuing their route south, they climbed over the Pfitzer Jock Pass to Sterzing, where Garnett and Hobson left by train for Verona. Frieda and Lawrence renewed their journey to Lake Garda. Beyond Meran they were stranded high up in the mountains, 'Frieda dead with weariness' and Lawrence 'furious for having come the wrong way, the night rolling up filthy and black from out of a hell of a gulf below' them, with 'a wind like a razor, cold as ice'. After sleeping in a room over a pigsty at Bozen, they moved on to Trient. (These towns – Merano, Bolzano, and Trento – were then in Austrian territory.) They then travelled by train to Riva, at the head of the lake. Frieda received new clothes and hats from her sister Johanna, and Lawrence a cheque for fifty pounds from his publisher Duckworth, much to their relief. Soon they obtained a flat at Gargnano, a straggling village with vineyards, olive woods, and lemon gardens. High rocky mountains made it unapproachable except by steamer. They had a grand view over the lake, and a kitchen with a large open fireplace and two charcoal braziers where Lawrence enjoyed cooking; he often had to come to the rescue during Frieda's domestic initiations. Their landlord sent them 'weird' fruit, baskets of figs and grapes, and 'queer' fermenting grape juice. Wine was trodden in the street and in the courtyard. The Italians were poor but they sang, and Lawrence felt how miserable English people were in comparison. His friend McLeod of Davidson Road School had sent him books at his request, but to read *Anna of the Five Towns* made Lawrence wish to 'wash off England, the oldness and grubbiness and despair'. His plan was to stay at Gargnano for the winter, finish *Sons and Lovers*, and start another novel.

Frieda claimed that she had 'more to do' with *Sons and Lovers* than with any other of his novels, and it seems certain that she accentuated its Freudian emphasis in the hope (once entertained by Jessie Chambers) that Lawrence would thereby secure release from his mother's psychic hold. The re-creation of the past brought no relief, however. He told Frieda that he would not have been able to love her if his mother had lived, and natural impatience moved her to retaliate with a skit called 'Paul Morel, or His Mother's Darling'.

In December life was the jollier for the arrival of Harold Hobson. The delay over the divorce imposed a strain which made it difficult for Lawrence to settle to new writing. He painted four pictures, and wished he had 'An Idyll' by him to make another copy, this time for McLeod. He could make little headway with a novel based on the life of Burns, the hero a Midlander, and Scargill Street, which runs almost opposite his birthplace, supplying its title. Despite their trials, Frieda's heartache for her children, and living alone in a foreign country, they had dug out a love deeper and deeper, he told Sallie Hopkin in two Christmas letters. He would write a novel about 'Love Triumphant' and do more for women than the suffragette movement could achieve; he would always be 'a priest of love' and preach his heart out.

By January 1913 Lawrence had a new play ready, had begun *The Lost Girl*, and was proclaiming his new religion of blood-consciousness. *Love Poems and Others* was published the following month, and he sent Jessie Chambers a copy. Then for some strange reason he sent her proofs of *Sons and Lovers*, inviting her to visit him and Frieda 'some time' should she care to do so. She did not know whether to laugh or to cry, and after taking counsel with her sister returned his letter without comment. Neither of them was interested in his proofs when they discovered no change of attitude towards Miriam, and they were promptly sent back. Lawrence was hurt, and told Edward Garnett that Jessie had always looked down on him spiritually. He would have welcomed a companion sometimes as a relief from Frieda, and wished he had invited Ada for Easter. He was writing assiduously, having a second novel, *The Sisters*, well under way. He regarded it as a 'pot-boiler' for *jeunes filles*, yet it was to develop into *The Rainbow* and *Women in Love*.

At the beginning of April, they stayed at San Gaudenzio, a farm high on the mountainside above Gargnano, in 'a situation beautiful as a dream', with vines, olives, a lemon garden, peach and pear blossom, and grape hyacinths and violets 'all over the mountains'. When they left, hoping that Frieda's divorce might be expedited by their visit to England, they travelled by train to Munich, staying with the Jaffes at Irschenhausen near Icking. Lawrence was sorry to leave Italy. Reading *The New Machiavelli* had nearly broken his heart; only through a 'making free and healthy' of sex could England be roused from her 'atrophy', he believed. He became quite euphoric about *The Sisters*, which he had almost finished; 'it is a wonder – but it wants dressing down a bit'. *Sons and Lovers* was published in May, and Lawrence wrote some short stories, including 'Honour and Arms', which was later inappropriately entitled 'The Prussian Officer' by Edward Garnett.

Back in England in June, he and Frieda stayed with the Garnetts at the Cearne, became acquainted with the Murrys (John Middleton Murry and Katherine Mansfield), and met Edward Marsh, editor of *Georgian Poetry* and Secretary to the Admiralty, who introduced them to Cynthia and Herbert Asquith, son of the Liberal Prime Minister. Lawrence stayed with the Hopkins at Eastwood for his sister Ada's wedding, but no progress was possible with the divorce, and Frieda was upset at seeing so little of her children, especially Monty at St Paul's School, despite her ruses and the assistance of Katherine Mansfield. She felt 'better of her trouble' when she and Lawrence returned to Irschenhausen in August. On her birthday she stood on the verandah in Bavarian peasant dress to receive presents from her niece and nephews, who walked in procession through the meadow towards her. Lawrence worked 'like a nigger' on proofs of his Italian sketches and the revision of *The Widowing of Mrs Holroyd*, the manuscript of which Garnett had held for nearly two years; subsequently he made good progress with *The Sisters*.

Frieda then went to visit her parents, while Lawrence set off for another walking tour through the Alps. After reaching Constance, and travelling down the Rhine to Schaffhausen by steamer, he left the Falls and made his way via Zurich and Lucerne up to Andermatt and the Gotthard Pass. He was affected so strongly by the 'cold materialism' and 'soulless ordinariness' of Switzerland that he was glad to leave the country. Even in a high valley among the Alps with their glamorous snow suggestive of death he saw the 'horrible, desolating' advance of industrialism. This conjunction of impressions and high feeling found its artistic expression in *Women in Love*. Mechanization and cosmopolitanism continued in Italy, but life was still vivid there. Frieda joined him in Milan. They stayed at Lerici, and found a four-roomed pink cottage among vines and olives at Fiascherino, a fishing village on the coast off which Shelley had been drowned. The house was cheap and Lawrence was short of money; unfortunately it was very dirty, and he had to do much scrubbing before the redness of its floor began to 'dawn'. Felice, who was sixty, loved to serve their meals, and her daughter Elide was very attentive to 'La Signora' and 'Signor Lorenzo'. The setting was beautiful: in the morning the dark pines were all 'mixed up with perfect rose of dawn'; all day long the olives shimmered, and fishing-boats and strange sails like Corsican ships appeared 'out of nowhere on a pale blue sea'; in the evening the sea was 'milky gold and scarlet with sundown'. Frieda was still troubled about her children, and Lawrence was unable to write much.

There was another reason for this. His reputation as an author was growing, and they had many social engagements with British residents in the neighbourhood. They became friendly with T. D. Dunlop, the British consul at Spezia. Three young poets, Lascelles Abercrombie, Wilfrid Gibson, and Robert Calverley, called when they were at a peasant wedding, bringing with them the artist Aubrey Waterfield. The novelist Ivy Low (a Lawrence admirer who became the wife of the Russian ambassador Litvinov) arrived by invitation, and stayed too long for Frieda. Before Christmas they were Waterfield's guests at his castle twelve miles inland, with 'the jagged Appennines prowling around'. On Christmas Eve they entertained sixteen peasants, and were invited out by the Huntingdons and Pearses, who read *Sons and Lovers* with admiration; the Pearses had 'a beautiful house where the Empress Frederick of Germany spent a winter with them – and Count Secken-dorf'. In the New Year Edward Marsh made a brief visit with a friend. Constance, Edward Garnett's wife, stayed at Lerici, and sympathized with Frieda's woes.

In the early months of 1914 Lawrence made great progress with *The Sisters*, but news of Frieda's divorce caused them to leave Italy sooner than was expected. Lawrence walked through Switzerland a second time, accompanying Lewis, a Vickers engineer from Spezia, via the St Bernard Pass and Interlaken; Frieda took the train for Baden-Baden, where she saw her father for the last time. They stayed in Kensington with Gordon Campbell, an Irish barrister whom Middleton Murry had introduced to them the previous summer, and met Catherine Carswell, Ivy Low, and the Freudian psychoanalyst Dr David Eder. Lawrence and Frieda were married at the Kensington Registry Office on 13 July, with Murry and Campbell as witnesses. 'Your most vital necessity in this life is that you shall love your wife completely and implicitly and in entire nakedness of body and spirit. Then you will have peace and inner security, no matter how things go wrong', Lawrence had written a few days earlier to his friend Dunlop. Katherine Mansfield was so impressed by his views on marriage, Richard Aldington tells us, that she decided forthwith to wear a wedding-ring, whereupon 'Frieda, no longer having occasion to wear the wedding ring of her first marriage, instantly presented it to her friend'.

*   *   *

At the end of July Lawrence heard hints of war with Germany from Edward Marsh without realizing how serious the situation was. The American poet Amy Lowell, who wished him to join her Imagist group, invited him to the Berkeley Hotel, where they dined with Richard Aldington and his wife H. D., also an American poet. They 'had some poetry', and Lawrence talked lightly on the European crisis. The next day he set off with three others, including S. S. Koteliansky, an émigré Russian Jew who became his lifelong friend, for a short walking tour in the Lake District, probably suggested by Lewis, the Vickers engineer who had accompanied Lawrence back to England. Lewis joined the party in the Lake District, and it was at his home in Barrow-in-Furness that they heard war had been declared.

The Lawrences decided to stay in England for a time, and rented a cottage near Chesham, Buckinghamshire, at a mere six shillings per month. Out of sheer rage with the war, he began his long essay on Thomas Hardy, and made rapid progress with it. He had little money until he received a grant of £50 from the Royal Literary Fund, and the cottage ('The Triangle') was damp and cold. Lawrence was ill at times, and let his beard grow; finding it 'warm and complete', he decided to keep it. The Murrys lived only three miles off at Lee, and other new friends included the novelist Gilbert Cannan and his wife (formerly James Barrie's) and their guest, the young painter Mark Gertler. Soon Lawrence was working hard again on *The Rainbow*, revising and rewriting in the hope that it would be finished by January, and that his new publisher would pay him enough on receipt for a return to Fiascherino. He was furious with Edward Garnett when his first volume of stories appeared under the title of 'The Prussian Officer'. In December he and Frieda stayed with his sister Ada at Ripley, Derbyshire, travelling

33

no doubt on the tramway that had been completed in 1914 to link up with the Nottingham–Eastwood line. Frieda took the occasion to meet Professor Weekley, who would not allow her to see the children, and was most unpleasant.

Lawrence changed his plans in the New Year. His novel had become unwieldy, and he suggested two volumes; he decided not to return to Italy, accepted from the poet Alice Meynell's daughter Viola the loan of a cottage at Greatham, in a beautiful tract of the Weald south of Pulborough, Sussex, and began to canvass his 'pet scheme' whereby 'twenty souls' could 'sail away from this world of war and squalor', and found a little island colony 'where there shall be no money but a sort of communism as far as the necessaries of life go', and where all is based on 'the assumption of goodness in the members'. He suggested that Lady Ottoline Morrell should form the nucleus of this community, which would initiate a life 'wherein the struggle shall not be for money or for power, but for individual freedom and common effort towards good'. Its communism would be based upon 'complete fulfilment in the flesh of all strong desire. . . . We will be aristocrats, and as wise as the serpent in dealing with the mob.' His utopian project was called Rananim after the opening of Psalm xxxiii, which Koteliansky often sang and Lawrence wrote down as 'Ranane Sadihkim'.

Lady Ottoline Morrell, daughter of the former Earl of Portland, lived at Garsington Manor, near Oxford. Her husband Philip, a Liberal M.P., was personally a man of moderation and tolerance, but his opposition to the war made the Bloomsbury clique think him for a time the leader of the pacifist cause. His wife's appearance was extraordinarily striking. She was very tall, and wore the most flamboyant clothes; her unusually long nose was foreshortened by the habitual uptilt of her face. She was an eccentric who courted admiration. Her ambition was to make Garsington Manor a centre of culture and social and spiritual reform, her role being that of patroness, while her home became a free house to the younger intellectuals, artists, and writers. She was susceptible, and not above infidelities. At this time she was still involved in a passionate affair with Bertrand Russell, the philosopher-mathematician, lecturer at Trinity College, Cambridge. The two came to see Lawrence in his refectory-like cottage (once a long byre) at Greatham. E. M. Forster followed, but he was not so sure of the Lawrences, and they were not so sure of him. Lawrence wrote at great length to Russell, arguing that Forster could not be a leader because he refused to know himself; a man must go to a woman to explore the unknown and realize himself before he could become a Prometheus unbound. Lawrence's ideas seemed to appeal to Russell, for it was soon arranged that they should meet in Cambridge to discuss the social revolution further. Lawrence had abandoned his island dream, and now believed that the economic panacea was widespread nationalization, with payment of wages to all, including the sick, the unemployed, and the retired; 'think what a splendid world we shall have, when each man shall seek joy and understanding rather than getting and having', he wrote to Lady Ottoline.

Shortly before his Cambridge visit early in March 1915, Lawrence finished *The Rainbow* and felt as excited about it as 'a bird in spring that is amazed at the colours of its own coat'. At the same time he began to feel depressed at the thought of meeting intellectuals at Trinity. The visit was a failure. He had little to say, and appeared cold and morose. Russell and John Maynard Keynes did their best to draw him out, but he told Frieda that they talked on matters like the Balkan situation of which they knew nothing. So dejected was he at home that he could not continue writing his 'philosophy'; the 'rottenness' or 'marsh-stagnancy' of Cambridge made him wonder how people 'so sick' could rise up. Some idea of his resentment and self-righteous rage at this time can be formed from his 'black fury' at having to listen to the endless talk (which Frieda enjoyed) of two young guests, David Garnett and Francis Birrell, the latter particularly: 'never a good or real thing said', each in his hard shell, with no outgoing of feeling or reverence. They made him dream of killing a beetle that bit like a scorpion; he could not bear the horror of 'little swarming selves' (19.iv.15). Sometimes he felt he would go mad. He was sick of visitors; he had begun to doubt whether the novel which represented three years' work would be published; he was threatened with bankruptcy if he refused to pay the divorce costs; and the war goaded him to frenzies of hatred – 'I would like to kill a million Germans – two millions.'

In the summer he and Russell discussed a series of autumn lectures in London, Russell on ethics and Lawrence on 'Immortality'. He urged Lady Ottoline to act as the centre-pin holding them together and the needle keeping their direction constant. They *must* not 'lapse into temporality'; the early Greeks had clarified his soul, and he must shed his 'Christian religiosity' and 'drop all about God'. Russell must give up his democratic beliefs; 'the idea of giving power to the hands of the working class is *wrong*'. Lawrence was opposed to tyranny, and insisted that women should be given the opportunity to rise to responsibility equally with men.

In August he and Frieda moved to the Vale of Health, Hampstead, where they witnessed the first big zeppelin raid on London. In deference to his literary agent J. B. Pinker he had deleted phrases from *The Rainbow*, but he refused to omit longer passages. He agreed 'to do the preaching' in Murry's *Signature*, with a 'sort of philosophy – the beliefs by which one can reconstruct the world'. His essay 'The Crown' appeared in the first three numbers, and the magazine died for lack of subscribers. The lecture scheme had been abandoned: he disagreed profoundly with Russell, told him that he was 'the enemy of all mankind', his will being 'false and cruel', and that it was better for them to 'become strangers'.

Realizing now that its cessation was remote, Lawrence could not bear the 'colossal and deliberate horror' of the new determination to wage all-out war; it was 'the real winter of the spirit in England'. When *The Rainbow* fell foul of the reviewers, he was hoping to leave for America. Early in November the book was banned, and an order issued for the destruction of all unsold copies. As Philip Morrell intended to raise a question in the House of Commons on the suppression of the novel, Lawrence felt he must stay 'to fight out this business'. Recently he and Frieda had been guests at Garsington Manor; the house seemed to him to typify the great past of England, and the falling leaves its passing into winter. Lady Ottoline sent him £30, and he hoped to sail straight to Florida, and not to New York, where *The Rainbow* was being published. At the end of the month he was at Garsington again. He had received £40 from his literary agent, but did not know that it included a gift from Arnold Bennett (subsequently refunded). From the Manor he wrote Lady Ottoline a lyrical letter, partly 'the vision of a drowning man, the vision of all that I am, all I have become, and ceased to be', finally of 'another heaven and earth – a resurrection'. The Rananim plan was revived for Florida before Lawrence discovered that he could not leave the country without military exemption. After a Christmas visit to his two sisters (whose husbands were on war service) and a quarrel with his brother George over politics and religion, he and Frieda left for the novelist J. D. Beresford's house in Cornwall, the loan of which had been arranged for them by Murry. Frieda had been jealous of Lady Ottoline, and her disapproval had startling results.

The Lawrences' first Cornish home, a 'big, low, grey, well-to-do' farmhouse, stood above a cove at Porthcothan, near Padstow. The waves came white under a low black headland, recalling 'Tristan and his boat, and his horn'. Philip Heseltine, a young musician whom they may have met at Garsington, was their guest for several weeks. He was joined by 'Michael Arlen', who had been interested in Lawrence's Florida project; later, by his 'Puma' (the 'Pussum' of *WL*). Lawrence's 'wintry inflammation' made him very ill; he corrected the proofs of his Italian sketches and, on receipt of the poetry manuscript books he had left with Felice in Italy, prepared *Amores*, a new selection of his poems ('a sort of inner history of my life from 20 to 26'). Lady Ottoline sent him books, and a counterpane; he read *Moby Dick* and wrote notes on Dostoevsky for Murry.

When Beresford's loan expired at the end of February 1916, the Lawrences moved into temporary quarters at the Tinners' Arms, Zennor, near St Ives. They soon rented a cottage at Higher Tregerthen for five pounds per annum, and hoped the Murrys would take the neighbouring house, and Heseltine one room in it. Heseltine, who was in London, decided not to return, or to collaborate further in a private publication of *The Rainbow*. The Murrys were at Bandol, and Katherine Mansfield wept when they left the Mediterranean sunshine for Cornwall. Murry enjoyed walks to St Ives with Lawrence when they were buying old furniture, but he was acutely embarrassed by Lawrence's irrational and persistent request that they should pledge their renewed friendship in a ritual *Blutbruderschaft*. He was to see three Lawrences then and later: the personal friend who radiated 'virtue' and with whom he enjoyed 'sheer, rich, simple human happiness'; the impersonal man of destiny or prophet; and a man possessed sometimes to the point of delirium, terrifying in his bouts of rage or hatred. Lawrence's quarrels with Frieda (symptomatic of deep-seated psychological unfulfilment) were not new. They were frightful to witness, but when the paroxysm was over the two were soon reconciled in love, and behaved as if nothing had happened. His reiterated announcements on phallic consciousness made Katherine Mansfield think that his home ought to be dubbed 'The Phallus'; Frieda agreed, we are told, and it was the only thing they did agree on, according to Murry's biographer F. A. Lea. Katherine was

37

miserable, and Murry was scared. They told Lawrence the climate was too bleak, and found a cottage in the south of Cornwall, at Mylor near Falmouth.

Lawrence became immersed in *Women in Love*. 'It comes rapidly, and is very good', he wrote to Lady Ottoline, adding: 'When one is shaken to the very depths, one finds reality in the unreal world. At present my real world is the world of my inner soul, which reflects on to the novel I write' (24.v.16). The same day Frieda reported a great 'rumpus' she had had with her 'dear Lady Ottoline'; she had told her that her spirituality was false, and her democracy, an autocrat gone sour. At the end of June, Lawrence had to attend a medical inspection at Bodmin for military service; he felt both relieved and humiliated at his rejection. His gaol-like examination angered him, and the recollection of it contributed to 'The Nightmare' (*K*.xii).

Amores was published in July. He had continued the reading of American fiction, and had started typing up *Women in Love*, though the last chapter was yet to be written. He was so penurious that he had to keep his expenses to the minimum, but soon he was tired and ill, and had to give up the typing. Murry sent him a copy of his book on Dostoevsky, and was promptly told he had put the cart before the horse. Among his birthday presents was a copy of Swinburne, sent by Barbara Low, who had stayed at Higher Tregerthen that summer. It pleased Lawrence immensely; he 'put him with Shelley as our greatest poet', described him as 'the last fiery spirit among us', and thought (self-consciously perhaps) how wicked 'the world' had been to jeer at his physical appearance.

One month later he informed Murry that he and Frieda had at last 'finished the long and bloody fight'; it had been 'horrible and agonizing', but 'a new Adam and Eve' had emerged. His new novel was 'terrible and wonderful', he told Pinker; Frieda believed it was by far his best book, and was happy with its presentation of her. At the end of September, Lawrence had wished to see Lady Ottoline; in November he told Koteliansky he had finished with her and the Murrys and 'all the rest'. People and the world were foul and obscene, and his Rananim, his Florida idea, had been right. He was worried lest Lady Ottoline, who had heard she was the villainess of his novel, should see the manuscript.

Early in 1917 he prepared the collection of poems which was published as *Look! We Have Come Through!*; he thought he would call them

'Poems of a Married Man'. They were 'real'; and in them will be found feelings which animated much in his letters and fiction of the Zennor period. As there was no hope of finding an English publisher for *Women in Love* and he had little money (he would have starved, he says, if an American – Amy Lowell – had not given him £60), he applied for visas to New York. They were refused, and he wrote 'The Reality of Peace'. In April he visited his sisters at Ripley, was indisposed in London, and called at Hermitage in Berkshire to see Dollie (Mrs Ernest) Radford (who had befriended the Lawrences in Sussex) before returning to Cornwall, where he found Frieda ill. Growing more food was a necessity for him as for others; he enlarged the garden, took over a large corner of a neighbouring field, and worked hard to raise crops. The lambs ('those symbols of Christian meekness') ate off his broad bean plants in May, but the results in summer more than matched his expectations until massive storms created havoc. Called up for re-examination at Bodmin in June, he had been registered C3. He helped his farmer friend William Henry Hocking, particularly at harvest time, and began writing studies of American literature. The Lawrences had hardly any close acquaintances in the neighbourhood, and aroused suspicion, principally because Frieda was German and received letters from Germany. Occasionally they met the composer Cecil Gray, one of Heseltine's friends, who lived at Bosigran Castle above the cliffs four miles to the west. The crisis came one evening when they were there, and a light was detected through an uncurtained window overlooking the sea where German submarines often lurked (cf. *K*.xii). On 12 October police visited the Lawrences' house, ransacked it, and ordered them to leave Cornwall in three days; they were to avoid any prohibited area, and report their movements. 'We are as innocent even of pacifist activities, let alone spying of any sort as the rabbits in the field outside', Lawrence wrote to Lady Cynthia Asquith. They left for London by train; from Plymouth it was full of soldiers and sailors. Frieda, who sat opposite her husband, was glad to get away; he sat there 'pale, in a kind of after-death', and something, she thought years later, changed in him forever.

They stayed, first at Hampstead with Dollie Radford, then at Hilda Aldington's in Mecklenburgh Square (Richard was serving in the army), where Lawrence began *Aaron's Rod*, a novel in which Aldington was to notice that all those who had done anything to help the author in London were 'mercilessly satirised'. As a result of the representations he had made to Lady Cynthia Asquith, Lawrence had hopes of returning to Cornwall before Christmas. At the same time, assuming the end of the war that winter, and a grant of £1000 from Gray, he was planning another Rananim on the east slope of the Andes, in Paraguay or Colombia. Numbered with the Lawrences in the group of the elect were Eder and his wife, Hocking, Gray, probably Hilda Aldington, possibly Koteliansky, Dorothy Yorke (an American girl who, like Hilda Aldington, came from Pennsylvania, and lodged with her), and the Carswells (though Catherine was expecting a baby). A few days later Lawrence had fallen out with Gray and Frieda.

When Aldington returned on long leave, the Lawrences made the Radfords' cottage at Hermitage their home. They spent Christmas with Ada at Ripley, and then stayed four months in poverty at Hermitage. He continued working on his American essays and *Aaron's Rod*. The country around Hermitage reminded him of *The Woodlanders*, 'all woods and hazel-copses, and tiny little villages that will sleep for ever'. He wished he were a fox or bird when the question of taking another house arose; 'but my ideal now is to have a caravan and a horse, and move on for ever, and never have a neighbour. This is a real after-the-war ideal. There is a gipsy camp near here – and how I envy them – down a sandy lane under some pine trees.'

In April Mrs Clarke (Lawrence's sister Ada) found a house which she thought he and Frieda would like. They went to inspect it, and she rented it for a year. It was Mountain Cottage, Middleton, above Wirksworth and Cromford. Its high windows overlooked the deep Via Gellia valley, with the small village of Slaley beyond, on the shoulder of heights extending above Matlock. On moving in at the beginning of May, the Lawrences felt 'lost and queer and exiled', but soon they discovered their surroundings were really beautiful.

Lawrence continued writing his essays on American literature and reading Gibbon's *Decline and Fall*. He grew vegetables, cut the croquet lawn, and carried water down from the well in the field above the thicket-covered slope beyond his gardens. Among the Lawrences' visitors were his two sisters and their children, and Vere Collins, who came to discuss the writing of a school textbook on European history for the Oxford University Press. Dorothy Yorke stayed two weeks in June, when the rhododendrons and peonies were out and rock-roses were lovely in the fields. Lawrence was pleasantly surprised to find that he could return to Eastwood without his usual antipathy, and doubtless the agreeableness of his visit owed much to the hospitality of the Hopkins. His financial difficulties were eased by a grant from the Royal Literary Fund, though he regarded it as only 'a miserable £50'. In August, after visiting London and Hermitage, he travelled with Frieda to the Forest of Dean, to see the Carswells and their baby son.

On his birthday, soon after his return to Derbyshire, Lawrence received instructions to attend his third medical examination for national service. The banning of *The Rainbow* had given him a notoriety which excited much comment and condemnation in his home country, and there can be little doubt that his reputation preceded him, and accounts for the curiosity and titters which his rather frail physique provoked when he was examined at Derby on 26 September 1918. It was far worse than anything he had encountered at previous inspections; he hated the Midlands now, and the experience became the climax of 'The Nightmare'. He was graded C2 and fit for non-military service. Immediately he wrote to Lady Cynthia Asquith, stressing his qualifications and experience as a teacher; he hoped to secure a post under the Ministry of Education, 'not where I shall be kicked about like an old can'. The long war ended on 11 November, when the Lawrences were staying at Hermitage; but, though the Forces could be gradually reduced, they could not be disbanded, and losses over the years had been so catastrophic that shortage of man-power at home was still desperate. As if to prove himself, Lawrence accepted an invitation to write for *The Times Educational Supplement*. He wrote the first four essays of 'Education of the People', but they were rejected; and reluctantly he continued his work on European history as Christmas approached. His *New Poems* had appeared in October, and discussions on Socialism and local industry with Willie Hopkin were probably the mainspring behind the writing of his play *Touch and Go* in the autumn.

In the New Year the weather was extremely cold, and there were heavy falls of snow on and off until late March. Lawrence was very ill in February, but his financial position had improved. He had received payments for magazine acceptances, and £16 from the sale of his furniture in Cornwall. £50 was due for *Movements in European History*, which had just been completed; (for obvious reasons it was published as the work of Lawrence H. Davidson). When March opened he was suffering again from influenza at Ripley, and was so 'sick' of Frieda's 'bullying' that he refused to return to Mountain Cottage without Ada. Murry, who had become editor of *The Athenaeum*, invited him to contribute. Lawrence looked forward to such a collaboration, and wrote 'Whistling of Birds', an essay with a winter-spring Shelleyan theme of an emergence into new life after the horrors of war (P.3–6). Murry's later rejection of 'Adolf' seemed to Lawrence another sign of his unreliability.

At the end of their year's lease, the Lawrences returned to Hermitage. Edward Marsh sent him £20 from the Rupert Brooke memorial fund, and Lawrence thought of living in America, where his publisher would arrange for him to lecture. He had thought of going to Palestine with Dr Eder. By the end of June, when the peace treaty with Germany was concluded, Amy Lowell had convinced the Lawrences that America was not ready for them. During August they stayed at Myrtle Cottage, Mrs Baynes's home at Pangbourne, where Lawrence revised some of Koteliansky's translations from the Russian. They had lovely days in September while they waited for their passports. After refusing to go to Germany with Frieda, Lawrence went to the Midlands (where his sister was ill), and left for Italy in November. England, with a shroud of snow on the Downs, looked like a 'dreary-grey coffin sinking in the sea' (*K*.xii) as he sailed from Folkestone. In Italy three days later he felt transported: 'a blazing, blazing sun, a lapping Mediterranean – *bellezza*! The south! the south! The south! Let me go south', he wrote to Lady Cynthia Asquith. He was on his way to Florence, where he was to meet Frieda.

*   *   *

Lawrence had stayed two nights in Turin at the home of Sir Walter Becker, and found himself out of his element. Frieda's arrival in Florence was postponed, and Lawrence stayed there three weeks, meeting Norman Douglas and his hanger-on Maurice Magnus. From Rome the Lawrences moved to a farmstead in the mountains above Picinisco; the owner had served as a model to Sir Hamo Thornycroft, and it was the sculptor's daughter Mrs Baynes who arranged the visit that provided memorable scenes in *The Lost Girl*. Picinisco was so 'icy-mountainous' that the Lawrences escaped to Capri, where they had rooms with wonderful views at the top of an old palace on the neck of the island. They met Compton Mackenzie, Francis Brett Young and his wife, and

Mary Cannan, whose tales about the cosmopolitan life of Capri would
have made Suetonius blush and Tiberius feel that he had been 'a flea-
bite'. Lawrence found the place 'a stewpot of semi-literary cats'.
Mackenzie was friendly, but wished the Lawrences would 'sometimes
say a good word for somebody'. He remembered Lawrence's obsession
with phallic consciousness and the difficulty of achieving perfect sexual
consummation. At the end of February, not many days after visiting
Magnus at Monte Cassino, Lawrence crossed to Sicily in search of a new
home. Brett Young and his wife travelled with him, but his impressions
of Lawrence were not commendatory: 'a more timid, shrinking, sensitive,
violent, boastful, brazen creature it would be impossible to conceive', he
wrote to Martin Secker, Lawrence's future publisher.

Eventually Lawrence found quarters near Taormina, and telegraphed
Frieda to come. He rented the upper floor of Fontana Vecchia, an old
farmhouse on a green height above the sea. It was roomy, and the blue
kitchen (which Frieda loved) had been built by a rich Dutch family.
There was an old Greek temple in the garden, where an ancient fountain
still ran 'in a sort of little cave-place'. The almond blossom was over, but
the peaches were in bloom; Etna, 'deep hooded with snow', looked
lovely; and 'the snowy, shallow crest' of Calabria was visible beyond the
blueness of the sea. Lawrence enjoyed Sicily, but soon found he was out
of sympathy with most of his countrymen in Taormina; whether
virtuous or vicious, they were all weeds, 'cultivating their egos hard, one
against the other'. Soon he had reached agreement with Secker to
publish *Women in Love* (which he thought his best novel) followed by
The Rainbow. Else Jaffe sent *The Lost Girl* manuscript; after completing
it, he began *Mr Noon*. The spongeing, high-living Magnus had turned
up at Fontana Vecchia, and the Lawrences met him again on a trip to
Malta which they had been persuaded to take with Mary Cannan in the
second half of May.

So hot was it at the peak of summer that Lawrence used to 'live in
pyjamas, barefoot, all day'. Frieda wished to visit Germany, but once
again he would not accompany her, as he had heard that it was still
'inhospitable to foreigners'. Instead he travelled in Italy, where he
frequently witnessed political unrest, violence, and Fascist demonstra-
tions. At San Gervasio, in the hills above Florence, he stayed in a villa
belonging to Mrs Baynes, and wrote the first of the poems which were
finally collected in *Birds, Beasts and Flowers*. When Frieda joined him in

43

Venice, he was 'still stuck in the middle of *Aaron's Rod*'. Soon after their return to Sicily, they heard the news of Magnus's suicide in Malta. His creditors sent the manuscript of his *Memoirs of the Foreign Legion* to Lawrence, who agreed to prepare it for publication on their behalf.

At the opening of 1921 he and Frieda made 'a dash' to Sardinia, a fortnight's excursion which they enjoyed, though they did not think the island 'a place to live in'. In less than two months he had finished a lively descriptive account, first published in New York with coloured illustrations by Jan Juta. Meanwhile the Murrys continued to excite some of the worst in Lawrence. A year earlier he had written to Katherine Mansfield, 'I loathe you. You revolt me stewing in your consumption.' 'Spit on her for me when you see her, she's a liar out and out', he now wrote to Mary Cannan, adding that he had heard *The Athenaeum* lost £5000 a year 'under our friend', and he would know in whose pockets to look for it – 'Vermin, the pair of 'em'. When he heard that Murry was giving the Oxford lectures which were to published as *The Problem of Style*, he commented, 'So the Murrain is renewing his bald youth like the vulture . . . and stuffing himself with Oxford garbage.' Lawrence had grown 'tired of Taormina, of Italy, of Europe', and longed to go to America.

Hearing that her mother was ill, Frieda left for Baden early in April. Lawrence had been sceptical about the report but, finding himself lonely, decided to join her, making a number of calls on the way. In Capri he met the American painters Earl and Achsah Brewster, and discovered that they had honeymooned at Fontana Vecchia. Achsah remembered the lithe precision of Lawrence's walk, and how the sun shone on his 'warm brown hair', and made his beard 'flicker in red flames'. Lawrence travelled cheaply, making his way to Rome and Florence, where his admirer Rebecca West met him. She had been dining with Norman Douglas and Reginald Turner, and they all went to the poorish hotel where Lawrence was staying. Douglas was certain that he would already be typing an article about the city, and laughed like a satyr to find his expectations fulfilled. The next day, he and Rebecca walked in the country with Lawrence, and found him the embodiment of 'the renascent quality of the day' after heavy rain. He moved quickly and joyously, talking on the Etruscans, Maurice Magnus, and the hatred and malice of the Sicilians. Three miles from Baden, at Ebersteinburg, where Frieda's mother was recovering, he completed *Aaron's Rod* and wrote (much of it in the woods) the first draft of *Fantasia of the Unconscious*, a sequel to his *Psychoanalysis and the Unconscious*, which had just been published in New York. Frieda's mother grew very fond of Lawrence in her later years.

In the summer he and Frieda lived with her younger sister Johanna and her family at Thumersbach, across the lake from Zell, high up in the Alps south of Salzburg. Nusch's husband was a former army officer, but the marriage had been a failure, and was nearing its end. This situation and the setting contributed largely to 'The Captain's Doll', which Lawrence wrote in the autumn. At Florence, on his way back to Sicily, he composed the two poems 'Bat' and 'Man and Bat'. When he arrived home he was tired of travel, and glad to turn his back on the north. He could not: *Women in Love* had not been well received in England, and Heseltine threatened legal action; first impressions of *Aaron's Rod* were not very favourable. In 'a world of *canaille*' and 'stink-pots', he was in 'a hell of a temper'. Fortunately the writing of short stories amused him, and he found some of the Sicilian novelist Giovanni Verga's fiction so fascinating that he wished to translate him.

So cold was it in January 1922, when his introduction to Magnus's *Memoirs* was complete, that Lawrence looked forward to being in New Mexico by March in response to the invitation of Mabel Dodge Sterne. The almond blossom and magenta anemones were 'sparking out', but Etna was a 'shrouded horror'. The Americans would *love* a book on their own country, he imagined; with mountains and deserts, Indians and Mexicans, there was plenty for him to write about and Jan Juta to paint. Suddenly he changed his mind; he still wanted to get away from Europe, but he would go to Ceylon, where Earl Brewster was studying Buddhism at first hand. It struck Lawrence that to qualify for his great onslaught on western civilization, he must experience the reality of the inner world. There and then he wrote to make arrangements for sailing from Naples. When, on 27 February, the second day of the voyage, he saw Etna for hours 'like a white queen or a white witch', he 'wept inside' with 'grief of separation'. The ship was like a luxury hotel; Frieda was in bed with a cold, and the service of the steward and stewardess made civilization appear 'a beautiful and fine thing'. All the afternoon of the next day Crete was visible with snow on the mountains. Lawrence enjoyed this voyage, especially through the Suez Canal. He talked a great deal with some Australian passengers, but was most impressed with desert scenes, finally by Mt Sinai, a symbol of the Law, of 'iron will and ideal', the enemy of life, 'like a dagger that has been dipped in blood and has dried long ago and is a bit rusty and is always there like something dreadful between man and his lost Paradise'.

When they reached the Brewsters', and saw the forests with Kandy Lake in the distance on the one hand and the Great Elephant River on the other, Frieda thought it the most wonderful place in the world; Lawrence said, 'I shall never leave it.' The season was unusually hot, and he soon discovered he could not endure it. There were birds and flowers of gorgeous hues, but the teeming wild life of the jungle horrified him. One unforgettable experience was the Perahera, with the Prince of Wales, pale and dispirited, high on an elephant above the torch flares. The heaving elephant procession was impressive, but the tom-toms, the weird singing, the flames, and the devil-dancing, made Lawrence feel that the Buddhist substratum was barbaric, and suspect that its 'high-flownness' existed 'only on paper'. Earl Brewster was startled to hear him say that man created the sun and moon, and found him generally more compassionate, and both gayer and sadder, than he appeared in his books. Lawrence told Achsah that he had been unjust to his father in *Sons and Lovers;* accepting his mother's view of him, he had not realized 'his unquenchable fire and relish for living'. When his father came in after drinking with his friends, she never allowed him to go quickly and quietly to bed, but reviled him while he told the children they had nothing to fear.

Lawrence did not enjoy much of his time in Ceylon; he disliked the swarming populace and 'hideous little' temples, and he 'never felt so sick' in his life. After six weeks he and Frieda left for Australia; they had no clear reason for going, except the prospect of a cooler climate. On the way Lawrence continued the translation of Verga which he had begun in Sicily. After two weeks in West Australia, first at Perth and then at Darlington (on the edge of the bush country), where he met Mollie Skinner, they travelled by boat to Sydney, calling at Adelaide and Melbourne. They rented a bungalow (facetiously named Wyewurk) overlooking the Pacific at Thirroul, a small coal-mining bungaloid town rather more than thirty miles to the south. Almost immediately Lawrence began *Kangaroo*, using his Australian impressions to introduce a political theme based less on the pre-election campaign out there than on his own views. Except for the closing chapter, it was completed in seven weeks. At the end of August, during his voyage to San Francisco,

he grew tired of the passengers, and was shocked by the amorous behaviour of a film-producing group which came on board at Tahiti.
There was much to be said for the loneliness he had enjoyed at Thirroul,
but his destination was Taos.

Mabel Sterne believed she had been willing Lawrence there; she
hoped that he would write about New Mexico as he had done about
Sardinia, publicizing her artists colony at Taos and her enterprise as
doyenne of the Indians. She was rich, and from the time the Lawrences
reached San Francisco they were to be her guests. After three marriages
and the cosmopolitanism of Europe and New York, she was now living
with Tony Luhan, an Indian who acted as her chauffeur. He drove
Mabel to meet Lawrence at Lamy station but, as a result of a breakdown
on the return journey, they had to stay overnight at Santa Fé, the
Lawrences lodging with Witter Bynner, a local poet who taught at the
University of California. They had hardly arrived at 'the charming
adobe house' Mabel Sterne had built for them, when she insisted that
Tony should drive Lawrence 120 miles to see the Apache fiesta described
in 'Indians and an Englishman' (P.92–9). Lawrence thought it 'rather
like a comic opera played with solemn intensity'. Soon, escorted by an
Indian, he was trotting on a bay pony to the pueblo which stood like
heaps of 'earth-coloured cube-boxes' at the foot of Taos Mountain. The
Rockies were not far distant, beyond a plain 7000 feet high and greyish-
white with sage brush. Lawrence, who soon tired of people, was much
more impressed with the natural scenery than with the Indians or the
dude-ranch atmosphere of the 'adobe pile' where Mabel Sterne lived.
Generous and well-meaning though she was, he resented her direction
and will, just as later he was critical of her attempts to 'save' the Indians
in a way that appealed to her. He suggested that she wrote a novel on her
experiences from the time of meeting her last husband to her settling at
Taos with Tony Luhan; it was to include the 'expulsion' of Sterne and
the 'fight' with Tony's wife. From his own observations, Lawrence wrote
the episode describing her arrival in New Mexico by train; but Frieda was
jealous of Mabel from the start, and the collaboration did not go far.

Tired of his *padrona* and of the artists who called on him from Taos,
Lawrence accepted her offer of an old abandoned ranch below Lobo Peak,
among woods of pine, piñon, spruce, and cedar, and with a panoramic
view of stretches of *mesa* streaked with canyon rifts. Two Danish artists,
Knud Merrild and Kai Gótzsche, helped to remove the remains and

47

droppings of animals, and agreed to stay and assist as winter guests. The next day they heard that Mabel wanted one of the cabins for her son. Lawrence then rented two cabins further down at Del Monte Ranch in the higher, forested foothills of the Rockies, seventeen miles from Taos. The Danes lived in the smaller three-roomed cabin. Together they worked on repairs and decorations, and cut down trees for fuel. It was very cold, particularly at night. The scenery was 'marvellous', but it was all outdoor life, Lawrence complained. They would ride off to the hot springs in the Rio Grande Canyon and bathe there. His collection of stories *England, My England* had appeared, and Seltzer, his American publisher, visited him at Christmas.

More memorable were the Indian Christmas dances at the Taos pueblo (P.145–7). Lawrence felt that he was in touch with a pure, cosmic religion far greater than any associated with gods. It seemed strange that the Red Indians should make him aware of a living religion which he had not experienced 'in holy Kandy, in Ceylon, the holy of holies of southern Buddhism'. Later he realized that New Mexico changed him for ever. 'Curious as it may sound, it was New Mexico that liberated me from the present era of civilization, the great era of material and mechanical development'. He had never experienced 'a *greatness* of beauty' such as he felt in 'the fierce, proud silence' of the Rockies, looking far over the deserts to the mountains of Arizona, 'blue as chalce-dony', or round to the ponderous Sangre de Cristo mountains on the east. It was more than aesthetic splendour; it combined beauty with terror. 'Ah, yes, in New Mexico the heart is sacrificed to the sun and the human being is left stark, heartless, but undauntedly religious' (P.142–3).

Lawrence's first impressions were more superficial. He worked hard in menial tasks but, however inexpert at first, 'just wouldn't be told anything'. His feelings were unpredictably variable, 'like the wind, blowing in all directions, sometimes like a hurricane', Merrild wrote. Whatever his later views, the soullessness of the landscape was apt to depress him, but he loved the sunsets, the beauty of trees, and animal life. It was in January 1923 that he met two men carrying a dead lion (CP.401–2). Another experience commemorated in verse that winter relates to a blue jay and Lawrence's dog Bibbles (CP.375). His anger that she should go off with the rancher's Airedale reached an indescribable pitch of fury and punitive cruelty; Frieda too was the subject of his rage here as elsewhere. After such displays of uncontrollable temper, Lawrence expressed his contrite apologies to the Danes in gifts of baked bread and cakes which he brought himself without a word of regret. Hearing that Katherine Mansfield had died, he promised to meet Murry in England; it had been 'a savage enough pilgrimage these last four years', he added. He had not been able to write much at the ranch, but he revised *Studies in Classic American Literature* and completed *Birds, Beasts and Flowers*.

With a new novel in mind, Lawrence travelled with Frieda the long mountain journey south by rail to Mexico City in March. His early experiences, notably the bull-fight, provided the opening of *The Plumed Serpent* just as brief initial impressions of Australia were used as an introduction to *Kangaroo*. At Teotihuacán, he wandered among the pyramids, showing special interest in the stone images of Quetzalcoatl. Mexico was restive with Bolshevism, Fascism, and revolution, but the Indians remained unchanged, he observed, 'like black water, over which go our dirty motor boats, with stink and noise – the water gets a little dirtier but does not really change'. He was writing to his mother-in-law, with whom he had become very cordial. The catastrophic depreciation of the mark made him send presents of money to her and Else Jaffe.

After showing annoyance with the Secretary of Public Education for breaking a lunch engagement with him, Lawrence travelled in search of a home, first to Guadalajara, then thirty-five miles on to the lakeside village resort of Chapala, where he was successful. He was joined by Frieda, and began writing *The Plumed Serpent* at the beginning of May, hoping to complete 'its first rough form' by the end of June. Witter Bynner and his friend Willard Johnson, who had joined them in Mexico City, arrived and stayed in a hotel; and news came of Mabel Sterne's sudden marriage to Tony Luhan. Meanwhile the theme and background of Lawrence's novel were becoming clear: if only the Mexican Indians had a new faith, they might be 'a new, young, beautiful people', he informed Frieda's mother. Such was the danger of robbery and bandits, they were not allowed to walk outside Chapala, which was guarded by twenty soldiers, and they had an armed man on the verandah to protect them by night. More revolution being expected, Lawrence made plans to leave at the end of June for New York and England.

In New York he refused to accompany Frieda when she sailed on 18 August. Before travelling to Baden, she proposed to see her children in London, and he asked Murry to 'look after her a bit' in his absence. Lawrence took her on board; she attempted to change his mind, and they parted in anger. He went back to his hotel to continue his proof-reading; he had had no less than *Kangaroo*, his translation of Verga's *Mastro-don Gesualdo*, and *Birds, Beasts and Flowers* to check. On his way back to Mexico he called at Buffalo to see Mrs Freeman, an old friend of Mrs Luhan whom he had met at Taos. He visited Chicago, which he found 'more alive and more real' than New York, and spent a month in Los Angeles, where he met Merrild and Gótzsche. He was not happy, especially in a hotel, and thought of hiring a ship for the three of them. Gótzsche was persuaded to accompany him on a long and arduous route, by rail and road, to Guadalajara. When they came to Mexico they followed western roads through 'wild lost places' and beautiful country so strange that Lawrence felt out of this world. At times Gótzsche thought him crazy, a state Lawrence attributed to the changing air. At Guadalajara in October the days were 'so pure and lovely, like an enchantment, as if some dark-faced gods were still young', that he would have stayed on a ranch for the winter if only Frieda would come. She refused. He worked on and off from Los Angeles at the novel which Mollie Skinner had allowed him to modify for publication. It needed greater unity, rhythm, and 'psychic development' in the hero, and considerable changes at the end; he suggested 'The Boy in the Bush' for the title. His revision seems to have been completed at Guadalajara. From there a letter to Frieda's mother betrays his megalomaniac proclivity. He was 'no Jesus that lies on his mother's lap'; his wife kept asking for love, and he needed above all 'courage and strength and weapons' to fight (10.xi.23). His confidence asserted itself with Mabel Luhan; he had won her submission. She must leave the world to him; in the fight against it, he would be as the serpent, 'the serpent of the Sun' (20.xi.23). His valour in spirit was supported by the religion of his unfinished Mexican novel.

From Mexico City he journeyed to Vera Cruz, where he sailed for Plymouth. Frieda, Murry, and Koteliansky met him at Paddington Station. Soon London, fog and filthy air, and a bad cold, made him feel as if he were in his tomb. The essay 'On Coming Home' (P2.250–6) shows that Lawrence was depressed by more than the weather. He was 'flabbergasted' by the rot that afflicted a country 'pretending to direct the destinies of the world'. 'Look at us now. Not a man left inside all the millions of pairs of trousers.' Here was another embarrassment for

Murry: 'On Coming Home' was intended for his new magazine *The Adelphi*, and he had to reject it.

Frieda had been disappointed to find her children growing up and less emotionally responsive than she expected. She had fallen out with Lawrence, and been rebuffed by Murry. Visiting Freiburg in September (to consult a specialist on the neuroticism of T. S. Eliot's wife), he had accompanied her to Germany, and discovered they were in love. He had rejected her proposals; it was 'the one and only great renunciation' of his life, but he could not be false to Lawrence. *Aaron's Rod* and *Fantasia of the Unconscious* had renewed his faith in him; they were 'the pinnacle' of his achievement, and he had launched *The Adelphi* as his 'lieutenant'. Lawrence, however, had no great faith in Murry's venture; he urged him to 'attack everything' and join him in America. He had, he was convinced, won Mabel Luhan's submission, and believed that Rananim could be realized in New Mexico.

After spending Christmas with his sisters, Lawrence visited Pontesbury, Shropshire, to see Frederick Carter, whose manuscript of *The Dragon of the Alchemists* had fascinated him in Mexico (18.vi.23, P.292ff). His mood had changed. They must cultivate *insouciance*, he told Mabel Luhan; his gods had 'a bit of a natural grin on their face' like the great god Pan (9.i.24). He would attack the world with horse-hoofs and horse-laughter; Willard Johnson's magazine *The Laughing Horse* had already prepared the way for 'St Mawr'. After staying in Paris (a regal museum which provoked thought on natural aristocracy, P.119–22), Lawrence and Frieda travelled to Strasbourg and Baden, where he wrote 'A Letter from Germany', ominously prophetic of the aftermath of German economic collapse (P.107–10). They returned to London towards the end of February.

The dinner Lawrence arranged at the Café Royal sems to have taken place soon afterwards. His guests were the Carswells, Mary Cannan (with whom Frieda had stayed in London), Murry, Koteliansky, Gertler, and Dorothy Brett. There was much drinking, and Lawrence was soon ill; he persisted, made a speech on his struggle with the world, and invited them to join him in New Mexico. All agreed except Mary Cannan. Murry kissed Lawrence, who put his arms round his neck and said, 'Don't betray me.' In effect Murry replied, 'I love you, Lorenzo, but I won't promise not to betray you.' The Last Supper overtones of this maudlin scene were ridiculously fulsome. Shortly afterwards Lawrence slumped forward and was sick on the tablecloth; Frieda sat coldly aloof. They sailed in March for New York, accompanied by one Rananim disciple, the Hon. Dorothy Brett, daughter of Viscount Esher.

Murry's explanation was that he could not guarantee to keep the cause of Lawrence's suffering concealed. He was aware of Lawrence's suspicions, and subsequently wrote that, if he had gone to New Mexico, Frieda would have become his and there would have been a strange *ménage à trois*. Lawrence's jealous dislike of Murry (with whom there had been a strong love-hate relationship almost from the first) simmered, and took its revenge in a number of short stories, the first of which had already been written at Baden.

Although he had wished to return and finish his novel in Mexico, Lawrence stayed on at Taos. Mrs Luhan offered him her son's ranch as a gift, but he refused it. Frieda then accepted it, and gave her the manuscript of *Sons and Lovers* in exchange. The ranch was 8600 feet high, below Lobo Peak and more than two miles above Del Monte Ranch. It comprised two log-houses, a small cabin, and one hundred and sixty acres of forest and clearing, long uncultivated. Three Indians and a Mexican carpenter were employed to assist in the work of restoration, especially of the three-roomed cabin in which the Lawrences were to live. The one-roomed cabin became Brett's, and the two-roomed was reserved for the Luhans. Lawrence renamed the ranch Kiowa. He was too busy to write much, his principal work being the essay 'Pan in America' (P.22–31).

Dorothy Brett was a painter with whom the Lawrences became acquainted in London towards the end of 1915. She was deaf, and had a habit of flourishing her ear-trumpet whenever anyone spoke. Inevitably storms developed from Frieda's jealousy of her and Mabel Luhan, but she was amazingly patient and loyal. She remembered Lawrence in a blue shirt, white corduroy pants, and a big pointed straw hat, sitting as he wrote with his back to the tall pine which dominated his cabin. They had five horses, and much time was spent riding, into the forest, or down to Del Monte Ranch for milk, butter, eggs, and letters. Lawrence showed great courage in horse-management, chopped wood, carried water, and tried to improve irrigation in order to grow food. He often assisted in cleaning and cooking, and had an adobe oven built outside by the Indian Geronimo and his one-eyed wife. Frieda enjoyed working at the wash-tub, and was habitually seen with a cigarette hanging from the corner of her mouth. Brett typed for Lawrence; first 'The Woman Who Rode Away', then 'St Mawr'. In August the Lawrences and the Luhans visited Arizona to see the Hopi snake dance (*MM*.vii). One day Brett and her friend Rachel Hawk of Del Monte Ranch rode with Lawrence up the San Cristobal Canyon to a razor edge, and saw a wonderful view of high ranges, with the Red River shining far off, and Columbine Lake, blue-green and dark, deep down in the valley. Lawrence used the scenery for the setting of 'The Princess', the last story he wrote at Kiowa Ranch.

By autumn when the aspens high on the mountains were 'like a fleece of gold' Lawrence was anxious to leave. He had just had news of his father's death, and bronchial weakness made him more anxious than ever to escape the 'corpse fingers' of cold winds. With Frieda and Dorothy Brett he travelled to Mexico City, and then on to Oaxaca for the winter. Writing to Rachel Hawk's husband, he reported that the climate was perfect, and his chest and throat better. He loved the flowers, and enjoyed market visits, though Indians sometimes called 'Christo! Christo!' after him. Convinced that Chapala had been too tamed and 'touristy' to reveal the spirit of Mexico, he revised what he had written of *The Plumed Serpent*, and finished the novel by the beginning of February 1925, in addition to four *Mornings in Mexico* sketches. Dorothy Brett had typed for him, and they had gone into the desert, Lawrence to write and she to sketch, until jealousy flared up and she had to go. Brett stayed at Del Monte Ranch, and forwarded the Lawrences' letters, among them some from Murry, which provoked an abusive reply (28.i.25; cf. 17.xi.24). Lawrence was ill, suffering from malaria and dysentery. He had thought of returning to England, but tuberculosis was diagnosed in Mexico City, and he was told that a sea voyage just then could be fatal. It was during his illness in Mexico City that he wrote the fragment 'The Flying Fish', the visionary creation of one so near death that he was unable to continue it. The Lawrences reached Del Monte Ranch on 1 April, and stayed there a few days until Kiowa was ready for the invalid. Dorothy Brett stayed on at Del Monte Ranch, where she had her own house and friends.

Frieda was delighted to be in her home again, but there were cold winds, and Lawrence suffered. He would lie in the porch when it was sunny and warm, 'with the pine-trees round, and the desert away below, and the Sangre de Cristo mountains with their snow pale and bluish' blocking the view south to Mexico. The Indian Trinidad and his wife did most of the work on the ranch. Soon Lawrence was busy writing his play *David*, the idea of which had come to him from a discussion with the actress Ida Rauh, a friend of Mabel Luhan. It was finished in May; later he wrote 'Reflections on the Death of a Porcupine' and other essays (P2). Health was his major preoccupation, and he spent as much time as he could out of doors. He had acquired poultry; he had his horses to attend to; then he bought Susan, a black cow he often milked himself. When there was water, he improved the irrigation, making a garden, and producing more fodder in the field of alfalfa which had been sown by a previous rancher. Dorothy Brett's painting interested him, and occasionally he indicated with supreme confidence how she could impart greater life to her pictures. He avoided Taos. Frieda's nephew 'Friedel' Jaffe stayed at the ranch in the summer while Lawrence recuperated. Winter there was out of the question, but Lawrence did not look forward to visiting England, and regretted having to leave Kiowa, his horses, 'black-eyed Susan', the cat Timsy Wemyss, and the white cock Moses. In New York, after travelling by train via Denver and Chicago, he met his new American publishers, the Knopfs. He and Frieda attended a play at Greenwich Village Theatre, and ate mutton chops by a driftwood fire one night on the shore of Long Island. They were back in London at the beginning of October; it was foggy, and the general air, with a million and a quarter unemployed, was disconsolate.

*   *   *

Frieda was anxious to see her children again, but their 'suburban bounce and *suffisance*' were too much for Lawrence. Of 'the old crowd' of friends they saw only the Carswells and Eders; Compton Mackenzie and his wife lunched with them at their hotel. They then visited the Midlands, staying two weeks with Lawrence's sisters, and motoring 'all over' his 'well-known Derbyshire'. He had refused to visit Murry and his wife and baby on the Dorset coast, and was pleased to tell Dorothy Brett (still in New Mexico) that *The Adelphi* editor had 'got Jesus, badly and nastily' and *The Nation* had compared him to Pecksniff. He came to see the Lawrences just before they left London to stay with Frieda's ageing mother at Baden. Thence they moved to Spotorno, west of Genoa, where Lawrence received from Vere Collins a copy of his European history suitably amended for Irish schools, together with Murry's work on Keats, which inspired the subtle denigration of 'quite good . . . but oh heaven, so die-away – the text might be: Oh lap up Shakespeare till you've cleaned the dish, and you may hope to swoon into raptures and die an early but beautiful death at 25'. Soon afterwards Lawrence rented the three-storeyed Villa Bernarda at Spotorno from Angelo Ravagli, Frieda's future husband.

Lawrence immediately informed Murry that there was room for him and his family. The invitation was neither warm nor explicit (19.xi.25), and nothing came of it, to Lawrence's exasperation. Dorothy Brett was in Capri, and offered to do more typing; Lawrence sent her 'Sun' and, at the end of the year, 'Glad Ghosts'. She probably typed the anti-Murry story 'Smile' about the same time (cf. 29.vii.26). When Murry asked him to share *The Adelphi* with him, he told him to throw it to the devil, and not to take himself so seriously; there was no sense in trying to ram oneself down people's throats. Perhaps Lawrence already felt that his zeal had carried him too far in *The Plumed Serpent*. He still dreamt of life on a ship, now in the Mediterranean, visiting 'the Isles of Greece' and passing through the Bosphorus; Rananim was 'sunk out of sight'. Barbara Weekley's visit at the end of the year led to the writing of 'The Virgin and the Gipsy'. Early in 1926 Frieda began translating *David* enthusiastically into German; *The Plumed Serpent* was published, and she thought it Lawrence's best book. It rained; the house was fireless and cold, and Lawrence had influenza. When his sister Ada came on a visit with a friend, she made her disapproval so evident that Frieda took the first opportunity, when both her daughters arrived, of joining them in their hotel and staying with them until Ada left.

Lawrence also left, spending a week with his sister at Monte Carlo on her way home; he then visited the Brewsters in Capri, and helped them to pack for India. Mackenzie was away on his Channel island, but Dorothy Brett was pleased to see Lawrence again, and accompanied him on the mainland (where they met Millicent Beveridge, who had painted his portrait in Sicily) until she had to leave for Naples to collect her papers for readmission to the States. Lawrence's visits to friends led him to Rome, Assisi, Pisa, Florence, and Ravenna, before he returned to Frieda and her daughters at Easter. 'One must be able to forget a lot and go on', he wrote to his mother-in-law (4.iv.26). It amused him to see Frieda's daughters 'fly at her very much in her own style'; the effect was to make her less overbearing and more appreciative of him.

They all stayed in Florence until Elsa and Barbara Weekley left for London. Then Lawrence rented the upper half of Villa Mirenda at Scandicci, seven miles from the city, as a centre from which to study the old Etruscan places. Here they became very friendly with the artist Arthur Gair Wilkinson and his family. Brett had returned to America to take care of Kiowa Ranch. In July the Lawrences went to Baden to celebrate the Baroness's seventy-fifth birthday. In early August they were in London. After meeting Frieda's son Montague, now twenty-five and quick to notice his step-father's accent, Lawrence set off for Scotland, to stay with Millicent Beveridge at Newtonmore. Except for 'one perfect day', it was very wet, but they made an excursion via Fort William and Malaig to Skye. A holiday of more than two weeks with Frieda and Lawrence's sisters followed at Sutton-on-Sea, Lincolnshire. It was a coast he had always liked, and he found he liked England again, especially the common people. There was something 'twinkling and nascent' about them; they were 'not finished'. Miners were still out when he returned to Eastwood, though the General Strike was over. He went over the old ground with Willie Hopkin; by the pond at Felley Mill he looked across to Haggs Farm, and 'a terrible look of pain' crossed his face. Asked at the end of the walk when he would come again, he answered 'Never! I hate the damned place.'

There is a tradition in the Sitwell family that the Lawrences visited Renishaw Hall. Lawrence would certainly have been interested, after meeting Sir George and Lady Ida Sitwell at the Castle of Montegufoni in June (?) 1926 (CL.917,923), and an unpublished letter shows that he had hoped to see the Sitwells at Renishaw (cf. 29.vii.26). Wragby Hall and its surroundings in *Lady Chatterley's Lover* certainly have distinctive features which are to be found there, and Lawrence's return to the Midlands twice within a year provided searing impressions of the socio-economic contrast and conflict which are at the heart of the 'short long story' or 'little novel' he began soon after his return to Scandicci. He wrote much of the early part in the woods. This venture, like the second he began at Villa Mirenda, was destined to revive, magnify, and perpetuate the notoriety associated with his name. He had been busy painting the house ('windowframes by the mile, doors by the acre') when Aldous Huxley and his wife Maria arrived in their new car, hoping Lawrence would buy their old one. He was not interested, but he accepted the four old daubed canvases Maria wanted to dispose of, and he tried his hand at pictures. He called the first 'Unholy Family' because 'the *bambino* – with a *nimbus* – is just watching anxiously to see the young man give the semi-nude woman *un gros baiser*'. His next picture was a scene from Boccaccio's story of the gardener and the nuns. Painting was 'fun', and a change from writing; he enjoyed expressing his ideas and feelings on canvas so much that he went on and on, painting 'no picture that won't shock people's castrated social spirituality'. This, whether it was intended originally or not, became a leading objective in *Lady Chatterley's Lover*; when he finished the first version of the story in March 1927, he was certain that it would never be published.

While Frieda was on a visit to her mother, Lawrence stayed with the Brewsters at Ravello (above Amalfi), and then visited Cerveteri, Tarquinia, Vulci, and Volterra with Earl to inspect Etruscan tombs. He had read much on the subject, and hoped to make further inspections. Seeing a toy white rooster escaping from an egg in a shop window on this Easter tour, Brewster remarked, 'The Escaped Cock – a story of the Resurrection'. The story which became 'The Man Who Died' was already germinating; the first part, soon finished, was called 'The Escaped Cock'. Achsah Brewster remembered Lawrence's gaiety; his knowledge of German, French, and English folk-song seemed endless. He still used the rainbow as a symbol of fulfilment in marriage. Two essays written in the spring of 1927 provide testimony to his delight in flowering scenes around Scandicci, and in the song of nightingales that hardly ceased during spring and summer (P.40–58).

He had already begun the second version of *Lady Chatterley*. Bronchial colds and malaria in May made it impossible for him to attend the London production of *David* or return to his ranch, as Brett wished. He began writing his Etruscan essays in June, but a visit to Aldous and Maria Huxley at Forte dei Marmi on the Ligurian coast, and sea-bathing there, aggravated his condition, and in July he suffered a series of bronchial hemorrhages. The heat was too much for him, but he managed to 'crawl' into a *wagon-lit* and travel with Frieda to the Austrian Tyrol, where the cooler climate soon brought relief. Frieda's sister Johanna was staying near; she had exchanged her army officer husband for a banker, and was still unhappy. On wet days Lawrence continued translating Verga. At Irschenhausen, where they all joined Else Jaffe (and where the Lawrences had stayed in 1913), he finished *Cavalleria Rusticana* towards the end of September. At Baden he refused to enter a sanatorium, and resorted to inhalation treatment an hour every morning. By the late autumn he was weary of Italy, and pined for New Mexico: 'anything to shake off this stupor and have a bit of fun in life. I'd even go to Hell, en route.' After thinking of publishing it privately, he began to write *Lady Chatterley's Lover* all over again, and finished it early in January.

Switzerland was recommended for Lawrence's health, and he and Frieda spent seven weeks at Les Diablerets, where they met Aldous Huxley, his brother Julian, and their wives. Lawrence prepared a slightly expurgated version of his novel for the general public, and sent copies to his two publishers. He had decided to publish an unexpurgated edition privately, and Mrs Carswell in London and Maria Huxley prepared the complete typescript between them. Julian Huxley's wife read the manuscript and strongly disapproved; she told Lawrence 'rather savagely' that the title might just as well be 'John Thomas and Lady Jane', and Lawrence promptly accepted it. He took the complete typescript to his publisher Orioli in Florence soon after his return to Villa Mirenda in early March, and was not surprised to hear that his English publisher Martin Secker had rejected the novel.

Barbara Weekley arrived suddenly, and suggested that Dorothy Warren might like to exhibit Lawrence's pictures in London. He wrote, expressing an interest, and enclosing a few order forms for his 'nice new phallic novel'. He had continued his painting at Villa Mirenda: one small picture called 'Dandelions' showed a man urinating; another, in oil, of the rape of the Sabine women, might, he suggested, be called 'A Study in Arses'. For one who had consistently spurned worldly wealth, the business acumen which accompanied his eagerness to sell his most daring book may seem a revelation. Undoubtedly it reflects his pugnacity, but mercenary motivation is clear. He hoped he could afford to sail with Frieda in the autumn to San Francisco, stay in Santa Fé, and return to his ranch in the spring; deep down, he must have been worried at the increasing health expenditure which he could see looming ahead; even more, about Frieda's future.

When the Brewsters came to Florence in May, they were shocked at Lawrence's appearance, and decided they must accompany him and Frieda to Switzerland in June. They were at the Grand Hotel, Chexbres-sur-Vevey, when his copy of *Lady Chatterley* arrived; it was a handsome volume, and he was very pleased with it. The weather proving too hot, they moved up to Gsteig-bei-Gstaad, where the Brewsters stayed at a hotel, while the Lawrences occupied a peasant chalet on the mountain side higher up. Lawrence was not fit for strenuous walking, and the Brewsters often called. Sometimes he read essays which he was writing for newspapers. (They were included in *Assorted Articles*; 'Insouciance' presents a scene at the Grand Hotel, Chexbres, and indicates the kind of authorial renunciation Lawrence had made since the completion of *The Plumed Serpent*.) He was at the centre of correspondence dealing with the tricky business of distributing his phallic novel without creating a public stir; but booksellers were cancelling orders, police raids were rumoured, and steps had to be taken to have unsold copies in England safely stowed. Lawrence thought of raising the price. By the end of August he estimated that the gross receipts were £980 and the expenses about £300. His sister Emily arrived with her nineteen-year-old daughter, and Lawrence had to hide the novel like a skeleton in the cupboard. He painted several pictures at Gsteig, wrote 'The Blue Moccasins' and the second part of 'The Escaped Cock', and took an active interest in preparations for his London 'picture show'. Koteliansky was 'scared stiff' at the prospect, and warned Lawrence that his enemies were waiting to pounce. Before leaving for Baden in September, Lawrence heard what huge profits dealers were making on his book in America, and raised the publishing price to four guineas.

He relinquished Villa Mirenda, and by the middle of August had joined the Aldingtons (Richard Aldington and Dorothy Yorke) at the 'fortress' on the island of Port-Cros near Toulon. His month there was not a happy one. He disliked islands, and he caught a cold from Frieda; reviews of his last book of stories, *The Woman Who Rode Away*, were not encouraging, and English papers had begun their attack on *Lady Chatterley*. He read furthermore Aldous Huxley's *Point Counter Point* (in which he appears as Rampion) and the first part of Aldington's *Death of a Hero*, and the nihilism of both (their relish for murder, suicide, and rape) made him feel ill.

With memories of Katherine Mansfield, the Lawrences spent their winter on the mainland, at the Hôtel Beau Rivage, Bandol. He was glad to renew friendly correspondence with Lady Ottoline Morrell, but anxious that she should not misunderstand the aim of his latest novel. Questions arising from its distribution were still to the fore, and he wished he had many more copies of the cheaper edition to undersell pirate presses. He prepared a long introductory essay for an American edition of his paintings, and continued the lucrative writing of short essays for London newspapers. More important was the series of *pensées* ('pansies'), a light verse divertissement, 'nice and peppery', which he finished by the end of the year.

The surreptitious distribution of *Lady Chatterley* in England had not escaped the attention of the Home Secretary, Sir William Joynson-Hicks ('Jix'); copies were seized and sent, with the manuscripts of *Pansies* and of the introductory essay on painting (which Lawrence had mailed to his literary agent), to the Director of Public Prosecutions. One outcome was the omission of fourteen poems in the edition of *Pansies* which appeared in the summer of 1929.

In the meantime he had written the story 'Mother and Daughter', been visited by Ada (who was depressed and wished to get away from the Midlands), and had left Bandol. Frieda visited her mother while he was in Paris negotiating a popular edition of *Lady Chatterley*. He stayed a week with Aldous and Maria Huxley at Suresnes and, with Frieda, visited Harry Crosby at Ermenonville. (Crosby and his wife managed the Black Sun Press, Paris, and published Lawrence's 'Sun' and 'The Escaped Cock'; Lawrence admired Crosby's poetry, and wrote a preface to his *Chariot of the Sun*, P.255–62.) They then decided to try Majorca, but Lawrence found it expensive and disliked the dead mask-like Spanish faces (rather like city English, he thought), while Frieda preferred Italy. Hearing he was ill, Murry suggested a visit to Majorca, but Lawrence told him not to think of it; they were 'a dissonance', and it was better 'to let one another alone, for ever' (20.v.29). He continued writing the 'More Pansies' poems. Frieda broke her ankle among the rocks after bathing, and went to London about the middle of June to receive specialist attention and visit Lawrence's exhibition at the Warren Gallery. He stayed with the Huxleys at Forte dei Marmi (CP.625), and then proceeded to Florence, where he learned on 10 July that thirteen of his exhibited pictures had been seized by the police. He did not wish them to be burned, as seemed inevitable if he opposed the law, and advised that the exhibition be wound up 'soon'.

With Frieda he left Florence for Baden; he enjoyed listening to orchestral concerts, but hated the bourgeois crowds, and was unhappy higher up at the Plätter, where they stayed to please the Baroness. It proved wet and cold; the hotel was crowded, and Lawrence was bored and thoroughly depressed. He was in Baden when the 'trial' of his pictures began. No legal decision on the question of their obscenity was reached, for they were withdrawn with the assurance that they would never be exhibited again. Lawrence was provoked to write some 'nice stinging nettles', and on 25 August, a fortnight after Frieda's fiftieth birthday, they left for Bavaria.

There was a steady, if not increasing, demand for *Lady Chatterley*, *Pansies*, and *Collected Poems;* and a *sub rosa* unexpurgated London edition of five hundred copies of *Pansies* was soon sold out. Lawrence loved the pastoral scenery and life among the mountains at Rottach-am-Tegernsee, but suffered increasingly, especially from asthma, and resorted to a health cure which was of no avail. Frieda was luckier; a bone-setter did what specialists in London and Baden had failed to do. Lawrence wrote the pamphlet 'Pornography and Obscenity'. His sister Emily informed him that she had found the manuscript of *The Rainbow*, and he wrote to Brett to ascertain what manuscripts remained at Kiowa Ranch. He realized that he might not live much longer, and was anxious for Frieda. He was probably conscious of the nearness of death when he wrote 'Glory of Darkness' (CP.973–5), the first sketch of 'Bavarian Gentians'. Frieda had listened at night to ascertain that he was breathing, and in the dim dawn the enormous bunch of gentians she had put on the floor by his bed seemed the only living thing in the room. When he reached Bandol, where it was decided to stay the winter because he had been relatively well and happy there the previous year, he stated, in an invitation to the Brewsters, that he had had an 'awful' feeling of certain death in Germany.

The Brewsters were the only ones who remembered his forty-fourth birthday. They arrived in Bandol a month later than the Lawrences, who had rented Villa Beau Soleil, a bungalow with central heating, and with heliotrope walls and golden-framed mirrors which made Achsah think it must have been designed for some lady-love. Frieda was happy there. Lawrence's room presented a wide view of the sea which he associated with the adventurers of ancient Greece. He wrote 'A Propos of *Lady Chatterley's Lover*', an expansion of his introduction to the Paris edition of the novel. Frederick Carter stayed in Bandol during the second half of November, and they discussed writings on the Apocalypse which he had sent at Lawrence's request. Lawrence wrote his *Apocalypse* as a commentary or introduction. Here and there it contains the finest expression of his central faith in life, but the best writing of his final period will be found in the 'pure serene' of some of his *Last Poems*, which form a spiritual autobiography of his approach to death. News of Harry Crosby's suicide upset him very much: 'That's all he could do with life, throw it away. How could he betray the great privilege of life?'

Harwood, the daughter of the Brewsters, had been a favourite with Lawrence. When she returned from school in England for Christmas she brought hampers of presents from Lawrence's sisters, and typed his *Apocalypse*. Her parents had taken a house about four miles from Beau Soleil, but had to stay on for weeks at the Hôtel Beau Rivage before they could afford to furnish it. Their aim was to help and comfort Lawrence all they could. In the New Year he informed Brett that the winter made him certain he would die if he stayed on 'like this' in Europe, and that he hoped to return to New Mexico in the spring. Among his visitors were Orioli and Norman Douglas (whose 'on the holiday razzle' spirit depressed him), the Brett Youngs (who irritated him because their income was an easy £4000 a year), Else Jaffe, and Barbara Weekley. Both his sisters wished to come, but Lawrence persuaded them to wait. Dr Andrew Morland, who was on holiday on the Côte d'Azur and knew from Koteliansky and Gertler how seriously ill he was, examined him and found he had suffered from pulmonary tuberculosis for several years. Lawrence was extremely emaciated, but his resistance was remarkable. Dr Morland insisted that he must have complete rest, especially from people. Bandol was too exposed for one with such acute bronchitis, and he recommended the Ad Astra sanatorium at Vence, above Nice.

Lawrence did not wish to leave home but, after about two weeks, he 'submitted' and applied for a room at the sanatorium for one month. He still attended to business matters, sitting up in bed to correct the proofs of *Nettles* on the morning of his departure for Vence. It was a long, difficult journey by road and rail. He was accompanied by Frieda and Earl Brewster, and Achsah almost filled the car with almond blossom when she saw them off. Frieda stayed at a hotel in Vence, and decided to give up Beau Soleil, where her daughter Barbara was staying, and live with her in a hotel at Cagnes from which she could travel by bus to Vence; they were joined by Ida Rauh. Brewster brought masses of orange flowers to counteract the 'awful blue' walls of Lawrence's room, and found books in the sanatorium library for him to read, including French translations of Scott. Lawrence enjoyed sitting on the balcony, gazing across to the Mediterranean; the almond blossom was beautiful, and a mimosa 'all out, in clouds' reminded him of Australia. He thought Dr Morland was wrong in advising complete rest, and accepted his new consultant's suggestion that he should go down to lunch, even though there were two steep flights of stairs. Yet 'the bronchial-asthma condition' tired him, and he lost his appetite.

H. G. Wells visited him. At his suggestion, the American sculptor Jo Davidson came and modelled Lawrence's head in clay. Aldous and Maria Huxley travelled from London and, seeing how ill he was, decided not to leave. Then the Aga Khan called with his wife. Brewster had gone to India, expecting to see Lawrence when he returned in two months' time. Towards the end of February Lawrence wrote to him, and to his sister Ada, that he was no worse. Yet his pain increased; he thought he had influenza, but Dr Morland diagnosed pleurisy. Lawrence did not wish Frieda to leave him, and she stayed by his bedside several nights. Then, at his insistence, they moved to Robermond, a rented villa in Vence; for the first time he allowed her to put on his shoes. The next morning (Sunday, 2 March 1930) he asked her to remain by him; he was reading a life of Columbus. After lunch he was in agony, and he told the Huxleys he ought to have morphine. Aldous fetched a doctor to give an injection, after which Lawrence, who had asked Frieda to hold him because he did not know where he was, said he was better. At ten o'clock that night he was more peaceful, when suddenly his breathing became irregular, and soon he was dead. Two days later he was buried at Vence. There were ten mourners, among them Frieda and Barbara, Achsah Brewster, Aldous and Maria Huxley, Ida Rauh, and the poet Robert Nichols. No service was read, but posies of freesias, mimosa, violets, and primroses formed a fitting tribute. Many sprays of mimosa were dropped on the coffin, and Frieda said simply, 'Good-bye, Lorenzo'.

*   *   *

A phoenix after Lawrence's design was commissioned for the headstone, and executed in pebbles of rose, white, and grey from the beach at Bandol. Louie Burrows had not forgotten the man to whom she was once engaged; she visited his grave on two occasions, the first not long after his death.

Middleton Murry did not delay his pilgrimage to Vence; it led to the consummation of his love for Frieda. With her, he wrote, he knew fulfilment for the first time. Ernest Weekley offered to marry her again. In the spring of 1931 she returned to her New Mexican ranch with Angelo Ravagli, owner of Villa Bernarda, who had six months' leave from the Italian army.

In the absence of a will, letters of administration were granted to Lawrence's brother George, and Frieda received no royalties. It was Murry's testimony that Lawrence had drawn up a will in her favour, and in terms identical with those of his own on behalf of Katherine Mansfield, after the outbreak of the 1914–18 war, which secured Frieda the estate Lawrence's brother seemed willing to appropriate.

After the successful conclusion of this case in the Probate Court, Frieda visited Westminster Abbey and thought that Lawrence ought to be there among his equals; then, in the British Museum, she conceived the idea of building 'a simple shrine at the ranch in New Mexico for her husband's ashes'. In 1935, in accordance with her wishes, Ravagli had Lawrence's remains cremated in Marseille. He had endless difficulty in getting the urn which contained the ashes through the customs at New York and, after meeting Frieda at Lamy station, travelled twenty miles towards the ranch before realizing that he had left it on the railway platform. It was recovered and taken to Kiowa Ranch, where, on the wooded slope above, in a spot dear to Lawrence for its wild flowers, the main structure of a small open chapel had been built. Mrs Luhan, who had never been a friend of Frieda Lawrence, was probably critical; she and Dorothy Brett thought that Lawrence would have preferred the ashes to be scattered over the ranch. Frieda was convinced that there was a plot to steal the urn from the chapel. Not to be beaten, she had Lawrence's remains mixed in with the cement which was used to form the chapel altar.

Ravagli procured a divorce which was not valid in Italy. When he and Frieda married in 1950, they acquired American citizenship which enabled him to visit Italy without fear of arrest. Frieda died in 1956, and was buried in front of the Lawrence chapel.

An expurgated British edition of *Lady Chatterley's Lover* appeared in 1932. The unexpurgated text was published in England for the first time in 1960, as a challenge to the Obscene Publications Act. The trial which followed secured the removal of the ban on the novel, and obviously did much to create a disproportionate and often misdirected interest in a work which is now available in all its three versions.

Thought-Adventures

Lawrence's ideas animate many scenes in his fiction, and are implicitly or explicitly expressed in his poetry. He believed that the only genuine form of thought is instinctive or intuitive, since life is beyond mental analysis and, in the words of D'Annunzio, anatomy presupposes a corpse (*K*.xvi). 'The thought-adventure starts in the blood, not in the mind' (P2.618). Lawrence's basic views developed very rapidly and, though subject to changing emphases, never altered radically; the best expression of them occurs at the end of *Apocalypse*, his last important work:

> What man most passionately wants is his living wholeness and his living unison, not his own isolate salvation of his 'soul'. Man wants his physical fulfilment first and foremost, since now, once and once only, he is in the flesh and potent. . . . For man, as for flower and beast and bird, the supreme triumph is to be most vividly, most perfectly alive. . . . But the magnificent here and now of life in the flesh is ours, and ours alone, and ours only for a time. We ought to dance with rapture that we should be alive and in the flesh, and part of the living, incarnate cosmos. . . . But I *can* deny my connections, break them, and become a fragment. Then I am wretched. What we want is to destroy our false, inorganic connections, especially those related to money, and re-establish the living organic connections with the cosmos, the sun and earth, with mankind and nation and family.

Given the full perspective, it is easy to see that Lawrence's ideas are rooted in his own experience. It goes back to Eastwood: to reflections on his upbringing and education; to 'the tragedy' of sons and lovers; and to an industrial blight in the lives of English workers and families, the economic and political repercussions of which still bedevil us.

'Without Contraries is no progression', wrote Blake. Lawrence's ideas burgeoned through marriage and a realization of how much his own life and other people's had lost through the predominance (as Matthew Arnold saw it) of Hebraism over Hellenism. The principle of evil, Lawrence emphasized, was not 'anti-Christ or anti-Jehovah, but anti-life'; eating of the Tree of Knowledge rather than of the Tree of Life caused man to think of himself as an isolate, and crave for a God as an intermediary between himself and the cosmos. Through false education and ideals, therefore, and through not 'knowing in terms of togetherness, which is religious and poetic', we are 'cut off from the earth and sun and stars, and love is a grinning mockery, because, poor blossom, we plucked it from its stem on the tree of Life, and expected it to keep on blooming in our civilized vase on the table' ('A Propos of *Lady Chatterley's Lover*', P2.504).

Lawrence's questioning of orthodoxy began to develop before his marriage. His own experience, his observation of nature, and his reading (of Swinburne and Schopenhauer, for example) built up a complex of views ranging from the penumbral and tentative to clear conviction. Criticism of teaching in schools and of his own education underlies his belief that most of our thinking is barren because it is based on conventional opinions and second-hand knowledge; he suggests (15.xii.08), admitting that his phraseology is vague and impossible, that real knowledge of 'the most vital parts of the cosmos' is unconscious and to be gained by touch. God is impersonal, an immanence; not a spirit, but 'a vast, shimmering impulse which waves onwards' towards some unknowable end. This impulse is indifferent to the individual, but humanity as it dies falls back like raindrops into 'the big, shimmering sea of unorganised life which we call God' (9.iv.11).

Not until he settled with Frieda at Gargnano did he formulate his 'great religion', a belief in blood-knowledge, instinct, and intuition rather than in the intellect: 'We have got so ridiculously mindful, that we never know that we ourselves are anything.' We ignore the flame of life within us, and are obsessed with ideas about the outer world; with ideal, rather than real, knowledge. The question facing us is 'To be or not to be'; and nearly every Englishman says 'Not to be' (17.i.13).

Lawrence elaborated these views in 'The Lemon Gardens' and 'The Theatre' (*TI*). The disappointment of Signor di Paoli in having no children gives Lawrence the opportunity to preach and underscore his predilection for a people who live the life of the senses. The northern nations feel superior, with their science, industrialization, social reform, and education. But the will which dominates and drives us towards 'the great mechanized society' exhausts and dehumanizes us. Education serves to promote the same process of 'self-reduction'.

Right living, on the other hand, depends on advancing fulfilment; and this requires the seeking of two Infinites, the Original or Creative Infinite which is the source of darkness in the self, and the Ultimate Infinite which makes us aware of the living cosmos. Lawrence expresses the two Infinites in a series of antithetical terms and symbols such as the Father and the Son, the Dark and the Light, the Senses and the Mind, the Eagle and the Dove, the Tiger and the Lamb. Man must know both Infinites, though they are opposite; 'the lion shall never lie down with the lamb'. Excluding one, he excludes the whole; confusing the two, he makes 'nullity nihil'. The northern nations tend to exclude one; the Italians, the other.

The subject was resumed after Lawrence had seen *Ghosts* and *Hamlet* at the theatre in Gargnano. Both plays revealed a mental and perverted interested in sex, the northern or Christian Infinite having 'supplanted the old pagan Infinite, wherein the self like a root threw out branches and radicles which embraced the whole universe, became the Whole'. Conversely the Italian, dominated by woman (the Magna Mater) developed only his phallic or sensual self. 'His real man's soul, the soul that goes forth and builds up a new world out of the void, was ineffectual.' For his fulfilment man needs the old 'Dionysic' or 'Davidian' ecstasy, 'the becoming infinite through the absorption of all into the Ego'. Lawrence then returns to the Holy Ghost or 'mystic Reason' which unites both natures of God, the senses and the spirit. This Absolute forms 'a superb bridge, on which one can stand and know the whole world, my world, the two halves of the universe'.

Lawrence sees an inevitable link between self-fulfilment and social reform. If 'the greatest idea of the self' is fulfilled, the self is 'kingly, imperial, aristocratic'. Only intrinsically aristocratic people can lead and renew society. The supreme emphasis in social and political reform has been on the 'Not-me, the other'; the 'governing factor in the State' has been 'the idea of the good of others', increasingly at the expense of the individual. The implications of 'democratic' for Lawrence are less political than human; democratic movements tend towards egalitarianism, a flattening-out of individuality. In this, as in more psychological matters, one may suspect the influence of Frieda and German intellectualism. Lawrence's confidence in his genius as a Salvator Mundi was expressed in hope, with the Noachian rainbow as its symbol. Ursula at the end of *The Rainbow* is renewed in spirit, like a kernel freed from its husk at the end of winter and striving to take root, 'to create a new knowledge of Eternity in the flux of Time'. 'She knew that the sordid people . . . were living still, that the rainbow was arched in their blood and would quiver to life in their spirit . . .'. The fulfilment of body and spirit in unison can create a new vision of life, but no millennium. With continuing obsolescence and corruption, the struggle for amelioration must go 'on and on', and will always require leaders who can communicate the vision of what it is to be 'most vividly, most perfectly alive'.

*   *   *

Lawrence believed that, as a result of a closer relationship between men and women, a stronger intuitive sense of human suffering and joy would develop, leading to advancement in both civilization and art (2.vi.14). Fulfilment in marriage would 'give peace and inner security, no matter how many things go wrong. And this peace and security will leave you free to act and to produce your own work, a real independent workman' (7.vii.14). When the 1914–18 war broke out, he declared that there could be no vision (or right leadership) until man's soul was 'fertilised by the *female*', and he re-emphasized the importance of the unknown life-force within us, 'the tremendous *non-human* quality of life'. Not to submit to it leads to human impoverishment (21.ix.14). This vital inspiring force is the wind of 'Song of a Man Who Has Come Through'; if only one is sensitive and yields to it, 'The rock will split, we shall come at the wonder, we shall find the Hesperides'.

Lawrence's *Confessio Fidei* (18.xii.14) or gospel on the subject is the lengthy 'Study of Thomas Hardy' (P.398–516) which he wrote soon after the outbreak of the war. Why cannot people, he asks, live in the 'fulness of wisdom' like the phoenix before it bursts into flame and expires in ash? Without ever 'bursting the bud, the tight economical bud of caution and thrift and self-preservation', we 'rot and crumble away'. We even (to use the Erewhonian metaphor) store our goodness like coin to invest in the life after death. Instead of unfolding like the gay red poppy, we remain hidebound like the cabbage, 'tight shut', the will holding us 'immovable'. Yet the final aim of every living thing is 'the full achievement of itself'. On the quality of one's living depends the quality of our work and of our children.

Laws should interfere with the individual as little as possible. They do nothing to cure the sickness from which society suffers, to create sound human beings, 'sex-whole and money-healthy'. We throw our lives away in war, since they have become of so little value to us. The only good that can come out of this disaster is the realization that 'self-preservation is not the final goal of life' and that we must have the courage 'to *be*, to risk ourselves in a forward venture of life', and renew growth after 'this winter of cowardice' that will not 'let us *be*'. In the advancement of mankind, we should be the outposts, like kindled bonfires on the edge of the unknown.

Man's rhythm does not follow that of the seasons; with him every day is a blossoming, if he will; he is 'a well-head built over a strong, perennial spring'. Work is only a means to an end. Man wants to be free from routine, the known and the mechanical; he wishes to be himself. Insofar as machines save us from drudgery and give us more time to be ourselves, they are an advantage to the human race; used not just for our needs but to satisfy the lust for money-making, they reduce us to slaves. All need enough and something to spare; there is a normal or healthy money appetite; but 'why can't we really grow up, and become adult with regard to money as with regard to food?' The individual is greater than the State. Three or four hours' work a day would produce 'supplies of ample sufficiency'. Man could have 'half an eternity of pure leisure' were he not goaded on by the idea that 'riches are the means of freedom'. We have 'circumscribed, hampered, imprisoned ourselves within the limits of our poor-and-rich system, till our life is utterly pot-bound'.

Work is 'one of the inevitable conditions of man's existence', but one must avoid routine in order to develop. Man attains his individuality through the extension of his consciousness and awareness of outer reality. In the emergence of orders and species, evolution shows that the process of individualization will continue. Yet the growth of individuality does not imply selfishness; the opposite, in fact, because a selfish person is 'impure'; he wants 'that which is not himself'; 'the finer, the more distinct the individual, the more finely and distinctly is he aware of all other individuality', and of the impurities, the extraneous ideas, the mass-mindedness, which prevent others from attaining that

69

individuality. Here Lawrence goes a long way towards reassuring those who quite justifiably take issue with the unqualified assertions he makes in explaining his 'great religion' (17.i.13):

> The real way of living is to answer to one's wants. Not 'I want to light up with my intelligence as many things as possible' but 'For the living of my full flame – I want that liberty, I want that woman, I want that pound of peaches, I want to go to sleep, I want to go to the pub and have a good time, I want to look a beastly swell today, I want to kiss that girl, I want to insult that man.'

The central belief in the essay around Hardy is that human awareness 'flows on to the very furthest edge of known feeling', and beyond, in the sexual act of love. Every man's desire is that all he does, in mind and body, 'shall be the pulsation outwards' of the stimulus which comes from the sexual act, that 'the woman of his body shall be the begetter of his whole life'. When he knows that his achievement derives from 'the woman of his body', he knows what fundamental happiness is. This is the ideal result, but 'since no man and no woman can get a perfect mate, nor obtain complete satisfaction at all times', he must have a God or an idea which makes him strive towards perfection.

The fanciful interpretation of religions and artists which follows in terms of male and female is based on the axiom that man seeks his complement outside marriage; that the male spirit is the Will-to-Motion, and the female, the Will-to-Inertia. The latter produced Monism and the Ten Commandments. 'Christ rose from the suppressed male spirit of Judea', and the 'great assertion of the Male was the New Testament', the gospel of 'love thy neighbour as thyself'. The Old Law says, 'In the life of the body we are one with the Father'; the New Law declares that in the body we must die as Christ died on the Cross. It is now time to end the post-Renaissance schism which opposes Father and Son. For the body is the *via media* to consummation of body and spirit; in the act of love that which is mixed becomes pure, the female in man being imparted to the female, the male in her being received by the man. This is the 'singling away into purity' which creates the two-star equilibrium in marriage (*WL*.xvi). 'There must be marriage of body in body, and of spirit in spirit, and Two-in-One'; the two marriages must be reconciled.

This reconciliation of Father and Son implies a fusion of the Law (natural law, functioning in the body) and Love. We have to learn that individual natures differ, but can be reconciled once the lesson of love is learned. 'Thou shalt love thy enemy' is the Christian recognition of 'the law of the other person', but it is 'the hardest thing for any man' to know that the true natural law of his neighbour is different from his own. He should 'seek out the Holy Spirit, the Reconciler' who 'drives the twin principles of Law and Love across the Ages'. The creation and fostering of this Two-in-One principle between individuals and nations is impossible unless men are mature and fulfilled, and this depends on the Two-in-One relationship in marriage.

The development of individuality, maturity, and wisdom from a full awareness and experience of life, especially in sexual love, is Lawrence's major original contribution in this essay. That it was written euphorically may be seen in some of the concluding paragraphs:

> After Sue, after Dostoievsky's *Idiot*, after Turner's latest pictures . . . there is no further possible utterance of the peace that passeth understanding, the peace of God which is Perfect Knowledge. There is only silence beyond this. . . . So that . . . there comes over us now, over England and Russia and France, the pause of finality, now we see the purity of Knowledge, the great, white, uninterrupted Light, infinite and eternal.

When this was written, the 1914–18 war had only just begun.

*   *   *

Initially the idea of Rananim was the formation of a small community in which the new religion could be *lived* as a preparation for disseminating its gospel in the post-war era. Instead of struggling for money or power as in the contemporary world, people would, it was hoped, strive for 'individual freedom and common effort towards good', for 'communism' based on 'complete fulfilment in the flesh', and for the creation of 'aristocrats' or 'Sons of God' as wise as the serpent in dealing with the mob (1.ii.15). Functionally Lawrence's religion is similar to that of the Positivists such as John Stuart Mill: the immanent God or Great Will 'which is working itself out in all things' can achieve human progress only through right human vision and action. The belief that God or Providence would make all things right without human agency is that of the unbeliever 'affirming belief'; 'every *living* soul believes that, whatever the conditions, there will be that conjunction between the conditions and the soul itself which shall fulfill (*sic*) the Great Will' (14.v.15).

Later in 1915 Lawrence agreed to write for Middleton Murry's short-lived *Signature*, preaching 'the beliefs by which one can reconstruct the world'. The result was 'The Crown' (P2.365–415), six essays in which the mythopoeic trend of Lawrence's philosophizing becomes more evident. Universal darkness breeds universal light, 'for there cannot exist a specific infinite save by virtue of the opposite and equivalent specific infinite'. We are the beginning and the end, conceived and nourished in the darkness of the Father and Creator, realizing also the infinite light of 'unblemished being'. 'The darkness builds up the warm shadow of the flesh in splendour and triumph, enclosing the light' (as in Assyria and Egypt at their zenith). 'Then the light, wrestling within the vessel, throws up a white gleam of universal love' (as in St Francis and Shelley). There is no reconciliation between the darkness and the light which meet in us; one flows back to the beginning, the other to the future. They sustain 'the fight of Creation' within us, and their consummation is like the meeting waves of two oceans. 'And the clash and the foam are the Crown, the Absolute.' It is 'the music between the cymbals'; 'the rainbow, the iridescence which is darkness at once and light'.

The Crown is not the prize for victory; it is the *raison d'être* of both the lion and the unicorn, and is set upon 'the perfect balance of the fight' between the two forces within us which they represent. It is the 'holy spirit between the opposite divinities', 'the Timelessness into which are assumed the two Eternities'.

The waves of the Eternities which meet and mingle with no consummation are 'the myriad lives of human beings which pass in confusion of nothingness'; they are 'the uncreated lives'. In mortal man 'the light of the seed' seeks 'the infinite darkness, the womb of all creation' by way of the blood. Woman is 'the doorway . . . the gate to the dark eternity of power'; in sexual consummation man is with 'the dark Almighty of the beginning'. He is then new-born, and sees 'the infinite light of the Spirit'. If 'the seed of light never propagates in the darkness', the 'unconsummated soul . . . will seek to make itself whole by bringing the whole world under its own order'. 'Consummated in one infinite, and one alone', it will 'assert the oneness of all things'. 'This is the infinite with its tail in its mouth.' Such a partial soul establishes 'One God, One

Way, One Glory', and this is the false crown which the lion or the unicorn puts on whenever either triumphs. Whichever triumphs perishes. 'The moment power *triumphs*, it becomes spurious with sheer egoism, like Caesar and Napoleon. And the moment democracy triumphs, it too becomes hideous with egoism, like Russia now.'

One does not come really into being until the two Eternities, from the End and from the Beginning, are 'transfused into oneness'. Until then, one is an inferior being, a self-conscious ego. It is evil when this 'temporal and relative' self 'asserts itself eternal and absolute'. Being is not attained at birth but (if at all) 'in the midst of life, just as the phoenix in her maturity becomes immortal in flame. That is not her perishing: it is her becoming absolute: a blossom of fire.' Hidebound like cabbages, people of our civilization cannot flower; and the threshing about caused by the flower in the corruption within them becomes our life, and leads collectively to war. The tiger rises supreme; the deer melts away. 'Within the closed shell of the Christian conception, we lapse utterly back, through reduction, back to the Beginning.' The process resembles 'the serpent lying prone in the cold, watery fire of corruption', his belly white with the light flowing from him, his back 'dark and brindled where the darkness returns to the Source'. Darkness and light are kept apart; the darkness lapses into 'stone darkness' and the light becomes 'keen and cold as frost' (cf. African knowledge and northern knowledge, p. 173 and *WL*.xix).

The inferior mortal who is 'unborn' but thinks himself absolute assumes he has reached the limit of human perception and development. His ego makes him hate every other ego, and wish to conquer the universe. 'So circumscribed within the outer nullity, we give ourselves up to the flux of death, to analysis, to introspection, to mechanical war and destruction, to humanitarian absorption in the body politic, the poor, the birth-rate. . . . It is the continued activity of disintegration', a process of reducing everything to equality. Our devitalization makes us seek 'sensational gratification in the flesh, or sensational gratification within the mind'. This 'reducing activity is draped in alluring sentimentalism', with the result that our heroines get younger and younger and, in the movies, more and more childish. Being fully alive, subject to the Holy Ghost or Crown, means a constant change of 'flowering'; at present, 'safe within the mundane egg of our self-consciousness and self-esteem', we cannot change.

'Egoistic sex-excitement means the reacting of the sexes against one another in a purely reducing activity', and its continuation leads to perversity and degradation. Then come alcohol and drugs and, last reduction of all, the desire for war or violent revolution and death.

We must have faith, and that means an ultimate reliance on something more than our will. When the war is over, shall we be satisfied with 'the barren triumph of the will' or with the equally barren triumph of inertia and irresponsibility? If corruption induces a higher form of life, it is divine. In the 'marshy chill heat' of reptiles there is 'the sign of the Godhead'. 'When the swan first rose out of the marshes, it was a glory of creation.' Life is a process of destruction and creation; progress involves growth and decay, and the absolute is 'the pure relation, which is both'.

'But let us watch that we do not preserve an enveloping falsity around our destructive activity, some nullity of virtue and self-righteousness, some conceit of the "general good" and the salvation of the world by bringing it all within our own conceived whole form.' In the 'enveloping falsity' of our world one can see arrested growth such as is found in the natural world: aristocrats like vultures, high and remote, but carrion birds with heads 'fast-locked, like stone'; democrats like carrion dogs and hyenas, prowling 'among the bare stones of the common earth . . . their loins cringing, their heads sharpened to stone'; and financiers and millionaires of the intelligence order of the baboon, 'almost a man, or almost a high beast'. The stony head of the vulture and the stony fixity of the hyena's loins are emblems of 'the last state into which man may fall', 'the triumph of the will and the triumph of inertia, the state of the animated sepulchre'.

The two eternities of the Past and the Future meet in life, and this is the eternal flux. We pass away, but this relationship remains; it is the Absolute. 'God is the utter relation between the two eternities', the flowing together and the flowing apart. Immortality is not a question of time, but of consummate being; it means 'undaunted suffering and undaunted enjoyment', and both through submission to divine grace. The Holy Spirit dwells within the fulfilled soul, and this is our immortality.

This revelation of God 'within the body, or within the soul' is the vital part of the timeless flux. It is the 'quick' of life, in nature and in art. One cannot *live* on the 'stale memory' of revelations of God. Nor is it necessary to resort to war to destroy their hold on us. Why not create a new revelation instead of merely seeking to destroy the old? For 'the one glorious activity of man' is 'the getting himself into a new relationship with a new heaven and a new earth'.

In much of this sermonizing, Lawrence's earlier ideas can be seen writ large. His religiosity makes him more rhapsodic than practical, but his undeviating faith in life is to be admired. He is a prophet whose vision keeps alive those 'kindled bonfires on the edge of space' which mark 'advance-posts' in the progress of mankind.

*   *   *

The plan for Lawrence to lecture with Bertrand Russell on the post-war world came to nothing. Lawrence told him that there must be 'an aristocracy of people who have wisdom' and 'a Ruler: a Kaiser: no Presidents and democracies' (?7.vii.15). The idea of giving power to the working classes was wrong; workers could elect their local representatives (15.vii.15). He opposed tyranny, and insisted on women's rights; women should be represented side by side with men at all legislative levels, including the highest (26.vii.15). Lawrence soon concluded, however, that Russell, in wishing to impose his will, was 'false and cruel' (14.ix.15). He was one of those who wished to bind mankind in 'enveloping falsity', in accordance with his own conception of the 'general good'. Although his own insistencies have their Platonic analogues, Lawrence thought Russell wrong like Plato, in giving his will to mental consciousness and ignoring blood-consciousness. This, he contended, was the tragedy of our time (8.xii.15), for, as he argued in 'The Crown', the suppression of one or the other consciousness meant the virtual extinction of vitality. Lawrence, it should be added, thought too much in terms of Eternity for the anti-metaphysical Russell; and his assertion at this time (?7.vii.15) that the early Greeks had clarified his soul, and that he was 'rid' of his 'Christian religiosity', is significant.

The altruistic power of love is destroyed by the spirit of war, Lawrence maintained; when it prevails, it is 'the great creative process, like spring, the making of an integral unity out of many disintegrated factors' (2.xi.15). Christian and Shelleyan in spirit, it is the directing principle of 'The Reality of Peace', seven short essays which Lawrence completed by the beginning of March 1917. The first four were published the following summer in *The English Review*, but what happened to the remainder is not known. Their purpose was to make people think about '*a new world, a creative peace*', and Lawrence thought them 'very good, and beautiful'. The change of style is noticeable from the outset, though it was well-nigh impossible for Lawrence to avoid Biblical metaphor and allusion altogether. He loses no time in asserting that no one can prescribe for the future. Our intelligence will be shown in the adjustments we make to avoid obstructions and wrong turnings. We must abandon our assurance, 'our conceit of final knowledge'. To yield our will to the unknown requires greater courage than to smile contemptuously in the face of death (like the Red Indian). Any class struggle for domination will be deathly, for 'all strife between things old is pure death'.

'When we know the death is in ourselves, we are emerging into the new epoch.' Decay or corruption inevitably accompanies creation and growth; they are 'the systole–diastole of the physical universe'. 'If there is a serpent of secret and shameful desire in my soul, let me not beat it out of my consciousness with sticks. It will lie beyond, in the marsh of the so-called subconsciousness, where I cannot follow it with my sticks.' Let it be accepted calmly as part of one's natural self. It is the secret fascination which is the fearful tyranny, and freedom from this comes with a sense of proportion, for 'the Lord is the lord of all things, not of some only'. 'The timeless quality of *being* is understanding; when I understand fully, flesh and blood and bone, and mind and soul and spirit one rose of unison, then I *am*.'

Lawrence longs for the death in the multitude of the quality that makes them impervious to change. They are sheep, with heads down, intent on feeding fat. 'It is very natural that every word about death they will decry as evil.' Today we have to fear not 'the overweening individual' but the will of the masses. Lawrence ends his third section with a prayer that the 'glassy rind' or fixed notions of humanity may be smashed, and that a few 'pure and single men' may emerge who see clearly what needs to be destroyed and what created.

The fourth section contains nothing remarkably new except the image of the orbit. Lawrence regards the mass of humanity as beetles or ants, 'one monstrosity of multiple identical units', 'one big, self-absorbed unity'. Freedom means the right of the individual, nonetheless, to choose his own path to his own goal; no one has the right to dictate to him. Like the lines of longitude, the paths of men are all separate, but all are linked to the poles of destruction and creation, of death and heaven on earth. In all are the forces which can be represented as the lion (or the tiger) and the lamb, the leopard and the deer, or (as in 'The Crown') the lion and the unicorn. It is by the equipoise of the two 'in perfect conjunction' that one passes into the 'glad absolution of the rose'. Just as the earth pulses round her orbit by 'a law of dual attraction and repulsion', so when 'drawn by centripetal force into communion with the whole' and by an 'equivalent centrifugal force away into the splendour of beaming isolation' one 'suddenly, like a miracle' finds the peace of one's orbit.

There is a hint that one topic in the remainder of 'The Reality of Peace' was the critical relation between man and woman (11.xi.16), but it seems a fair inference that the final three sections contained hardly a new idea, and that their significant features will be found elsewhere in Lawrence. One thing is clear: whatever he thought of the masses (cf. 27.xii.15), the charge of Fascism which was levelled against Lawrence by Russell is absurd (see p. 287).

Even so, the stress which Lawrence lays on individuality may seem to be more than offset by his general attitude towards the masses and his views on education. 'Education of the People', which he completed in 1920, shows no change in his main principles. People are born unequal, and most are unsuitable for academic education; yet the individuality of all should be given every opportunity for development. Lawrence's disillusionment as a teacher is soon evident. 'He is caught between the upper and nether millstones of idealism and materialism', between the theory of individual uniqueness and the insistent pressure to prepare children for jobs. Nothing can solve this educational problem until the fear of not being able to earn a living is removed.

'Our present system of education . . . turns out a lot of half-informed youth who despise the whole business of understanding and wisdom, and who realize that in a world like ours nothing but money matters.' The small minority of the instructible will soon be like Lilliputians in 'the grimy fist' of 'the uninstructible Brobdingnag'. Having 'got ourselves thoroughly entangled in a vast mob which may at any moment start to bolt down to the precipice Gadarene-wise', we need a new educational system. Lawrence outlines one (P.597–9), the supreme aim of which is 'to recognize the true nature in each child, and to give each its natural chance'. 'Each individual is to be helped, wisely, reverently, towards his own natural fulfilment.'

Lawrence insists on State education for all, based on elementary education from the age of seven ('five is too soon') to twelve, to 'give us a common human basis, a common radical understanding'. Afterwards there is selection, the non-academic spending more time on crafts which will be useful for life than on mental education; at fourteen they serve as apprentices, giving half their time to education for two years. The more academic are divided into two groups at the age of fourteen, the less proficient being similarly drafted into part-time, two-year, semi-professional training. The most academically gifted proceed to college at sixteen to take more general courses at first, with emphasis on particular studies for special aptitudes. At all these stages, it should be noticed, physical education and the crafts are not neglected. Finally, scholars at the age of twenty are given two years' highly specialized professional training (in medicine or the arts, for example).

Whatever the practical difficulties of his scheme, it shows that Lawrence was well in advance of his age. In some respects it provides a better preparation for life than the present system of education in England: we should all be happier and wiser, less dependent and more vitalized, if we were more manually proficient in both arts and crafts, for leisure and our everyday needs, especially in an era of mass-production. The Lawrence of 'Let us be Men' would find much to expostulate against in the passivity of our television addictions.

The only human equality is that every man counts as one, and this is a 'pure intellectual abstraction'. Every man should be himself, and the business of teachers is not to let children make their own decisions but to ensure that courses are chosen which will enable them as far as possible to attain fulfilment according to their true natures; the ideal should be 'living, spontaneous individuality in every man and woman'. Yet the masses will always be 'almost expressionless by themselves', and true democracy will find its utterance in 'the great individuals of their race and time'; 'no populace will ever know, by itself, what to do with its own soul. Left to itself, it will never do more than demand a pound a day, and so on.' Like Plato, Lawrence combines high idealism with a disillusioned evaluation of the human race in general.

No individual can develop in isolation; he accomplishes his individuality through interaction in society. Society inevitably implies the acceptance of traditional values, but man is given intelligence to evolve a morality more in accordance with changing conditions and discoveries about life.

For educational progress, one must realize that the awareness of the very young proceeds from 'the great affective centres, volitional and emotional', which act 'direct and spontaneous, without mental consciousness or interference'. Initially therefore no attempt should be made to educate the child mentally. Having suffered from mother-love, Lawrence denounces it, and especially its idealization. 'A mother should have ten strokes with the birch every times she "comes over" with soul or yearning love or aching responsibility'; 'it is a vice which threatens the ultimate sanity of our race' (cf. pp. 86–7). The natural relation of mother and child is instinctive, 'non-personal, non-ideal, non-spiritual'. It is effective at 'the great primary centres'. The great mistake in our education is to attempt 'deliberately to provoke reactions' in these affective centres, and 'to dictate these reactions from the mind'. The result is self-conscious perversion and attitudinizing.

All our radical knowledge comes from the primal consciousness or life-circuit which is established between the affective centres, but its spontaneity and impact have been weakened by mental consciousness and direction. We are self-consciously deliberate; even our passional life has become auto-suggestive. Individuality has diminished in the prevailing light of mental consciousness, just as the stars are extinguished in the light of day. The oneness of a group is the 'one element held in common by many individuals', and the larger the group, the smaller the element common to all. The *quick* of the individual which we should aim at fostering is something far richer and more complex. The aim is not the promotion of anarchy and disorder, but of '*manifoldness* of being' like that of the stars, each one 'flashing with singleness'.

Lawrence emphasizes the importance of developing beauty of spontaneous movement in the very young. We must prevent 'their degenerating into physical cloddishness or mechanical affectation or fluttered nervousness', even if it means a tussle with them. A bird does not attain poise and control in all conditions without 'long, keen pain of learning' and being on the *qui vive*. In the correction of children there should be no discussion of morals. Parents and teachers should exert their responsibilities. 'A parent *owes* the child all the natural passional reactions provoked', whether compassion or wrath. Rows are wholesome, provided the disagreement be 'spontaneous and natural, without fixities and perversions'; and love without a fight is degeneracy.

The child should learn self-dependence as soon as possible; he should take pleasure in doing things for himself, not for ideal reasons, but because the activity is its own reward, and ultimately he will find pleasure in being independent. If people make their own clothes in the style which pleases them instead of following fashion, so much the better. 'Let every individual be single and self-expressive; not self-expressive in the self-conscious, smirking fashion, but busy making something he *needs* and wants to have just so, according to his own soul's desire.' Craft work should not be mind-work. With practice one attains a facility whereby the fingers 'almost live and think by themselves'; and this absorption or forgetfulness in work is one of 'the joys of life'. Just as handwork should not be muddled with mind-work, so mental work (as in arithmetic) should remain an abstraction, he adds.

Although the motive of emulation introduces an element of meanness in the classroom, it is a natural factor in sport and games, and far better for the individual than self-conscious exercises in physical training. Physical culture should be restricted to training for competitive sports or for the expressive dance. Man is a fighter, and the 'old male spirit' should be revived. Lawrence then proceeds to condemn modern warfare, but thinks that, with no explosive weapons or League of Nations, we could fight our enemies face to face. 'Think what we've missed: the glorious bright passion of anger and pride, recklessness and dauntless cock-a-lory.'

Having lost a great deal of steam on mother-fixations, and much of what remained on convincing himself that man is justified in fighting when he feels like it, Lawrence ends his disproportionate and rather inadequate treatise with the delegation of responsibility in modern life. The idealization of women and the child and democracy is not the way to progress. In the forward march, men must go 'beyond their women' and regain the 'old passion of deathless friendship between man and man'. Marriage is 'the centre of human life'; deathless friendship is 'the leap ahead'. This is 'the last word in the education of a people', Lawrence concludes, having raised the question at the end of *Women in Love*. It is an important element in his next two or three novels.

In 'Democracy' (P.699–718) Lawrence argues that the State (whatever political form it takes) and Leagues of Nations are concerned only with the means of life. He ridicules the concept of the 'average man'; this idea illustrates the idealism which hampers progress. He sees it in the One Identity, the En-Masse of Whitman's democratic vision. One man is 'neither equal nor unequal' to another; he is different, unique. When men attain their true selves, the material necessities of life can easily be adjusted to give general satisfaction. The principal aim of government should be to ensure the maximum freedom for the spontaneous development of the individual until he reaches fulfilment of life.

* * *

Some of Lawrence's knowledge of Freudian psychology came from Frieda; much more subsequently from Dr David Eder and Barbara Low. His own was largely intuitive and egoistically inspirational, the product of a mythopoeic, anti-scientific imagination, stimulated by readings in anthropology and ancient philosophy. It ranged from his blood-consciousness to the Creation. This cosmic psychology was first formulated in 1917–18 in 'The Two Principles' (P2.227–37) as a basis for the work which became *Studies in Classic American Literature*.

Fundamental to Lawrence's mature philosophy is the conviction that pagan forms of religion are superior to Christianity in creating vital links between the material cosmos and the human psyche. Within the universe there is always a creative presence, as in the first division into primordial fire and water. The next division produced the four elements, earth, air, fire, and water. It is the primary division which is fundamental, however, since everything is created from the consummation of fire and water. First came the sun, 'the great mystery-centre'; towards it the invisible fire and the invisible waters steal, and from it new waters are shed and new fire floods into space. The waters and the fire 'swirling on their way' to this 'great central conjunction' become 'entangled' to form the lesser worlds and stars. Creation is accompanied by disintegration, inanimate matter being 'released from the dead body of the world's creatures'.

Lawrence associates the 'eternal waters' with woman, and fire (the sun) with man. Yet, in a statement which evokes Gerald Crich in *Women in Love*, he says that some races, men and women alike, derive primarily from the sun, while others, 'blonde, blue-eyed, northern, are evidently water-born, born along with the ice-crystals and blue, cold deeps, and yellow, ice-refracted sunshine'.

Sexual union may be delicate and purely creative, or it may be a clash of opposites. The first produces harmonious souls; the second, disintegrative. The second preponderates in eras of disintegration, when the reductive process eventually leads to a break in sexual polarity, and 'habitual or deliberate' sexual intercourse takes the place of dynamic.

A 'perfect and fulfilled' human being lives in 'fourfold creative activity'. Both a horizontal and vertical polarization of the living body are imagined. The centres of spiritual awareness are in the upper zone; of the sensual, in the lower. The frontal zones are sympathetic, but the spinal are assertive or voluntary; the former make us seek union with the outer world; the latter express our will in resistance or in the desire for mastery.

'Through the gates of the eyes and nose and mouth and ears, through the delicate ports of the fingers, we pass into oneness with the universe, our great extension of being, towards infinitude.' In the lower body 'the contiguous universe is drunk into the blood'. 'Here is the world of living dark waters, where the fire is quenched in watery creation. Here, in the navel, flowers the water-born lotus, the soul of the water begotten by one germ of fire. And the lotus is the symbol of our perfected first-being, which rises in blossom from the unfathomable waters.' It is the 'magnificent centre' of the self 'wherein all life pivots', 'a state portrayed in the great dark statues of the seated lords of Egypt' (cf. *WL*.xxiii). 'In the blood we have our strongest self-knowledge, our most powerful dark conscience.'

Only when a balance is achieved between the spiritual and the sensual do we reach 'full consciousness in the mind'; but complete fulfilment requires strength of will as well as sympathetic growth. In such a state of development, a man 'knows the sweet spiritual communion, and he is at the same time a sword to enforce the spiritual level; he knows the tender unspeakable sensual communion, but he is a tiger against anyone who would abate his pride and his liberty'.

The typing of *Psychoanalysis and the Unconscious*, one of the most disciplined of Lawrence's works, was completed in March 1920, soon after he had settled in Sicily. His case is that psychoanalysis is 'out, under a therapeutic disguise, to do away entirely with the moral faculty in man', and he thinks it is time 'the white garb of the therapeutic cant was stripped off the psychoanalyst'. He had been impressed by Trigant Burrow's assertion that Freud's unconscious represents our *conception* of 'conscious sexual life as this latter exists in a state of repression'. Sin enters when sex becomes mental; the incest motive, for example, is not a pristine impulse, but an idea which has been applied to 'the affective-passional psyche' by the mind of modern man. 'The Freudian unconscious is the cellar in which the mind keeps its own bastard spawn', but the 'true unconscious' derives from the God who bade Adam and Eve not to eat from the tree of knowledge.

The motivizing of sex by mental consciousness is 'the death of all spontaneous, creative life, and the substituting of the mechanical principle'. We should discard the concepts superimposed on the unconscious by psychoanalytical reasoning, and live according to the spontaneous promptings of the known but unanalyzable 'integral unconscious' which makes every individual unique. A religious attitude to life and creation would make us not less scientific but more complete.

The integral consciousness of the child in the womb is non-cerebral; it lies beneath the navel which links it with its mother, and it remains the principal centre of sympathy after birth. The child gradually asserts its independence, however. Individual growth is impossible without this polarity of sympathy and self-assertion. (The physiological details which Lawrence gives at this stage to explain child-development add nothing essential to the concept of the 'fourfold creative activity' which leads to human fulfilment through the 'sympathetic' and 'voluntary' nerve centres on the higher and lower planes.) Sympathy creates a sense of 'at-oneness' with the beloved or with the universe, but it is the voluntary centres which produce a sense of realization: in the upper plane, of existence in the outer world; in the lower plane, of one's self. As long as the sympathetic mode predominates (as Lawrence thought it did among the northern races, and as it did between him and his mother), the individual is divided and denied fulfilment.

The unconscious, in short, is the life within us, and the whole of life is 'one long, blind effort' to establish a harmonious relationship with the outer world, both human and non-human. In this we fail; we are bedevilled by 'a whole set of india-rubber ideas and ideals and conventions'.

Mind is no more than the 'terminal instrument' of our dynamic, fourfold consciousness. 'It transmutes what is a creative flux' into ideas, which are thrown off 'as leaves are shed from a tree, or as feathers fall from a bird'. With the will as driving-force, it can subject 'everything spontaneous to certain machine-principles called ideals or ideas'. Mental consciousness is not a goal, but it provides us with the 'means to adjust

83

ourselves to the external universe', and to subdue 'the external materio-
mechanical universe to our great end of creative life'.

In 1921, after completing *Aaron's Rod*, Lawrence wrote *Fantasia of
the Unconscious*, describing it as a continuation of *Psychoanalysis and
the Unconscious*. In substance much of it is a repetition; the difference
is in the style, which is informal, topical, personal, spontaneous and
sprightly, 'chirping' with insouciance. He claims that his 'pseudo-
philosophy' was 'deduced from the novels and poems, not the reverse';
the novels and poems came 'unwatched out of one's pen'. Yet the more
closely one studies *The Rainbow* and *Women in Love*, the more it will
be seen that the philosophy was an integral part of the shaping spirit of
Lawrence's imagination. His convictions coloured his vision of life,
providing the 'dynamic idea' or 'metaphysic' on which his art depended.
Philosophy had come to interest Lawrence more than people (23.v.17),
and inevitably affected his presentation of life. He was a novelist with a
purpose.

The best of *Fantasia of the Unconscious* is not to be found in the
elaboration of planes of consciousness with reference to ganglia and other
physiological centres but in the more random remarks on life. Lawrence
improvises freely at times; he sits at the foot of a fir-tree on the edge of
the Black Forest, waiting for thoughts to come and digressing because the
problematical nut he has been gnawing squirrel-fashion has proved to be
empty. Bitterly opposed to the ideal consciousness and the damage it can
do to growing psyches, he wishes he could be one of the mindless trees a
while, and is glad 'to be with them in their silent, intent passion, and
their great lust' – their great 'root-lust'. He can understand why Jesus
was crucified on a tree (iv).

He has much to say on parenthood. The child has a tripartite being,
'the mother within him, the father within him, and the Holy Ghost, the
self which he is supposed to consummate, and which mostly he doesn't'.
Mother-love is generally more evident, but it is 'ultimately on the remote
but powerful father-love that the infant rests', for 'in the male the
dominant centres are naturally the volitional centres, centres of responsibility, authority, and care'. A mother may develop too much spiritual
love in a child, but an equilibrium between the two modes of love is
necessary for a child's healthy development. 'The flashing interchange
of anger between parent and child is part of the responsible relationship',
but right relationships depend on wisdom, a state of soul, not a set of

precepts. The attempt to impose one's will on a child is a form of bullying, which is hateful. 'Ideal' bullying is criminal; it produces 'impoverishment and distortion and subsequent deficiency'. As a result of 'the all-famous love and charity ideal', the 'great sympathetic centre of the breast becomes exhausted', and the lungs diseased. Lawrence is here generalizing from the cramping effects of the possessive maternal love (and will) from which he suffered. 'Would God a she-wolf had suckled me, and stood over me with her paps, and kicked me back into a rocky corner when she'd had enough of me. It might have made a man of me', he had written in 'Education of the People' (P.632). Nowadays, he noticed, 'men have a stunt of pretending that children and idiots alone know best. This is a pretty piece of sophistry, and criminal cowardice, trying to dodge the life-responsibility which no man or woman can dodge without disaster.'

The chapter on the five senses reveals some amusing eccentricities in illustration of Lawrence's insistent conviction that we live too much in our sympathetic centres, and neglect the lower sensual planes of consciousness for the upper. We should be happier if we had 'sharp and vivid' teeth like wolves, but we are 'sympathy-rotten, and spirit-rotten, and idea-rotten. We have forfeited our flashing sensual power. And we have false teeth in our mouths.' There is a sensual way of beholding, as may be seen in the savage or the horse: 'The root of his vision is in his belly, in the solar plexus. And he fights with his teeth, and his heels, the sensual weapons.' Music at one time 'acted upon the sensual powers direct. We hear it still in savage music, and in the roll of drums, and in the roaring of lions, and in the howling of cats.'

The educational views which Lawrence links with his physiology of 'the great primary centres' and their development are largely those of 'Education of the People'; despite a core of progressiveness, they are even more hopelessly reactionary. '*The great mass of humanity should never learn to read and write – never*', he emphasizes (partly to 'prevent their eating much more of the tissues of leprosy, newspapers and books'). Immorality, vice, and crime are due to a suppression or collapse at one of the great primary centres, and one of the main reasons for the damage is the forcing of children into 'a set of mental tricks' at school. After a few years of this, they are turned loose 'like so many inferior Don Quixotes, to make a mess of life'. There should be no schools for children before the age of ten; then all should be sent to public workshops and gymnasia for domestic crafts, technical industry or art, and for training in 'primitive modes of fighting and gymnastics', up to the age of fourteen. Further education (university included) should be free, but the critical question of how far the decision to allow young people to pursue higher courses should rest with parents is not raised.

Lawrence repeats his warning against the encouragement of 'so-called self-expression' in children; it results in self-consciousness and falsity. He wants a natural development, and the same is true in sex-education. It is 'ten times criminal to tell young children facts about sex'. Nothing should be hidden; 'if a child occasionally sees its parent nude, taking a bath, all the better'. The worst happens when the 'shadowy dynamic realities' which find a natural place in the strong but evanescent sex-awareness of the child are 'dragged' into mental consciousness. Similarly 'to talk to a child about an adult is vile'. Undoubtedly Lawrence condemned his mother when he wrote: 'It is despicable for any one parent to accept a child's sympathy against the other parent. And the one who *received* the sympathy is always more contemptible than the one who is hated.'

The importance of 'The Birth of Sex' chapter is in its clear but unavowed formulation of Lawrence's main purpose as a writer. Many readers will have wondered how a civilization can be made whole through sexual fulfilment. Lawrence argues that it makes man purposive, and that only when 'the sex passion submits to the great purposive passion' is a man truly fulfilled. No great purposive passion, he adds, can last long unless it is based on the fulfilment of 'true sexual passion' in most people. Lawrence concludes with the assertion of his 'passionate instinct' to save the working man, 'save him alive, in his living, spontaneous, original being'; he would like 'the responsibility for thought, for direction', so that he could restore to the working man his insouciance, spontaneity, and fullness of life.

In the chapter on parent love, Lawrence returns to the problem-tragedy of *Sons and Lovers* (though his reference is to John Ruskin). When a mother and her adolescent son are 'intensely linked in adult love-sympathy and love-will, on the upper plane', the 'deep sensual centres' are roused sooner or later. Finding no polarization with another person, they are experienced through 'the *upper* channels', and sex-consciousness and sex-curiosity follow. 'This is the secret of our intro-version and our perversion to-day.' The love of a mature woman is fine

86

for the son 'till he is faced with the actual fact of sex necessity'; it can make him flare up 'like a flame in oxygen'. 'No wonder they say geniuses mostly have great mothers', Lawrence adds. 'They mostly have sad fates.' For such a love can outlive the mother, and may be invested with a glamour that marriage cannot equal.

Habitual association of ideas drives Lawrence into some ridiculous generalizations on motherhood. The modern babe never drinks one mouthful of the milk of human kindness. 'There is no mother's milk to-day, save in tigers' udders, and in the udders of sea-whales.' The idealism which substitutes 'the sterilized milk of human benevolence' is responsible for modern inventions such as poison-gas. More Lawrentian gall overflows in 'Oh, ideal humanity, how detestable and despicable you are! . . . How you deserve to perish in your own stink.' The baby is reduced to 'an ideal-born beastly little entity with a devil's own will of its own, benevolent, of course, and a Satan's own seraphic self-consciousness, like a beastly Botticelli brat'. After this splenetic outburst Lawrence turns over a new leaf, concluding incongruously that one's business is not to save anybody's soul or put anybody in the right, but to attain, and remain in, 'the stillness and solitude' of one's soul.

He then turns to cosmology. Lawrence has more faith in a witch-doctor than in science, and he creates his own universe. The fundamental article of his cosmographical belief is that the first cosmic reality consisted of nothing but 'living, incorporate individuals'. The cosmos as we know it is 'nothing but the aggregate of the dead bodies and dead energies of bygone individuals'. 'The living soul partakes of the dead souls, as the living breast partakes of the outer air, and the blood partakes of the sun.' Every living soul is polarized with the sun, and the sun is 'the soul of the inanimate universe'. Materially it is formed of 'all the effluence of the dead', but the *quick* of the sun is polarized with 'the solar plexus in mankind'. Similarly the moon is polarized with the lumbar ganglion, so that in this Lawrentian universe human beings, like the earth, are polarized between the sun and the moon, the moon's attraction counter-acting the sun's and asserting our 'terrestrial *volition*'. She 'burns white with the intense friction of her withdrawal into separation' from the 'sun-stuff', for the 'sun-principle' and the 'moon-principle' correspond to primordial fire and water. The saltness of the sea makes it respond to the moon, which is a 'strange coagulation' of 'water-born substances' such as salt, soda, and phosphorus. When we die, 'our radiance is flung to the sun, our marsh-fire to the moon'. 'We fall into the earth', and 'earth, sun, and moon are born only of our death'. The sun is 'the centre of our infinite oneing in death with all the other after-death souls of the cosmos'; the moon is the meeting-place of 'cold, dead, angry souls' from the earth only.

There is 'a pure polarity' therefore 'between each living individual and the outer cosmos' and between the living and dead. Lawrence seems to be on the point of saying something on the dreams that matter when 'something *threatens* us from the outer mechanical, or accidental *death*-world', but nothing comes of it, and the implications of his terms here (as elsewhere) are not elucidated. He turns to physical causes of dreams, repudiates once more the Freudian incest-wish, and explains fear-dreams about horses and bulls. The former show 'some arrest in the deepest sensual activity' of the male; the latter, a female desire, 'not from the centres of the lower, sensual self, but from the intense physical centres of the upper body'.

Our life alone supports the moon. It is the planet of our nights, 'the mother of darkness', 'the tide-turner' which 'calls us back, back out of our day-self, back through the moonlit darkness of the sensual planes, to sleep'. It is the planet of women, whose deepest consciousness is in the loins and belly; 'intelligent' women are therefore a perversion. Woman is really polarized downwards, towards the centre of the earth', just as 'man is polarized upwards, towards the sun and the day's activity'. The sexes must be kept pure, and woman must 'yield once more to the male leadership'. 'Sex as an end in itself is a disaster', but 'an ideal purpose which has no roots in the deep sea of passionate sex is a greater disaster still'. Lawrence warms at the thought of man coming home to a wife who *believes* in him and submits to his purpose in life. There can be no happy sex relationship 'without a relationship of men towards men in a spirit of unfathomable trust and responsibility, service and leadership, obedience and pure authority'. There must be a system of 'culminating aristocracy, society tapering like a pyramid to the supreme leader'.

Lawrence's cosmic fantasies are more amazing than his elaboration of planes of consciousness and sex in terms of polarization, circuits, magnetism, and electricity, but the main ideas of *Fantasia of the Unconscious* cover old ground and take us no further than *Aaron's Rod*.

Some interesting 'footnotes' may be found in Lawrence's letters to the American psychoanalyst Dr Trigant Burrow. 'Those *Unconscious* things of mine hardly sell at all, and only arouse dislike', he writes. 'People are too dead, and too conceited. *Man is the measure of the universe.* Let him be it: idiotic foot-rule which even then is nothing' (6.vi.25). 'I, who loathe sexuality so deeply, am considered a lurid sexuality specialist', he writes on Christmas Day, 1926. Very significantly he regrets 'the absolute frustration' of his 'primeval societal instinct' and thinks 'societal repression much more devastating' than sexual repression (13.vii.27). He never got beyond the stage reached by Birkin at the end of *Women in Love.* The same regret is voiced a little later, after reading Burrow's *The Social Basis of Consciousness;* Lawrence is so 'cut off' that he cannot 'link up with the social unconscious'. There will never be a millennium; it is 'the time between Good Friday and Easter', and Dr Burrow's book is a chink of light in the door of the tomb. 'I'm not sure if a mental relation with a woman doesn't make it impossible to love her', he continues (3.viii.27).

He had never read a book more 'in sympathy' with his own thinking, and he made it the subject of a review (P.377–82). Dr Burrow had realized that the application of Freudian theory in psychoanalysis was a 'mechanistic' process, and discovered that the root of modern neurosis is the sense of separateness which dominates every man. Self-awareness destroys spontaneity; and living according to the image of the 'normal' created by man, and not in accordance with one's true self, is the cause of division and derangement. Dr Burrow had found that the mass is more neurotic than the individual, and Lawrence finds 'the last great insanity of all, which is going to tear our civilization to pieces', in class-hatred. It hardly exists between man and man, yet it is regarded as 'normal' and 'social'. Self-seeking leads to sexuality (see *WL*.iii, where the mirror image is used for the mental obsession with sex that leads to 'porno-graphy'), and 'the mirror in which we all live grimacing' must be shattered if we are to recover 'true relatedness'.

*   *   *

Studies in Classic American Literature took its final form in 1922–3. In 'Nathaniel Hawthorne and *The Scarlet Letter*' Lawrence reverts to the 'beastly apple' of the Fall. The sin was in the self-consciousness; 'the mind and the spiritual consciousness of man simply *hates* the dark potency of blood-acts'. And, with a pessimistic finality that is unprece-dented on this particular subject, he states that blood-consciousness and mind-consciousness will always remain antagonistic. 'That is our cross', he adds. Yet the creed which he reached before he was thirty never basically changed, and he states it quite intransigently in 'Benjamin Franklin':

That I am I.
That my soul is a dark forest.
That my known self will never be more than a little clearing in the forest.
That gods, strange gods, come forth from the forest into the clearing of my known self, and then go back.
That I must have the courage to let them come and go.
That I will never let mankind put anything over me, but that I will try always to recognize and submit to the gods in me and the gods in other men and women.

Here the uniqueness of the individual, the manifoldness of the self, and the importance of the lower sensual plane of consciousness are expressed with poetic lucidity. 'I want them all, all the gods. They are all God', Swinburnian Lawrence had written in the winter of 1912–13 (P.307). 'I am sick to death of the Jewish monotheistic string. It has become monomaniac. I prefer the pagan many gods, and the animistic vision', he wrote to Rolf Gardiner from his New Mexican ranch (4.vii.24).

In this letter he links the monotheism of the western world with the *willing* of 'world unison'. He had realized that a perfect world meant the cessation of growth and individualism. 'The spirit of place ultimately always triumphs', and there was no more unison among men than among the coyotes, chipmunks, porcupines, deer, and rattlesnakes with which he was familiar. The crumbling of the old order with its 'white ideas' gave him hope; it meant 'life' and 'all sorts of wonder coming through'.

A 'new part' of Lawrence's soul 'woke up suddenly' in New Mexico, and 'the old world gave way to a new'. A sense of living religion came from the beauty and terror of the landscape, to be reinforced by the ritual dancing of the Red Indians. He felt in touch with 'a vast old religion' which preceded god-concepts and images. It was a religion in which there were no gods, for all is God; it was both cosmic and Darwinian, bringing one into direct contact with elemental life (P.141–7). The Indian belief that rays from 'the first of suns' make men strong and glad through linking the known and the unknown convinced him that westernized man, restricted by his consciousness and will, needed to submit to 'the great origin-powers of his life, and conquer them (*MM*.vii).

Lawrence enlarges on the subject in 'Reflections on the Death of a Porcupine' (P2.460–74), stressing as uncompromisingly as the Erewhonian oracle the inexorable law of nature on the survival of the fittest. Just as one creature preys on another, man has to fight for his place against the lower orders wherever he establishes himself. 'As far as existence goes, that life-species is the highest which can devour, or destroy, or subjugate every other life-species against which it is pitted in contest.' Man, he continues, is 'less than half grown'; he will have to 'start budding' or he will be 'abandoned as a failure in creation'. 'No man, or creature, or race can have vivid vitality unless it be moving towards a blossoming'; and man cannot blossom until he reaches 'a pure, *new* relationship with all the cosmos'.

The subject is brought to a practical conclusion in 'Aristocracy' (P2.475–84). After much that is unintentionally amusing here and there on the natural aristocrat – the man who is most alive and life-giving, most related to all living things, including his fellow-men, and to 'the circumambient universe', especially the sun – Lawrence describes 'the democratic mass, capitalist and proletariat alike', as 'a vast, sluggish, ghastily greedy porcupine, lumbering with inertia. Even Bolshevism is the same porcupine: nothing but greed and inertia.' A new aristocracy, a 'confraternity of the living sun' without reference to nationality, shall rule the world, he proclaims, 'making the embers of financial internationalism and industrial nationalism pale upon the hearth of the earth'.

Lawrence found this aristocratic spirit in Etruscan tomb paintings and, though he did not believe that the masses could be 'more than a little aware' of it, he was convinced that their lives could be vivified; they could live more abundantly; they could even be whole, 'body and mind and spirit, without split', as he writes is his vision of a Utopian Eastwood (P.830).

Frederick Carter's manuscripts on St John's 'Revelation' prompted Lawrence to write *Apocalypse* and an introduction designed for the publication of Carter's work. Commenting on the loss of the old cosmic awareness in this essay (P.292–303), Lawrence reflects on the 'miserable thought-forms' which education has substituted for the wonders of the natural world. The moon 'that pulls the tides' is not dead, but 'maybe we are dead, half-dead little modern worms stuffing our damp carcases with thought-forms, that have no sensual reality'. Lawrence is on the side of Rousseau, Wordsworth, and Keats; and he has excellent support from the philosopher A. N. Whitehead, particularly in the last chapter of his *Science and the Modern World* (1926).

It is said that in the midst of death we are in life. There is no finer testimony to the sincerity of Lawrence's inspiration than the burning belief in life which he showed in the months before his death. In 'The Real Thing' he wrote (P.202):

What makes life good to me is the sense that, even if I am sick and ill, I am alive, alive to the depths of my soul, and in touch somewhere in touch with the vivid life of the cosmos. Somehow my life draws strength from the depths of the universe, from the depths among the stars, from the great 'world'. Out of the great world comes my strength and my reassurance. One could say 'God', but the word 'God' is somehow tainted. But there *is* a flame or a Life Everlasting wreathing through the cosmos for ever and giving us our renewal, once we can get in touch with it.

'We ought to dance with rapture that we should be alive and in the flesh, and part of the living, incarnate cosmos', he wrote at the end of *Apocalypse*. It recalls the 'Dionysic' or 'Davidian' ecstasy of *Twilight in Italy*, and Browning's

How good is man's life, the mere living! how fit to employ
All the heart and the soul and the senses, for ever in joy!

The Poetry

Most of Lawrence's poetry is intimately related to his life or thought. In his preface to *Collected Poems* (1928), he states that he tried to arrange his poems in the order in which they were written because 'in their fragmentary fashion' they constitute 'a biography of an emotional and inner life'. This is true, but serious difficulties are encountered from the outset, since he altered many of the early poems for the collected edition, some being entirely rewritten, some recast. In consequence, the question often arises whether the revised version represents the youthful Lawrence or the Lawrence of 1928. He instances 'The Wild Common' and 'Virgin Youth', claiming that 'the wild common, the gorse, the virgin youth are here and now, the same: the same me, the same one experience. Only now perhaps I can give it more complete expression' (CP.850).

If Lawrence had merely recalled the earlier experiences, his assurance would be less open to question. A comparison between the two poems in *Amores* (1916) and their final form leads to different conclusions. The second 'Virgin Youth' does not remain true to the 'demon' that was shy in his adolescence; it reveals the rather obsessive and even absurd 'demon' that prompted the address to 'homunculus' in the second version of *Lady Chatterley's Lover* (xi). The first version of the poem is truer to Lawrence's youthful feelings, and more psychologically interesting (CP.909). That of 'The Wild Common' (CP.907–8), based on the saying 'When gorse is out, it's kissing time', ends, after a point of some imprecision, with a convincing adolescent integrity. The poet feels the exhilaration of spring, and imagines that the water which sways the reflection of his naked self is the pulsing blood of a heaving woman who holds him and thinks his supple body a 'rare glad thing, supremely good'. Exhilaration is conveyed not only through the general imagery of the scene but through rhythm and kinetic vigour; at the outset, for instance, the 'quick sparks on the gorse-bushes are leaping', and the hill 'bursts and heaves' under the 'spurting kick' of the rabbits. It is the thought which changes. The revised version reaches a conclusion reminiscent of Browning's 'How good is man's life, the mere living!' and 'God's in his heaven'. The dog image for the reflection of the water is unnecessary and fanciful; frequent repetition of 'Here' combined with its rhymes causes one verse to founder; and (as happens often in Lawrence's poems) rhyme requirement leads to ludicrous inadequacy: 'Oh but the water loves me and folds me,/Plays with me, sways me, lifts me and sinks me, murmurs: Oh marvellous stuff!' Nothing in the original sinks to this banality, though its final words approach it. Similarly the changed ending of the dialect poem 'Whether or Not' creates a new poem. The Lawrence who wrote it was more tired of the ache of amorous love which he had belittled in Whitman than the young policeman of the story, or the young unmarried Lawrence who wrote the story, could ever have been. Each poem has its validity, but the later Lawrence does not utter 'the real say' of the younger (cf. CP.76–85 and 935–42).

Much of Lawrence's early poetic expression is found in the descriptive prose of *The White Peacock*. His association of the setting with Meredith's 'Love in the Valley' may be seen in 'Renascence'. Lawrence's love, however, is linked with cruelty, and has strong Darwinian overtones, especially in 'Love on the Farm'. The quickening that comes from love in 'Renascence' makes the poet aware of the stir of animal and bird life on and around the farm, including one of its horrible manifestations. So his awareness of nature spreads, as if the valley were 'fleshed' like him 'With feelings that change and quiver/And clash and yet seem to tally'. In 'Love on the Farm' the same setting and theme provide a fictional scene. The language is equal to the subject in this dramatic monologue, and imagery is interwoven to give design and unity rarely equalled in Lawrence's rhymed verse. The wound of love, for example, is seen in the redness of the evening sky. As the lover approaches, the swallow reveals her red and flies away; the water-hen hides her scarlet blushes and lies 'still as dead'; the rabbit spurts with terror, and is caught in a springe. He kills it, flings it on the table board as he enters, and embraces the woman who awaits him. His hand is an uplifted sword against her bosom; his glance, like a broad blade, demands a welcome. His caressing fingers smell of the rabbit's fur, and the woman is snared as he fingers her 'pulse of life' and noses like a stoat eager for blood. As he kisses her, his bright dark eyes come like a hood over her mind. She drowns in a flood of 'sweet fire', and finds 'death good'. The darkness and sweet fire of this conclusion are suggested menacingly but with admirable appropriateness in the fanciful imagery of the opening lines: 'What large, dark hands are those at the window/Grasping in the golden light/ Which weaves its way through the evening wind/At my heart's delight?'

Many of the earlier poems relate to the tangle of Lawrence's pre-marriage love life, most of them belonging to the Croydon period. His first love, Jessie Chambers, is the Eve of 'Renascence'; his longing for her is deeply expressed in 'Dog-Tired', though the poem (written or imagined after a day in the hayfields at Greasley) promises an excellence of form which is not fulfilled. 'Cherry Robbers' is based on a scene at Haggs Farm which was elaborated poetically as a prelude to Miriam's self-sacrifice (*SL*.xi). Written in the mood which made Lawrence tell Louie Burrows, 'Some savage in me would like to taste your blood', it has overtones of love and cruelty, in the blood-stained birds and the curt concluding 'I will see/If she has any tears', far sharper than those of 'Love on the Farm'.

'Dreams Old and Nascent', 'Discipline', and 'Baby-Movements' were the first of Lawrence's poems to be published (p. 20). They are all Croydon poems, and Jessie Chambers is the 'darling' of the first two in both their original and final forms. It is well for her, he reflects in 'Letter from Town: On a Grey Morning in March', with younglings at the farm and in the fields, but he is in a desert of rocks without water. He imagines her in the woods or 'out by the orchard, where violets secretly darken the earth'; and the song he is trying to write is like tears and swords to his heart, 'arrows no armour will turn or deter'. In 'Letter from Town: The Almond-Tree' the violets she had promised to send him are a pledge of their 'early love that hardly has opened yet', and he thinks of her unbearable tenderness and sparkling eyes 'so wide with hereafter'.

The realization or conviction that she shrank physically from passion is the subject of 'Lightning'; it is at the root of his dislike for the grieving 'Of the she-dove in the blossom, still believing/Love will yet again return to her and make all good' in 'Sigh No More', a poem where rhyming leads to a final bathos which recalls the 'supremely good' and 'marvellous stuff' in the two versions of 'The Wild Common'. In the moon images of 'Aware', 'A Pang of Reminiscence', and 'A White Blossom' there is a hint of 'the first white love of my youth, passionless and in vain'.

'Scent of Irises' evokes a happy memory of Jessie and Lawrence amid a 'yellow incantation' of flowers (for 'the cowslips of the meadow above' cf. *WP*.II.vii); he thanks God that the 'healing days' can close the gulf between them. In 'Reminder' he wonders how different life would have been if only she had 'unlocked the moon' and 'taken' him in November 1910, when his mother was dying, just before he became engaged to Louie Burrows. 'Last Words to Miriam' is remarkable for its imagery. In 'Anna Victrix' (*R*.vi) physical fulfilment is a purifying fire which creates a golden radiance; here its fire removes bodily 'deadness and dross' to produce a lovely painted window. The image of the cross in an early version of the poem (CP.946) anticipates its use in *Studies in Classic American Literature* as a symbol of the conflict between spirituality and sex. The mood of the poem is one of failure and guilt: 'I should have been cruel enough to bring/You through the flame.' In 'Ah, Muriel' (CP.735) Lawrence confesses that he did Jessie Chambers 'an injury'. Soon after breaking his engagement to Louie Burrows, he met Jessie again, wondering (in the words of 'After Many Days') 'how make the best reparation'. She was 'kindly cold', and he could not forgive her. 'Hymn to Priapus' (previously entitled 'Constancy of a Sort') refers to Orion, the most significant constellation for Paul and Miriam (*SL*.viii), as 'the star of my first beloved/Love-making./The witness of all that bitter-sweet/Heart-aching'.

The position of most of the poems relating to Louie Burrows indicates that Lawrence's order is not always reliable. Although 'Snap-Dragon' follows 'After Many Days', a copy of it was handed with a significant glance to Jessie Chambers in the summer of 1907 (p. 16). The opening stanzas attain a narrative ease and quiet splendour of incidental imagery rather in the style of Yeats, but the poem becomes involved in fanciful analogies, especially when Lawrence attempts to express blood-consciousness. Lack of grasp and improvization result in metaphorical extravagance, unevenness, and disproportion. The 'reiver/rover' cuckoo which takes possession of the poet's heart 'in a heat of love' is *'this rich/ Sumptuous central grain;/This mutable witch,/This one refrain/This laugh in the fight,/This clot in the night,/This field of delight'. 'This clot of night'* is 'This clot of light,/This brown core of night' in an earlier version.

Lawrence is catching at expression; inevitably, because the experience has not clarified. The antagonistic movement with which the poem ends suggests once again a sadistic streak in the imagination of a sexually frustrated writer.

After this highly-charged but rather cloudy verse, 'Tease' expresses a welcome light-heartedness, making good-humoured play of Louie's anxious personal curiosity. Like 'Kisses in the Train' (on the dizzying success of Lawrence's impulsive proposal), the poem achieves a stylistic adequacy and completeness of form which are unusually satisfying. 'Come Spring, Come Sorrow' opens admirably, but soon descends to a less demanding level of verse, as Lawrence plies a sexual theme and announces his developing cosmic theories: 'from the golden sun/A quickening, masculine gleam floats in to all/Us creatures', and 'Fine thrills' fly from our 'full-sappy' earth to quicken the spheres. Lawrence's love for his 'gipsy' is the theme of 'A Love Song' and 'Twofold', but Louie Burrows was too respectable to respond fully to his nature, and her self-repression is presented with physical vividness in 'The Hands of the Betrothed'.

The Trespasser was founded on the last phase of the love-story between Helen Corke and her violin-teacher. Its fatal conclusion is the subject of the dramatic monologue 'Red' (CP.898–9). Perhaps some critical situation in that story, told by Helen or imagined by Lawrence, was the inspiration for the complementary dramatic lyrics 'A Winter's Tale' and 'Return', which seem to introduce the Helen poems. The 'drink–shrink' antithesis of 'The Appeal' (a poem related to the ardour of 'Mystery') presents their general theme. 'Lilies in the Fire' gives the problem more specifically: 'You love me while I hover tenderly/Like moonbeams kissing you; but the body of me/Closing upon you in the lightning-flamed/Moment, destroys you, you are just destroyed . . . . like lilies flagged and sere/Upon the floor, that erst stood up so fresh.' In 'Lotus and Frost', which reveals the same frustration, Helen is the 'moon-faced lover' while the lotus symbolizes sensual passion (cf. p. 82 and P2.235–6). 'Repulsed' shows Lawrence like 'an empty dandelion stalk, bereft of connection, small/And nakedly nothing 'twixt world and heaven' (cf. pp. 82 and 91). Fanciful, disproportionate, and distracting imagery is probably the most notable feature of the poem, the sky being like 'a cat's distended pupil' that sparkles with stars, and the lights of two towns gushing upwards like breath from the nostrils of a beast 'crouched across the globe' but ready to pounce on 'the cat in heaven's hostile eminence'. 'Coldness in Love' is an imaginative reconstruction of Helen Corke's experience when she and Lawrence stayed at a boarding-house near the harbour at Seaford one October weekend in 1910. His quandary as they returned that same autumn from Nottingham, where Helen had been staying with Jessie Chambers, is the subject of 'Excursion Train'. The origin of 'The Yew-Tree on the Downs' can be seen in *The Trespasser* (xxxi). Though the reasoning may have suffered in the revision, 'Release' is a reduced and improved form of 'Reproach' (CP.877–9), and rather remarkable for its sustained imagery. 'These Clever Women' expresses impatience with a relationship which seemed entirely on the upper plane: 'Am I doomed in a long coition of words to mate you?' Lawrence asks. The conclusion, which has all the bluntness of his later self, should be compared with the earlier ending, in 'A Spiritual Woman' (CP.950). His reproach in 'Passing Visit to Helen' is that she continues her old game, keeping him like a glowing brazier at which she can 'warm her hands and invite her soul', a priestess or spiritual lover 'Sprinkling incense and salt of words/And kisses pale, and sipping the toll/Of incense-smoke that rises like birds'; for Lawrence she was another Sue Bridehead (see CP.888–9, where much of the expression is identical).

The overriding love of Lawrence's youth was for his mother. Her illness and death occasioned him the greatest sorrow of his life. Without her he was anchorless and rudderless, and it is no wonder that, after drifting this way and that, he took the first opportunity to live with a mature woman who could satisfy the yearning he felt, initially at least, for both mother-love and marriage. In 'Monologue of a Mother', he expresses with sympathetic insight his mother's fear of losing him (probably to Jessie Chambers); each suffers, and the pain of one and the guilt of the other are well conveyed in:

I must look away from him, for my faded eyes
Like a cringing dog at his heels offend him now,
Like a toothless hound pursuing him with my will;
Till he chafes at my crouching persistence, and a sharp spark flies
In my soul from under the sudden frown of his brow
As he blenches and turns away, and my heart stands still.

'End of Another Home Holiday' recalls the ache of leaving her 'so lonely, greying now'. A haunting sense of guilt affects the poet's impressions of the outer scene. He thinks of the moon pursuing her lonely way without anguish, but 'the yearning-eyed/Inexorable love goes lagging' ever at his side. Other forms of life enjoy isolation at times of growth, and the corncrake (repeated with other features of the outward scene in *SL*.xi) insistently voices another call (as in 'The Overtone').

At Croydon, Lawrence continually thought of his mother's suffering ('Suspense', 'Endless Anxiety'); his own gethsamene is referred to in 'Reminder'. In 'The End' he thinks of the tribulations of her life; 'The Bride' presents her death-bed picture (as in *SL*.xiv). The ambivalence of 'The Virgin Mother' is repeated in reverse at the end of *Sons and Lovers*, and the 'void' in which Paul finds himself is expressed by Lawrence after his mother's funeral in 'At the Window'. Of the other poems written soon afterwards (CP.104–11) the most felicitous is 'Sorrow', which gives dramatic expression to unutterable feelings in an apparently casual manner worthy of Browning (for the recollection see *SL*.xiii). The image of 'Troth with the Dead' is strikingly unusual, and far more impressive than the poetical fancy of 'Submergence'. Some of the poems written in memory of his mother show little inner compulsion, rather a poeticizing proclivity. This seems true of 'Brother and Sister', though its rhetorical accomplishment is obvious. The lure of imagery is a bane in 'The Shadow of Death', contrasting forcibly with the lighter touch and genuine feeling conveyed by the best of 'Call into Death'. Lyrical eloquence, even nearer to speech rhythms, marks 'On that Day', Lawrence's birthday salute to his mother. She is remembered also in 'Elegy', 'Everlasting Flowers', 'All Souls', and 'Spirits Summoned West'; but the most memorable poem with which she is linked is 'Piano', born after long gestation from a poem clogged with secondary (but biographically interesting) detail (CP.958). Only the very heart of its inspirational experience has been retained and refined. Strong feeling is awakened, but it is artistically controlled, and there is no sentimental excess, though Lawrence weeps 'like a child for the past'.

Brief minor poems like 'Gipsy' and 'In Trouble and Shame' (to take examples which differ in type and mood) have a clarity and completeness which make many of Lawrence's rhymed poems seem forced rather than finished. His verse can be laboured and dull; it can lose distinctness of outline through the continued efflorescence of distracting metaphor. Figurative elaboration at the opening of 'The Shadow of Death' is utterly confusing compared with the 'littered lettering of trees and hills and houses' which can no longer be read when darkness closes the book of landscape in 'Red Moon-Rise'; the conceit here may be fanciful, but its fascinating originality prints it on the memory. In the octet of 'Baby Running Barefoot' the figurative images, though delicate individually, ultimately blur the picture; with sense-priorities rightly ordered in the sestet, subordination presents resemblances clearly, and with maximum effect through emphasis on the link-words 'cool', 'firm', and 'silken': 'And I could feel her feet in either hand/Cool as syringa buds in morning hours,/Or firm and silken as young peony flowers'.

'Corot' and 'Michael Angelo' were written after Lawrence's visit to the Tate Gallery with Helen Corke. The second is too much an imitation of Blake to create a convincing impression, and comparison with 'The Tyger' suggests that its relative lack of imaginative power (and compression) is due largely to Lawrence's proneness to explain the mysteries of creation. Its ends vaguely, in rhyme-determined factitiousness which lacks the significant clarity of the original (CP.933). 'Corot' opens with an impression one can share, and has a greater and more subtle appeal, but unity and intensity are reduced through Lawrence's urge to say something on Life, which leads to the incidental inadequacy of 'it silently sweeps to its somewhere, its goal' and to the vaguer grandeur of epithet in a portentous conclusion: 'Imitate the magnificent trees/That speak no word of rapture, but only/Breathe largely the luminous breeze'.

By and large the Croydon and London poems suggest literary exercises or sketches. Sensitive classroom scenes ('The Best of School', 'A Snowy Day in School') and incidental outdoor imagery are memorable, but it seems hardly possible that some of the forced and tired writing of this and the subsequent period can be the work of the poet who wrote 'Ballad of Another Ophelia'. The difference is between kinds of experience, for, as Coleridge pointed out, the vitalizing power of the poetic imagination is inseparable from 'musical delight' in words. Analysis of this ballad in terms of sound and rhythm will not explain how the words came as they did, or how they combine with the imagery to create the right psychological effect. The poem is one of Lawrence's supreme imaginative triumphs. It has 'the quality of a troublesome dream that seems incoherent but is selected by another sort of consciousness. The latter part is the waking up part, yet not really awake, because she is mad' (31.vii.14).

'Two Wives', one of Lawrence's most ambitious poems, presents the antithesis between the merely spiritual and the more sensual love. The spiritual wife is dead, and the darkness of failure is in her eyes; she gains her husband only when death releases his spirit; she has kept his virginity intact for him, and now at last they are one. The idea is implicit in the deathly pallor of the scene. To reinforce it, Lawrence added the last two sections when he prepared *Collected Poems*. The second wife, who bore the husband's children, can now triumph over the first, for whom he is no more than a dream. All the first had done was to rouse his mind and burn away his heart; but she must stand back and not dare to touch his body, 'for he hated you/To touch him, and he said so, and you knew'. The rejoinder is dramatic, and makes the poem more explicit; yet it creates a less rounded whole than the original conclusion.

This death-bed scene is the setting for a subject which has its counter-part to some degree in the more parochial tragi-comedy of 'Whether or Not', a dialect poem in varying moods. Lawrence had a flair for this kind of verse. Of the three other dialect poems, 'The Collier's Wife', 'Violets', and 'The Drained Cup', the first is the best and most true to life. No stroke is wasted in this dramatic sketch, which recalls a scene at the open-ing of *SL*.v; it is a kind of ballad where the humour of situation and surface harshness intensify whatever tragic feeling escapes.

Several poems towards the end of the 'rhyming' group reflect Law-rence's attitudes to the First World War. 'On the March' and 'The Attack' have nothing to do with the soldiers or the battle-front. The first, probably the most artistically satisfying of these poems, expresses a desolating and unrelieved sense of futility. 'The Attack' suggests a sudden access of pseudo-inspiration which made Lawrence think of war sacrifice as a kind of transubstantiation. The blossoming of 'every black tree' is made clearer in a letter to Lady Cynthia Asquith (2.xi.15): 'Let all the leaves fall, and many branches. But the quick of the tree must not perish. There are unrevealed buds which can come forward into another epoch of civilisation, if only we can shed this dead form and be strong in the spirit of love and creation.' 'Dreams Old and Nascent' is a complete recast of an idea which came to Lawrence in a mood of euphoria with his Croydon class (CP.922–6). With the war in mind, he looks forward to the time when people wake up from 'the foul dream' of industrial greed and envy, break out of the prison and illusions of materialism, and find fulfilment in flesh and spirit:

For the proper dream-stuff is molten, and moving mysteriously,
And the bodies of men and women are molten matter of dreams
That stirs with a stir which is cosmic, as ever, invisibly
The heart of the live world pulses, and the blood of the live world teems.

The subject of destruction for the sake of renewal recurs in Lawrence's letters (see ?3.viii.15 and to Catherine Carswell, 16.vii.16).

*   *   *

One can readily see why Lawrence ignored the chronological principle to begin the second main group of his poems with the fulfilment theme of *Look! We Have Come Through!* Why he describes the two groups as 'rhyming' and 'unrhyming' is a mystery, though his introduction to the American edition of *New Poems* (CP.181–6) does suggest that he came to associate *Look! We Have Come Through!* with free verse. Most of the poems in this volume are rhymed, though it ends with the kind of free verse which is characteristic of Lawrence.

Three brief introductory poems are significant. The first is clearly influenced by the opening of Keats's *Endymion;* 'perfect, bright experience never falls/To nothingness'. It outlasts death, as 'Elegy' shows with reference to Lawrence's mother. Finally, how much better it is to forget oneself, and to feel at one with the universe.

The honeymoon poems are introduced by 'Hymn to Priapus' and 'Ballad of a Wilful Woman'. The change in title of the first from 'Constancy of a Sort' is a wry admission of guilt, for the first beloved with whom he associated Orion was Jessie Chambers: 'And something in me has forgotten,/Has ceased to care./Desire comes up, and contentment is debonair.' The picture of Lawrence's bountiful new love ('The big, soft country lass,/Like a loose sheaf of wheat') is a less happy translation than his image of the old: 'My love lies underground/With her face upturned to mine,/And her mouth unclosed in the last long kiss/That ended her life and mine.' Yet the poem contains some of the most haunting, bardic verses Lawrence ever wrote. The ballad tells the story of a woman 'trying the various ideals – Aphrodite, Apostle John, etc.' (28.x.13), and the interest is in the 'etc.', for it hints premonitorily at Frieda's 'troubling about the children' (cf. ?26.x.13) and her committal to 'restless wanderings'.

Frieda's mourning for the children she had abandoned was a source of irritation to Lawrence for many years, and his honeymoon was hardly

over before he gave expression to the *saeva indignatio* which his unsym-
pathetic, self-centred jealousy roused in him. In 'She Looks Back' she is
'Lot's Wife – Not Wife, but Mother' and a 'pillar of salt accursed'. This
is the first of Lawrence's more substantial poems in free verse, and it
hardly conforms to what he wrote so lyrically on the subject in his
introduction to the American edition of *New Poems*. Many poets have
captured the magic of the moment, and preserved it in traditional forms
of verse. Greater technical freedom gives a poet a greater opportunity for
avoiding false turns of expression; equally, it can lead to diminution of
both intensity and artistic discipline. As happened frequently with
Lawrence, free verse can also develop into more elaborate poems which
do not aim to capture the evanescence or 'momentaneity' of experience.
The imagery with which he refers to this kind of poetry dazzles judgment.
Nobody can dispute the general basis of Lawrence's contention:

> In the immediate present there is no perfection, no consummation,
> nothing finished. The strands are all flying, quivering, inter-
> mingling into the web, the waters are shaking the moon. There is
> no round, consummate moon on the face of the running water,
> nor on the face of the unfinished tide.

The critical question does not relate to the nature of experience but to
the form which poetry assumes, whatever kind of verse is chosen.
Lawrence writes excellently on 'clichés of rhythm as well as of phrase'
and on the irrelevance of all external laws to free verse. 'The law must
come each time from within.' It will vary according to subject, mood,
and poet. Lawrence's free verse is not Whitman's, which is less variable,
less conversational, and more rhetorical.

What it aspires to be may be gauged in a poem of moderate success
such as 'Bei Hennef'. It reaches much more ecstatic heights in 'Frohnleichnam'; and the poem has an excellence of form which depends on
structural integration through both repetition and the steady centri-
petalization of imagery, in words which give the ear, the imagination,
and the intellect, a pleasing sense of completion. The immediacy of the
experience, its 'creative quick' quality, is inescapable, but the supreme
test is artistic.

The vicissitudes of Lawrence's early marriage, its discords and resolu-
tions, are reflected in many poems, some of which may appear indefinite
in reference; in general their interest is biographical rather than poetical.

Excruciating experience achieves fine expression in the form and imagery of 'A Young Wife'. 'River Roses' ends in private symbolism ('Let it be as the snake disposes/Here in this simmering marsh'), on which light is thrown in 'The Reality of Peace' (P.677–9). 'I am Like a Rose' and 'Rose of All the World' are best explained with reference to *Women in Love* (see pp. 294–5). 'A Doe at Evening' is spoilt by one of Lawrence's intuitive imbecilities (seen more absurdly in 'Aristocracy', when he feels his 'bull's blood' responding to Susan, his cow). Several undistinguished and rather miscellaneous poems mark the middle section of *Look! We Have Come Through!*

One of the most memorable poems in the volume is 'Meeting Among the Mountains', but the sense of guilt which links Christ on the Tyrolean crucifix with the driver of the bullock remains a haunting mystery until one realizes (as Frieda disclosed) that the brown eyes of the driver which are 'black with misery and hate' recalled one whom Lawrence had admired as a teacher of French, and whom subsequently he had been instrumental in wronging, Professor Ernest Weekley. The highly wrought imagery of the poem has an artistic relatedness and consonance from beginning to end. Central to the crescendo of suffering, His own, the driver's, and Lawrence's, is the dead Christ on the crucifix; reproach is sensed also in the scene, from the cold mountains to the averted and scentless pansies by the road.

'Giorno dei Morti' is a beautifully organized and completely exterior picture which speaks for itself; unlike 'Sunday Afternoon in Italy', where the scene is described for the comment, and neither seems to have much of the substance of poetry.

'She Said as Well to Me' has a remarkably quiet beauty and dignity of tone, but is spoilt by the 'I tell you' style of the Lawrentian retort with which it ends. 'Song of a Man Who is Loved', on which Lawrence set much store (3.viii.17 and CP.852), suffers in comparison with 'Song of a Man Who Has Come Through'. Their juxtaposition confirms a coarseness of texture and inappropriate jauntiness of rhythm in the former, which is too 'instant' (though rhymed) and shows the bounce and assertion of which he complains: 'I am that I am, and no more than that: but so much/I am, nor will I be bounced out of it.' Self-expression often passes as poetry in Lawrence.

The 'Look! We Have Come Through!' theme of the volume has three aspects. It relates hopefully to Lawrence's marriage, as is seen in 'Spring

Morning'. 'One Woman to All Women' develops Lawrence's idea of man and woman in fulfilment as beings in union but separate, 'in glorious equilibrium' like stars. The thought is continued in 'Manifesto', a piece of free verse that falls rather flat at first, proceeding in orotund language to say simple things at great length, punctuated occasionally with bland conversational commonplaces such as 'So far, so good', 'our heaven, as a matter of fact', and 'quite beyond, if you understand what that means'. With 'pure existence', arising from fulfilment in sexual passion, it reaches higher levels, and in both idea and expression coincides with *Women in Love* (cf. end of xxiii). A 'star-equilibrium which alone is freedom' is reached, 'two of us, unutterably distinguished, and in unutterable conjunction'. So singleness or purity of being is attained – 'we shall love, we shall hate', 'the lightning and the rainbow appearing in us unbidden'. The poem, like the novel, was written at Zennor, but the concept of separateness in marriage union has an earlier origin (cf. P.468).

The second emergent idea relates to war. In 'New Heaven and Earth' Lawrence rejoices that he has risen above the taint of self which made everything around him a 'maniacal horror'. He delights not only in the death of his old self but also in the destruction of much that is hideous and foul. Despite the war horror, he finds that he is 'living where life was never yet dreamed of', and this new life and vision he attributes to fulfilment in marriage. Only the fulfilled can be 'pure' and 'single'. The poem is not always well or wisely expressed. Its principal thought is expressed poetically in 'Autumn Rain'; it assumes a negative form in *Women in Love* (v, xxxi), and a more positive expression (linked implicitly with thoughts of leadership) in 'The Reality of Peace' (P.686–7). Lawrence wishes to be released from 'the debased social body', be himself, and find others who are 'distinct and at ease in themselves like stars'. In 'Craving for Spring' he thinks excitedly, but not with unqualified assurance, of the new world that could arise after the war; the same hope and the same metaphor inspire 'Whistling of Birds', the essay Lawrence wrote when the war ended.

'Song of a Man Who Has Come Through' reveals the third transformation. Only in his pure and single self can Lawrence submit to 'the subtle new wind from heaven', the 'fine wind' that 'is blowing the new direction of Time'. Though some common aims may be seen in him and Blake, his cosmic religion is much nearer the 'wise passiveness' of the pantheist Wordsworth. The stress is not on 'mental fight' but primarily on the higher knowledge that comes 'of itself' from being in touch with the eternal. Lawrence's repudiation of the personal will as a reforming force is emphatic at the outset: 'Not I, not I, but the wind that blows through me!' (It is no wonder that he and Bertrand Russell found they were at cross-purposes.) He prays for that purity of self which will enable him to respond sensitively to the new vision. He wishes to be 'a good fountain, a good well-head' (cf. P.421–2), and recalls the three angels, as in *The Rainbow* (xi): 'Once three angels stood in Abraham's doorway, and greeted him, and stayed and ate with him, leaving his household enriched for ever when they went.' Lawrence's poem expresses the purpose to which he wished to dedicate himself, and this was to show how life can be lived more abundantly.

*   *   *

Birds, Beasts and Flowers was begun at San Gervasio near Florence in September 1920 and completed in February 1923. Most of the poems were written in Italy or Sicily, a few in other countries, and several in New Mexico. They are divided into nine groups, prefixed with quotations, mainly from the third edition of John Burnet's *Early Greek Philosophy*, a book which influenced Lawrence considerably, according to Richard Aldington. The title was recalled from the popular hymn 'Now the day is over' by S. Baring-Gould.

The order of poems in each section seems to be chronological by and large. The majority of the first were written at San Gervasio, as were 'The Evangelistic Beasts', an atypical group. The four beasts ('living creatures') of the Apocalypse (Revelation, iv. 6–8) belong to 'the last age of the living cosmos', before a God of the universe was created by man; their wings suggest that they command all space. With the dwindling of 'the cosmic idea', they eventually became associated with the Evangelist writers Matthew, Mark, Luke, and John (*Ap.* xviii), as in *The Book of Kells*. For Lawrence therefore their wings are spiritual, and a menace to life; the poems are a foursquare counter-gospel on the inadequacy of Christian idealism. Matthew, being a man, reiterates Lawrence's view that life needs to be lived on the dark sensual plane as well as on the spiritual; he is a 'traveller back and forth'. The lion represented by Mark has become 'the faithful sheep-dog of the Shepherd' and will soon be blind; once, a king of beasts, he lay in the sun, dreaming voluptuously, even of blood. After two thousand years of spiritual winging, the bull Luke is 'over-charged by the dammed-up pressure of his own massive black blood' and threatens war; 'the bull of the proletariat has got his head down'. John, the intellectual, sun-peering eagle ('In the beginning was the Word') now sits moulting and shabby-looking, waiting for a phoenix-change which will create a new conception of life.

Though more obviously characteristic of *Birds, Beasts and Flowers*, the tortoise poems in 'Reptiles' may also be considered as a unit. Lawrence regards the independence, isolation, and indomitable spirit of the baby tortoise with wonder and admiration; at times it looks comical, but it is 'a Stoic, Ulyssean atom' or a Titan under its battle-shield. The creative mystery is then presented with mathematical reference to the pattern of its shell, and to the symbolical cross which 'goes right through him'. The mutual indifference of the tortoise family makes Lawrence think the infant tortoise, 'all to himself', another Adam, 'wandering in the slow triumph of his own existence'. Then, by contrast, we see the male, 'crucified into sex', 'dragged out of an eternity of silent isolation' in comical courtship attendance on the female, his 'steel-trap face' opening occasionally to seize her scaly ankle until his consummation or crucifixion is heard again and again as he screams. In his strange yell, which seems to come 'from under the very edge of the farthest far-off horizon of life', Lawrence finds the 'cross' which breaks our integrity and tears a cry from us. There is a degree of ambivalence in the human overtones of this series; some nostalgia is felt for the happy innocent isolation or 'integrity' which is lost, but we are 'torn, to become whole', 'that which is in part' finding its integrity again 'throughout the universe'.

Lawrence's revulsion against sex-mindedness or sexuality is strongest in the 'Animals' section. In 'Bibbles' the polyandrous instincts of Lawrence's New Mexican dog (which drove him to demonic rages of jealousy) turn into a playful derisory indictment of the American 'live-by-love humanity' which he chose to see in the promiscuity of this 'little Walt-Whitmanesque bitch'. More amusing is 'The Ass', where the 'authentic Arabic interpretation' of his braying (mimetically produced), and the contrast between the wild ass of the steppes and the ridiculous figure of its submissive donkey successor, prompt an attack on its human counterpart. The ass, 'the first of all animals to fall finally into love', is, like man, 'always in rut'. By a convenient freak of fancy, associating in his habitual manner sex-mindedness with spiritual love and Christendom,

Lawrence sees the plight of western humanity as that of an ass, the triumphal entry into Jerusalem leading inevitably to the 'great cross', the conflict between the 'blood-self' and the 'nerve-brain' or spiritual self (*St.Am*.ix). 'He-Goat' presents another animal whose instinctive life is foiled. Occasionally one sees the God-gleam in his 'storm-lightning-slitted eye', but he has become a poor, stinking, lascivious, 'domesticated beast'. This is how Lawrence, in a Swift-like mood of disgust, typifies the 'procreant male' with his 'selfish will and libidinous desire'.

So *dégagé* is Lawrence's humour that, even when his main intention is serious, as in 'The Ass', he can present animals in their comical aspects. As soon as he detests her, his she-goat 'trips mild and smug like a woman going to mass', or he catches sight of her 'standing like some huge, ghoulish grey bird in the air, on the bough of a leaning almond-tree' at Fontana Vecchia, 'straight as a board on the bough, looking down like some hairy horrid God the Father in a William Blake imagination'. A light touch is found in the tropical humour of 'Purple Anemones'. Whenever Persephone gains her freedom, flowers spring up in her Sicilian tracks: Dis is after her. With a dramatic adaptation of Swinburne's 'When the hounds of spring are on winter's traces' to the flowering scene, Lawrence turns the subject into engaging ridicule of equal rights for women. It is spring, and Ceres and Persephone think they are enfranchised.

There are some strange inclusions. 'The Revolutionary' identifies Lawrence with Samson, a 'Lord of the dark and moving hosts' intent on bringing down the white rigid pillars which support the dome of lofty idealism. In another incongruous poem, 'The Evening Land', Lawrence defines the two spectres which keep him from America: its 'exaggerate', undifferentiated, general benevolence; and, even more frightening in its effects on the development of the individual, its faith in mechanization. 'Peace' is inspired by the same impulse as 'The Revolutionary'; Lawrence thinks of Etna again in eruption, its bright trail of lava moving like a royal snake down to the sea, to wipe out an old era, and create a new. He had described 'the new life' in terms of the truth and passion that come from the burning darkness at the earth's centre. 'But the dark fire, the hidden, invisible passion, that has neither flame nor heat, that is the greatest of all passion' (?1.iii.15). For Lawrence there could be peace only in the certainty of life's continuing renewal: 'My heart will know no peace/Till the hill bursts.' 'Tropic' and 'Southern Night' are comple-

mentary sun and moon poems. The first gives a preternatural vision of
the renewal taking place, not from the earth centre, but from 'the dark
heart of the first of suns. . . . Because from the first of suns come travelling
the rays that make men strong and glad and gods who can range between
the known and unknown' (*MM*.vii). It is the consciousness and will
commonly associated by Lawrence with northern races which is seen in
'the milk of northern spume', turned black in the veins by waves of
dark heat. The blood-dark moon of the southern night restores blood-
consciousness, healing a mind stung with memories of the 'white'
northern world. 'Spirits Summoned West' seems to have been drafted
into the last section, partly to illustrate the disconsolate ghosts of the
preliminary passage from Empedocles, partly to further the recurring
theme of non-fulfilment in the northern world.

In 'Guelder Roses', one of the first of his poems, Lawrence declares his
intention to seek for immortal fruit elsewhere than on 'the stems of
virginity'. He begins *Birds, Beasts and Flowers* with impish emphasis on
the vulval features of ripe fruits; yet he makes little of these subjects,
and their prominence is rather unfortunate, for, in retrospect, they
appear relatively dull. More typical poems give us graceful incisiveness
of incidental description, with witty asides, and hints of themes related
to life or the contemporary world, the tone ranging from the chirpy to
the oracular and beautifully poetical. More of these qualities are found
in 'Medlars and Sorb-Apples', with its autumnal suggestion of departure
and isolation, of an Orphic farewell and a Dionysiac 'intoxication of final
loneliness' in the exquisite underworld darkness. The thought is continued in 'Grapes': 'Close the eyes, and go/Down the tendrilled avenues
of wine and the otherworld.' For the vine is the 'invisible rose' of the
pristine world when men enjoyed an audile and tactile sensitivity like
that of tendrils. We could be on the brink of 're-remembrance', Lawrence
thinks; but, with 'the agonised perverseness of a child heavy with sleep,
yet fighting, fighting to keep awake', we still clutch 'at our vistas
democratic, boulevards, tram-cars, policemen', and all the sober values
of our 'pale day'. To the same period as these poems belong two written
at Fiesole. Tuscan cypresses recall 'the delicate magic of life' which is
buried with the Etruscans. Only one evil exists, and that is the denial of
life, Lawrence holds. He wishes he could restore the meaning which life
held for them, and which is now 'inviolable in soft cypress-trees'.
'Turkey-Cock' presents a colourful and amusingly depreciatory study

of an imperfect species, one impression graphically embodying the spirit of insistence or assertion ('A raw American will, that has never been tempered by life'). Lawrence wonders whether this 'slag-wattled' bird must go through the fire again until it is 'smelted pure' or whether it will become the bird of the west.

At Zell-am-See (p. 45) he wrote 'Fish'. He is thrilled by its movement:

> To have the element under one, like a lover;
> And to spring away with a curvetting click in the air,
> Provocative.
> Dropping back with a slap on the face of the flood.
> And merging oneself!

As with the tortoise in its Adam-like isolation, he envies the fish its life of sheer sensation ('You and the naked element,/Sway-wave') and its freedom from love. The world of the fish is beyond human ken; '*His God stands outside my God.*' Man is not 'the measure of creation'. The poem concludes with a hint of teleological significance. Jesus was called 'The Fish' because he had 'the other consciousness of the Ocean which is the divine End of us all', Lawrence writes in 'The Proper Study', envisaging a new relationship, with men 'like fishes on a great wave of the God of the End, swimming together, and apart, in a new medium', a 'new whole' (P.721–3). The two bat poems he wrote at Florence, on his way back to Sicily, are at the other extreme, in being devoid of ulterior meaning. They exemplify an amazing genius for recalling impressions, and the dramatization of 'Man and Bat' has the effect of total experience. The Lawrentian 'I would have had to kill him if he'd bitten me' recalls 'Rabbit Snared in the Night'.

Sicilian impressions are memorable, none more so than the visual re-creation of 'Snake'. Its rhythmic ductility accords felicitously with physical movements but, as a whole, the poem seems rather contrived, as if written to give concrete expression to ideas expressed in 'The Crown' (P2.407):

The snake is the spirit of the great corruptive principle, the festering cold of the marsh. This is how he seems, as we look back. We revolt from him, but we share the same life and tide of life as he. He struggles as we struggle, he enjoys the sun, he comes to the water to drink, he curls up, hides himself to sleep. And under the low skies of the far past aeons, he emerged a king out of chaos, a long beam of new life.

It is in comparison with arrested forms of life like the vulture (p. 74) that the snake appears a king. He is held down by the moist earth, but 'the sun in him would fain rise half-way, and move on feet' (CP.348). He is in exile in the underworld; in his emergence he shares the beauty of the swan when it first rose out of the marshes; he represents a spirit of corruption which is pure and divine because it seeks new life (P2.403). For Lawrence this urge is inseparable from the dissolution which accompanies creation in the universe; the snake typifies the principle of pure or 'living' corruption (P.678–9).

More distinctive and purely poetical is 'Almond Blossom'. In Sicily (a centre of Greek civilization 'in the world's morning') the almond is 'in exile, in the iron age'. But it offers encouragement as its blossom bursts from iron-like branches in January:

> Think of it, from the iron fastness
> Suddenly to dare to come out naked, in perfection of blossom,
>   beyond the sword-rust.
> Think, to stand there in full-unfolded nudity, smiling,
> With all the snow-wind, and the sun-glare, and the dog-star
>   baying epithalamion.

It inspired Lawrence to write in the first version of *Studies in Classic American Literature*:

> Even the buds of iron break into soft little flames of issue. So will people change. So will the machine-parts open like buds and the great machine break into leaf. Even we can expect our iron ships to put forth vine and tendril and bunches of grapes, like the ship of Dionysos in full sail upon the ocean.

The mood of 'Bare Fig-Trees' is mocking. Under 'the many-branching candelabrum' of one of these 'wicked' trees with 'many secrets up its sleeve', Lawrence sees in the sky-pointing of its twigs a representation of democracy, 'equality over-reaching itself', each 'intent to hold the candle of the sun upon its socket-tip'.

Repeating the dominant image of 'Purple Anemones', 'Sicilian Cyclamens' presents the 'dawn-rose' flowers 'Arching/Waking, pricking their ears/Like delicate very-young greyhound bitches', as in that

'Mediterranean morning' of Grecian splendour 'when our world began'. With 'Hibiscus and Salvia Flowers' we encounter another age, another mood: Lawrence is disgusted to see Sicilian bolshevists with flowers of the noble hibiscus and flaming salvia in their Sunday suits. If he could burn the world with 'flame that licks it clean', he would wear salvia, and burn these louts too. He will not be put on 'a cabbage-idealistic level of equality' with them; he is their superior, and salutes the hibiscus flower as a 'sign of life, of lovely, dangerous life/And passionate disquality of men' (cf. P2.384–8).

An overweening sense of his own superiority is seen in the sublime arrogance which concludes 'Elephant'. The main part of the poem is an elaborate processional picture of the Perahera at Kandy in Ceylon. The Prince of Wales sat high up in a pavilion, pale and dispirited, hardly noticing the 'huge homage' of the shadowy beasts below. At the end Lawrence senses the disappointment of the elephants and natives. He sees the crowds like thick wild rice, and the repeated rice-field image recalls the opening theme-picture of an elephant advancing along a dyke between paddy-fields. Lawrence had stood aside on the bank to let him pass, but the slim naked rider had slipped down, hooked the huge creature's knee, and made him salaam to the white man. At the Perahera the people had come to see royalty; they saw 'a weary, diffident boy' whose motto was *Ich Dien* ('I Serve'). Lawrence ends by wishing that he had been aloft in his place. He would have held the three feathers 'above the world' and said, '*Serve me, I am meet to be served./Being royal of the gods*', and he would have told the elephants, the 'first great beasts of the earth', to 'crook the knee and be glad', for a prince had come back to them.

Somehow the Australian kangaroo failed to kindle Lawrence's imagination (cf. end of *K*.xvii), but he makes great play with Bibbles, the 'Little black snub-nosed bitch with a shoved-out jaw/And a wrinkled reproachful look' which appropriated him in New Mexico. Indiscriminate affection makes her 'Walt-Whitmanesque', but the poem ripples with good humour from first to last. (It is Merrild and Götzsche who are 'taken in' by her fawning when she runs away after being switched with a juniper twig for her filthy tricks.) Lawrence's affection for this provoking animal is communicated in the relish with which he brings to life, in picture after picture, its extraordinary facial expressions and fierce, sudden movements.

New Mexican poems are miscellaneous in subject and quality, and it seems strange that Lawrence had difficulty in bringing 'Eagle in New Mexico' to a successful issue. A more explicit and regal presentation (CP.780–3) asserts the theory of 'the God-thrust' transmitted from the fire at the earth centre (cf. *PS*.xiii, xxii; *MM*.vii) up through the cedar and 'the iron feet of the eagle' in 'thrills of fiery power'. It is pleasant to think of the red-bearded Lawrence hearing the demon voice from the pueblo, *Thin red wolf of a pale face,/Thin red wolf, go home*, and replying, when he hears the name of the Indian spirit is 'Star-Road', that 'he can go back the same gait'; then declaring that, since he has 'trotted at the tail of the sun as far as ever the creature went west', he will be 'red-dawn-wolf' and sit on his tail waiting for the sun to return. The most impressive of the 'Ghosts' poems is 'Autumn at Taos', the features of the scene suggesting animals and the golden hawk. The aspens on the slopes of the Rockies are 'Like yellow hair of a tigress brindled with pines'; the sage of the mesa is 'An ash-grey pelt/Of wolf all hairy and level'; and the pines Lawrence rides under are 'the hairy belly of a great black bear'. He is glad to emerge and proceed past 'the otter's whiskers' to 'the fur of the wolf-pelt', then look back at the rounded sides of the Rockies, 'Tigress brindled with aspen,/Jaguar-splashed, puma-yellow, leopard-livid slopes of America'. 'Make big eyes', he tells his pony; 'these skins of wild beasts won't hurt you. Fangs, claws, talons, beaks, and hawk-eyes are nerveless now.' More moving is the lament for the mountain lion Lawrence saw being carried down the Lobo canyon:

> So, she will never leap up that way again, with the yellow flash of
> a mountain lion's long shoot!
> And her bright striped frost-face will never watch any more, out
> of the shadow of the cave in the blood-orange rock,
> Above the trees of the Lobo dark valley-mouth! . . .
> And I think in the world beyond, how easily we might spare a
> million or two of humans
> And never miss them.
> Yet what a gap in the world, the missing white frost-face of that
> slim yellow mountain lion!

Lawrence's anti-Americanism has been noticed in 'The Evening Land' and 'Turkey-Cock'; it is drawn into the conclusion of 'Cypresses'. A special broadside is reserved for 'The American Eagle', the final poem in *Birds, Beasts and Flowers*. The dove of Liberty hatched an eagle and,

113

having been gratified with the demise of the imperialistic eagles, found it was the only eagle in the world. Then it tried to look like a pelican, and plucked feathers out of its plumage to feather the nests of all the 'new naked little republics come into the world'. It grew and grew until it became 'a startling big bird/On the roof of the world'. The American Eagle had better make up its mind, says Lawrence, whether it is a sucking dove, a pelican, a prosperity-gander laying golden eggs, or really an eagle. There is too much 'all my eye' in the bird with the 'Me-Almighty eye'. The eagle is the bird of 'men that are masters', creative of splendour and royalty; a 'young Cock-Eagle' can't 'sit simpering/With an olive-sprig in his mouth'.

*   *   *

In retrospect one can see that Lawrence had achieved his aims in the best of his poetry. Essentially they had never changed; he had moved from more traditional forms to free verse to achieve them more fully. He had decried 'plaster-cast' poetry and vagueness for the sake of musicality; 'I do not worship music or the "half-said thing" ' (17.vii.08). His ambition was to write 'live things, if crude and half formed, rather than beautiful dying decadent things with sad odours' (20.i.09), but he found it hard to get his verse 'cut close to the palpitating form of the experience' (?15.xi.10). To Edward Marsh, whose ear was more attuned to Flecker's *The Golden Journey to Samarkand*, he wrote: 'I think . . . that my rhythms fit my mood pretty well . . . I have always tried to get an emotion out in its own course, without altering it. It needs the finest instinct imaginable, much finer than the skill of the craftsmen. . . . Remember skilled verse is dead in fifty years' (18.viii.13); and again, 'I think I read my poetry more by length than by stress – as a matter of movements in space than footsteps hitting the earth. I think more of a bird with broad wings flying and lapsing through the air, than anything, when I think of metre' (19.xi.13). During the First World War Lawrence wrote, 'The essence of poetry with us in this age of stark and unlovely actualities is a stark directness. . . . Use rhyme *accidentally*, not as a sort of draper's rule for measuring lines off' (?11.i.16). T. S. Eliot thought that Lawrence's statement on stark directness, without 'a shadow of deflection anywhere', expressed what he himself had long aimed at as a poet: 'poetry which should be essentially poetry, with nothing poetic about it, poetry standing naked in its bare bones, or poetry so transparent that we should not see the poetry'. Writing towards the end of his life, Lawrence declared that 'the new spirit of poetry' would be a dauntless 'naïveté', 'a real thing, the real creature of the inside of the soul'. 'Why try to whitewash ourselves? . . . All we have to do is to accept the true chaos that we are, like the jaguar dappled with black suns in gold' (P.262).

From the time that he left Sicily, early in 1922, Lawrence wrote little poetry until he settled in New Mexico; it had become less an avocation than a literary by-product. He does not appear to have written any for nearly six years after January or February 1923, when *Birds, Beasts and Flowers* was completed. 'I am doing some little *Pensées* – sort of poems, but really *thoughts* – all in snatches: rather amusing. Impossible to paint in poky hotel rooms', he wrote from Bandol on 10 December 1928. (Painting, it might be claimed, had usurped the place of poetry during the previous two years.) The first volume ('my *Pansies*, nice and peppery') was finished by the end of the year, but many poems were revised (?13.ii.29), and one at least ('England in 1929') added a few weeks later. Lawrence was in the mood he announced at the opening of 1924, when he said that one needed 'the courage *not to care*', and that he would ride 'a laughing horse'. Undoubtedly he enjoyed shocking the Establishment, and in some less important matters showed an obsessive lack of proportion; in general, however, though his views had not changed, his inspirational fervour as a Salvator Mundi had waned, and he accepted more limited and basic objectives.

He had realized that thoughts simply and briefly expressed, each 'trotting down the page like an independent creature', could provide more effective propaganda than more extended and elaborate works of art. Thought in verse would 'nag' less than in prose, he argued, though some of the essays in *Assorted Articles* show that Lawrence was capable of presenting his ideas just as attractively to the general reader in prose. He may not have been guilty of nagging in *Pansies*, but he did not avoid becoming a bore; he had a few leading ideas, and seems to have assumed that saying the same thing repeatedly in slightly different ways made tactical sense.

That Frieda Lawrence shared most of his feelings is confirmed by Aldous Huxley in *Point Counter Point* (1928). 'It's factories, it's Christianity, it's science, it's respectability, it's our education', her counterpart Mary Rampion explained. 'They weigh on the modern soul. They suck

115

the life out of it. They . . .'. 'Oh, for God's sake shut up!' said Rampion. The reader may be forgiven if he sometimes feels likewise against Lawrence. In a cancelled introduction to *Pansies* (CP.417) he says, with reference to *panser*, that his poems could be regarded as 'tender administrations to the mental and emotional wounds we suffer from', 'each of them combining with all the others to make up a complete state of mind'. In the gradation from theme to theme (most of them recurring), he is apt to repeat himself 'like the flushing of a W.C.', to quote his own phrase. His main subjects are sex in the head and not in the loins, bourgeois conformity, industrialization and the machine, the money-curse, four-lettered words and *Lady Chatterley*, and occasionally something finer and more positive. He would get rid of money, industry, machines, soviets, and working classes, and have 'men as men, and the work as merely part of the game of life' ('Why – ?'); he would 'betray the middle classes/and money and industry/and the intellectual asses/ and cash christianity', but not the England that made him 'the stuff of a man' ('As for me, I'm a Patriot'); and it is this man-stuff which indulges in some rather crude verse, towards the end of the volume, against the 'fat-arsed' upper classes. Whether all this writing 'came out of Lawrence's nerves', as Richard Aldington thought (CP.595), is arguable; giving vent to his feelings in 'real doggerel' (as Frieda described it joyfully) must have been a pleasant pastime for Lawrence. Most of his aims are summed up in a letter to Charles Wilson: the whole scheme of things was rotten; it was time for an *enormous* revolution; money and the *possessive* spirit should be smashed, but Marxist materialism was no better. 'What we want is life and *trust* . . . if men trusted men, we could soon have a new world, and send this one to the devil.' Social injustice, as he saw it in the rich English on the Riviera, nauseated him (28.xii.28).

Lawrence wrote too easily, and in a deliberately low key. Occasionally a subject inspires poetic flow and completion, as in 'Beautiful Old Age'. Implicit is the theme of integrity, which takes poetic form in 'Courage', and is continued less felicitously in 'When the Ripe Fruit Falls', where the swan image evokes the idea of new creation in space, to which the souls of those who die fulfilled continually contribute. The idea of 'Spray' creates a fine audio-visual image. In some of the opening poems (as in 'Twilight') the image and idea merge into a single sea picture, the meaning of which is apparent to anyone familiar with Lawrence's dark concepts of blood-consciousness on the sensual plane (see *PS*.xiii for a more explicit presentation). Sometimes, as in 'Ships in Bottles' and 'Know Thyself, and that Thou Art Mortal', a new conceit takes his fancy, and he exhausts it in prosaic verse. As a contrast, one can point to 'Salt of the Earth', where the idea in the image is expressed with a freshness of wit which pleases, inducing one to linger in reflection. 'Fidelity' has more developed imagery but, both in movement and expression, it sustains a pitch of poetry which is more characteristic of Lawrence than most of *Pansies*.

Lawrence's programme of reform is Utopian, and based on a mystifying religion. He assumes mutual trust between workers, contentment with 'the modesty of simple living', free homes, heating, and food ('Money-Madness', 'Kill Money'), and freedom from 'the terror of earning a living' ('Men are not Bad'); 'A man should never earn his living,/if he earns his life he'll be lovely' ('A Living'). Lawrence wants 'some sort of communism', without wages, or buying and selling, and based on 'a religion of life'. He reiterates the deceptiveness of the intellect and science; to be in touch with the quick of the universe, one must develop blood-consciousness. 'Man is an alternating consciousness' ('Climb Down, O Lordly Mind'). He must overcome the fear of life ('The Risen Lord'); 'poor mental worm', he is the only creature who is afraid of life and 'terrified of his own possible splendour and delight' ('Cowards'). All one needs is contact with 'the sun of suns', 'the exquisite orgasm of coition/with the Godhead of energy that cannot tell lies'. Given the pure vitality of this passion and its cool truth, the soul's next passion is to 'embrace the extant body of life/with the thrusting embrace of new justice . . . between men and men, men and women, and earth and stars, and suns' ('The Primal Passions'). So each one may be resurrected ('Sun in Me'), 'receiving from the great one/his strength and his promptings,/and refusing the pettifogging promptings of human weakness' ('Sun-Men'). A woman will 'open/like a marigold to the sun,/and thrill with glittering rays' when a man 'with sun in his face' looks upon her ('Sun-Women'). The individual is fulfilled, and becomes a 'sun-aristocrat': 'I am that I am /from the sun,/and people are not my measure' ('Aristocracy of the Sun'). 'It is a question of getting into contact again with the *living* centre of the cosmos. And how are we to do it?' Lawrence asks at the end of 'The Real Thing' (P.203). He supplies no clear answer. It was the axis of his faith (cf. *PS*.xiii).

The swan is the symbol of new vitality, which is to be found more in women than in men ('Swan', 'Leda', 'Give us Gods'). Lawrence wonders whether man will 'brace himself up' to change the world, whether the flood of dissolution which precedes change will bring him to an Ararat, to 'start a new world for man', or whether the 'new Day' (see pp. 251–2) will come from man's supersession by a new species ('To Let Go or to Hold On – ?').

However mystified or sceptical one may be about Lawrence's cosmic philosophy, nobody can challenge the moral implications to be drawn from his distinction between life and anti-life. The irony of 'What Matters', for instance, applies even more to the modern world than to Lawrence's age. What people 'thrill to' is not limited to intellectuals and fiction or films; through television it has invaded most homes and become an addiction for many. The complementary poems 'When I Went to the Film' and 'When I Went to the Circus' give some idea of what Lawrence had in mind in his differentiation between a life of lies and real life or 'pure vitality'. The response of children at the circus indicates that they are cheated of their birthright. Perhaps, he writes in 'Aristocracy of the Sun', 'if we started right, all the children could grow up sunny/and sun-aristocrats./We need have no dead people, money-slaves, and social worms.'

Lawrence condemns anything that makes man passive or enslaved, but (as we have seen) he would not dispense with labour-saving machinery which gives people more time to live. Lifeless work is to be avoided ('All That we Have is Life'), but 'Give, and it shall be given unto you/ is still the truth about life'; if we can 'transmit life into our work', life 'rushes into us to compensate'; we kindle 'the life-quality where it was not/even if it's only in the whiteness of a washed pocket-handkerchief' ('We are Transmitters'). In teacher-preacher style, with three instances of 'as a matter of fact', he continues the subject in 'The Combative Spirit'. Work is 'the clue to a man's life', and 'one free, cheerful activity stimulates another'. Men are not naturally mean, he concludes; they are 'so much better' than the system allows them to be. The competitive system kills trust, the 'generous flow' that is indispensable for true living ('Being Alive'). On socio-economic problems generally, one line sums up Lawrence's earnest demand: 'For God's sake, let us be men' ('Let us be Men').

Artistically Lawrence's pictures are of little importance; they were exhibited to challenge, rather than educate, public opinion. The prosecution which followed provoked *Nettles*, a slim volume of rather raw verse which is inferior by and large to the worst of *Pansies*. It attacked the British public, the government, the police, the magistrate Mr Mead, the critics (for Thomas Earp, see CP.680), editors of the press, and, as a slight make-weight, the industrial system for its devitalizing effect on the masses. The best item is on the 13,000 who visited the exhibition: 'and I'll tell you what/all eyes sought the same old spot/in every picture, every time,/and gazed and gloated without rhyme/or reason, where the leaf should be,/the fig-leaf that was not, woe is me!'

Two sets of poems were published posthumously under the title of *Last Poems*. The less important consists of further verses of the *Pansies* class with several *Nettles* rejects and varying versions or little cycles throughout. Lawrence's *bêtes noires* remain constant, with special emphasis on the plague of industry; and his hammering away at ideas rarely produces a poem which it is an unqualified pleasure to read and re-read. His brief reflections are little more than warmed-up prose, devoid of epigrammatic wit and sparkle. 'Full Life' reads: 'A man can't fully live unless he dies and ceases to care, ceases to care'; and 'Non-Existence': 'We don't exist unless we are deeply and sensually in touch/ with that which can be touched but not known'. More memorable, but only as a thought, is the relationship drawn between the bourgeois and the bolshevist: 'The bourgeois produces the bolshevist, inevitably/as every half-truth at length produces the contradiction of itself/in the opposite half-truth.' A sympton of Lawrence's growing impatience with the world is his emphatic re-assertion of *hoi polloi* doctrine. He repudiates the masses; their job is to serve ('Fellow-Men', 'The Sight of God'). The desire 'to be alone, to possess one's soul in silence' is evident at the outset: attempted friendships had led to 'trespassed contacts'; those who had loved him had not really known him, only an image they mistook for him ('Image-Making Love'). Most people are 'chimaera', 'fantasies of self-importance', and 'sphinxes of self-consciousness'. He can renounce Middleton Murry with cheerful self-satisfaction: 'A miss is as good as a mile/mister' (cf. 'Correspondence in After Years' and 20.v.29); and, in one of his wittier poems, dismiss woman's love as self-love, a mere desire for a flattering reflection of her own image (cf. 'Intimates' with 'Know Deeply, Know Thyself More Deeply' in *Pansies*), an idea which goes back to Paul's assessment of Clara Dawes (*SL*.ix).

The irony of the title 'Amo Sacrum Vulgus' (recalling *Vox populi,
vox Dei*) is confirmed by its euphoric metre. Lawrence saw no 'golden
fields of people', 'all moving into flower' as a result of being saved from
the 'mowing-machines' of industry and 'middle-class money-power'.
In a real democracy 'the many must obey the few that look into the
eyes of the gods' ('False Democracy and Real'). It will be a 'democracy
of touch', and with its coming the industrial machine and war will
wither away. Only men who have 'died', found 'living connection with
the cosmos', and learned to be alone, can 'come into touch' ('Initiation
Degrees', 'The Breath of Life'; cf. 'The Uprooted'). The many will be
ground small by the mills of God 'to fertilise the roots' of future people
('Multitudes'). For one 'eternal division' of 'The Cross' is between 'the
base and the beautiful', the hordes of inferiors who must be 'thrust down
into service' and the natural élite whom they must obey; 'the time has
come to cease to be kind any more/to the robot classes and masses'
('Impulse'). When men cease to be robots, they can live only by the
gleam transmitted from the faces of 'vivider men/who look into the
eyes of the gods' ('Worship', 'Classes').

In 'Two Ways of Living and Dying' Lawrence contrasts these 'vivider
men', flowering at times like gods, with those whose energies derive
wholly from their will, which drives them like machines until their
final breakdown (cf. *LC*.xiii). To those who live vividly, death is an
adventure, and Lawrence turns to it eagerly as to beauty ('So Let me
Live'). In 'the dark sunshine of death' he feels that he is unfolding to
'something flowery and fulfilled, and with a strange sweet perfume'
('Gladness of Death'). Here we have an introit to the purer spirit of
Lawrence's final poems.

However much Lawrence derived from religions and philosophies,
his beliefs grew from convictions born of experience; they were co-
ordinated and extended to form an original whole which must surely
constitute one of the most extraordinary philosophies ever conceived
in a scientific age. In this his self-confidence was never shaken. How
genuine his beliefs were may be seen in the inspired re-affirmation of
his views in the last months of his life, and in the serenity with which
he prepared for the adventure of death. Death was an inevitable part of
life, and Lawrence's faith, like Wordsworth's, looked through death.
He had said that man was the only creature that was afraid of life; now,
in 'Only Man', he asserts that he is the only creature that can 'fall from

God'. Despite Lawrence's denial of orthodox evolution in his foreword to *Fantasia of the Unconscious*, his God is an evolutionary Life-Force, 'the great urge that has not yet found a body/but urges towards incarnation' ('The Body of God'). It is not a Mind (a Logos) but a great, unconscious urge. While emphasizing the beauty of new emergent forms of life, Lawrence, unlike Hardy, accepts it unflinchingly in all its aspects, destructive and creative. There is 'no end to the birth of God' ('God is Born'), the 'tremendous creative yearning' which blossomed at last in the red geranium and mignonette, or in Helen and Ninon, 'any lovely and generous woman at her best and her most beautiful', or in 'any clear and fearless man'. 'The lovely things are god that has come to pass. . . The rest, the undiscoverable, is the demi-urge.' Man falls out of the hands of God through ungodly knowledge, and this is self-centredness, self-analysis, and self-will. There is no bottom to the abyss down which man slips 'writhing and twisting' in 'all the minutiae of self-knowledge' ('Abysmal Immortality', 'Only Man'). The one evil is anti-life.

Looking at the Mediterranean from his room at Bandol, Lawrence was continually reminded, as in 'Sicilian Cyclamens', of the 'morning, when our world began'. To live imaginatively with the Greek adventurers meant release from the weight 'heavier than leaden linings of coffins' which depressed him when he thought of the industrial masses. The quickening excitement of Lawrence's poems as he thinks of the Argonauts and the ships of Cnossos comes, however, from no mere romantic evocation of the past but from their identification with his confidence in a renewal of life to come. The present cannot be overlooked (an ocean liner from the western world, 'leaving a long thread of dark smoke/like a bad smell' looks like 'a small beetle', an image of abomination for Lawrence), but the Greeks keep appearing, 'a hail of something coming', over the rim of the sea. The 'smoking ships/of the P. & O. and the Orient line and all the other stinkers' may cross the Minoan distance like clockwork, but

> the Minoan Gods, and the Gods of Tiryns
> are heard softly laughing and chatting, as ever;
> and Dionysos, young and a stranger
> leans listening at the gate, in all respect.

Dionysos stands for life; his *ego sum* ('Medlars and Sorb-Apples') is 'a stranger' to the *Cogito, ergo sum* ('Climb Down, O Lordly Mind') and deadly mechanization of modern life. He remains young, and waits to enter our lives. The Mediterranean symbolizes the life-source; it is the 'Middle of the World' and like 'the birth of God' it has no end:

> This sea will never die, neither will it ever grow old
> nor cease to be blue, nor in the dawn
> cease to lift up its hills
> and let the slim black ship of Dionysos come sailing in
> with grape-vines up the mast, and dolphins leaping.

'Even we can expect our iron ships to put forth vine and tendril and bunches of grapes, like the ship of Dionysos in full sail upon the ocean', Lawrence had written (see p. 111 and *K*.ix).

So Lawrence looks forward to a time when people will live; he hears laughter as the bearded Greek heroes return, men with the slim waists of warriors and the long feet of 'moon-lit' dancers (the moon 'only cares that we should be lovely in the flesh'). Their faces are scarlet, 'glowing as of god', for they are like the Etruscan kings (*EP*.iii):

> kings who are gods by vividness, because they have gathered into themselves core after core of vital potency from the universe, till they are clothed in scarlet, they are bodily a piece of the deepest fire. . . . They, in their own body, unlock the vast treasure-house of the cosmos for their people, and bring out life, and show the way into the dark of death, which is the blue burning of the one fire.

Here we can see the link between death and life's continuing renewal, between 'Bavarian Gentians' and the sea that will never die: 'The dawn is not off the sea, and Odysseus' ships/have not yet passed the islands, I must watch them still'. He must not be disturbed ('wait, wait, don't bring me the coffee yet, nor the *pain grillé*'), for it is good to contemplate 'the birth of God' and feel 'the presence of the living God/like a great reassurance': 'All that matters is to be at one with the living God/to be a creature in the house of the God of Life.'

In 'Maximus' we find Hermes, the messenger of the gods, in place of Dionysos. He had waited (as Dionysos waits) for the invitation to enter ('Give, and it shall be given unto you/is still the truth about life'). He sits by the hearth, before 'the fire of life', where one feels 'the presence of the living God' ('Pax'). In this context Hermes is more appropriate than Dionysos because he represents the rays that travel from 'the first of suns' and make men 'strong and glad', 'gods who can range between the known and the unknown' (*MM*.vii); the unknown is that which is about to become, the demi-urge or God striving for 'incarnation' ('The Body of God'). Hermes' entry evokes the experience of loveliness, such as that felt by the man of Tyre when he sees a woman emerging from the sea and thinks her Aphrodite; it is his god-given delight which makes her 'godly and lovely'. Yet 'God is one and all alone and ever more shall be so'; he is present in the mating of the whales in the depths of the sea. Aphrodite is the delight they feel, the sense of loveliness which transports the dolphins as they leap round the ship of Dionysos ('They Say the Sea is Loveless'). Taking its initial inspiration from Melville's *Moby Dick*, Lawrence's free verse attains a lyricism and limpidity in 'Whales Weep Not!' which he rarely equalled (cf. *St.Am.*xi).

In this second group of his last poems there is a wide range of poetic levels. Several poems are in his more ordinary, didactic voice. An expository group extends the cosmology of his philosophy a little. Salt is scorched water, produced in the 'eternal opposition' of primordial fire and water (p. 81). It is therefore associated with division; and Lawrence enlarges on the role of the Sunderers (angels with sharp black wings, as opposed to 'angels of creation') in 'Walk Warily'. They cause strife between individuals, put salt in our mouths and hearts, and create 'hotness' and 'currents of excitement in our limbs', preventing the love and peace which one knows in 'the presence of the living God'. A scientific alignment with the contention of Anaxagoras that there is an element of blackness in snow is dismissed with contempt ('Anaxagoras'). Life is for daimons who put honey on our lips, and demons who put salt; but it is not for 'the puerility of contradictions/like saying snow is black, or desire is evil' ('Kissing and Horrid Strife'). Lawrence combines two forms of arrested nature in 'Evil is Homeless' (the 'grey evil' of corpse-eaters such as the vulture and the hyena, and of men who sit in machines, 'in an apotheosis of wheels'), and has a last fling at unreal abstractions that divorce us from God in 'What Then is Evil?' and 'Departure'. He finds 'pure evil' only in man and his machines, particularly in the principle of the wheel. The mind constructs it, to be driven by the will, 'on the hub of the ego', the conscious self becoming absolute in its disconnection from sun, earth, and moon, and strife and kisses. To be saved, one must turn from the will, the wheel, machines, and money-making; and be released from such abstractions (modes of thinking that take us away from the reality of life) as finance, science, education; jazz, film, wireless; and the politics of our era.

The higher philosophy of dissolution-creation ('the sharp winds of change/mingled with the breath of destruction' in 'The Breath of Life') finds personal expression in the autumnal sweetness of 'Shadows'. If he wakes refreshed 'like a new-opened flower', Lawrence has been 'dipped again in God, and new-created'; but if in the weeks ahead, as autumn deepens, he feels the pain of falling leaves and stems that break in storms, and of deep shadows folding around him, or falls into sickness, and his strength is gone, though he enjoys snatches of lovely oblivion and renewal, then he will still know that he is in God's hands, and that God is breaking him down 'to his own oblivion', to send him forth 'on a new morning, a new man'. The philosophy of dying into new life takes its final form in 'Phoenix'.

'Shadows' is a far more lyrical and successful poem than 'Silence'. In both there are Keatsian overtones: the nightingale, 'dissolution', and 'drowse' of the first, and the 'bride of quietness' allusion in the other. The 'huge, huger, huger and huger pealing' of God's thunderous laugh, the 'tremendous body of Silence', and the final 'Lift up your heads, O ye Gates!' (after what appears to be a hint of the Communion in 'meet' and 'very fitting') seem rather bogus, as if reminiscent of Congregational services at Eastwood. By contrast, the tone of 'Pax' is wholly unexceptionable, the parallel with the cat, asleep and at one with the master of the house, having an aptness and charm which would have appealed to religious writers of the seventeenth century.

There is a graceful allusion to death in 'Butterfly', where the wind blowing seaward has a symbolism which recalls T. S. Eliot's later poetry. The garden wall may allude to the body, as in 'All Souls' Day', and the butterfly to the soul, as in Greek philosophy. The poet asks the butterfly if it will leave his 'warm house', and climb on big soft wings 'as up an invisible rainbow', till the wind slides it 'sheer from the arch-crest' and it goes out seaward 'in a strange level fluttering'. 'Farewell, farewell, lost soul!/you have melted in the crystalline distance,/it is enough! I saw you vanish into air.' 'Invocation to the Moon' is a prayer to the goddess who soothes and heals the spirit. Although her mansion is the nearest in space, it is the last to be reached, in the hour of need before death; 'the Villa of Venus the glowing' is far and forgotten (she is the 'lingering lady who looks over the distant fence of the twilight'); the golden house of the sun (the life-giver, 'the lion with the golden paws') is behind, in the gulfs of space, together with the four great lords (Mars, Saturn, Jupiter, Mercury). All six have given the poet gifts, and wished him god-speed, and he now implores the lady of the Moon to open the garden gate leading to her silvery house. A spiritual healing is sought, but the poet who wrote this original dramatic lyric is already, one feels, a 'healed, whole man'. No false note in word or rhythm mars his ecstasy, and the reader's sense of transport is heightened by delightful echoes of a nursery-rhyme garden adorned with silver bells and cockle-shells. With this one may contrast 'Bavarian Gentians', a poem undoubtedly inspired by Lawrence's admiration for the Etruscan kings as 'life-bringers and death-guides' who 'show the way into the dark of death, which is the blue burning of the one fire' by which they had lived so vividly. He imagines the ribbed gentians as torches, their 'blaze of darkness' spreading blue in Pluto's realm (suggested by the Etruscan tombs), and himself guided by the light of one down the ever-deepening stairs, even where Persephone goes, a mere voice or a 'darkness visible enfolded in the deeper dark/of the arms Plutonic'. Imaginatively it is a most impressive poem, but it has less personal involvement than 'Invocation to the Moon'; the fanciful quality of its theme is more apparent in the wedding-guest ending of another version (CP.975), which completes and clarifies the poem more satisfactorily than does its ancillary 'Lucifer'.

A number of poems derive from the Etruscan custom of placing a little bronze ship with other treasures in the burial chamber of a chief or Lucomo; it was the 'ship of death that should bear him over to the other world' (*EP*.i). All Souls' Day, 1929, made Lawrence think of the spirits unappeased and peregrine, the dead who sought their old haunts with 'cold, ghostly rage'; he wonders how much woe they cause in the modern world, and urges, 'Be kind, Oh be kind to your dead/and give them a little encouragement/and help them to build their little ship of death.' Warm memories and love from 'still-loving hearts' could waft them 'far from the grey shores of marginal existence' to the 'pivotal oblivion/where the soul comes at last, and has utter peace'. 'The Ship of Death' which Lawrence wrote with his own end in mind is weakened somewhat by a digression on Hamlet and suicide, and is, on the whole, less poetically sustained than the shortest version (CP.979–80). With 'Now it is autumn and the falling fruit/and the long journey towards oblivion', it begins in perfect elegiac tone. The apples rot on the ground and release seed for a new life, just as the soul is released from the body at death. Spiritual peace is needed for the long journey to oblivion. Build then the ship of death, 'and furnish it with food, with little cakes, and wine', 'And die the death, the long and painful death/that lies between the old self and the new'. On the sea of death 'the fragile soul in the fragile ship of courage' sails darkly, without direction, until all seems lost. Yet 'out of eternity' a thread separates on the blackness and proves to be dawn. 'And the little ship wings home, faltering and lapsing/on the pink flood,/and the frail soul steps out, into her house again/filling the heart with peace.' Lawrence's hope is humbly expressed at the end of 'Difficult Death':

> Maybe life is still our portion
> after the bitter passage of oblivion.

Novels

THE WHITE PEACOCK

Written sporadically (most of it several times) from 1906 to 1909, *The White Peacock* provided Lawrence with a ready medium for his prodigal early efflorescence. Had he been more interested in the action, it could have been a greater novel. Lawrence's 'daimon', however, made him impatient of constraints at all times, and he was drawn more to natural description and the on-going of life than to plot, which 'bored' him (as it always would). His novel was to be 'a mosaic, a mosaic of moods'. First it was *Laetitia*, then *Nethermere*. He thought the former the only important result of his college career, and describes it banteringly in terms of sentiment (all about love), rhapsodies on spring, heroines galore, no plot, and nine-tenths adjectives (15.iv.08). Two months later he attaches more importance to 'fine scenes and effects' than to reality in his characters (another pointer to the future). In his first term at Croydon, before he began the *Nethermere* version, he realized that his protracted dialogues could be reduced in narrative or descriptive form, and that there was too much 'metaphoric fancy' and talk for the sake of 'talk about themes'. He no longer believed that Lettie broke off her engagement to Leslie (11.xi.08).

Jessie Chambers did not think highly of this first version, in which George married Lettie, a superior young lady who had been shabbily treated by the 'still more socially superior' Leslie. (Lettie had found herself pregnant by Leslie, and it is this, rather than a marriage of social incompatibility comparable to her own, which explains Mrs Lawrence's pained reply, 'To think *my* son should have written such a story', when Jessie asked her opinion of the novel at Robin Hood's Bay in 1907.) Jessie thought the story romantic despite its sentimentality, and found a kind of epitome of it in the poem 'Love on the Farm'.

Most of the weaknesses diagnosed by Lawrence are still evident. His immaturity of judgment is reflected in the artificiality and forced wit of the dialogue, which is often little more than the clever display of a pedantic adolescent who finds literary, classical, and artistic references irresistible. Yet, despite callow excesses, this pretentiousness accentuates by contrast the tragedy that runs through the book. The refinement and superficial 'brilliance' of Lettie's little world seem to intensify those true feelings which she occasionally expresses but chooses to ignore for the sake of social ambition. Like Catherine Earnshaw in *Wuthering Heights*, she plays a taunting role to her bucolic lover and, like Catherine's, her ambition 'led her to adopt a double character without exactly intending to deceive anyone'. Her marriage to Leslie and repudiation of an instinctive bond with George are the cause of his moral collapse and decline, which form a more normal analogue to Heathcliff's developing madness.

Life on the farm is the reality, and George's chance collocation of 'ladies' accomplishments' and remarks on calving is significant. Lettie teases him for being bovine, but Greiffenhagen's 'Idyll' makes them look 'nakedly' at each other in torture, their blood coursing madly. Admiring his physique as he mows the corn, she tells him he is 'picturesque' and 'quite fit for an Idyll'; he is 'like some great firm bud of life' to her, in Lawrence's view. Fanciful imagery, reminiscent of Charlotte Brontë's in *Jane Eyre*, but never as intense, points the way to the tragic division, which is again highlighted by contrasting the trivial flashiness of intellectual conversation and the real life of the farm, the Atalanta and 'Blessed Damozel' ideas of the one, and the naturalness of the other, with George's father 'opulently asleep, his tanned face as still as a brown pear against the wall', and the golden turnip chips gleaming on the earthen floor of the barn. The undercurrent of George's jealous passion is expressed with profound psychological insight in the milking scene which follows. Twice the natural kinship of Lettie and George is seen in the exhilaration of the dance. Just before the Christmas of her disastrous engagement to Leslie, they kiss under the mistletoe of the orchard; the light of the lamp which he holds up to illuminate the trees seems 'to hold them as in a globe', and once again they see the truth in each other's eyes. In the following scene Lettie wears hot-house flowers

128

in preference to those which are an expression of love. The engagement is signalled first with a Hardy-like image of death (ix), then with dialogue and divertissements of the world of cultural make-believe. George complains that Lettie has awakened his life, and left him at a loose end; she tells him that they can't help themselves – 'we're all chessmen' and (with another Hardy echo) 'what is done, is done'.

Lawrence's Rousseauistic view that man is the only creature which is corrupt is expressed by the gamekeeper Annable, with an obvious authorial reference to Lettie. His motto is 'Be a good animal, true to your animal instinct'. His children can be 'like birds, or weasels, or vipers, or squirrels, so long as they ain't human rot'. They are numerous, and he refers to them as 'a lovely litter . . . natural as weasels . . . bred up like a bunch o' young foxes'. There seems to be an ambivalence here, for his children, left to the care of an overburdened, distraught wife, are a perpetual discord. An unconvincing accident removes him as soon as he has served Lawrence's moral purpose. The first stage of his funeral occasions a long poetical passage which turns into a keen. A sallow like a pale gold cloud with a fairy busby on every twig, a spink flashing past in triumph with a fleece from a bramble, the bright ecstasy of a nesting thrush and the darting of a jenny wren into a bush (both birds observed in confidential tones which recall George Eliot), are features of an antithetical prelude to the wheeling plovers which cry and complain, heralding 'like shadows in the bright air' the procession of mourners soon to appear over the brow of the hill. 'They are like priests in their robes, more black than white, more grief than hope, driving endlessly round and round, turning, lifting, falling and crying always in mournful desolation, repeating their last syllables like the broken accents of despair.' The elegiac description follows an outworn pastoral tradition; it has its rhythmical appropriateness, but it is overdone, to the point almost of sentimentality.

In Part II the novel loses some of its tension for a while. There is no radical change of situation, and the 'mosaic' composition becomes more evident. Initially Lettie and Leslie draw closer together. She 'shut out all distant outlooks' and peeped only occasionally 'from her tent into the out space'. In the meantime George has turned to the *Rubáiyát* and cousin Meg at the Ram Inn. He would emigrate to Canada but, when Lettie refuses to accompany him, decides he will stay and marry Meg. In 'Kiss when She's Ripe for Tears' nothing happens to make one think

Lettie has changed, or to validate Cyril's view that George has stupidly missed his opportunity. The tenor of the novel and the implications of its title do not accord with his argument 'You should have insisted and made your own destiny'. Subsequently the tension increases. In 'The Fascination of the Forbidden Apple' Lettie wishes she could be free again; as always, she tauntingly hints that the blame for inaction is George's. The blossom she insists on gathering for herself is pretty but, as she bitterly remarks, it produces only crab-apples. Nature is hymeneal, heavy bees swinging down in 'a blunder of extravagance among the purple flowers', and she imagines the tree-trunks rising to hold an embroidered care-cloth over them, with bird-song and scents and the hum of bees an accompaniment for their wedding. She complains that, when the threads of her life were untwined, George did not take them and twist them into a 'chord' with his. Now it is being twisted by another, as is his, and they can no longer get free. It is the last passionate scene between them. 'A Poem of Friendship' follows; it is more Lawrence's regret for departed days than a necessary part of the novel. The section concludes with 'Pastorals and Peonies', a sketch in which the idyllics of classical verse (cf. p. 18) and a romantic legend contrast with the reality for George, the havoc caused by rabbits to the young crops, and his own sick thoughts.

Lettie's marriage is soon followed by George's, and at first all bodes well for him. He rejoices in 'a place of his own, a home, and a beautiful wife' who adores him. In a Hardyan manner characteristic of earlier scenes, Lawrence harmonizes situation and natural background, harvest bounty reinforcing the sense of George's happiness. But the course marked out for him (rather arbitrarily) is essentially one of unbroken moral and physical decline. More and more he takes to drink, wastes his money in trading horses, and becomes brutal and indifferent to his family. The unreality and affectation of Lettie's life makes him a Socialist until, like Lawrence, he grows weary of the movement. Like Lawrence again, having stepped out of his class, he finds that he belongs to 'no class of society whatsoever'. The 'scarp slope' of dissoluteness leads to 'the marshes of Lethe'. Perhaps the spirit of Lawrence's mother drove him down this headlong course; like Lawrence's father he is made a 'spectacle' for his children and a 'disgusting disgrace' for his wife. In the end everyone including Cyril is alienated by him, and he sits apart and obscure 'like a condemned man'.

This moral narrative is wholly fictional. George's physical splendour as seen by Lettie and Cyril in his undegenerate days reflects Lawrence's admiration of his friend Alan Chambers, however. It culminates in 'A Poem of Friendship', the recollection (partially coloured by fictional needs) of a love 'more perfect than any love I have known since, either for man or woman'. 'Life was full of glamour for us both', Lawrence writes as Cyril-narrator. Emily had long known that Cyril thought more of her brother George 'than anybody'. The relationship between her and Cyril never rises above close friendship, but it contains hints of the Jessie Chambers ('Muriel') whom Lawrence regarded as another Jane Eyre, demanding his soul (3.xii.10). In her soulfulness Emily is like Burne-Jones's damsels. The scene where Cyril thrusts stalks of ruby guelder-rose berries in her black hair (I.vi) recalls 'Guelder Roses', one of the first poems Lawrence wrote: their 'dreamy chaplets' are 'like the thought-drenched eyes/Of some Pre-Raphaelite mystic queen', and he proposes to wait for 'immortal fruit', not on 'stems of virginity' but on those of life-lovers (a subject developed at length in *Sons and Lovers*). Emily is spared 'the torture' of modern life, and finds her place and happiness as a farmer's wife.

The White Peacock suffers from a lack of homogeneity. Scenes are presented at various levels, from the vividly imaginative and poetic (but often overwritten) to the plain and surprisingly prosaic. In places the mosaic method of composition produces patchwork. Realistic scenes such as those at the gamekeeper's home and at the Ram Inn tend to be drab and tedious. Attempts to impart comic relief rarely bring them to life. Only when its significance is relative to the main story does Lawrence's humour have a semblance of success, as in the short scene with 'the Parrot' (III.ii); none of it has a relish equal to that in the description of the feeding piglets, which provides an apt illustration of George's ill-luck in the lottery of life (II.vi). The last part of the book suggests revision at Croydon. Cyril writes in exile in Norwood, his eyes on the Crystal Palace, and recalls a succession of colourful images from Lawrence's London poetry. The story reminds him of Tchehov and Maupassant; reference is made to George Moore's *Evelyn Innes* and indirectly to *Toil of Men* (by the Dutch author Querido), two novels admired by Lawrence at the time of writing. The picture of Meg like a Madonna over her baby, and of its toe-balls like 'wee pink mushrooms' (III.iv) are based on observations in the Croydon home where he lodged. The

Embankment scene (III.v) combines memories recorded in two poems (CP.143–5). The thought that Nethermere has lost its romantic spell renews the pathetic fallacies of poetic prose (III.vii), but poetic images or fancies (such as cornfields with shocks of wheat 'like small yellow-sailed ships in a wide-spread flotilla') are rare and isolated compared with their profusion in earlier chapters. An imaginative revival marks the ending of the novel. George is 'lamentably decayed' and talks 'stupidly, with vulgar contumely of others, and in weak praise of himself'. Like a falling tree, rotten and clammy with fungi (the development of an image in 'A Poem of Friendship'), he leans against a gate, outside the 'flow of thick sweet sunshine'. Life and work and splendour continue. Harvesting goes on, and Emily's husband works with Arthur, unloading a wagon 'in an exquisite, subtle rhythm' amid stacks of bright gold. So it had been with George.

Cyril's admiration for the George of old and Annable long since dead may indirectly express Lawrence's regard for a father whose vitality and love of the countryside and wild life had secured his affection before it was maimed and well-nigh extinguished by his mother. Mrs Lawrence was a cultured intellectual with a degree of pavonian superiority. Like Lawrence's father, Annable and George were admired for their physique, but Lady Crystabel preferred to see Annable in an aesthetic light, as if he were a Greek statue rather than flesh and blood. She became 'souly', and he was merely her 'animal', her *boeuf*, as Lettie regarded George when she teasingly tried to elevate him from a bucolic to a cultural plane. Annable distinguishes between 'lady' and 'woman'; Cyril comments, as he watches Emily bathing Meg's baby (III.iv), that a woman is 'so ready to disclaim the body of a man's love'; 'she clings to his neck, to his head and his cheeks, fondling them for the soul's meaning that is there, and shrinking from his passionate limbs and body'. The ideas of *Fantasia of the Unconscious* are already adumbrated, but the plane of ideality in *The White Peacock* is more socio-cultural than spiritual, its artificialities, evasions, and fatal consequences contrasting with what is natural and life-giving. It is Lettie's doom to see only manners and, when she finds life generally 'worthless and insipid', to live vicariously, for her children. Woman, Lawrence comments, escapes the responsibilities of her own development, living in self-abnegation like a nun, for God, or some man, or her children, or some cause (III.v). Lettie is like the Lady of Shalott, her life 'a small indoor existence with artificial light and padded upholstery'. Her artistic world continues to blow bubbles of 'floating fancy and wit' as in her pre-marriage days, but Cyril has grown to loathe it.

Lettie's choice of life on the upper plane harms not only George and Leslie but her children, who look 'like acolytes'. She insists on doing her duty, but George, who is rudderless, cannot accept his, and neglects or ill-treats his family; it is Meg who rules. Annable, who had been proud of his body, was humiliated when Lady Crystabel denied him children; his subsequent cynical choice of an 'animal' life leads him to despise parental duties, and his 'brats' suffer the consequence.

Remembering how the aesthetic Lady Crystabel had worshipped him as a Greek statue and denied him fulness of life, Annable sees a symbol of woman in the Hall peacock which makes a pedestal of a carved angel in the neighbouring churchyard and fouls it: 'all vanity and screech and defilement', he says. The defilement refers to the havoc such women work in men's lives. For Lawrence love is pure and whole only when it develops naturally on the sensual plane. Its 'idealization' is the evil, and Annable gives a hint of it when he says that his children 'shan't learn to dirty themselves wi' smirking deviltry'. Like the gull's cry in later novels, 'screech' has a sub-human connotation; it may refer obliquely to the artistic prattle of Lettie. After their honeymoon, she and Leslie talk 'brightly about a thousand things' and, as she chatters on Paris, pictures, and new music, George admires her 'culture and facility'. Annable's reflection, at the end of his Lady Crystabel story, 'I suppose it wasn't all her fault' evokes Cyril's comment 'A white peacock, we will say'. This has no implication of innocence, for her or Lettie, but it does suggest that they are controlled too much by heredity and circumstance. Lawrence's personal involvement in the question can be seen in Lettie's belief that her mother's disastrous marriage produced 'death in her veins for me before I was born' (I.iii).

White peacock overtones (social vanity and life-denial) reach their climax after Lettie's marriage. The first we see of her is her white hand; then the whiteness of her face, as she throws back her hood and smiles in triumph at George, while Leslie kneels at her feet; when the three walk on, she flings her draperies 'into loose eloquence', and there is a glimpse of her bosom 'white with the moon'. Indoors she lets her cloak 'slide over her white shoulder and fall with silk splendour of a peacock's gorgeous blue' over the arm of the settee, while she stands 'laughing and brilliant with triumph', 'her white hand upon the peacock of her cloak'.

Annable has one idea, 'that all civilization is 'the painted fungus of rottenness'. He hates any sign of culture, and the decay of mankind is uppermost in his thoughts. This is the theme of the novel, and the danger of idealization from culture divorced from the fulness of life is its 'white peacock' feature. Nowhere are decay and corruption, as opposed to the fresh air of life, more manifest than in the abandoned, falling church near which the peacock yells and defecates. Close by, in the Hall, lives the squire responsible for the devastation of crops on the Mill farm. This and the consequent departure of the Saxtons provide another illustration of the theme. Close association of the two menaces (II.ii), the actual and the symbolical, is significant. For in the old days (as Lawrence proclaims rhapsodically at the opening of *The Rainbow*) men lived lives of fulfilment in close union with nature. The first paragraph of *The White Peacock* is both retrospective and proleptic. The murmur of the stream falling through the millrace recalls 'the tumult of life' in 'the young days when the valley was lusty', as it might have been for George Saxton before 'the torture of strange, complex modern life' supervened. George's decline may have generic overtones, for his name suggests husbandry (see p. 18) and the Anglo-Saxon tradition.

THE TRESPASSER

Helen Corke's diary of the holiday she spent with her music teacher, H. B. MacCartney of the Carl Rosa Opera Company, on the Isle of Wight provided the main inspiration for *The Trespasser*. Almost every factual detail was preserved for story and settings, and the poetry of Helen's condensed descriptions was put to good account. She had resisted the love of the violinist, a married man with four children, but agreed to stay with him at Freshwater for sympathetic reasons. Depression and disappointment (aggravated possibly by sunstroke) led to his suicide on his return home. On the very day she travelled to meet him at Freshwater, Lawrence reached the Isle of Wight with his mother and sister for a holiday at Shanklin. His knowledge of the island and London background, his friendship and discussions with Helen, and outings with her from

Croydon, in the country where she had walked with her former frustrate lover, gave Lawrence all he needed to expand what the diary supplied.

According to Jessie Chambers, the first version of the novel was written 'in feverish haste between the Whitsuntide and Midsummer of 1910'; it seems to have been started rather earlier in the year, when the love-lorn Lawrence knew what it was to receive nothing beyond friendship and affection from the Helen with whom he had sympathized in her grief. Having recorded his frustrations in poetry, he could readily empathize with MacCartney, and translate his own feelings into the vicarious satisfactions of imaginative experience. The eroticism of the novel made him withdraw it from the publishers in 1911, and revise it at the beginning of 1912, during the convalescence which occurred at the end of his teaching career. Even then he was afraid it contained too much of his 'naked self'; it was also 'too florid, too *chargé*', and at the proof-stage he promised Edward Garnett he would 'wage war' on the adjectives. 'A Game of Forfeits' was eventually settled as the title, but 'The Trespasser' was retained by oversight. As the title appears (30.xii.11) to be a contraction of 'Trespassers in Cythera' (a reference to the island of Venus), the suggestion that it hints at death (Fr. *trépas*) loses its cogency. For the thought of death weighs continually only on Siegmund's mind; on the way home he realizes that Helena is a 'foreigner' to him, and death is not the way for her. Suicide could not have entered her reckoning when she thought of the wondrous harmonies woven by a Master-Fate who is 'too great an artist to suffer an anti-climax' (xiv).

The original title was 'The Saga of Siegmund', and the novel is strewn with Wagnerian references, the principal reason being MacCartney's enthusiasm for *The Ring*. He played in Wagnerian performances at Covent Garden, and Helen, with her friend Agnes Mason, saw *Das Rheingold*, *Die Walküre*, and *Götterdämmerung*. Later, in October 1909, Lawrence attended *Tristan und Isolde*, and was very disappointed; in November 1911 he visited Covent Garden to hear *Siegfried*, one of the Ring cycle he had not heard. No doubt George Moore's *Evelyn Innes* encouraged him to think that he could use the contemporary Wagner cult to advantage in fiction.

The novel moves with commendable economy at the opening, from a scene in Helena's room at the time when Lawrence became interested in the story (February 1910) to a resumé of the events, recalled by Siegmund, which preceded his holiday assignation. Helena's arms are still inflamed from the sunburn of August; she still broods and lives in the past; and her longing for Siegmund's violin fills Byrne (Lawrence) with envious resentment. On the eve of his departure for 'Sieglinde's island', the moonlight reminds Siegmund of Helena's whiteness (a contrast to the 'drab and dreary' impression of his home), and the two images are associated with the sea when he crosses.

Helen Corke's diary for the 'burning' days of 1–4 August 1909 is the basis for the narrative and much of the description and dialogue from the evening of Siegmund's arrival (iii) to the contemplated departure (end of xix). A key image is the sea-mist which surrounds the lovers and excludes the outer world (cf. iii, xiv). 'The curtain of the Mist Spirit is thinning', Helen Corke wrote in her diary, and this development of the image appears when the end of the holiday is in prospect. 'Six hours,' thought Helena, 'and we shall have passed the mist-curtain. Already it is thinning. I could break it open with waving my hand. I will not wave my hand' (xix).

Helen Corke gave the novel her approval. 'The intuition it shows, the rare symbolism, fill me with wonder', she wrote, hinting at its two main features. The detail of the story is less striking than the fecundity of its imagery, from the minute and incidental to the elaborate and symbolical. Even so, the novel is less imaginative than many scenes in *The White Peacock*. For the most part Lawrence's imagination works on decorative and enriching effects; it is applied rather than inherent and structural. The numerous Wagnerian references are of course integral to the Siegmund story, and they are reinforced occasionally with a pleasing psychological aptitude: as the musician waits drearily at Newport station for Helena, the wind moans 'like the calling of many violoncellos'; she thrills 'beneath his mouth' like 'a violin under the bow'; for Helena, near the end of the story, it is 'the bow of the wind' which causes the tree-tops to flutter. The most frequent descriptive images have no overtones. Houses and cottages appear wandering like white, red, and black cattle, or crouching, or huddled together in sleep. Floral similes are common in the earlier chapters: women move gaily 'like crocus flowers, in white and blue and lavender'; the sea is as blue as a periwinkle, and the wake behind the ship carrying Siegmund trails 'myriads of daisies'; his hands hang listless in the evening fire-glow like two scarlet flowers; the next morning his eyes are like cornflowers, shining warmer than the sea; sunlight makes the waves golden and rich with a velvety coolness, like cowslips; Helena revives like 'a white pansy flung into water', and laughs like 'a fringed poppy that opens itself to the sun'; when the holiday is almost ended, another hour falls 'like a foxglove bell from the stalk', and only two red blossoms are left.

Here and there the prose is overburdened with imagery. An opening paragraph (xv) runs lucidly: Siegmund's afternoon sleep on the beach, 'evanescent' and 'irised with dreams and with suffering'; Helena's thoughts, breaking on the shore of her drowsiness like little waves, each ripple tinged as it ran 'with copper-coloured gleams as from a lurid sunset'. Intuitively one feels with Helena that 'the sun was setting on her and Siegmund'. Lawrence cannot resist another image, however, and the thought, which is repetitive, is lost in pictorial complication: 'the sun was wheeling down, tangling Siegmund and her in the traces, like overthrown charioteers'. This example of a tendency is unexceptionable compared with the bewildering profusion of associated images in the description of sunrise on Siegmund's last morning (xxvii: the paragraph, 'The day was pushing aside the boughs of darkness . . . the moon was like a dead mouse which floats on water').

Perhaps a note in Helen's diary on bees droning accounts for the recurrence of bee imagery. It is used in a variety of ways with reference to thoughts and sex; best perhaps when Lawrence expands Helen's note into a picture of a bee which lazily lets go a white clover-head, and booms 'in a careless curve out to sea, humming softer and softer' as he reels along in 'the giddy space', to prompt Siegmund's reflection that he has 'flown out into life' beyond his strength to get back (xix); most interestingly in an overwrought skyscape which turns into the poetry of Siegmund's metaphysical musings on life and the absorption at death of the individual into the undying life of the universe (xxi).

Moonlight diffuses calm; 'amid the blonde heavens' the moon seems to 'transcend forgetfulness', and Siegmund associates it with Helena and the sea (ii). After a long passionate embrace, he is soothed and feels 'like the sea, blue and hazy in the morning'; she has given him 'this new soft beauty'. It is eleven o'clock, and they are drawn to the sea. The moon wades through shallows of white cloud into a clear depth of blue, and they follow the 'moonpath' down to the bay. (These exterior details and the time are taken from the diary.) Helena begins to share the harmony he feels. His attention is caught by 'the white transport of the water beneath the moon', and they stand 'folded together, gazing into the white heart of the night' (v). A white moon can also signify apartness (as it does basically here), even coldness in love (see CP.99, with reference to Helen Corke). When Helena and Siegmund realize that after the morrow they must separate, the sense of oneness departs. In the midst of this passion of fear, the rim of the moon rises red over the sea, emerging as an oval horn of fiery gold, and spilling its liquor in ruddy splashes on the distant waves. With majestic movement it is lifted overhead, 'letting stream forth the wonderful unwasted liquor of gold over the sea – a libation'. In time, as the immense libation pours out, the whitening cup looks frail and empty. 'If I have spilled my life,' Siegmund thinks, 'the unfamiliar eyes of the land and sky will gather it up again.' (The thought, which is similar to his cosmic reflections on death, and to those in the paragraph, 'Meanwhile the flowers of their passion. . .' (ix), will be found in 'Red Moon-Rise', CP.89.) He then looks at Helena, and finds her face as white and shining as the empty moon (xvi).

Whiteness is the dominant symbol; it occurs continually in association with Helena. She can never love Siegmund, though one night she indulges his passion completely. 'It restored in him the full "will to live". But she felt it destroyed her. Her soul seemed blasted.' She makes a charitable self-sacrifice, and the whiteness of her dress contrasts with his ruddy face and hands like scarlet flowers in the fire-glow which represents his passion. (Fire and white as symbols of passion and coldness in love probably derive from *Jane Eyre*.) Helena 'belonged to that class of "dreaming women" with whom passion exhausts itself at the mouth'; one of the titles Lawrence proposed for the novel was 'The Man and the Dreaming Woman' (1.iv.12). She could swoon on Siegmund's breast, and leave him like a 'balked animal'; her frequent endearments suggest nothing more than a pitying affection, and she becomes a Madonna to him. The difference between them is expressed in terms of the sea: he takes the sea 'in his arms', but she is 'no swimmer' and lies on the sand, 'where the cold arms of the ocean lifted her and smothered her impetuously, like an awful lover'. She prefers rock-pools; the 'white fire' of the sea reveals God to her, 'His fire settling on her like the Holy Spirit'. She is one of Lawrence's 'spiritual' women. He told another, Jessie Chambers, that he could neither think nor feel the same, nor write poetry, in her absence; and it is significant that Helena connects Siegmund with 'the beauty of things', as if she is 'the nerve' through which he communicates with the universe (vi).

Helena is not another Lettie, but basically the moral of the story for Lawrence is the same as that of *The White Peacock*, and it is stated explicitly: 'For centuries a certain type of woman has been rejecting the "animal" in humanity, till now her dreams are abstract, and full of fantasy, and her blood runs in bondage, and her kindness is full of cruelty' (iv). A queer 'young man' of thirty-five is engaged to give a lecturette on the subject, and his comments on the 'soulful ladies of romance' ('semi-transparent' and 'crystal' as opposed to 'gross and animal' or 'opaque') recall Annable and Lady Crystabel (xiii). Siegmund's yearning for the bucolic life (xiv) is a reminder of George Saxton in his early prime.

Compared with the central story, the final chapters are plain and straightforward. Lawrence employs scenes with narrative human interest to reinforce Siegmund's thoughts on Helena's foreignness (xx) and the nearness of death (xxi). Both preoccupations isolate him from her on the return journey; sunset leads to her comments on what life can offer them, and starlight, to his reflections on what life has given him and what it will be when he has gone. The story is pursued to the end with unflinching realism, tempered with the sympathy that springs from psychological perception. This is noticeable in brief situations between Siegmund and two of his children, the youngest especially (xxiii); but no scene is more moving than that between Helena's parents when they know that the crisis is past, and nowhere are the effects more simple (xxix). Neither disciplined economy nor humanity is a dominant quality in Lawrence, but both will be found in some of these chapters.

The last two are rather tepid and superfluous. They are there to satisfy readers that the future holds out hope for Helena and Siegmund's wife. For the boarders of the latter, Lawrence sketched teachers he knew at Croydon; the walk with Helena is based on the memory of one he took with Helen Corke in the neighbouring country from Riddlesdown to Sanderstead (see p. 98).

SONS AND LOVERS

Begun as *Paul Morel* in October 1910, when Lawrence realized his mother was dying, this novel developed in three stages, each influenced by a woman: Mrs Lawrence, Jessie Chambers, and Frieda Weekley. He intended it to be 'restrained' and 'somewhat impersonal', 'a novel', not (and he was thinking of *The White Peacock*) 'a florid prose poem, or a decorated idyll running to seed in realism' (18.x.10). By the middle of 1911 he had reached a deadlock with the opposition of Mrs Morel to the growing friendship of Paul and Miriam. Jessie Chambers, who had followed the novel stage by stage, describes it as a 'story-bookish account of Mrs Lawrence's married life, almost sentimental at times. A non-conformist minister was the foil to a brutal husband; Ernest was not included; and Miriam ('a sort of foundling') was placed in the identical bourgeois setting of Alvina in *The Lost Girl*. She insisted that the actual story behind all this was much more interesting and poignant, urged Lawrence to include Ernest, and rewrite the novel completely. He agreed, and asked her to send her recollections, which she began writing at once. The first draft of this 'colliery novel' was near completion in the spring of 1912. In July Lawrence received detailed comments on the text from Edward Garnett, and decided to 'slave like a Turk' on it, though he loathed *Paul Morel*. Living with Frieda in Germany, and in need of 'running money', he concluded that he must rewrite the novel and recast the first part altogether. Revision began in September; by the end of October, when he had done three-fifths, he suggested 'Sons and Lovers' for the title. The work of pruning, shaping, and filling in was finished in November, when Lawrence wrote enthusiastically to Garnett about the 'idea' which had given it final shape, revealing above all the Freudian influence of Frieda. 'It is a great tragedy, and I tell you I have written a great book. It's the tragedy of thousands of young men in England. . . If *you* can't see the development – which is slow, like growth – I can', he added (14.xi.12).

In January 1913 Lawrence wrote a foreword to *Sons and Lovers* which was not printed until after his death (HL.95–102). Most of it is turgidly irrelevant, anticipating passages in 'Study of Thomas Hardy' and 'The Crown'. At the very end it reaches its subject. The conflict of flesh and spirit ('the Word') in marriage may make the wife turn to her son, who becomes 'her lover in part only'; receiving no 'confirmation and renewal' in the flesh, he wastes away. 'The old son-lover was Oedipus. The name of the new one is Legion.' If the son-lover marries, his life will be 'torn in twain', and his wife will in turn hope for sons, 'that she may have her lover in her hour'.

A letter to Rachel Annand Taylor (3.xii.10) sets out graphically the subject Lawrence had in mind at the outset: the 'carnal, bloody fight' between the parents, the bond between him and his mother (almost 'a husband and wife love'), and his refusal to allow anyone to have his soul, which his mother 'has had'. In his letter to Garnett, on completing the novel, Lawrence states that the mother selects her sons as lovers, first the eldest, then the second. They are '*urged* into life' by the 'reciprocal love of their mother', and are unable to love when they grow up because their mother 'holds them'. William 'gives his sex to a fribble, and his mother holds his soul. But the split kills him. . . The next son gets a woman who fights for his soul . . . fights his mother. . . . The mother gradually proves stronger, because of the tie of blood.' The son leaves his soul 'in his mother's hands', and seeks passion. There is a second 'split', but the mother 'realises what is the matter, and begins to die. The son casts off his mistress', attends to his dying mother, and in the end is left 'naked of everything, with the drift towards death'. While showing its general plan and direction, this psychological abstract is not a true reflection of the novel as we have it, the main reason being the subordination of William's role as son and lover. This arose partly from the pruning of Garnett, who, to keep the novel in reasonable length, omitted eighty-eight passages of lengths varying from a few lines to several pages, the majority in the first six chapters, some relating to parental quarrels, more to William as a lover.

The danger of exaggerating the autobiographical element in *Sons and Lovers* is great, simply because the real settings are everywhere recognizable, and an immense amount of detail relative to Lawrence's early life and background has been included. It should be emphasized that actual events have been selected and often modified, and that much has been imagined and invented throughout, for artistic purposes, and in accordance with the design of the novel. At the factual level it is obvious, for example, that the Morel family is not exactly the Lawrence family: William is the eldest, and Annie (drawn from Ada) is five years older than Paul; it is Arthur, the youngest, who wins a scholarship to 'the Grammar School' in Nottingham. Again, Paul 'launches into life' before he meets Miriam. His dedication to painting, and the continuation of his career at Jordan's, besides many settings and much narrative in the later stages of the novel, are wholly fictitious. More significantly, Miriam is cast in a particular role for the sake of the theme from the very outset.

141

Artistic invention is apparent at the end of the first and second chapters. In the first the widening rift between the moral and religious Mrs Morel and her grosser, drink-addicted husband leads to her being bolted out at night. Her soul is inflamed with passion, and she becomes intensely aware of the child in her womb. Recollections of the quarrel which has just flared up come down again and again like a red-hot brand on her soul until 'the mark was burnt in, and the pain burnt out'. Then she becomes conscious of white lilies reeling in the cold moonlight, of their scent, and the whiteness of other flowers. The reeling of the lilies is a symbolical parallel to the delirium of her soul during its traumatic experience. She puts her hand into a 'white bin' of pollen, and drinks a deep draught of its scent. On recovering, she melts out like scent (as if she too were a lily) into 'the shiny, pale air'. The child also melts with her 'in the mixing-pot of moonlight', and she rests 'with the hills and lilies and houses, all swum together in a kind of swoon'. The whole passage marks a fertilization of the soul (see xii for Lawrence's use of this metaphor) which creates a prenatal psychic bond between Paul and his mother. The white symbolism is consistent with that in Lawrence's earlier poetry and fiction, but it is more complex, and related to other flower scenes in the novel. A simpler but no less effective kind is seen in the 'battle' which follows Paul's birth, when Morel flings a drawer at his wife, cutting her brow, and drops of blood soak into the white shawl of the baby, and later into its hair – a christening which creates an indelible impression of a child born in pain from which it will never recover.

This violent scene is preceded by one which contrasts with some of the serried factual detail of the opening chapters. Mrs Morel sits on the edge of the cricket-pitch one bright evening, with the baby Paul on her knee. Morel had kicked William, and she would never forgive him. She looks at the green field 'like the bed of a sea of light', the wheeling rooks, the players, and the red sunset. Across the field she sees mountain-ash berries fierily distinct, and beyond, a few shocks of corn standing up as if alive. She imagines them bowing, and thinks her son may be a Joseph. It was 'one of those still moments' for Mrs Morel, when 'small frets vanish, and the beauty of things stands out'. She notices the peculiar knitting of the baby's eyebrows, 'as if it were trying to understand something that was pain', and suddenly 'the heavy feeling' at the mother's heart 'melted into passionate grief'. Dimly she felt that she and her husband were guilty. 'A wave of hot love went over her', and she held the child to her face and breast. 'With all her force, with all her soul she would make up to it for having brought it into the world unloved.'

In later years Lawrence regretted that he had done his father an injustice in *Sons and Lovers*. Even so, there are moments and scenes when Morel, contrite and inexpressive in defeat or repulse, is most sympathetically presented. His manhood breaks; he is 'the more damaged' because he never expresses his sorrow, and the wound it causes makes him turn again to drink for alleviation. Some of Paul's happiest recollections are of his father working cheerfully at home; at such times he sings and, when his children are around him, shows great fondness. Such brief scenes have a moving resonance, which make all the bourgeois connections to which William rises seem superficial. It is there too in the love felt by Paul for his mother during an illness, when, after hearing the thud, thud of her iron on the ironing-board, he wakens fully and watches her face, 'with the mouth closed tight from suffering and disillusion and self-denial', and her blue eyes 'so young, quick, and warm'. It hurts him to think of his inability to mitigate her suffering, but it is delightful to see her spit on the iron, the little ball of saliva bounding, racing off the dark, glossy surface, then watch her kneel down 'warm in the ruddy firelight' to iron the lining of the hearthrug vigorously, with brisk, light movements. Such scenes are infused with poetry of experience felt and treasured in the memory, and communicate a far deeper sense of reality than the more extended recollections of Lawrence's first employment.

Morel's inarticulate suffering is felt once again at the time of William's death, which brings the novel's first movement to an end without giving a sustained or convincing demonstration that William's failure in love and his death are the consequence of his mother's hold on him. Despite the distance which has gradually grown between them, his attachment to his mother remains strong, and her heart has never been heavier than at the thought of his *mésalliance;* but the brief scene in which he rails at his fiancée surprises both the reader and his mother, who is angry and ashamed of him. The consequence which Lawrence intended is made far more strongly in the Paul–Miriam story, and with the first visit of Paul and his mother to Willey Farm before William's death Part I and Part II are bridged.

Readers familiar with Lawrence's two earlier novels will see that

Miriam is condemned from the start. Ultimately one sees that she has become an unconvincing amalgam of the vividly real and the designedly stereotypic. Physically afraid and unaware of her beauty, she lives in a world of literary romance, is religious like her mother, and inclined to be mystical; her name implies 'exalted'. As a result of her religious intensity she shrinks from the 'shimmer' of life which is the Lawrentian revelation of God (see p. 66), and sees the world as 'either a nunnery garden or a paradise, . . . or else an ugly, cruel thing'. To see her swooning in an ecstasy of love over her youngest brother fills Paul with frenzy. When she concentrates on algebra, he wants to know why she does it with her trembling soul, and not with her wits. The 'life-warmth' which inspires his painting comes from his mother, but Miriam urges 'this warmth into intensity like a white light'. The spiritual 'communion' which she wishes to share with him is centred in a straggling white rose which splashes the darkness of the wood with spilt stars of pure white, the virgin scent of which makes Paul feel 'anxious and imprisoned'. Their intimacy is 'utterly blanched and chaste'. Ironically Mrs Morel, afraid that her own spiritual hold on Paul may be weakened, categorizes Miriam as 'one of those who will want to suck a man's soul out till he has none of his own left. . . She will never let him become a man. . .'.

Two flower scenes express the communion the two rivals are able to establish with Paul before sex-awareness prevents the renewal of such harmonies. Before the walk to the Hemlock Stone, Mrs Morel calls him into the garden to share her rapture in the discovery of three scyllas in bloom; not far from the Stone, Miriam is delighted to find Paul withdrawn from his companions, and waiting for her to admire an old manor garden. She turns to 'the quiet lawn, surrounded by sheaves of shut-up crocuses', and 'a feeling of stillness, almost of ecstasy' comes over her. In the church at Alfreton on the next excursion he is 'a prayer along with her', his latent mysticism quivering into life, as her soul glows in an atmosphere created by religious light and the whiteness and scent of Easter lilies and narcissi. When she becomes conscious of the 'serpent in her Eden', she is ashamed and shrinks 'in a coil of torture'. First she prays not to love Paul; then (and the extra twist from Lawrence turns the passage almost into parody), if it is God's will, that she may love him self-sacrificially, as Christ died for men's souls. Paul's crisis is reached on the Lincolnshire coast at moonrise, when his blood concentrates 'like a flame in his chest', and her 'purity' makes him shrink from kissing her; 'his ease and naturalness' are destroyed, and he feels humiliated.

Tensions inevitably increase: Paul loves to sit next to Miriam in chapel but enjoys cruelly destroying her beliefs; his mother's jealousy towards her increases. From this imbroglio, when Orion, the constellation of the two young lovers, is hidden behind gathered clouds, Lawrence provides relief in recollected and more fully realized scenes of life at home. The greatest of these is a recension (see p. 267), beginning with the miniature drama of Morel's Friday evening bath when he is in good spirits; the realistic grimness of the scene is part of its humour, giving a relish to the geniality it radiates in a brief rekindling of fondness and admiration which suggest that the love between Mrs Morel and her husband is never quite extinguished. The share-out of the wages which follows has its own interest; its main function is to supply insights into the community life of a colliery village. The lively Beatrice Wyld, the burning of the bread, the love which may be seen in Miriam's French composition and her eyes, the cruelty of Paul in reading Baudelaire's 'Le Balcon', his mother's jealous complaints when he returns from escorting Miriam home, take us step by step from light-heartedness back to the crux of the novel. Mrs Morel works on Paul's emotions by saying she has never really had a husband. After a passionate embrace which assures her that she is his first love, she tells him to have Miriam if he wants her. She looks so strange that Paul kisses her again. Morel enters at this moment and, seizing the situation at a glance, utters the taunt 'At your mischief again?' It goes straight to its mark, and Mrs Morel's emotion changes to sudden hate. The fight which threatens between father and son recalls a similar scene with William as the mother's champion, stressing the connotative duality of 'Sons and Lovers'.

At the end of 'the first phase' of his 'love-affair', Paul still thinks that he belongs to Miriam, though Hamlet-wise he regards her as a nun. But the sex-instinct which she has 'over-refined' grows strong. 'Often, as he talked to Clara Dawes, came that thickening and quickening of his blood . . . warning him that sooner or later he would have to ask one woman or another.' The change is reflected most in flower scenes. 'You get 'em because you want 'em', Paul tells Miriam when she says that flowers are not harmed if you treat them with reverence. In his conversation with Clara, as they gaze at a sheet of bluebells which seem to have flowed over into a field from a wood, one can see the light and dark of

Lawrence's spiritual and sensual planes emerging. Paul wonders which was the more frightened among the old tribes, 'those bursting out of their darkness of woods upon all the space of light, or those from the open tiptoeing into the forests'. He belongs to Miriam spiritually, but now discovers his 'physical bondage'. He would have 'given his head' for 'a joyous desire to marry her', but he was inhibited: 'he could not have faced his mother' (xi). Paul is selfish; he wants Miriam sexually, and she, rather like Helena in *The Trespasser*, submits to a religious self-sacrifice. He can never 'melt out into the darkness' of his wood; she is 'never alive, and giving off life'; she is 'his conscience, not his mate'. Sensual symbolism is underlined in Paul's 'I like the darkness. I wish it were thicker – good, thick darkness'; and it is integral to the scene which marks his new resolution. A half-moon is sinking behind the black sycamore at the end of the garden as he passes the scented pinks and stands by a 'white fence' of flagging lilies (the weakening hold of spiritual sex; cf. p. 97). A corncrake in the hay-field beyond insistently voices nature's call, until Paul's attention is caught by a raw, coarse perfume. The lilies still have their appeal but, hunting round, he finds purple iris flowers, and touches their 'fleshy throats' and 'dark, grasping hands'. Unlike the lilies, they stand stiff in the gathering darkness, and their scent is brutal. The male is 'dominant' in Paul. On Sunday (an appropriate day) he will break with Miriam, he tells his mother, as he smells a pink from the garden; he then chews it, and spits it into the fire.

Passion with Clara Dawes is imaged in scarlet carnation petals sprinkled like 'splashed drops of blood' after Paul's embrace by the river. Just as significantly when Miriam meets the new couple at the Morels', Paul points out the white chrysanthemums which had come from her garden. At the performance of *La Dame aux Camélias* (see p. 17), he is lost as much in the 'insane reality' of Clara's flesh as in the play. He succeeds in awakening her love, but he can give himself to her no more than he had to Miriam, so strong is his mother's psychic hold on him. One dark evening by the canal, however, when Clara tries to soothe him in his misery, his 'naked hunger' is 'blind and ruthless in its primitiveness'. When he comes to, he is aware of life around him, from the thrust of the grass to the calling peewit and the wheel of the stars. For each it is an 'initiation'; they know their own nothingness in the 'tremendous living flood' which has borne them along and given them individual completeness. It is an experience which never recurs. Gradually some mechanical effort spoils their loving, or, when they have their 'splendid moments', they have them separately. Clara learns that she has never possessed Paul, that he has never sought her, only the woman in her. Unlike Baxter, the husband from whom she has parted, he can never escape himself. Gradually she is convinced that Baxter wants her for herself; and their reconciliation provides the most human and moving scene in the protracted and complicated episode which it culminates.

In the meantime Mrs Morel has died. The account of Paul's last vigil has all the authenticity of some of the earlier scenes which were likewise indelibly imprinted on Lawrence's memory; its audio-visual realism make a direct, moving impact. Subsequently Paul meets Clara in Nottingham; they have tea together, and are quite jolly again. His father sits sentimentalizing with Mrs Morel's relatives after the funeral, telling them he has striven to do all he could for her. Yet deep down within him the real tragedy goes on, and for Paul there is 'the gap in life, the tear in the veil', through which he seems to drift as if to death. A last sacrificial effort by Miriam is rejected. It is redundant; she cannot renew his life any more than he can renew hers. The future seems dead, and he gives her the freesias and scarlet anemones that have adorned his table. They are a token of the grinning mockery of love (cf. p. 66).

The novel does not end with 'the drift towards death'. Paul takes Miriam back to her cousin's, and returns to the country. He feels 'the vastness and terror' of the night-sky, and knows that his soul cannot leave his mother, wherever she is. The night in which everything is lost reaches beyond the stars, which are like 'a few bright grains' spinning on though daunted. So it seems while he is weakened by maternal attachment, but a sudden resolve not to be 'less than an ear of wheat lost in the field' makes him turn his back sharply on the darkness and walk 'quickly' towards 'the city's gold phosphorescence'.

With its emphasis on determination and quickness (life), the ending is in perfect accord with a passage contrasting Miriam and Paul in architectural terms (vii). She was drawn to perpendicular lines and the Gothic arch which 'leapt up at heaven and touched the ecstasy and lost itself in the divine', whereas for Paul 'the great levels of sky and land in Lincolnshire' meant 'the eternality of the will, just as the bowed Norman arches of the church, repeating themselves, meant the dogged leaping forward of the persistent human soul, on and on, nobody knows where'.

Lawrence was thinking of Lincoln Cathedral and Southwell Minster (see *R*.iv and vii).

There is enough in this passage for two imaginative scenes, and one cannot help wishing at times that Lawrence had given greater scope to his imaginative power by being more selective. Chapters of *Sons and Lovers* suffer from disproportionateness and inequalities, with sudden shifts from the intensely imaginative to relatively flat stretches of the realistic, and from scenes shimmering with life to those which are factitious. The unevenness is due sometimes to haste and facility, often to piecemeal composition in repeated revisions. Integrational weakness also reflects the combination of fact and fiction; the fiction is sometimes slanted, whereas the best of the real scenes are not. Frieda Lawrence, who said that she had 'more to do' with this novel than with any other of Lawrence's, probably had something of this in mind (with reference to Miriam) when she wrote to Edward Garnett from Fiascherino: 'it feels as if there were nothing *behind* all those happenings. . . It does not seem the deepest and last thing said; if for instance a man loves in a book the pretty curl on the neck of "her", he loves it ever so intensely and beautifully, there is something behind that curl, *more* than the curl; there is *she*, the living, striving *she*.' One suspects that Lawrence, in his wish to 'explain' or justify Paul, was guilty of putting 'his thumb in the scale, to pull down the balance to his own predilection'; and that, insofar as he overweighted the case against Miriam, there were times when he lost that 'trembling instability of the balance' which keeps the novel alive and morally true (P.528–30; cf. 'The State of Funk', P2.568).

THE RAINBOW

'But one sheds one's sicknesses in books – repeats and presents again one's emotions, to be master of them', Lawrence wrote to his former Croydon colleague A. W. McLeod with reference to *Sons and Lovers*, the novel in which he had tried to resolve a complex past which still plagued his conscience (?26.x.13). The resolution of more immediate experiences with Frieda often provides an imaginative core in subsequent novels, and is adapted repeatedly in *The Rainbow* and *Women in Love* to reflect currents in contemporary life. Superficially *The Rainbow* is a

(*left*) the Lawrence family. Children, left to right: Ada, Emily, George, David Herbert, Ernest   (*right*) Mrs Lawrence, a few months before her death

1

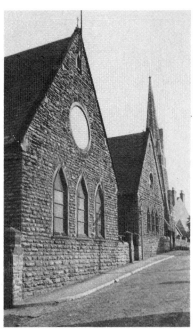

Eastwood: (*above left*) Lawrence's birthplace, Victoria Street (*above right*) the British School, Albert Street, below the Congregational Chapel (*below*) the Lawrences' home in the Breach

(*above*) the colliery at Brinsley where Lawrence's father worked
(*below*) Lamb Close

3

(*above*) Beauvale School   (*below*) Beauvale Priory

4

(*above*) Haggs Farm   (*below*) the pond at Felley Mill

5

D. H. Lawrence: (*left*) on his twenty-first birthday (*middle*) in 1908, while at Nottingham University College (*right*) in 1912-13

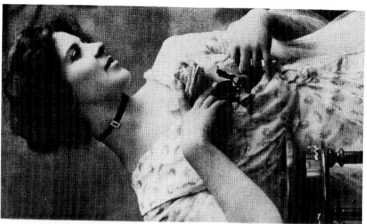

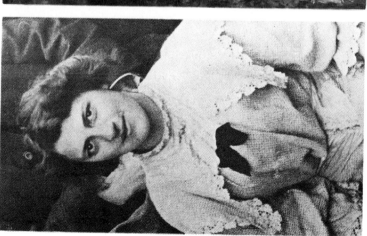

(*left*) Jessie Chambers, from a photograph of the teaching staff at Underwood National School, 1907 (*middle*) Maurice Greiffenhagen's 'An Idyll' (*right*) a studio photograph of Louisa Burrows

7

Nottingham: *(above)* workroom at J. H. Haywood's. Castle Gate *(middle)* Goose Fair *(below)* University College

8

Cossall: (*above*) the church (*middle*) Louisa Burrows', home (Will and Anna Brangwen's) (*below*) Marsh Farm (also in *The Rainbow*)

9

(*above left*) the Rev. Rodolph von Hube of Greasley　(*above right*) Frieda Weekley in Bavarian costume, 1913　(*below left*) Professor Ernest Weekley　(*below right*) William Hopkin

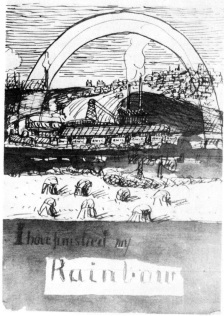

(*above left*) Southwell Minster : 'the dogged leaping forward of the persistent human soul, on and on, nobody knows where' (*above right*) Lincoln Cathedral : the perpendicular lines and the Gothic arch which 'leapt up at heaven and touched the ecstasy and lost itself in the divine' (*below left*) Lawrence's *Rainbow* sketch (the letters on the coal trucks are B W & Co : Barber, Walker & Co) (*below right*) Garsington Manor

11

(above left) Lady Ottoline Morrell   (below left) the Lawrences' cottage at Greatham, Sussex
(right) the Hon. Dorothy Brett

12

(*left*) on Lake Chapala, Mexico, 1923 (*right*) market scene by the steps leading to the Church of Soledad, Oaxaca, Mexico, December 1924, Lawrence and Frieda in the centre foreground

13

Kiowa Ranch: (*above left*) the kitchen (*above right*) the adobe oven at the back (*below left*) Lawrence with two of the ranch horses (*below right*) with Susan, the black cow, Frieda's nephew assisting

14

(*above left*) Villa Bernarda, Spotorno   (*above right*) with Ada Lawrence at Mablethorpe in 1926   (*below*) in the sun near Villa Mirenda, Scandicci; under this tree
part of *Lady Chatterley's Lover* was written

15

(*above*) Lawrence's grave at Vence   (*below*) his memorial chapel, with Frieda's tomb in front (left), at Kiowa Ranch

16

family chronicle covering three generations; fundamentally it is a creative analysis of the inner life of society during a period of change and disintegration.

These two related novels were written in pursuance of an aim which Lawrence described as 'Love Triumphant' when he told Sallie Hopkin that he would achieve something better for women than the suffrage (23.xii.12). Only through 'a readjustment between men and women, and a making free and healthy of this sex' would England 'get out of her present atrophy', he told McLeod: 'Oh, Lord, and if I don't "subdue my art to a metaphysic", as somebody very beautifully said of Hardy, I do write because I want folk – English folk – to alter, and have more sense' (*postmark* 26.iv.13).

Not until January 1915 did Lawrence decide to make two volumes of the work which began as 'a pot-boiler' at the end of 1912, changed in character and design, and grew, initially as *The Sisters* and then as *The Wedding Ring*. The former is related to *Women in Love*, the latter to the story of Ursula, her education, and her love-affair with Skrebensky. The first generation story of *The Rainbow* was, it seems, the last of the three to be contemplated. *The Sisters* had been intended for *jeunes filles*, but Lawrence found he could write only on what he felt strongly, and *the* problem for him was 'the relation between men and women'. Half-way through, he described it as 'all analytical – quite unlike *Sons and Lovers*, not a bit visualized' and 'so really a stratum deeper than I think anybody has ever gone, in a novel' (11.iii.13). The 'first crude fermenting' was Lawrence's theorizing and 'Frieda's God Almightiness'; and Frieda recognized herself in the 'superior arrogant females' (CL.207–8).

A more artistic, less flippant version was then written in the third person. Comparing it with *Sons and Lovers*, Lawrence felt that the 'Laocoön writhing and shrieking' had disappeared from his new work; he had begun to feel 'something of the source, the great impersonal which never changes and out of which all change comes' (CL.241). This work, *The Wedding Ring*, was abandoned near completion early in 1914, when Lawrence learned that Garnett was disturbed by the apparent lack of artistry in the first half of the manuscript; he no longer wished to create vivid, emotional scenes, and preferred 'permeating' to 'incorporated' beauty (beauty in a shapely novel, 'a story with a plot', 29.i.14). Without delay he began the novel about Frieda and himself for the seventh time, having 'quite a thousand pages' of manuscript to burn (3.iv.14). 'Now you will find her and me in the novel, I think, and the work is of both of us', he wrote in a letter of protest to Garnett, who had described the new work as 'common', and recommended a reversion to the tone of *The Sisters*. The germ of the novel ('woman becoming individual, self-responsible, taking her own initiative') had been in the old, but it was flippant. Lawrence insisted that he was primarily 'a passionately religious man', and that his novel must be written from the depth of his religious experience (22.iv.14). He finished the work in May, and recommended 'The Rainbow' as its title.

In another letter of disagreement with Garnett, he explained that something of what he was after could be seen in Marinetti's 'profound intuitions of life', which together, 'in their illogical conception', form 'the general lines of an intuitive physiology of matter'. He was more interested in the 'non-human' element in humanity than in the old-fashioned moral conception of character. People change: 'You mustn't look in my novel for the old stable *ego* – of the character. There is another *ego*, according to whose action the individual is unrecognisable, and passes through, as it were, allotropic states which it needs a deeper sense than any we've been used to exercise, to discover are states of the same single radically unchanged element.' 'Don't look for the development of the novel to follow the lines of certain characters', he reiterated: 'the characters fall into the form of some other rhythmic form, as when one draws a fiddle-bow across a fine tray delicately sanded, the sand takes lines unknown' (5.vi.14). Lawrence's relations with Edward Garnett were virtually at an end, for, in England a few weeks later, he accepted a lucrative offer from a new publisher. However, further revisions proved necessary, involving some strenuous rewriting, which began in late November and did not end until the opening of March 1915. Further objections were raised to phrases and passages. Lawrence deleted the former, but refused to alter any of the latter; and publication proceeded with unfortunate consequences.

Lawrence's recollection of his final revision is chronologically inaccurate, but he maintained that *The Rainbow* was (substantially) 'all written before the war', and thought that its 'pre-war statement' remained unaltered (27.vii.17). Yet the final writing led to such expansion that he decided two novels were necessary adequately to present the corruptive processes in a society which had created the First World War. He knew that he was writing a 'destructive' work, and the growing

realization of ultimate aims which led to the writing of the first phase of
The Rainbow helps to explain why his nostalgia for the more organic life
of England in the past is more deeply felt here than in *The White
Peacock*, and why it produces some of his greatest prose poetry.

Lawrence does not paint the kind of idyllic picture of the past which
(influenced by Carlyle's *Past and Present*) he had suggested in the
opening paragraph of *The White Peacock*. Already signs of modernity
and disintegration are appearing: first the raised canal for coal-transport,
then a colliery, a railway, and rapid urbanization. The Brangwens are
eager for the unknown; the women look out to the world beyond,
determined, if they cannot reach it, that their children will. Yet the
men live 'full and surcharged' lives, in such an intimate and active
communion with the natural world of earth and heaven and animals
that the thought of their blood-consciousness lifts Lawrence to lyrical
ecstasy.

The Brangwen men, whose homestead is 'just on the safe side of
civilization', face inwards to 'the teeming life of creation', whereas the
women are aware of the 'lips and mind' of the world beyond. For Tom's
mother the key to success lay in knowledge or education. He had to
attend a grammar school, and it is significant that he was a failure, though
anxious to succeed for her sake. Yet he was more 'sensuously developed'
and more 'refined in instinct' than most of the other boys; he hated books
but responded deeply to imaginative poetry. Woman was the symbol of
'that further life which comprised religion and love and morality', but
when Tom had lost both parents he had no one to whom he could turn.
He got tipsy at times, and went jaunts on horseback to the nearest
towns. At Matlock he met a girl and a foreigner whose manners he
admired. Theirs was the life for him; but it was never realized, and he
became a bout-drinker. Then he met Lydia Lensky, a Polish widow,
and at last his existence became real. For each it was a rebirth. Lydia felt
at home in England; her father had been a landowner, and she was
happy at Marsh Farm. She and Tom were foreign to each other, but a
power greater than their individual selves kept them together at all
times. (In this relationship Lawrence thought of himself and Frieda.)

Lydia's Polish child Anna was educated at a ladies' school in Nottingham, but she grew to mistrust herself and the outer world, and was
always happiest at home, though she retained her 'splendid-lady ideal'.
At eighteen she fell in love with her cousin Will, Tom Brangwen's

nephew, who had come to Ilkeston from Nottingham as a junior draughts-
man in a lace factory. He was devoted to Ruskin and church architecture,
and set on marrying Anna, who was swept off her feet by his talk until
'the land seemed to be covered with a vast, mystic church, reserved in
gloom, thrilled with an unknown Presence'. Tom Brangwen, who loved
Anna, was angry, but provided handsomely for their marriage. It was
not a happy one. Anna became the mother of a large family. Will
Brangwen was a craftsman of very limited outlook, and the rift between
the spiritual and the physical is soon apparent in him.

Their eldest child Ursula knew 'what it was to live amidst storms of
babies, in the heat and swelter of fecundity'. She craved for spirituality
and stateliness, finding the latter in *Idylls of the King* and the world of
dreams, and the former in the Church, until the ecstasies and sufferings
of the annual Christian cycle lost their appeal, and 'the religion which
had been another world for her' became an illusion. Meeting Skrebensky
'brought her a strong sense of the outer world. It was as if she were set
on a hill and could feel vaguely the whole world lying spread before her.'
He was one of those Sons of God of whom she had dreamt. Their moonlight love-scene on the evening of her uncle Tom's wedding at Marsh
Farm is as ominous as the earlier one between Will and Anna. Ursula's
education is similar to Lawrence's. She matriculates at a Nottingham
grammar school, becomes a teacher, and then attends Nottingham
University College. Glamour soon departs from academic studies.
Skrebensky returns; they buy a wedding-ring, and a life of 'delicious
make-belief' begins for these two 'sensuous aristocrats' in London and
Paris. She fails her final examinations, and becomes increasingly aware
of her incompatibility with Skrebensky, though 'still fiercely jealous of
his body'. Their *de facto* marriage ends in Ursula's spiritual death.
Though she has rejected it, she is the victim of will-power, after being
nauseated with dehumanizing processes in school and industry. Through
education and travel she has escaped her parents' parochialism, but the
community sense of earlier generations has gone, and widening circles
have ended, for a time at least, in bleak disillusionment and isolation.

These are the main externalities of the story, but Lawrence's interest,
unlike that of acknowledged contemporary authors such as Galsworthy,
Bennett, and Wells, is in the inner drama of forces which create life or
destroy it. It would be a mistake to regard it as psychological; it is
something deeper, more whole, and more vital. A hint of it is found in the

contrasting views of Ursula and her friend Maggie Schofield, a suffragette (xiii). For Ursula the suffrage question was unreal. She has 'within her the strange, passionate knowledge of religion and living' which far transcends 'the limits of the automatic system' that contains the vote. This 'fundamental, organic knowledge', which as yet is undefined in Ursula, is the kind of experience which forms the major expression of *The Rainbow*. A second contrast between the two girls supplies a key to the theme of the novel. They talked of love and marriage; for Ursula 'love was a way, a means, not an end in itself, as Maggie seemed to think'.

Referring to *The Rainbow*, and fully aware of Lawrence's views and intentions, Frieda wrote: 'For perfect love you don't only have two people, it must include a bigger, universal connection.' This supra-personal life-force may be expressed explicitly, as with Lydia and Tom. Her impulse was strong against him, but she was drawn by 'one blind instinct'; he was held back by fear, but 'driven by a desire bigger than himself'. It finds expression in metaphor: Lydia unfolds, 'asking, as a flower opens in full request under the sun, as the beaks of tiny birds open flat, to receive, to receive'. Or (as in Hardy) inner forces are externalized. Something greater than any personal will drives Tom to the vicarage to make his proposal. The trees wave wildly in the roaring wind; his entry into the kitchen is an 'invasion of the night'. After their first embrace, the 'strange, inviolable completeness of the two made him feel as sure and stable as God'. Superficially they were strangers, and the conflict between his sense of foreignness and his passion is mirrored in the 'vast disorder' of the sky, with the moon 'running liquid-brilliant into the open for a moment, hurting the eyes before she plunged under cover of cloud again'. Here, with effects which are all the more impressive for being completely natural, Lawrence transmits 'the tremendous *non-human* quality of life' (21.ix.14):

It is not the emotions, nor the personal feelings and attachments, that matter. These are all only expressive, and expression has become mechanical. Behind in all are the tremendous unknown forces of life, coming unseen and unperceived as out of the desert to the Egyptians, and driving us, forcing us, destroying us if we do not submit to be swept away.

Marriage made life new for both; despite intervals of apartness, as, for example, during Lydia's pregnancy, when he felt 'like a broken arch thrusting sickeningly out from support', Tom was controlled by 'something bigger in him'. When he hankers after the 'polite visionary world' which he has seen in the home of an educated woman, his brother's mistress, Lydia's intuitive, heartfelt perception is admirable. She is transfigured, and takes the initiative. Something in Tom resists until he lets go 'his hold on himself'. Their consummation is complete. 'She was the doorway to him, he to her.' A power greater than themselves had taken possession; 'they had joined hands, the house was finished, and the Lord took up his abode'. They did not think of each other, nor did they worry about the future. All were assured; Anna, with whom Tom had found much happiness, was no longer required to sustain the broken end of the arch. 'Her father and mother now met to the span of the heavens.' This change in metaphor, from the man-made to the natural and divine, anticipates the rainbow, and expresses the 'universal connection'.

Such a union is never the lot of Anna and Will. Before their marriage, she is in ecstasies; religious fervour makes him feel that their falling in love is as if the hand of the Almighty had thrust burning-bright out of the darkness and gripped him. The moonlight harvesting scene does not express pure rapture, however. Anna responds naturally to the moon as if she were a wave, but at the end Will cannot understand her passion. It is his drumming will which brings them together after a succession of rhythmic sheaf-carrying movements, and his triumph is keen, his heart 'white as a star' as he drives his kisses nearer until he wants her sexually. They must marry; and his soul crystallizes inalterably. As the moon becomes brighter, he grows hard like a gleaming, bright pebble. His eyes are bright and inhuman like a hawk's when he tells his uncle and aunt that he and Anna propose to get married. His voice is that of the conscious will; Anna's comes from afar, 'out of her unconsciousness'. Elsewhere Lawrence distinguishes between the light of the mind and the darkness of the senses. Aphrodite, the queen of the senses which have become 'a conscious aim unto themselves', is the goddess of cold consuming fire. Flesh, Lawrence continues, becomes self-conscious, seeking gratification; but 'the fire is cold, as in the eyes of a cat'; it is 'fluid, electric' (see p. 293). Will's catlike voice and grin, and the 'electric state' of his passion, are noted at the beginning of his courtship. The symbolical darkness of the senses is continually associated with him. He and Anna remain 'separate in the light, and in the thick darkness married'; their love becomes 'a sensuality violent and extreme as death'.

During their honeymoon they seem to be 'at the heart of eternity', while time roars 'far off, towards the rim'. Will hates Anna when she wishes to return to the outer world and the normal round of life; he is 'electric with fury'. She cannot understand his religiosity; his soul is inhuman, unrelated to humanity and to his own self. Love alternates with conflict; he is cruel and hawk-like, and she retaliates. Life flows for her when he is out of the way, or when they have tea at the Marsh on Sundays, and she regains a 'lighter world, that had never known the gloom and the stained glass and the ecstasy of chanting'. Will's quasi-mystical yearnings reach their consummation in Lincoln Cathedral, 'clinched in the timeless ecstasy' at the apex of soaring pillars and arches. The 'jewelled gloom' is 'spanned round with the rainbow'; the altar is 'the mystic door, through which all and everything must move on to eternity'. Anna also is overcome with awe, but at length she remembers the open sky above, and realizes that the altar is barren. She wishes to escape the 'fixed, leaping, forward-travelling movement' conveyed by the architecture, and be free like a bird in the air. The carved imps tell her that the cathedral is not the absolute, and that many things have been left out of 'the great concept of the church'. Gradually she destroys Will's illusions, until he regards the Church as 'a world within a world', and realizes that a temple is never perfect till it is 'ruined and mixed up with the winds and the sky and the herbs'.

He had no spiritual faith but still loved the Church as a symbol, and worked more than ever to maintain it. He lived simply by Anna's 'physical love for him', knowing that he was unfulfilled; 'there was a darkness in him which he *could* not unfold' and 'which would never unfold in him'. Neither was Anna quite fulfilled, though she loved her child Ursula dearly. She looked from her 'Pisgah mount' and saw the faint gleam of a distant horizon, and a rainbow which was only 'a shadow-door with faintly coloured coping above it'. The feet of her rainbow were the dawn and the sunset of each day; she lived in the present, and 'relinquished the adventure to the unknown'. Rearing children, in her 'sleep of motherhood', she was happy, 'a door and a threshold' from which they could peer out 'for the direction to take'. Gradually the children became less important in the lives of their parents. Ursula, it is true, was light playing within her father's darkness, but only the darkness set him free, and Anna responded. When she was cold to him, he attempted to seduce a girl in the Park at Nottingham. Unsuccessful, he returned home, 'the sensual male seeking his pleasure'. His wife had changed; the old moral order meant nothing. They were strangers to each other, and each sought 'gratification pure and simple'. There was 'no tenderness, no love between them any more', only the sensual exploration. The body of woman had become his 'supreme, immoral, Absolute Beauty'. Anna sank to his level. Their 'shameful, natural and unnatural acts of sensual voluptuousness' freed Brangwen, and he devoted more and more of his time to parish work. All he did was magic to Ursula, but 'some dark, potent secret' overshadowed her mind.

The 'terrible' beauty which Lawrence agrees can be found in 'secret, shameful things', and which Will Brangwen realized, is not Lawrence's justification of them. He condemns them as 'immoral', 'shameful', and 'unlicensed'. Will is unredeemed. Arrayed in ironical white at the church organ, he is a key figure in Lawrence's depiction of a corrupt society. He cannot think for himself and, after losing his spiritual illusions, is quite soulless. Outwardly decent, he evades life in work and activity, and lives for his own sensual gratification.

Ursula was less than sixteen when she first met the army officer Skrebensky, and thought him 'one such as those Sons of God who saw the daughters of men, that they were fair'. Their early love began challengingly, self-assertively. 'And after all, what could either of them get from such a passion but a sense of his or of her own maximum self, in contradistinction to all the rest of life? Wherein was something finite and sad, for the human soul at its maximum wants a sense of the infinite', Lawrence adds. Sexual assertion is the key-note of the second wedding celebrations at Marsh Farm. The presiding spirit is Ursula's uncle Tom Brangwen, and he seems to fan the flames of physical desire. 'The bride was strongly attracted by him, and he was exerting his influence on another beautiful, fair girl, chill and burning as the sea, who said witty things which he appreciated, making her glint with more, like phosphorescence' (see p. 293). Ursula wished to escape into the starlit night, but Skrebensky would dance with her; it was 'his will and her will locked in a trance of motion'. When the moon rose, she wanted more and more communion with it, but Skrebensky put a cloak round her, and held her hand. 'Oh, for the cold liberty to be herself!' she felt. The dance continued; 'his will was set', but she remained 'cold and hard and compact of brilliance as the moon itself, and beyond him as the moonlight was beyond him'. When the dance was over, they walked out, she 'bright as a steel blade'. Among the new stacks of corn, the atmosphere was electric with cold, glimmering, whitish-steely fires. Suddenly the impulse came to reduce him to nothing. She tempted him, but remained 'burning and brilliant and hard as salt, and deadly'; she was fierce and 'corrosive as the moonlight' as she destroyed him with a kiss. Afterwards she relented; she wished to be kind. He kissed her, but he had lost his indomitable, triumphant spirit, and her soul was 'empty and finished'. Here as elsewhere, motivation, yearning, and feelings which are rarely articulated in experience, are unforgettably communicated in intensely vivid scene, metaphor, and symbol.

Ursula suffered successive disillusionments. She came to loathe the Winifred Inger she had loved, concluding that the right place for this perverted woman was with Uncle Tom in the corrupt mechanized milieu of Wiggiston. Though marriage meant nothing to him, he wanted children, and Winifred was a suitable companion. All his desires had ended in 'a disintegrated lifelessness of soul', and he had reached 'a stability of nullification', caring for neither God nor humanity, and believing in neither good nor evil. He had 'the instinct of a growing inertia' and 'would let the machinery carry him'. 'A traveller' who 'must go on and on', yearning for some unknown ideal, Ursula was repelled by the limitations of her mother's complacent physical life, and rejected a rural life of the senses with Anthony Schofield (xiv). She tried teaching and a college education, and was disgusted with the mechanical, life-denying horror of the one and the sterility of the other. 'Always, always she was spitting out of her mouth the ash and grit of disillusion, of falsity.' Her positive self lay unrevealed, like a seed in dry ash. Her world was like a lighted circle, but in the surrounding darkness she was aware of shadow-shapes, wild beasts and angels, which the 'illuminating consciousness' fenced out. Skrebensky might have been her angel, her 'doorway', she thought in her dejection.

The Skrebensky who returns is more alien than the youth Ursula knew. 'He seemed made up of a set of habitual actions and decisions', and she sensed a 'dark, heavy fixity' in his animal desire. He talked of Africa, and gradually transferred to her 'the hot, fecund darkness that possessed his own blood'. Her sensual subconsciousness made her regard the ordinary citizen as a 'subdued beast in sheep's clothing', a 'primeval darkness falsified to a social mechanism'; and this seems to sum up Skrebensky. The long 'dark kiss' that follows on a 'turgid, teeming night, heavy with fecundity' contrasts with the corrosive moonlight kiss of their early courtship. She is 'will-less' and carried away 'into the pristine darkness of paradise'. Yet their unlicensed honeymoon contains 'a developing germ of death', and she finds that she is 'very rich in being alone', in contact with the natural world. His tense fixed will, his belief in democracy, and his eagerness to join the governing class in India, anger her. Both are repelled by the meaningless activity and rigid torpor of mechanical England, but Ursula's preference of the downs and 'their intercourse with the everlasting skies' to the 'energetic courage' of the tiny train that tunnelled the earth 'blindly and uglily' applies to Skrebensky, who can no longer arouse any 'fruitful fecundity' in her, or 'connection with the unknown', or 'reverence of love'. On the Lincolnshire coast she wishes to be alone with the 'salt, bitter passion of the sea' and 'its indifference to the earth'. One evening she and Skrebensky are confronted by a 'terrifying glare of white light' like a blast over the sea from an incandescent moon. She wants to go she knows not where; her face is metallic in the moonlight, her voice ringing and metallic, like that of a harpy or the scream of gulls (cf. Gudrun, *WL*.xviii). Suddenly she seizes him, and kisses him with a 'fierce, beaked, harpy's kiss' till she has the heart of him. Their fight for consummation in the moonlight is 'terrible', and in the morning they are like dead people. When they left, Skrebensky was happy; it was easy to get rid of her. In two weeks he had married his colonel's daughter. Ursula was not informed; and a week later Skrebensky and his new wife sailed for India.

When she found herself pregnant, Ursula saw her mother in what appeared 'a just and true light'. 'What was her flesh but for childbearing, her strength for her children and her husband, the giver of life?' She wrote to Skrebensky, hoping to join him in India. The strange, frightening, almost phantasmagoric scene with the horses which follows is related by Lawrence to the 'seething' which 'rose to madness' within her when she received no reply. She sees the horses' haunches pressing repeatedly to burst some grip upon their breasts, till their inability to free themselves makes them go mad. Lawrence explains a similar appearance of horses in dreams as the 'secret yearning' of 'the spontaneous self' (in the male) for 'the liberation and fulfilment of the deepest and most powerful sensual nature' (*Fan*.xiv). Anton Skrebensky is a soldier, and (like Gerald Crich) 'a great rider', with 'a horseman's sureness' and 'some of the horseman's animal darkness' (xv). The pregnant Ursula sees no alternative but to accept her mother's role, become subjugated to Skrebensky, and bear his children. She has plumbed the depths; the 'concentrated knitted flank of the horse-group' stirs uneasily, 'awaiting her, knowing its triumph'. In the delirium which followed her escape, the question of herself and Skrebensky persisted in various forms. If she could not escape the compression of his world, she would go mad. The 'corrosion of him burned in her till it burned itself out'; it had not, however, changed her true self. She had to break out of reality 'like a nut from its shell'. The world was a bygone winter, discarded; the only reality was the kernel, 'free and naked and striving to take new root, to create a new knowledge of Eternity in the flux of Time'. Ursula then discovers that there is to be no child, and hears that Skrebensky is married. She can repudiate the past. The rainbow image that follows is a symbol of regeneration in the future. It is a cosmic symbol, 'making great architecture of light and colour and the space of heaven'; unlike the cathedral, it excludes nothing, and represents 'a living fabric of Truth'; it is 'the earth's new architecture'.

The rainbow presupposes a flood, and the flood, evil. Its pedestals are 'luminous in the corruption' which is seen in the prisoned or coffined lives of people in Beldover, Lethley, and Hainor (names suggesting age and decay, death, and the horrible). For Lawrence dissolution and creation are 'the systole–diastole of the physical universe' (p. 76). In 'The Crown' (v) he writes more explicitly on some of the forms of corruption which he embodies in *The Rainbow*, the static will of Skrebensky and his adherence to democratic beliefs, the growing inertia of Tom Brangwen in his industrial niche, for example. Woman's significance is not the bearing of children; her 'supreme and risky fate' is to 'bear herself' and 'drive on to the edge of the unknown' (P.441), as Ursula continues to do. The flood in *The Rainbow* is a recurring image rather than a symbol with large imaginative overtones. In actuality at Marsh Farm it marks the end of an era. The fact that Tom Brangwen is sometimes tipsy like Noah seems to be coincidental or irrelevant, for Noah was saved, and Tom is one of the antediluvian Sons of God. He rises to their stature, and Lawrence's memorial to him runs: 'he had made himself immortal in his knowledge with [Lydia]. So she had her place here, in life, and in immortality. For he had taken his knowledge of her into death, so that she had her place in death. "In my father's house are many mansions"' (ix). What the rainbow signified in married life for Lawrence was achieved by Tom and Lydia; their house finished, 'the Lord took up his abode'. Anna was supremely happy: 'Her father and mother now met to the span of the heavens, and she, the child, was free to play in the space beneath, between.' The most explicit references to the flood relate to Will Brangwen, who 'ignored the human mind and ran after his own dark-souled desires, following his own tunnelling nose' (an image which is varied in association with Skrebensky, p. 158). At first Anna was the Ark to him; without her he was afraid of drowning in the heaving flood of sensuality which gave him no rest. Ultimately she was reduced to his level, and their love was perverted by conscious will into nothing beyond sensual gratification, 'a passion of death'. The timing of the Marsh Farm flood at this point has an obvious significance. It is worth noting, too, that the climax of decadence in Will and Anna occurs at the end of 'The Child' chapter, which concludes ominously with the shadow of 'some dark, potent secret' in which Ursula seemed to run. At the Marsh she was frightened by the bestial expression in her uncle Tom, in whose eyes his mother discerned 'the black depths of disintegration'. He seemed to kindle a flame of physical desire at his brother's wedding. He danced with the bride, 'quick and fluid and as if in another element, inaccessible as the creatures that move in the water'. Passing the fire into the darkness, the shadowy couples created a vision of 'the depths of the underworld, under the great flood'. When Tom first met Winifred Inger, 'he detected in her a kinship with his own corruption'. Ursula noticed their 'ghoulish satisfaction with the state of things in mechanized Wiggiston. Instinctively aware that Winifred had become her uncle's lover, she longed to escape their 'soft' corruption, which affected her like the fetid air of a marsh. Ironically she and Skrebensky sat together in church on the morning after their first love-encounter, listening to the lesson on the Flood. Ursula sported with classical fancies when she heard the words 'and the waters shall no more become a flood to destroy all flesh'. She was 'surfeited' with the God who uttered them, and with the Ursula who 'felt troubled about God'. 'She felt she now had all licence', just as Anton believed that 'his own things were quite at his own disposal' when he listened to the sermon. It is after enjoying licence and sickening of his physical passion that she has her terrifying experience with the horses. Rain and marshland maintain the suggestion of flood and corruption;

160

she is 'dissolved like water'. Yet when she plumbs the depths she is 'inviolable and unalterable' like a stone at the bottom of a river. She yearns for a new life, reaches (as it were) a new shore, and sees the rainbow, its feet luminous in the corruption of her familiar world (see p. 295). It is 'a pledge of unbroken faith between the universe and the innermost' (*K*.viii).

The general deterioration in society is reflected chiefly in marriage. The marriage of Tom and Lydia reaches Lawrence's ideal; they were 'transfigured'; 'she was the doorway to him, he to her'. At the wedding of Will and Anna, Tom enunciates in his simple way what Lawrence writes on his and Lydia's immortality (ix) and (anticipating 'The Man Who Died') on the Resurrection (x). He implies that true marriage is both spiritual and physical, and that man knows spiritual fulfilment most in marriage. With succeeding Brangwen representatives, the spiritual is lost in the descent to willed, self-seeking, sensual sex: the men live by it; Anna succumbs to it; and, after a giddy licentious round, Ursula rejects it for something greater in life. Lawrence would have us believe that industrial conditions in Wiggiston are such that, one man or another, one woman or another, it is all the same in marriage.

The decline is seen in adult relationships with children. With her parents' fulfilment, Anna 'played between the pillar of fire and the pillar of cloud in confidence, having the assurance on her right hand and the assurance on her left'. One of the most realistic and touching scenes in the novel shows Tom Brangwen, when Lydia is expectant and Anna misses her, carrying the querulous child one evening out into the barn in one arm, gaining her attention as he prepares food and feeds the cows with the other, then sitting in the barn and listening to the cows in the adjoining building until she relaxes and falls asleep. His patience and love show a profound imaginative sympathy. And how Anna loved 'bowling along' with him in the trap to Nottingham and Derby! A happy relationship appears when she asks for the Sunday collection and takes it, on the morning of Will's first appearance. Tom's love for Anna and his dislike of Will make him angry and unbearably miserable in an unforgettable pictorial scene, as he hears her, a mere girl to him, protesting her love in the dimly illuminated loft. Ursula is less fortunate. At first she is everything to her father; when he was old he could never bear to think how dear she had been to him when she was a mere toddler. Then she was the light that 'played within his darkness'. There was a strange alliance between them, and his clasping her woke her too soon from 'the transient unconsciousness of childhood'. One of her earliest memories was of setting potatoes with him; the scene is a wonderful presentation of the gap between a child's impressions and the insensitive judgment of a self-centred unimaginative father. Other offences of which she was not conscious filled him with rage, until he was part of an 'outward malevolence' against her. For a time their attachment grew, but Ursula hardened. His wild escapades with her by the canal and at the fair reveal a cruel streak in him. It is no wonder that the child's mind was darkened by a shadow on which she preferred not to dwell, and that, talking with her grandmother of the distant past, she felt she was in paradise. Unlike her mother, she grew up looking beyond for freedom and self-fulfilment; everything she tried proved barren, but hope in the ultimate remained.

It is characteristic of Lawrence's attitude to his theme that only the first part nourishes humour. The wedding at the Marsh elicits free comment and amusing recollections which are not discordant with Tom Brangwen's lofty views of marriage. They keep us down to earth and, though a little saltier, recall instances of Hardy's humour. An *Under the Greenwood Tree* current follows in the carol-singing which Tom organizes as a benediction to the honeymoon couple in their home. It is not only familial and local; it helps to give a sense of the wholeness of life. And it has a wistful suggestion of a vanished past. From such scenes, and Tom's fuddled monologue as he rides happily home on the night of the flood, to the bitter struggle of Ursula in a Board of Education school brings us not only to the twentieth century but to a world as bleak as that of *Hard Times*. One suspects the influence of Dickens (and in the satirical extremism of the Wiggiston sketch). There is hardly a sign of caricature, however, in the presentation of Ursula's experience; it is humanly and completely realized by one who knew how dehumanized, dehumanizing, and mechanically barren State education at its worst could be. So absorbingly real are the scenes that they form an episode which seems almost self-contained, and certainly out of proportion to the novel as a whole.

Far removed in style from the brilliance of Lawrence's metaphorical moonlight scenes, they stand out nonetheless because they are in the conventional mode and outside the main current of *The Rainbow*, though obviously related to its vitalistic theme. Others (such as those already referred to in the adult life of Tom Brangwen), sometimes brief but equally memorable from fusion with deep feeling in focal characters, are more vividly imaginative and colourful. A bright, happy scene is created when Ursula, accompanied by Skrebensky, talks to the canal bargee and his wife, and is captivated by the baby. It is happily placed, redolent of goodness and honesty, and in clear contrast to the vacuity of Skrebensky in the conversation which precedes it, and the kind of love-making they pursue after Fred Brangwen's wedding. No scene, however, is more tense and moving than that at the farm on the night Tom is drowned, when growing anxiety is not only felt but loudly heard. It is set firmly amid indications of the disintegrative influences which his son Tom derived (we are told) from his mother's foreignness. Even so, Brangwen assumes in death an inviolable grandeur which attests Lawrence's reverence for life.

The banning of *The Rainbow* seems quite incomprehensible, more so than that of *Lady Chatterley's Lover*. The novel reveals the increasing devitalization of a society, particularly in marriage. It is inspired by a belief in the 'positivity' of women, and the importance of their role in the regeneration of man. The ban, the continuation of the war, and other disillusionments combined, however, to weaken Lawrence's optimism. 'You ask me about the message of *The Rainbow*', he wrote to Lady Cynthia Asquith (7.ii.16). 'I don't know myself what it is: except that the older world is done for . . . and that it's no use the men looking to the women for salvation, nor the women looking to sensuous satisfaction for their fulfilment. There must be a new world.'

WOMEN IN LOVE

Women in Love is not just a continuation of *The Rainbow*, although in some form or other parts of it originate in the first version of *The Sisters* (1912–13) and more of it was undoubtedly written before Lawrence decided to make two novels of his work. It began to take final shape in the spring of 1916, when he settled in Cornwall. Soon afterwards, Frieda had a great 'rumpus' with Lady Ottoline Morrell, telling her what she thought of her spirituality and democratic notions. Wayward and often hostile impressions of people the Lawrences met in England, and strong feelings exacerbated by the War (27.vii.17), direct and darken a novel which had to be self-contained after the suppression of *The Rainbow*. The reductive aspect of love which is central to the latter is therefore continued in the Gerald–Gudrun relationship as a foil to the Birkin–Ursula progression. The new novel came rapidly to Lawrence, who described it as 'the book of my free soul'. Most of it was completed by the end of June 1916, and all except the last chapter was sent to his literary agent by the end of October. In a foreword, apparently intended for the American edition, Lawrence states rather ambiguously that the novel was 'altogether re-written and finished in Cornwall in 1917' (P2.275). The title had been changed to 'Women in Love'; Frieda thought it should have been 'Dies Irae' (cf. 24.v.20). Lawrence told his friend McLeod that the work was 'a masterpiece' (21.xii.16). Nobody dared risk publication, however; and it had to wait until 1920 before it first appeared, in New York, and 'for subscribers only'. It was first published in England in 1921.

A reference in a discarded section (P2.92–108) to a type of Cornishman suggests that this was the opening of the novel which Lawrence began in Cornwall. The 'prologue' throws light on *Women in Love* and on Lawrence's premarital frustrations with 'spiritual' women. The central figure is Birkin, a school inspector, who believes that without a greater 'idea' nothing can be done to improve education 'in the winter that has come upon mankind'. One had to wait for decomposition to generate new growth. He found Hermione Roddice's spiritual love and moonlit ecstasies devitalizing, and became hostile towards her. He knew sexual desire, but had no desire for women. Rather he was drawn to men, though he realized it only in their presence. Extreme types, light and dark, attracted him: the former, 'keen-limbed', with 'eyes like blue-flashing ice and hair like crystals of winter sunshine'; the latter, heavier and sensual but ultimately revolting. Gerald Crich, whom he most admired, belonged to the former group. Birkin's incapacity to love a woman 'positively, with body and soul', tortured him; he yearned 'to love spontaneously', 'to be moved by a power greater than oneself'. He was a man of integrity, who would never sacrifice 'the sensual to the spiritual half of himself' or 'the spiritual to the sensual half'. These words sum up the 'message' of *The Rainbow* with reference to the personal relationships and outlook on which every aspect of society depends.

Women in Love begins colourfully, but one soon realizes that vividness of setting, or of dress (which we always associate with Gudrun) is more than offset by industrial defacement and the gathering shadows of moral disease which reach their climax in the deathly whiteness of the Tyrol. At the opening Gudrun expresses Lawrence's feelings on his return to the region of his birth shortly before he began *Women in Love*. Both wanted to go away, and not to know that it existed. No rainbow shone over Beldover, Lethley, and Hainor. Both were fascinated by the 'strange, dark, sensual life' of the colliers, but their utterly materialistic outlook made Lawrence feel he could scream; Gudrun was tortured by the ugly meaninglessness of their community (cf. 27.xii.15). Lawrence looked for new life abroad, and the immediate hope of Birkin and Ursula is to escape. The positive values they display are unable to counteract degenerative influences; they are no more than the Lawrentian key to a sane society in some vaguely distant future.

The exfoliation of *Women in Love* at first suggests a novel in conventional style, and a superficial reader may conclude that characters in action are extreme and even unreal at times. As one would expect from *The Rainbow*, the main stream of events relates to those inner forces which (in Lawrence's eyes) are responsible for the decline of civilization, or on which its upsurgence depends. More than any of his previous works, *Women in Love* is a novel of ideas. In such fiction, the author's major problem is to find or create an action which embodies and illustrates his theme. Lawrence did not know to what conclusion he was working when he began (?4.v.16), and the novel has no end, except for the climax of Gerald's death. Like life, it goes on; Lawrence's thought had not finalized, and the theme is continued in other novels. His imagination works in scenes or episodes; the action of *Women in Love* consists of related units rather than a rounded whole. Continuity depends on narrative links, but imaginative coherence comes continually from the repetition and enlargement of ideas through forms of symbolism, sometimes recurring, sometimes in more complicated conjunction. Thematic allusiveness in scene, imagery, and other details is characteristic of Lawrence; it is very strong in *The Rainbow*, but it combines with a far less linear plot in *Women in Love* to engender greater imaginative unity than is to be found in any other of his novels.

Details of conversation which are almost insignificant at first assume grave meaning when seen against the background of the novel as a whole.

A discussion starts at Breadalby (viii) on education; it is regarded as knowledge, and its limitations are reflected from different angles. The athletic Gerald Crich considers it a form of gymnastics for producing a vigorous mind, and agrees with Hermione on its uplifting potential. 'It's like getting on top of the mountain and seeing the Pacific', he says. In the end he can see no way out of the cul-de-sac in the mountains; if only he could have gone on, he might have been living in spirit with him, Birkin laments. A tedious 'old hat' question (ii) comes to life as Gudrun, after indulging in a daydream of Gerald as 'a Napoleon of peace, or a Bismarck', realizes that 'the advance was like having a spurious half-crown instead of a spurious penny', and that nobody would care for the national ideas of England any more than for its 'national bowler hat' (xxix). Again, at Breadalby, the little Italian countess breaks into the conversation to promote a loud laugh at an absurd translation of a tiny phrase in Turgenev's *Fathers and Children*. This not only implies an ironical ignorance of inevitable social revolution (the 'loud laugh' which comes from the Baronet, and signifies 'the vacant mind' in Goldsmith, 'rattled out like a clatter of falling stones') but hints at the ultimate moral void of nihilism which is portrayed in Loerke. Birkin's interest in the red catkins is pedagogic and obsessive but, in conjunction with the implications of his fierce attack on Hermione (and its parallel to the Lettie–George complex in *The White Peacock*), this apparently obtrusive image assumes tragic overtones for Gudrun, as she realizes the emptiness of her life with Gerald, and envies Ursula's happiness with Birkin. Gazing at the peaks above the 'blind' valley they had reached, she '*knew* how immortally beautiful they were, great pistils of rose-coloured, snow-fed fire in the blue twilight of the heaven'. She could see their loveliness; 'she knew it, but she was not of it. She was divorced, debarred, a soul shut out.'

Incidental narrative details may reflect moral judgments. Before Ursula reaches accord with Birkin, she half-agrees with Gudrun that he is overbearing, too much of a preacher; she then realizes the falsity of this summing-up. They see a robin singing shrilly, and describe him as 'a little Lloyd George of the air', but some yellowhammers darting along the road make Ursula change her mind. It is an impudence to think the unknown forces of life can be measured in human terms, and she turns again in spirit towards Birkin (xix). When his father is dying, Gerald Crich feels repulsion; Gudrun agrees that it is better to dance than wail, and trembles from the proximity of the man who suggests 'the same black licentiousness' that rises in herself. Riding in Birkin's car, they are amused when he says that he prefers a marriage contract to love, particularly free love. Gerald tells Birkin that he is over-refined, and the car runs through mud (xxi). Later, Gerald's love brings him to Gudrun's bedroom muddied from the clay of his father's grave. They follow the road to spiritual death, whereas Ursula and Birkin work their way painfully towards fulfilment in life. Sudden jealousy of Hermione makes Ursula attack Birkin furiously. She throws his precious rings at him, and they fall into the mud of the road. Then she walks off. Birkin knows that the spirituality of his past with Hermione had been a kind of self-destruction from which he is not wholly free, but Ursula's emotional intimacy is just as dangerous to his marriage ideals, a kind of tyranny which nauseates him. He picks up the rings, and wipes them unconsciously; to him they are tokens of 'the reality of beauty, the reality of happiness in warm creation'. Soon a contrite Ursula returns with the gift of a flower. This simple life-token dissolves all complexity, and reconciliation follows in tenderness and peace (xxiii).

Thematic ideas are vitalized in dramatic scenes of varying intensity Birkin regards marriage as a bond in which the partners maintain their integrity like 'two single equal stars balanced in conjunction'. The 'Mino' cat illustration in support of the need to create a 'pure stable equilibrium' or 'transcendent and abiding *rapport*' seems rather forced and feeble, like Birkin's explanation of Mino's 'volonté de pouvoir'. The scene of 'A Chair' is full of human interest; its sardonic realism underlines Birkin's dread of the conventional, home-centred, 'love-and-marriage' ideal, which was adequate for Gerald (see xxv for the likeness to Skrebensky's). Like Lawrence, Birkin did not wish to submit to the 'tyranny of a fixed milieu' and possessions; he wanted a complete relationship with Ursula, but something beyond, including a perfect relationship with man, and freedom to reach it. It is the subject of *Aaron's Rod*. The nature of Gudrun and Gerald is illustrated more vividly. His unremitting, almost mechanical ruthlessness in compelling a frightened mare to face up to a clanking locomotive at the railway crossing is for Ursula a horrible revelation of his 'lust for bullying', his 'Wille zur Macht' (cf. 27.xii.15); for Gudrun the subordination of the mare under his weight and indomitable thighs has a deep subconscious sexual appeal, comparable to her reaction when she sees the girl and the stallion, 'rigid with pent-up power', in the picture of Loerke's statuette (xxix). Her blood-affinity with Gerald is seen in her sudden spring to open the gates for him. The gull-like voice in which she cries 'I should think you're proud' is heard again in 'Water-Party' and 'Rabbit' (it has inhuman connotations for Lawrence, P2.105; cf. Ursula, R.xv). Gudrun also is animated by a will which can be violent. She has a sudden impulse to drive back a group of long-horned Highland cattle and dance before them, as if in a state of sexual hypnosis. Just as suddenly she rushes at them and, when warned of the danger by Gerald, smacks his face. 'You have struck the first blow', he says. 'And I shall strike the last', she retorts involuntarily, revealing the sexual aggressiveness of her deeper self. The 'league' between them is fully revealed in 'Rabbit'. His 'white-edged wrath' recalls the white fire of the poem 'Rabbit Snared in the Night'; Gudrun responds with 'white-cruel recognition'. Their 'hellish' or 'underworld' sense of mutuality, in association with her vindictive seagull's cry, recalls her witch-like screaming as she watched Gerald master his mare. Just as she empathized with the horse in subjection to his strength, she is now 'a soft recipient of his magical, hideous white fire'. Though the Crich family is in mourning, she has come gaudily dressed like a macaw, and even Gerald, immediately before sanity returns with Winifred's tender concern for the rabbit, is shocked to read in Gudrun's eyes the nonchalance or nihilism of her suggestiveness. Appropriately, in the end, she finds her kinship with Loerke.

Though never as optimistic as at the end of *The Rainbow*, Lawrence is not a prophet of doom in *Women in Love*. Like Shelley ('If Winter comes') he believed that corruption and dissolution are inevitable forerunners of regeneration. In 'The Crown' (p. 74) he had distinguished between 'divine' corruption which leads to new life, and a corruption which is uncreative by force of 'static will'. There is a hint of the former in Birkin's reference to the geese in a Chinese drawing which he is copying; their 'lotus mystery', or 'fire of the cold-burning mud' which enters their blood corrosively, has the strange effect of making Hermione feel the ghastliness of the dissolution to which she and her society are subject despite her 'static' will (viii). The most active form of corruption in *Women in Love*, as in *The Rainbow*, is the conscious pursuit of sensual gratification in sex. In 'The Lemon Gardens' (*TI*) it is associated with Aphrodite and cold white fire (the moon), sea phosphorescence, electric sensation, the will, and the loins. This sex-awareness is repeatedly emphasized in Gudrun as she contemplates 'the festering cold of the marsh' (x; cf. P2.407) and feels its 'turgid fleshy' growth 'as in a sensuous vision'; it is immediately linked with her sudden recognition of Gerald, as he seems to start 'out of the mud' in his boat. She notices the movement of his white loins, and his hair glistening white like 'the electricity of the sky'; as he moves towards her in the rocking boat he seems like surging marsh-fire or a phosphorescence. Her first reaction had been instant, 'a keen *frisson* of anticipation, an electric vibration in her veins', more intense than she had ever known in the strange 'underworld' glamour of the miners and the voluptuous dark resonance of their voices. Gerald is her escape from their 'heavy slough' (cf. ix), but their first embrace is significantly willed by her under the lonely colliery railway bridge where young miners brought their sweethearts when it rained. Another marsh prompts Birkin's discourse on the 'dark river of dissolution' (xiv). 'And our flowers are of this – our sea-born Aphrodite, all our white phosphorescent flowers of sensuous perfection, all our reality, nowadays.' These 'marsh-flowers – and Gudrun and Gerald' are 'born in the process of destructive creation'. It is 'a fearful flower of corruption' when man is regressive, and returns to 'cold, bygone consummations' of the evolutionary past (P2.403). The 'cold' return suggests a willed sensuality; in *Women in Love* its climax is reflected in the Tyrolean snow, which Ursula hates for its 'unnaturalness' and the 'unnatural feelings' it promotes.

Birkin wishes there were 'roses of happiness' among the 'fleurs du mal'; like the Lawrence of 'New Heaven and Earth', he is tired of 'the life that belongs to death – our kind of life'. (The difficulty of communicating imaginatively by symbol and metaphor is admitted at this point: Ursula and Birkin know that 'words themselves do not convey meaning', and are but a gesture or dumb show.) The subject is continued in the Pompadour, when representatives of the cultural world make fun of Birkin's letter on 'the Flux of Corruption' which terminates in mindless sensation, a state emblemized in Halliday's wood-carving of a savage woman in labour. Gerald sees Minette in it (vii); above all, the novel shows its relationship to Loerke and Gudrun.

With Loerke the regressive process goes further than with Gerald, who is the embodiment of depersonalizing will and mechanical industrial efficiency. Loerke is inhuman; his amoral abstract mind sees beauty in factories and machine-labour; in its representation of life his art is repulsively brutal (see p. 300). The more Ursula knows of him, the more she yearns to escape from the 'ghastly glamour' of the snow-world, with its 'terrible, static ice-built mountain tops' – the 'cold death' and 'glamorous snow' of 'The Return Journey' (*TI*) – to the 'dark fruitful earth' of the South. Gudrun supports Loerke, however: 'life doesn't *really* matter – it is one's art which is central'. In him she found 'the rock-bottom of all life'. He was a moral void, with no ideals or illusions; he existed only as 'a pure, unconnected will, stoical and momentaneous', caring fundamentally about nothing. To Birkin he was 'a rat, in the river of corruption, just where it falls over into the bottomless pit'. Gerald, endowed with purpose and attached to his world, was too limited for Gudrun; their 'sheer blind force of passion' could no longer satisfy her. With Loerke she could play a game of 'infinite suggestivity', 'mystic frictional activities of diabolic reducing down, disintegrating the vital organic body of life'. Their talk was full of evasions and suggestive vagueness; they never discussed the future, but delighted in 'mocking imaginations of destruction' or in sentimentalizing about the cultural past. Loerke believed in 'neither heaven nor earth nor hell'; he had no allegiance and, by 'abstraction from the rest', was 'absolute in himself'. Lawrence's reactions to the period may be exaggerated and atrabiliar, but they register the abhorrence of a writer whose faith in life and burning desire for improving the quality of living were the source of his greatest inspiration.

Death of one kind or another is never far removed from Gerald Crich and his family. When Mrs Crich tells Birkin that she would like her son to have a friend, he quotes Cain and realizes that, if anybody was Cain, it was Gerald, though he had killed his brother accidentally. At the end of the scene (ii), Birkin's view that one should 'act spontaneously on one's impulses' is challenged by Gerald, and the argument reaches the syllogistic conclusion that he must have a lurking desire to have his throat cut. Referring to his modernizing zeal, Ursula tells her sister that he will have to die when there is nothing left for him to improve; conversation then turns to the shooting of his brother, and Ursula thinks there could have been 'an unconscious will behind it' (iv). The thought is not so much a prolepsis as a pointer to the will in Gerald which subjugates the individual, and denies life and spontaneity. The death of Diana Crich at the water-party hastens her father's death. His Christian charity toward miners and their dependants made his wife despise him, but she was like a hawk which is sullen in submission. Their relationship was one of 'utter interdestruction', for the 'terrible white, destructive light that burned in her eyes only excited and roused him', so that his love for her was 'keen as death' and 'vitality was bled from within him'. When Gerald succeeded, efficiency and mechanization became the rule, and the miners were reduced to 'mere mechanical instruments'. His reductive sensuality appeals to Gudrun, and is countered by 'an unconquerable desire for deep violence against him'. Their love is deadly. She sought to *know* him with her 'subtle and intelligent hands', as Eve reached for the apples on the tree of knowledge; and this conscious awareness was 'a death from which she must recover' before she continued 'harvesting . . . upon the field of his living, radio-active body'. When Gerald came to her from his father's grave, 'the terrible frictional violence of death filled her, and she received it in an ecstasy of subjection'.

In the cul-de-sac among the mountains Gerald knew that he had lost Gudrun. His passion was bronze-like; 'his heart went up like a flame of ice, he closed over her like steel'; and she did not know him. To Ursula the air seemed 'conscious, malevolent, purposive in its intense murderous coldness', but Gudrun had at last reached her place, and wished to climb 'the wall of the white finality' into the 'frozen centre of the All'. One morning when Gerald accompanied her 'with the fine, blind face of a man who is in his state of fulfilment', they were in 'perfect static unity'; but she had discovered her kinship with Loerke, and decided she must fight Gerald until either he or she triumphed. She becomes 'stark and elemental', and treats him with 'a diabolical coldness'; it is always a 'see-saw', one destroying the other, until he feels 'torn open' like a victim. He is maddened with the desire to kill her, and she feels how maddening it would be to live with him day after day in 'dead mechanical monotony and meaninglessness'. Gerald's end comes after words from Loerke have arrested his attempt to strangle Gudrun. Will-motivated, he goes blindly on, weakened and nauseated, until he drifts unconsciously, his purpose being to keep climbing mechanically. Suddenly he sees a half-buried crucifix, and thinks somebody is about to murder him. A blow seems to descend, and he wanders till he slips and falls in death. When Birkin saw him 'like clay, like bluish corruptible ice', he remembered a dead stallion he had seen, a 'mass of maleness, repugnant'. Gerald had been a 'denier', and Birkin compares the 'cold, mute Matter' of his 'last terrible look' with 'the beautiful face of one whom he had

loved, and who had died still having the faith to yield to the mystery';
no one could remember it 'without the soul's warming with new, deep
life-trust'.

Lawrence's use of metaphor is so sustained that his moral theme is
almost allegorical. The positive complement is found in Birkin's development with Ursula. He is hostile to the dominating Hermione because
she is another Lady Crystabel or Lady of Shalott. Her passions and
instincts are intellectualized and spiritual, and her will is merely a
mirror which reflects her conscious world. Birkin tells her that sex in
the head is a form of pornography, like 'watching your naked animal
actions in mirrors'. Between 'the actual sensual being' and 'the vicious
mental-deliberate profligacy our lot goes in for', with 'the electricity
switched on' to watch ourselves, there is all the difference in the world,
he argues. In stating that Birkin 'sounded as if he were addressing a
meeting', Lawrence admits the reiteration of an obsessive theme (iii).
One of his metaphorical scenes shows Birkin's affinity with the natural
world, and the superficial absurdity which can result from this kind of
narrative. After Hermione's hatred of him has reached its violent
consummation, he rolls naked among hyacinths, covers himself with
fine wet grass 'more beautiful than the touch of any woman', and finds
it all 'very good, very satisfying'. (The anticlimax of expression recalls
some of Lawrence's poems.) Characteristically, Birkin thinks that Hermione was right to 'biff' him, simply because she wanted to. More
abstractly (and appropriately withdrawn to an island) he argues, in
disgust with humanity, 'If we want hate, let us have it – death, murder,
torture, violent destruction', adding that it would be better if mankind
were eliminated. Elder-flowers and bluebells – even the butterflies
(which had engaged Ursula's interest while Gudrun was absorbed in
the rank growth of the marsh) are 'a sign that pure creation takes place',
while mankind 'never gets beyond the caterpillar stage'. Self-consciously
Lawrence makes Ursula regret that Birkin's rare vital quality should be
combined with the stiff priggishness of 'a Salvator Mundi and a Sunday-
school teacher'.

In love Birkin wishes to rise above an emotional, personal plane, in
response to a 'law of creation' which insists on irrevocable conjunction
'in mystic balance and integrity – like a star balanced with another star'.
Love is neither subservient nor free; it is 'never pure until it is irrevocable'. For Birkin (Lawrence) the first step towards a new world is such

Novels

a 'mystic' union in marriage. He and Ursula, in revolt against the
willed and mechanical, wish to submit to the unknown (xiii, xv).
Realizing in her depression that 'the body is only one of the manifestations of the spirit', Ursula cannot bear to be 'cut off from living'; better
to leap into the new tide of life, like Sappho (P.673). 'No flowers grow
upon busy machinery, there is no sky to routine, there is no space to
a rotary motion.' The thought of domestic love and children, with a
dominant wife, repels Birkin. In their different ways, Hermione and
Ursula had assumed the Magna Mater role towards him (Ursula as 'the
queen bee' recalls Frieda in *Sea and Sardinia*). A talk with Gerald makes
him suddenly realize 'the problem of love and eternal conjunction
between two men'; he proposes *Blutbruderschaft*, as Lawrence did with
Murry, but nothing comes of it beyond the physical intimacy of a casual
wrestling bout.

The pond reflection of the moon which Birkin tries to destroy represents Cybele, a goddess identified with the Magna Mater and men's
sexual sacrifice. His action is a vehement protest against male subservience
in conventional love. It is because hope of reconciliation between them
is waning that the moon appears white, deathly, and triumphant as
Ursula approaches; for Birkin the whiteness of the moon's reflection and
the light-fragmentation he creates has a cold, destructive significance,
which is related to woman's will. Yet the scattered flakes of light in
the water suggest rose petals which keep drawing together, seeking to be
whole and composed like a rose, a symbol of complete love, when man
and woman are singled into 'purity and clear being' (xvi), and each is
'absolved from desire and made perfect' (P.680). Ursula wants 'pure
love', but her views make it impossible for Birkin to discuss it with her;
it is 'a paradisal bird' that can never be netted.

He can accept neither the old, purely sensual, unspiritual African way
of 'mystic knowledge in disintegration and dissolution, knowledge such
as beetles have' – the expressions recall company in the Pompadour
Café (vi, xxviii) – nor the northern way to 'ice-destructive knowledge'
and 'snow-abstract annihilation' (the way of Gerald and, even more, of
Gudrun). There is only one way for him, 'the paradisal entry into pure,
single being' in which the individual accepts 'the obligation of permanent
connection' in love, to achieve 'a lovely state of free proud singleness'
stronger than any emotion. Eventually it comes, but Lawrence's stock-
in-trade is not equal to it. As Ursula kneels in the Saracen's Head and

173

embraces Birkin, 'a new current of passional electric energy' is released, 'with floods of ineffable darkness and ineffable riches' from 'the source of the deepest life-force . . . at the back and base of the loins'. Repeated references to 'the sons of God in the beginning' reinforce an impression of facile factitiousness and subsequent critical failure. A lack of humour is suspected in the picture of Birkin driving the car 'like an Egyptian Pharaoh', and seated 'in immemorial potency' like a huge Egyptian statue, knowing what it is to be awake in the 'basic', 'deepest physical' mind. He steers with 'a sort of second consciousness', his upper body being Grecian, and 'a lambent intelligence' playing 'secondarily above his pure Egyptian concentration in darkness'. This darkness has its obvious ambivalence, for Birkin is 'dark and magic', Ursula is 'dark and fulfilled' and, after a brief stop, they drive on again 'into the darkness'. Their consummation in Sherwood Forest is mutual; they achieve the freedom of 'star-equilibrium', 'the immemorial magnificence of mystic, palpable, real otherness'. Beside this heavy verbalizing and many of the cumulated effects in this uneven episode a passage in 'Flitting' is exquisite, and one feels at last that theory is based on felt experience. The immanence of beauty in Ursula is like a 'strange, golden light' to the resurrected Birkin, and a spiritual oneness supervenes which transcends their individual selves. It is ineffable, but Lawrence conveys it convincingly. The golden 'paradisal glow on her heart' and the 'unutterable peace' in his, as they cross the Channel in thick darkness, is 'the all-in-all'. This transit is metaphorical as well as actual, but joining Gerald and Gudrun in the Tyrol is a mistake, and Ursula wishes to move on to the 'dark fruitful earth' beyond the Alps. Her marriage is shameless, but there is no suggestion that it is unnatural, like that of her parents. Birkin knows that his spiritual union with her is eternal, but regrets that his life is incomplete without 'eternal union with a man too'. His faith in life remains undiminished, nonetheless. Even if humanity 'ran into a *cul de sac*, and expended itself' (as Gerald had done), some new race would continue. 'To be man was as nothing compared to the possibilities of the creative mystery.' 'The fountain-head was incorruptible and unsearchable.'

The novel is not therefore 'purely destructive', as Lawrence wrote, but its major ideas undoubtedly stem from the effect on Lawrence's 'soul' of the war in Europe – a 'deluge of iron rain' with 'no Rainbow', 'the rushing of the Gadarene swine down the slope of extinction'

(27.vii.17) – and, even more perhaps, from his disgust at the lack of faith and ideals, or the moral negativism and anarchy, he found among intellectuals on his return to England from Italy. Intellectuals at Cambridge made him wonder how 'so sick people rise up', and the 'marsh-stagnancy' of the place filled him with deep gloom (?19.iii.15). Younger representatives, full of ideas and chatter, but devoid of feeling and 'reverence', drove him mad, and made him think of beetles (19 and ?20.iv.15). It is the image he associates with the Bohemians who meet in the Pompadour. Birkin feels like one of the 'damned' when, on his way to meet Halliday 'and his crowd', he travels by train through 'the disgrace of outspread London'. While Gerald believes that life centres in 'the social mechanism', he holds with Browning that 'Love is best', and quotes significantly from 'Love Among the Ruins' as they approach a city of 'death'. Beetles live 'purely within the world of corruption and cold dissolution' (xix), and the Pompadour is the 'small, slow, central whirlpool of disintegration' where 'the Flux of Corruption' and *Fleurs du Mal* are a joke. The taste in art and attitude to life of its habitués are an anticipation of Loerke, one (hardly human in appearance) who hates ideals and lives simply for the present, a 'negation, gnawing at the roots of life', to whom love is a mere convenience. Lawrence's impressions of Lady Ottoline Morrell and some of her guests may be seen in Hermione and the Breadalby group. She is 'a leaf upon a dying tree', a priestess 'suckled in a creed outworn', who believes that intellectually and spiritually she is one of the elect, though her 'universals' are a sham, and, in the last resort, her allegiance is to Mammon, the flesh, and the devil (xxii). Talk at Breadalby is frequently political or sociological, but 'curiously anarchistic'. Everything being 'thrown into the melting-pot, Ursula sees the speakers as witches, and Birkin becomes violent in his denunciation of Hermione's 'universals' on the brotherhood of man. (An extension of his argument is found in 'Democracy', P.699ff.)

Although the novel at this point approaches Peacock's satirical method, Lawrence's presentation is psychological. Hermione looked at Birkin with 'leering eyes', but this is his impression. 'He could feel violent waves of hatred and loathing of all he said, coming out of her.' In the revelation of inner forces and states of mind, Lawrence repeatedly changes from direct (literal or figurative) to oblique narrative or reflected experience; and the pointed vitality of his prose (at its best) makes it an excellent medium for the inner drama of Ursula, for example, when she sits 'crushed and obliterated in a darkness that was the border of death' (xv), or of her and Hermione, as conversation lapses and they drift into reverie (xxii). The excitation of Hermione's sustained anxiety when Birkin fails to appear at the wedding with which the novel opens is felt in the frequent repetition with which clauses begin; and (in 'Snowed Up') Gudrun's scorn of Gerald, and the thought of life with him at Shortlands, of wheels within wheels of people, and the mechanical succession of day after day, make her think feverishly of the tick-tack of time and the twitching hands of the clock, until she is wearied out with Lawrentian thoughts on the multiplication of wheels in the development of Gerald's industry, and of his likeness to an intricate chronometer-watch.

Technically more dramatic, *Women in Love* never quite reaches the magic of certain scenes in *The Rainbow;* its critical quality is harder and more insistent. Its main inspiration is inherent in the connective imagery which conveys its thoughts, but there are surprising lapses of style, even at climactic points. Could Lawrence have intended seriously the grammatical justification of 'whom' in a bedtime discussion between Ursula and little Billy? And what signifies 'of all things' in conjunction with 'a venison pasty' which looks 'noble' to Ursula at the height of her bliss? The prose is frequently repetitious, and sometimes turgid and tautological. It has been seen that Lawrence can look at himself and his ideas with critical detachment, if not with some amusement, but carelessness rather than lack of humour must account for the retention of 'she moved upon the firm vehicle of his body' (Gudrun and Gerald) and 'he gathered her like a belonging in his arms' (at the opening of a rare passage on the ecstasy of Birkin and Ursula).

Reference has been made to essays by Lawrence which throw light on creative ideas in the novel. One passage of particular importance in the letters (21.ix.14) discusses the fertilization of man's soul 'to vision or being', and the superhuman quality of life Lawrence found in Egyptian and Assyrian sculpture' (see p. 153). Two rather strange poems, 'New Heaven and Earth' and 'Manifesto', are contemporary with *Women in Love* and closely related to it. In the first Lawrence feels that he and his corrupt world have been indivisible; he rejoices that he has crossed into another world through resurrection in marriage, and that the old world is being destroyed. The principle of dissolution-creation is implied. 'Manifesto' continues the theme of the new life which comes with attainment of individual singleness in marriage, as in Birkin's 'star-equilibrium'. The assumption is that, when all are fulfilled, a sane society will emerge. The symbolism of the concluding lines is inexplicit, and for assurance one can turn to 'The Reality of Peace' (P.687–94); see also pp. 76–7 and 105.

THE LOST GIRL

'The first part is readable, the middle . . . sheer tosh, the end admirable. What a descent after the beauty of *Sons and Lovers* and the magnificent beginning of *The Rainbow*. . .'. So wrote Francis Brett Young, who was no great admirer of Lawrence. This overemphatic assessment calls attention to the undoubted unevenness and disunity of *The Lost Girl*. But for the War it would have been substantially different; it was begun in the winter of 1912–13 and not finished until 1920. The initial impetus came from reading Arnold Bennett's *Anna of the Five Towns*. Lawrence was happy at Gargnano, and Bennett's novel depressed him. The grubbiness and despair of England, and literary defeatism since Flaubert, made him feel that 'tragedy ought really to be a great kick at misery (6.x.12). When he began *The Insurrection of Miss Houghton* (as the novel was first called) is uncertain, but after completing two hundred manuscript pages he put it aside, probably in March 1913, to begin the pot-boiler which grew into *The Rainbow* and *Women in Love*. He describes the fragment as 'lumbering' but 'fearfully exciting' (?18.iv.13, probably the end of April).

When Lawrence came to England in 1914, he left the manuscript with Else Jaffe in Germany. He had probably found time to extend it, for the new title was 'Mixed Marriage', which suggests the completion of the exotic Natcha–Kee–Tawara episode. The idea of the troupe may have come from George Moore's *A Mummer's Wife*, in which the heroine deserts a family drapery business to marry an actor whose company she joins (C. Heywood, *English Studies*, 1966). With the opening of the new tramway from Nottingham to Eastwood in 1913, and its extension to Ripley via Langley Mill the following year, Lawrence had kept his story up-to-date (vii). The novel was considerably revised when it was resumed in Sicily, however, for Mr May is clearly founded on Maurice

Magnus (see pp. 254–6), as a comparison with Lawrence's introduction to *Memoirs of the Foreign Legion* will show (P2.303ff.). He decided to complete his story ('three parts done') after his memorable stay in the mountains near Picinisco (16 and 27.xii.19); and the transmutation of his most vivid recollections undoubtedly created the finest part of the book. 'The Bitter Cherry', a title suggested by his publisher (from Cicio's actual name 'Mascara') does not accord with Lawrence's intention, especially at the end. Anxious to write a 'perfect selling novel', after the banning of *The Rainbow* and the delay in the publication of *Women in Love*, he had subdued the sex element, and thought the story 'passable, from Mudie's point of view'. One page was rewritten. Sales were disappointing but, ironically, thanks no doubt to Rachel Annand Taylor, the novel was awarded the 1921 James Tait Black Memorial Prize (21.9.22). Lawrence's gratification must have been bitter-sweet, after the rejection of his two greatest works.

To become a successful novelist in 1920, Lawrence needed to be discreet. Almost inevitably certain situations excited his views but, if they animate his narrative, it is only spasmodically, and generally at a reasonable temperature. Sometimes he airs them with authorial freedom. When Miss Frost broods over the life of the unhappy Mrs Houghton, we hear about 'the *reductio ad absurdum* of idealism' and the puerility of howling like a baby in the bath for a 'soap-tablet', not so much of happiness as of being made happy, the expectation of 'every woman in Europe and America'. On the subterranean forces at work in the colliers, threatening disaster, Lawrence writes with an ambivalence which must have mystified contemporary readers: 'The puerile world went on crying out for a new Jesus . . . another heavenly superman. When what was wanted was a Dark Master from the underworld' (iv). Another subject which has to surface is the denudation of individuality by the 'machine-friction' of routine work, so that everywhere people are almost drowned in 'perpetual floods of ordinariness' (vi). Alvina rebels against such a fate, and it is to accentuate it that Lawrence imports colourful cosmopolitan characters into provincial Woodhouse. Two of them serve to express his views; Mr May, comically. He likes the *angel* in woman, but dreads a 'coming-on' disposition, and can speak amusingly on being married to a vegetarian who expected him to be elevated with a Shavian pamphlet, and bear the questioning of her Fabian friends, for eugenic reasons, on his private morals. (Lawrence sketches a memorable picture of him 'like a dove-grey, disconsolate bird pecking the crumbs of Alvina's sympathy, and cocking his eye all the time to watch that she did not advance one step towards him'.) May has an interesting but unconvincing explanation of the popular preference for films to live-show: films have no life except in the minds of the viewers, who love to identify themselves with heroes and heroines, whereas successful artistes excite only envy. Madame, the presiding genius of the troupe, holds Lawrentian views on the non-tragicality of Sue Bridehead and Anna Karenina, and is convinced that the practical kindness of English women comes from the head, not from the heart.

More vital are Lawrence's predilections in making his heroine choose Cicio, a rather repellent creature at first, whose mandoline-serenading suggests the howling of an amorous cat. Whether Lawrence intended this effect or not, he draws Cicio according to his Italian formula; he is a sensualist, one of the regressive type, his mind subservient to his senses, cat-like, tiger-like (*TI.* 'The Lemon Gardens'). Lawrence could not bear sex-jokes, and it is significant that Cicio starts the joke that changes Alvina's name to 'Allaye'. Such is his fascination that she prefers him eventually to material comforts and conformity. His appeal makes her powerless, and sexually he 'assassinates' her. Yet something seems to emerge in him, 'a potent, glamorous presence' with 'a certain dark leopard-like pride in the air about him' which drew attention in England. One might conclude that Alvina's cherry was bitter, but his love for her grows, even though his masculine mind has its home in the open air and piazza. Unlike Bennett's Anna she is deprived but happy. She loves to be with Cicio, and finds even his silence 'rich and physical'.

What Alvina refuses to submit to is presented with a degree of comicality. First of all there are the limitations of Woodhouse and a sheltered upbringing. She seems destined to be numbered among the old maids who find 'cold comfort in the Chapel'. She is attracted by Alexander Graham, but her mother does not like him, and Miss Frost disapproves. They become engaged, but he has only six weeks in England, and Miss Frost has little difficulty when he leaves in assuring Alvina that she does not like him, and that it is selfish and heartless of him to want her to join him in Sydney, especially as her mother would never see her again. Having submitted against her inclinations, Alvina soon becomes intolerable, and suddenly decides she wishes to become a nurse. Hospital experience in London, and association with young doctors, finish her youth and tutelage for ever. Her professional expectations come to little in Woodhouse, but unlike her mother she is not prepared to wait passively in the expectation of being 'made happy'. Miss Pinnegar thinks Alvina has found a most eligible man in Albert Witham, a teacher from South Africa, now studying for his degree at Oxford. He is an odd fish, who gives Alvina the impression that she looks at him 'through the glass walls of an aquarium'. She prefers his married brother Arthur, a Woodhouse plumber, but an amusing little interlude with the latter in the organ-loft, during which he accepts all her help and sympathy without any sense of gratitude, after falling from a pair of steps, reveals what a self-centred vulgarian he is, his main concern being to depart promptly before people start talking. At the evening service next day, Arthur is absent, but Alvina, looking down from her place in the choir, sees his wife Lottie, who had cultivated her acquaintance, sitting with Albert, and realizes how 'aggressive and vulgar' they look. Something in the appearance of Albert's head, as he stoops to pray, repels her and reminds her of Arthur. How could she have thought twice of him? Albert's attempts at courtship are ingenuously awkward, and she has no difficulty in shaking him off. Alvina now, in her twenty-eighth year, seems 'withering towards old-maiddom', as a result of 'reckless moods of irony and independence'. Perhaps there is too much incident in *The Lost Girl*. One suspects that Lawrence did not give himself the time to make the most of some of these scenes, and that they might have provided more delightful comedy, pungent or boisterous, in the hands of H. G. Wells or Arnold Bennett.

Mr May is entertaining but, finding new life in his company and the cinema, Alvina is regarded as 'carrying on' and *déclassée*. The Natcha–Kee–Tawara Troupe represents an unreal world to Miss Pinnegar (and to most readers), but she is such a spoil-sport that Alvina joins them after her father's death. When she is tired of them, she becomes a nurse at Lancaster, and meets the crotchety Dr Mitchell. For Lawrence he provided relief from an episode that was proving wearisome, and served as a foil to Alvina's choice of Cicio and the unknown. There is a short vivid scene of a workman eating the prescribed rice pudding (with which his moustache is copiously 'pearled') and telling the infuriated authoritarian doctor to take his 'titty-bottle' with him. The doctor proposes marriage, offering Alvina a splendid home and possessions, and falls ludicrously on his knees, after being violent through frustration at her

refusal of his diamond ring. Reluctantly Alvina consents to an engagement, but she procrastinates and becomes nurse to the expectant Mrs
Tuke. Here the comedy is both farcical and metaphysical. Mrs Tuke
regards herself as an intelligent victim who is 'prostituted' to the
unintelligent forces of nature. While one pain causes her to howl inside
the house, another makes Cicio howl 'Ma nun me lasciar' outside. As with
Birkin and the vagabond Lawrence, 'Love is best', and takes precedence
over home and comfort. Lawrence reinforces the point when he describes Alvina as powerless and will-less with Cicio, so that she felt like
'one of the old sacred prostitutes'. At this stage she is far more 'lost' than
in the Woodhouse days, after her father's death, when she shocked Miss
Pinnegar by inviting Cicio into her home or playing cards with Mr May
on a Sunday evening.

Other novelists would have found James Houghton, the dreamer of
Manchester House, a far more interesting figure than Alvina; and he is
probably more memorable. He appears in a comic rather than a tragic
role. The story of his decline is a crowded Woodhouse chronicle most of
which Lawrence had to present before he could begin his main story. On
the whole (and this is characteristic of him) *The Lost Girl* is unilinear in
construction, with no complication of plot. It is diversified by the introduction of a variety of minor characters and scenes. Alvina's visit to
Throttle-Ha'penny pit is more real than the 'atmospheric majolica'
impressions of Woodhouse which Lawrence attributes to her when she
returns to the surface. The description of the first-night variety show
is wonderfully well realized, and far more human and convincing than
anything Lawrence laboured to achieve with his mock-Indian troupe.
The most dramatic of the more incidental sketches is the bystanders'
composite running commentary on 'poor Alvina' at her father's funeral.
It is rich in unintentional humour, and has the added value of reviving
all the main events of the first half of the story. By and large, however,
the novel assumes three phases, of which the first and the last are real
and form a strong contrast in shade and tone, while the middle remains
transitory and colourful, a curious compound of the real, the exotically
bizarre, and the bogus. The beginning is compact but mainly unimaginative, lightened by an athletic style and a sense of humour; the ending is
colourful, and a graphic example of Lawrence's facility in adapting
recollected experience to fictional requirements.

England may appear like a coffin of winter sinking into the sea as

Alvina leaves for Italy, but Boulogne, instead of being gay and brilliant as she expected, is grey and dismal. When she arrives at Cicio's home, she feels utterly lost. There, on the edge of the Abruzzi, her psychic being is overthrown, and she swoons, as it were, into an earlier world. In her pregnancy she lives in an 'isolate' state of wonder. She is content, and Cicio and Pancrazio revere her because she is with child. Her happiness is expressed in the spring flowers, the green silken corn and maize, and and the budding vines. She feels vindictive presences of a pagan era in the loveliness around her, but new flowers bewitch her and restore her 'passionate nostalgia for the place'. Unfortunately the thought of his call-up hangs like doom over Cicio, but she gives him the will to return. All that matters at the end of the War is that they are together. The novel ends rather exquisitely on a single note of uncertainty, but there can be no doubt that Alvina has found herself, and that her faith in life is sure.

AARON'S ROD

'Philosophy interests me most now – not novels or stories. I find people ultimately boring: and you can't have fiction without people. So fiction does not, at the bottom, interest me any more. I am weary of humanity and human things. One is happy in the thoughts only that transcend humanity.' So Lawrence wrote to Middleton Murry (23.v.17). *The Lost Girl* hardly counts in the development of his fiction, since it was an early novel hastily finished after a long interval. The change of interest in Lawrence is most evident in *Women in Love*, which is inspired by ideas on life and anti-life manifestations rather than by interest in character. The trend continued, but not with the same sustained intensity, for Lawrence had entered a period when he no longer took the novel very seriously, though it might be useful to convey his ideas. Three months after beginning *Aaron's Rod*, he wrote, 'I am doing some philosophic essays, also, very spasmodically, another daft novel. It goes slowly – very slowly and fitfully. But I don't care' (21.ii.18). The essays eventually became *Studies in Classic American Literature*. *Aaron's Rod*, which began 'in the Mecklenburgh Square days' (November 1917) and amused Lawrence 'terribly' after he had written one hundred and fifty pages 'as blameless as *Cranford*' (?17.iii.18), was continued in Italy late in 1920 and finished in Germany in June 1921. Much of it is based directly or otherwise on the author's experience in London and northern Italy; for long sections it is a travelogue rather than a story. More often than not Lawrence's exceptional gift of vivid recall exceeded his creative powers, and the craving for new inspirational backgrounds was undoubtedly one of the impulses which drove him from place to place on his 'savage pilgrimage'. In the conclusion of *The Lost Girl* and most of *Aaron's Rod* we can see the recipe to which he was almost compelled to resort for much of his subsequent fiction: an extensive use of new scenes for narratives with hardly a plot and few events, but organized towards an artistic expression of thought.

Relieved to find that Lawrence had escaped the 'maelstrom' of 'sexual obsession' into which he sank in *Women in Love*, and anxious to atone for his strong denunciation of this novel a year earlier, Murry in August 1922 wrote that he had found 'beauty everywhere in *Aaron's Rod*', 'everywhere the careless riches of true creative power'. Lawrence's restoration to 'serenity' made him a 'big man' and excused his 'carelessness'. 'To read *Aaron's Rod* is to drink of a fountain of life'; it is 'the most important thing that has happened to English literature since the war'. Murry augured that Lawrence would 'go on from strength to strength', and described *Aaron's Rod* as 'simply the story of the effort of a man to lose the whole world and gain his whole soul'. Such overpitched claims and prognostications must have been based on more than literary insights. *Aaron's Rod* is a light novel, which would be easy to read were it not so boring at times. A careless rapture in the style often produces a satin sheen which is delightful after the adjectival clutter and repetitiousness of *Women in Love* at its worst, and an indicator of the best of Lawrence to come. Yet Lawrence's artistic carelessness is a mark of indifference to the reader, and the narrative is improvised to such an extent that the significance of parts can be realized only in retrospect, most of all at the end of the sermon which concludes the novel. Two ideas can be seen to determine its general direction, but Lawrence had acquired a light literary conscience, and no coherent imaginative design informs and vitalizes the work from first to last.

The first of the two related themes is personal: how to attain in marriage that individuality and uniqueness which for Lawrence is man's most precious goal in life. It is the question posed by Birkin in his two-star equilibrium theory. The situation in *Aaron's Rod* is very different. The radiance has gone; the blue ball of illusion which Aaron had cherished from childhood is smashed. Love has been soured by the demands of a possessive, querulous wife. He has developed a hard, resistant core, but can no longer escape reality in whisky, woman, or music. The bullying of the love-game nauseates him. Aaron may get drunk, but he does not participate in the gaiety of Christmas Eve; the additional illuminations are artificial, and all the opening scenes take place in natural darkness. A doctor's visit enables him to slip indoors from the garden shed where he has been lurking after a few days' absence from home, and escape unobserved with his flute and piccolo. He is next seen in London. Lawrence seems to be fictionalizing an unresolved problem in his own marriage. At the end of his Sardinian tour (*SS*.viii) he attends a theatre in Palermo and watches 'a very psycho-analytic performance' of which he could give 'a very good Freudian analysis'. The old witch who fills him with horror is the 'white, submerged *idea* of woman which rules from the deeps of the unconscious'. As the statue goes up in flame, the little boys yell. Men merely smile, knowing well enough the white image endures. The 'Andiamo' yelled out to gain the audience's attention for this act had stirred the old Adam at the roots of Lawrence's soul:

> Again the old, first-hand indifference, the rich, untamed male blood rocked down my veins. What does one care? What does one care for precept and mental dictation? Is there not the massive, brilliant, out-flinging recklessness in the male soul, summed up in the sudden word: *Andiamo*! Andiamo! Let us go on. Andiamo! – let us go hell knows where, but let us go on. The splendid reckless-ness and passion that knows no precept and no school-teacher, whose very molten spontaneity is its own guide.

Aaron sends what money he can to support his wife and children, but, after returning and finding that she still wants 'to win his self-betrayal out of him', he leaves London for northern Italy, regarding his action as 'a natural event'. One evening his thoughts return to her, the iron pressure of her persistent will, and her assumption that woman in her maternal role is 'the centre of creation' and man a mere 'adjunct'. She was certain there was nothing greater for him than 'to be perfectly enveloped in her all-beneficent love'; it was 'written in eternal letters, on the iron tablet of her will', that he must yield to her. His infidelity and a deadlock had resulted. Now he realizes that his very being is pivoted on his 'isolate self-responsibility', and that he will not sacrifice his integrity to her or anything. Feeling the need to air his views at this point, Lawrence takes over ('Don't grumble at me then, gentle reader, and swear at me that this damned fellow wasn't half clever enough to think all these smart things. . .'), and discusses the sacramental *idée fixe* that man is the gift and woman the receiver. 'Perhaps, truly, the process of love is never accomplished' but, as long as we prefer 'maudlin self-abandon and self-sacrifice' to the 'true goal, where the soul possesses itself in simple and generous singleness', love is 'a disease'. The 'splendid love-way' is imaged in the birds of Whitman's 'The Dalliance of the Eagles', each always being borne on its wings, even in mid-air consummation (xiii). Elsewhere, through Lilly, Lawrence states that 'possessing one's own soul' in union comes after 'a lot of fighting and a lot of sensual fulfilment'; it does not eliminate them, for it can flower only 'on top of them' (x).

Aaron and Lilly come from the same district, the same class, and have 'an almost uncanny understanding of one another'. They represent Lawrence's views; the difference is that Lilly has arrived, and Aaron is learning by painful degrees. Both agree with Josephine Ford that men are simply afraid to be alone. Lilly is learning to possess his soul in patience and peace, and hopes that his wife Tanny will have her Nirvana too; 'then there we are, together and apart at the same time, and free of each other, and eternally inseparable'. Only after his flute is smashed by the bomb does Aaron escape from 'the *cul de sac* in which he had been running for so long'. He had been untrue to himself more than once, yielding to 'the quicksands of woman or the stinking bog of society'. His flute-playing symbolizes his readiness to escape, to evade self-responsibility. His refuge at home, it had been supplemented by visits to the Royal Oak. At the opera-house, it relates to the distractions of a Bohemian set. A hint of its connotation comes from Josephine Ford's remark on the boredom of women: 'any fiddle, any instrument rather than empty hands and no tune going'. Significantly, after hearing this from Lilly, who believes that we should 'never let our own pride and courage of life be broken', Aaron takes to his flute. Lilly sarcastically remarks that Aaron's rod is putting forth flowers again, and makes it clear that he can have no further interest in his company at that stage. A vivid reminder of the contemporary world comes to Aaron in Milan, when a young Socialist scales the house opposite to haul down the national flag. The mob yells in triumph, and then scatters with the arrival of carabinieri, who cover the youth with uplifted pistols and force him to descend. Aaron turns to his music, and plays he knows not what. This leads to the acquaintance of two patronizing young men, one of whom finds his flute 'perfectly divine'. At Florence he meets other *déracinés*, including the American wife of an elderly, gnome-like *marchese*. Eventually his flute-playing gives her new life, and he begins to glory in his male 'super-power'. Lawrence's irony is unrelenting in the hyperbole which follows in terms of the strength of an eagle with lightning in its talons, Jove's thunderbolt, Aaron's black rod of power blossoming with Florentine lilies and fierce thorns, and the godliness of his passion in prospect. 'So he slept', the passage continues; and the meaning is more than literal. All his life he had 'slept and shelved the burden' of responsibility. The god proves victim to Cleopatra, but he has the sense to see that he is being used; he decides he is no Antony but will henceforth be himself. It is at this point that the explosion occurs which shatters his flute. He did not want another. 'The only thing he felt was a thread of destiny attaching him to Lilly.'

Of the strange concocted dream which follows, the most relevant part relates to the passage of the boat through the shallows, and Aaron's heedlessness as he allows his naked elbow to be struck by three of the stakes which mark his course. After the third blow he shifts his position, and the boat continues steadily until it reaches 'deep unfathomable water' again. The image of Astarte at the end suggests that all Aaron's mistakes have been made in love, with his wife at Beldover, Josephine Ford in London, and the *marchesa* in Florence. The community of miners, children, and wives in the early part of the dream, with the absurd figure of a man stuffed like a Bologna sausage for consumption by his fellows, refers to Aaron's life and work at Beldover, and more particularly to his loss of individuality within his miners' union.

The second of the two related themes which give an abstract coherence to this artistically unsatisfactory novel is political. As secretary of his union, Aaron had come to the conclusion that organized benevolence is 'all righteous bullying, like poison-gas'. For him all forms of good-will are the same, whether from the spokesman at the miners' meeting, the landlady of the Royal Oak, or his own wife. Lawrence associates love and dependence with Socialism, and it is significant that two prominent

186

members of the Bohemian group, Jim Bricknell, who aches for love
(cf. Whitman, *St.Am*.xii), and Josephine Ford, who seduces Aaron and
has 'had her lovers enough', both want a bloody revolution. Like the
neurotic woman in 'The Waste Land' who can only 'play a game of chess'
and wait for 'a knock on the door', she finds life a 'nothingness' (vii);
Jim feels he is alive only when he is in love, and is told by Lilly he needs
more self-reliance (viii). All men and women should stand by themselves. They can come together 'in the second place', but nothing can be
'good' unless 'each one stands alone, intrinsically'. Aaron's fall in
Covent Garden market and the illness from which Lilly helps him to
recover are related, allegorically rather than realistically, to his self-
betrayal with Josephine. Sitting by his bedside after massaging him
with oil, Lilly wonders why he bothers with him; his wife Tanny thinks
he wants power over others. He has finished with the Bohemian set. The
mob accept 'Lloyd George and Northcliffe and the police and money',
but 'Why can't they submit to a bit of healthy individual authority?'
Types worth knowing – the Aztecs and Red Indians – have been exter-
minated. 'All the rest are craven . . . only conceited in the mass.' 'A
man should remain himself, not try to spread himself over humanity.
He should pivot himself on his own pride', Lilly concludes, for a Jesus
must expect a Judas (ix).

There is no evidence that Lawrence thought very practically on
political questions. He takes his theory as far as he could at the end of
the novel. Levinson regards Socialism as inevitable, but for Lilly the
ideal of brotherhood and of all forms of equality is dead. He believes
that 'every man is a sacred and holy individual, *never* to be violated';
and it is precisely when he is emphasizing these principles that the
Socialist bomb explodes, as if in violent opposition to individual freedom.
'The anarchist, the criminal, the murderer, he is only the extreme
lover acting on the recoil'; the 'love-urge' flies back and becomes 'a
horror', Lilly holds. 'We've exhausted our love-urge, for the moment';
and we must accept 'the power motive', not Nietzsche's will-to-power
but 'living, fructifying power' which urges new growth. Instead of
crying out for love, there must be obedience to an 'incalculable power-
urge'. Men must submit to 'the greater soul in a man'; and women, to
'the positive power-soul in man'. Such is the Lilly-Lawrence message.
Aaron wishes to know to whom his soul must submit, and the answer is
'Your soul will tell you'. However unacceptable Lawrence's views, he

holds fast to his central principle: the absolute freedom of the individual to make his own choice.

The question is whether Aaron has reached maturity. In Novara his 'old sleepy English nature' was startled. The Alps gleamed fiercely like tigers, and there seemed to be 'a new life-quality everywhere'. There were many worlds, not one, but he failed to notice that one world was triumphing over the many, spreading a 'horrible sameness' like a disease 'from England and the north'. Subconsciously his own marital situation had defined itself; he had 'rolled out from the shell of the preconceived idea of himself' like a chestnut that was invisible, 'knowing, but making no conceptions'. But he had no new connections, nor was he 'moving *towards* anything' when he met Francis Dekker and Angus Guest in Milan; flattered by Francis, he could tell the tale of his life as if it were a comedy. In Florence he found himself in a new world, a city pre-eminently of men, but the resurgence of life within him betrayed his weakness. 'Whirled away' by society and a woman, he is robbed, and realizes the necessity not to 'sleep'. The desire for 'the magic feeling of phallic immortality' makes him a *marchesa*'s victim; it blasts his central life until he is able to stand apart, 'neither God nor victim: neither more nor less than himself'. Lawrence's presentation is not very convincing. The bomb coincides with the end of the intermediate stage in Aaron's life, and the dream suggests that he has passed the danger-zone. He feels his destiny is with Lilly, but cannot hear his views without questioning them. In consequence the novel ends rather equivocally, dramatizing an inconclusive issue.

Lawrence expresses various views incidentally. Lilly and Aaron agree that men should cease grovelling in married life, and stand up and stick together, since manhood is more important in human welfare than home and children. Anti-English satire is sparked off at many points, with comment on Englishmen abroad, and cheap jibes against the British nation. Resentment against the power of money is repeatedly expressed with reference to the Frankses; it is merely a part of the satire with which the Beckers were rewarded for entertaining Lawrence two nights in Turin (18.xi.19). Some of these views occur in authorial interpositions, the most unexceptionable being on the cinema, which invests us in so much splendour and heroics that everything life can offer is in danger of becoming stale. One comment applies half-apologetically to *Aaron's Rod*. Aaron writes a letter to Sir William Franks which (Lawrence tells us) states 'perhaps his greatest, or his innermost truth': his belief in 'the fight which is in everything', in love and against the world. 'Of all things love is the most deadly to me, and especially from such a repulsive world as I think this is. . .'. 'When a man writes a letter to himself, it is a pity to post it to somebody else. Perhaps the same is true of a book', Lawrence adds, admitting his artistic dilemma. 'A Man's life of any worth is a continual allegory', Keats wrote, and this is true of Lawrence's best fiction. In *Aaron's Rod*, however, he had embarked on a novel with ideas before embodying them completely in a co-ordinated imaginative design; his authorial intrusions and sermonizing, like the loose picaresque narrative, illustrate the hazards of fictional improvisation.

KANGAROO

The whole of *Kangaroo*, except the last chapter (which was written at Taos), was completed in six to seven weeks, after the Lawrences had settled in a furnished bungalow by the Pacific, south of Sydney. They had visited the bush country in Western Australia, and were now happy, Frieda at last in a home of her own, and Lawrence writing 'his head off'. As the men in the neighbouring community were coal-miners, he did not feel he was in an alien country until he discovered they cared for nothing but 'their own little egos'. 'The working people very discontented – always threaten more strikes – always more socialism', he noted soon after his arrival (28.v.22). It was winter; the days were sunny, the nights cold. A dark sky one day made him think of Cornwall. The sea was 'marvellous, so big, so many colours, with huge unfolding breakers and an everlastingly folded secret'. The air had an 'extraordinary *delicacy*', and the blue sky, the grey gum-trees with their pale trunks, 'pure silver dead trees with vivid limbs, 'weird bits of creek and marsh', the sand, the blue hills, with the 'subtly different distances, in layers, and such exquisite forms', reminded him of Puvis de Chavannes (13.vi.22). Work continued with few interruptions: 'We don't know one single soul – not a soul comes to the house'. This 'funny sort of novel where nothing happens and such a lot of things *should* happen' was 'half done' by 22 June; by 9 July it was 'nearly finished'.

One can believe that Lawrence wrote 'his head off'. After making steady progress for more than half its course, the novel suddenly breaks down; the story does not resume for more than a hundred pages, and then concludes rapidly. The first stopgap is 'The Nightmare'; then comes an extraordinary hotch-potch of material, varying from Australian newspaper extracts to the most inconsequential of Lawrence's thoughts and impressions. The novel does not require them; they are sometimes an exasperating hindrance, showing little progression of thought, and often (it might appear) no more than the megalomaniac doodlings of an exhausted isolate. Yet, in conjunction with much more in the remainder of the book, they are the most important record of Lawrence's thought during a difficult transitional period. Elsewhere there is much that is protracted in the dialogue. The story is thin, and moves slowly, with hardly any important incident; yet it creates suspense. Kangaroo is absurdly unreal, and the minor characters have only a slight interest. The most unfading recollections are of Australian scenes such as those of Sydney (where Lawrence stayed only one day before beginning the novel), the southern constellations, dawns over the Pacific, sea birds, dolphins suspended in a wall of rising green water, and, above all, of the bush, in visionary gleams or colourful splendour. They are rather incidental, sometimes repetitive, and often lyrical.

The main subject is a continuation of *Aaron's Rod*. From Europe, Italy in particular, Lawrence brought all his anxious political pre-occupations. In Australia he saw evidence of trade unionism ('the nastiest profiteering side of the working men' for Somers) and social indifference; but most of the political background of the novel, including the anti-Digger organization, was gathered from the columns of *The Sydney Bulletin*. The story of Kangaroo and his death as a result of a riot is Lawrentian fantasy. Kangaroo's repulsiveness is a projection of Lawrence's prejudices; they are partly anti-Semitic, but rooted pre-dominantly in the kind of opposition to practical Christian idealism which made him present Gerald Crich's father in an ambience of distasteful moribundity. Kangaroo poses as a father-figure, who believes in law and authority. Nevertheless, he shares some of Lawrence's views; he agrees with the thesis of 'The Crown', and insists on the need to obey the life-urge and oppose the static will. In the light of his benevolent ideas, he can appear as beautiful as a god; yet he is ugly in person, with pendulous face, forward shoulders, round belly, and large thighs. Lawrence's attempt to convey the warmth of her personality is ludicrous: 'You felt you were cuddled cosily, like a child, on his breast . . . and that your feet were nestling on his ample, beautiful "tummy".' He is an embodiment of Christian love, and, taking inspiration from Dostoevsky, wants to make Australia 'a kind of Church'. Yet, when withstood, he is a sub-human monster, a 'great Thing', a 'horror'. In the end Somers prefers Struthers' 'absolute of the People' to 'Kangaroo as God Himself', a kind of Jehovah.

Lawrence insists that a novel is 'a thought-adventure'; and his ideas in 'this gramophone of a novel' (xiv) are recorded principally by Somers. Fortunately he can present this person (in his own image) with some critical detachment; he is first seen as a 'comical-looking bloke', and his wife Harriet's views cannot be ignored, though he is 'a determined little devil':

> Him, a lord and master! Why, he was not really lord of his own bread and butter; next year they might both be starving. And he was not even master of himself, with his ungovernable furies and his uncritical intimacies with people. . . All he could do was to try and come it over her with this revolution rubbish and a stunt of 'male' activity. If it were even real! . . . He *wanted* to be male and unique, like a freak of a phoenix. And then go prancing off into connexions with men like Jack Callcott and Kangaroo, and saving the world. She could *not* stand these world-saviours.

Somers has grown tired of living and writing alone, without 'any connexion whatever with the rest of men', yet his attitude generally is a *Noli me tangere* one. He no longer wants the blood-brotherhood of a David and Jonathan relationship. The ready intimacy of Jack Callcott, with whom he has nothing in common, illustrates the 'treacly democratic Australia' he detests. After hearing Kangaroo, he wants to escape the 'cloy of human life' and to be 'exultantly ice-cold' and energetic like a fish. Kangaroo believes in a bond of spiritual love between men, but Somers wants something deeper, not the Son of Man but the 'unspoken God' who is 'just beyond the dark threshold of the lower self'. Here, in this 'sacred dark', there can be real communion between men. Similarly in marriage. Like Birkin, he renounces love which is 'bred in the head and born in the eye'. The idea of star-equilibrium (*WL*) or eagle dalliance (*AR*.xiii) revives in an image caught on the edge of the Pacific:

> Why should desire always be fretting. . . Why not break the bond

and be single, take a fierce stoop and a swing back, as when a gannet plunges like a white, metallic arrow into the sea, raising a burst of spray, disappearing, completing the downward curve of the parabola in the invisible underwater where it seizes the object of desire, then away, away with success upwards, back flashing into the air and white space?

Somers does not believe in revolution, yet the 'horrible staleness of Europe' makes him wish to clear the way for 'manliness' in men and women who can possess their souls and listen to the injunctions of 'the living life that is a rising tide in their one being'. He recognizes Whitman's love of comrades in Willie Struthers' appeal for a new bond between fellow-men, but absolute love or trust is perilous, since the prerequisite for living is the attainment of individuality. 'Two ships may sail together to the world's end', but 'lock them together in mid-ocean and try to steer both with one rudder, and they will smash one another to bits'. Human love is relative; the only absolute for 'the human heart' is the dark god who is 'the source of all passion'. 'And the spontaneous soul must extricate itself from the meshes of the *almost* automatic white octopus of the human ideal, the octopus of humanity.' Somers turns therefore to the dark gods (xiii):

> The long travail. The long gestation of the soul within a man, and the final parturition, the birth of a new way of knowledge, a new God-influx. . . . This time not a God scribbling on tablets of stone or bronze. No everlasting decalogues. No sermons on mounts, either. The dark God, the forever unrevealed. The God who is many gods to many men: all things to all men.

As 'the soul is withered at the source' in most people, this is another way of saying the obvious: we always need leaders with vision. Lawrence could make no further headway with this question, particularly when he spent so much of his time writing at prodigious speed. Somers therefore drifts into indifference, even to the landscape. Meaning becomes 'the most meaningless of illusions'. He likes nobody, is glad that Kangaroo is dying, wishes Harriet would neither speak nor feel, and prefers the company of animals. Ultimately both the call and the answer are found 'without intermediary' in lunar influxes swaying him and the sea; they are 'non-human gods, non-human human being' (xvii).

When (many pages before this) Somers had come to the end of his tether, and could have kicked himself for wanting to help mankind, still harder for frantically struggling with such questions as the 'soul', the 'dark god', the 'listener', and the 'answerer', Lawrence began stuffing the novel with 'bits'; anything that interested him, 'the sheer momentaneous life of the continent' as he found it in *The Sydney Bulletin*, for example. Telepathy in bullocks recalls *Moby Dick*, and his hero wishes he could be one of the 'phallic' whales, 'a great surge of living blood'. He keeps returning to philosophy: people all over the world are 'bits'; each is alone, and the dark God is beyond him. There are 'horrid millions' like ants, who are unable to listen, forming a new absolute like a teeming dust-heap or ant-heap which threatens to become a volcano. In contrast you have Erasmus, a listener, 'alone in the darkness of the cavern of himself, listening to soundlessness of inflowing fate'. So Lawrence renews the process of writing to himself which he acknowledged in *Aaron's Rod*. As in that novel, punning amuses him, and he takes care that the reader does not miss his joke: Somers thinks of the 'nauseating benevolence' of Kangaroo, and of him as a queen-bee (with all the other bees around him) 'buzzing with beatitudes'. 'Bee attitudes or. . .', Lawrence continues. 'Chapter follows chapter, and nothing doing', he resumes, telling the reader to give up the novel if he doesn't care for it. Elsewhere he makes use of chance impressions for transparently expletory purposes, but they usually have an acceptable scenic or human interest. Lawrence's irrelevance and skittish philosophizing at this juncture are much more a stumbling block than a source of entertainment; his short essay on marriage and 'the good bark *Harriet and Lovat*' (ix) is far more diverting, and most delightful compared with the later stages of his dissertation on mob-psychology (xvi).

There is no dross in 'The Nightmare'. Its link with the novel is obvious but tenuous and arbitrary, and for sheer quality of experience it must stand apart as one of the most valuable chapters of sustained autobiography Lawrence ever wrote. It is not altogether a product of persecution-mania, but highly subjective, the vision of a 'black soul' which brings back the war years with the force of a 'volcanic eruption'. His resentment of the inhuman treatment he suffered at the hands of 'insolent jackanapes, especially the stay-at-home military who had all the authority in England' is probably justified, and the effect of persistent suspicion and restriction is well compared to Poe's story 'The Pit and the Pendulum', where 'the walls come in, in, in, till the prisoner is almost squeezed'. The philosophy which follows has a special interest. 'Things *had* to go as they went' in the War, but it was not the workings of Hardy's 'Blind Fate'. Man is not a mere instrument, Somers argues, but lives according to his own idea of himself. When events run counter to this idea, he damns circumstances; when this 'running-counter' persists, he damns 'the nature of things'; and 'when it *still* persists, he becomes a fatalist'. The truth is that '*Fata volentem ducunt, nolentem trahunt. The Fates lead on the willing man, the unwilling man they drag.*' 'When a man follows the true inspiration of a new, living idea, he then is the willing man whom the Fates lead onwards', but when men persist in following a dead ideal (as they did during the War) they sooner or later find they have been 'sold', and demand revenge. The movements led by Kangaroo and Struthers appeal to the vengeful mob; Somers wishes to keep clear, and listen to his soul. He is ready to be a willing instrument of the dark god's will when 'true inspiration' comes.

The exhausting process of trying to 'disentangle himself' from the 'white octopus' of 'human love as an all in all' (the Whitmanesque spirit of Kangaroo's ideal Führer state; cf. also Lawrence's concept of Nietzsche, *AR*.xxi) causes Somers to drift into indifference to landscape, humanity, Harriet, home, and time; a state of soullessness, perhaps only 'the great pause between carings', when everything becomes meaningless 'like old husks'. The turmoil in his soul after Kangaroo's death and its effect on Harriet are conveyed in the cyclonic storm which imprisons them in claustrophobic darkness. Richard is a preaching hell-bird, and Australia, once her Paradise, now fills her with revulsion. In spirit she is already in America.

It seems that distance lent its enchantment when Lawrence wrote the final chapter in relative tranquillity after leaving Australia. Unlike Harriet, Richard fell in love with the continent again, hearing its call from fern-dark avenues which had once filled him with a sense of Australian torpor. In the bush against the soft, rose-pink evening sky, great gum-trees 'ran up their white limbs into the air like quicksilver', branching like nerves into the dusk. To think of Europe and its 'horrible human mistakes' made the landscape − 'bungalows, shacks, corrugated iron and all' − appear 'a sort of heaven'. When, soon after reaching Australia, he had walked into the bush, his hair 'began to stir with terror'; it happened again when he turned from peering at the 'weird, white, dead trees' and into 'hollow distances'. In the spring, before leaving, he and Harriet journeyed among the sunny, scattered trees of the upland bush, with its heath flowers and many varieties of golden mimosa. They brought home armfuls of flowers 'like angel-presences, something out of heaven'. Somers experienced a deep pang at leaving a country 'a man might love so hopelessly'. Nevertheless, whatever Lawrence felt, he could not deny the dark god that called him to Taos and Mexico.

THE PLUMED SERPENT

Once in New Mexico, Lawrence was inevitably drawn to Mexico. His interest in Aztec civilization and mythology is evident in his last two novels. Lilly is convinced that the element he seeks in life is to be found in the Aztecs and Red Indians (*AR*.ix; cf. *K*.xvi). In 'Cypresses', one of the earliest of the *Birds, Beasts and Flowers* poems, Lawrence asserts that the one evil is to deny life, 'As Rome denied Etruria/And mechanical America Montezuma still'. He read Prescott's *Conquest of Mexico* and other studies of Mexican history and mythology, one of his main sources for the latter being *Fundamental Principles of Old and New World Civilizations* by Mrs Nuttall, the 'Mrs Norris' of *The Plumed Serpent*. Extraneous elements entered the novel, from Indian dances in New Mexico to the central sun behind the visible sun of Madame Blavatsky's theosophical world. From Mexico City, where he visited the Aztec Museum, he made excursions to Aztec centres, including the pyramids at Teotihuacán, where he was fascinated particularly by the quadrangle of Quetzalcoatl and the coloured stone heads of the feathered snakes.

The novel was begun at Chapala in May 1923, with the account of the bull-fight which Lawrence and Frieda had watched, in the company of Witter Bynner and Willard Johnson, until they could bear it no longer. The first draft was left almost completed at the end of June. After a long break, revision was begun at Oaxaca late in 1924, and finished early in February, on the very day Lawrence was taken ill. Mexico cost him almost his life. The following May, two years after he began *Quetzalcoatl*, the title was questioned, and he suggested its translation, 'Feathered Snake' or ('more luscious') 'The Plumed Serpent'. He thought it his 'most important novel, so far', and said that it lay nearer his heart than any other of his works.

The Plumed Serpent is one of Lawrence's major novels, the most ambitious and successful of those he had written after *Women in Love*. The more capricious moods and outbreaks of *Aaron's Rod* and *Kangaroo* suggest that it is the product of a sustained effort to subdue his metaphysic to artistic composition. Lawrence's achievement is to be seen in proportioning and ordonnance throughout, and in the lucidity of his rhythmic prose. Only rarely does he intrude authorially, and by such gradations that there is no discontinuity or discord. In general his views are integrated with the action, issuing directly from human situations or forming part of ritualistic ceremonies. The novel is religious: extrinsically, in the revival of the old Mexican religion; essentially, in the enunciation of beliefs which Lawrence merged with that religion and which were cardinal for him in the regeneration of man. He was more assimilated to Mexican life than to Australian. In *Kangaroo* his impressions are intensely local or superficially general; his familiarity with Mexican scenes and people produces an endless variety of evocations in *The Plumed Serpent*. Many scenes in Mexico City or by the lake are based directly on experience; more remarkable is Lawrence's ability at all times to call up with consummate ease just those features of a setting, general or specific, natural or human, which are appropriate to his scene. The landscape has become part of his imaginative world, and it is presented vividly, whether in recollection or in re-creation, throughout the novel.

The central issue is one which was left unresolved in *Kangaroo*. It is expressed by Ramon. Political liberation always leads to enslavement of one form or another, he says:

There is no liberty for a man, apart from the God of his manhood. Free Mexico is a bully, and the old, colonial, ecclesiastical Mexico was another sort of bully. When man has nothing but his will to assert – even his good-will – it is always bullying. Bolshevism is one sort of bullying, capitalism another; and liberty is a change of chains.

He is 'nauseated with humanity and the human will', even with his own; he must abdicate from being god in his own machine, and achieve his manhood, something which the sceptical Kate would understand if she had found her womanhood. More and more she is impressed by the native Indians, and their ability to destroy the soul of the conquering

Spaniards, who had brought no new inspiration with them. The Mexicans believed in the return of Quetzalcoatl, the god of wind and rain whose breath was the fertilizing breath of life. 'He is not so dead as the Spanish churches, this all-enwreathing dragon of the horror of Mexico', she concludes, recalling Ramon's conviction that, men being still part of the Tree of Life, a dark forest would rise again, and overthrow the churches and American factories.

Kate is appalled by the degeneracy which the whites have created in Mexico. It is most apparent in the bull-fight with which the novel opens; four special bulls have been brought over from Spain for the occasion. The crowd is described as a mob; individuals prowl around like lost mongrels. Children and excited 'fat mammas' attend, but men predominate, and they are 'the mongrel men of a mongrel city', their heroes 'effeminate-looking fellows in tight, ornate clothes'. Kate expected a gallant show, and the only gallantry she experiences is from General Viedma (Don Cipriano) as she leaves in disgust. In the city she feels the contagion of a 'crawling' evil, and it is here in particular that Ramon and Cipriano have to contend with the resentment of centuries, the 'hidden malevolence of the Mexicans', coupled with the 'ugly negation of the greedy, mechanical foreigners, birds of prey forever alighting in the cosmopolitan capital' (xxv). Ramon has far less difficulty with his own people, near the haunts of the old gods, but two powerful singers employed at the opening of his religious campaign are men who had been reduced to singing in low drinking-dens in Mexico City. When Kate sees the revolutionary frescoes at the University, she wants to know what a policy based on hatred will do for 'the twelve million poor – mostly Indians', and decides that the artists are 'just half Spaniards full of European ideas', with 'no real bowels of compassion'.

In Europe 'she had heard the *consummatum est* of her own spirit'; in Mexico City, as she gazes from the roof of her hotel, first at a huge old church humped up like a crouching animal and then at the 'brownish tower-stumps' of the Cathedral, she feels that 'this heavy continent of dark-souled death' is more than she can bear. The page, once bright with love and flowers and stations of the Cross, ends in a grave, it seems. Soon the strange news of Quetzalcoatl's rebirth in the lake of Sayula appeals to her Celtic soul. Gods must be born again, even as we must. 'Out of the fight with the octopus of life, the dragon of degenerate or of incomplete existence', one must win the 'soft bloom of being, that is damaged by a touch', With her second husband Joachim, Kate had realized that only a man who fought 'to *change* the world, to make it freer, more alive' could win her love. Now, at forty, she wishes to be 'alone with the unfolding flower of her own soul, in the delicate, chiming silence that is at the midst of things'. As she proceeds towards the lake, she becomes aware of beauty and strength in the natives. She hears of banditry horrors but is convinced that, once free from contacts with agitators and socialism, the people will emerge 'rich and alive', breathing the Great Breath which comes from the sun behind the sun. Now they are incomplete ('bits' as in *K*.xiv), at the mercy of the 'fathomless lust of resentment, a demonish hatred of life itself' (viii). Hopefully, in the end, the air is mysteriously alive with a new Breath. The gentleness of the natives is seen in the way a cow and bull are persuaded into the hold of a boat from a breakwater wall; even more in the curious reassurance of the peon, when the ass-foal he has lifted to its feet begins to suckle for the first time. In the man's eyes Kate sees the foal, the mother, the drinking, 'the new life, the mystery of the shadowy battlefield of creation; and the adoration of the full-breasted woman beyond him'. 'How wonderful sex can be, when men keep it powerful and sacred, and it fills the world! Like sunshine through and through one!' she reflects. There is an ironic touch within this statement of the Lawrentian credo, for Kate is self-conscious; her old European heart still flutters with vanity, and she struggles to assert her will. She surrenders it voluntarily, nonetheless, and in so doing accepts 'the communion of grace' she first shared with the boatmen, when she felt the 'life-breath' on the lake of the gods (vi). The Pentecostal hymn sung by Ramon takes its particular significance from Kate's final choice: she asks for 'nothing except to slip/ In the tent of the Holy Ghost/And be there in the house of cloven flame,/ Guest of the Host'.

Native resentment against alien dominance breaks out from time to time in the volatile Juana, head of Kate's 'household'. Her moods vary from excitable kindness to 'heavy, reptilian indifference'. She can be deliberately provoking, having her children lice-pick in front of Kate's visitors, or making dart-like observations on the rapacity of *gringos* and *gringuitos*. Suppressed hatred breeds taunts and cruelty, Kate notices. Maria, who loves her, attends her at table, and is spitefully hurt by Concha, who thereupon breaks into 'a loud, brutal, mocking laugh, like some violent bird'. Two young urchins throw stones at a water-fowl which they have tethered for their sport. Growing up in a world where the elements are 'monstrous and cruel', they seek revenge against animal life, and inherit a hatred of foreigners. Mexico is a country of victims and victimizers, where the victims find satisfaction in victimizing. The 'terrible obstinate ponderosity' of Mexican life, with its blindness to 'the sympathy in things' is the background against which one should judge the natural kindness of the peons at the end of the novel. Ramon is opposed to political programmes because they foment hatred. He tells Carlota that Christianity has failed, and that 'the white Anti-Christ of charity, and socialism, and politics, and reform' will finally destroy Mexico. The reformers, 'surcharged with pity for living men, in their mouths, but really with hate – the hate of the materialist *have-nots* for the materialist *haves*', are the Anti-Christ, a 'Christ with real poison in the communion-cup'. In his fourth hymn, 'What Quetzalcoatl Saw in Mexico', Ramon attacks the people for accepting foreign exploitation, industrialization, trains, automobiles, aeroplanes, and cinemas. He believes with Lawrence that the spirits who 'mastered the forces of the world' live at peace after death; those who have mastered nothing prowl in 'the back streets of the air', seeking garbage and 'biting with venomous mouths' like masterless dogs (an image which recalls the 'men like lost mongrels' at the bull-fight). 'Conquer!', therefore, is the message of the Morning Star; and the hymn turns into a commination against the 'inert ones'.

In his foreword to *Fantasia of the Unconscious*, Lawrence states his belief that 'the great pagan world' had a 'vast and perhaps perfect science' of life, which was taught esoterically in all the countries of the globe, including the lost Atlantis. What remains of it can be judged from surviving myths, symbols, and ritual. With a strange sense of the humanity which existed in Mexico before the glacial era, Kate dimly experiences a 'non-cerebral', 'vertebrate' consciousness like that of this 'pre-Flood world', when 'the mind and the power of man was in his blood and his backbone' (cf. *K*.xvi). The Mexicans still had this mode of consciousness, but they had been subjected to the 'mental-spiritual' world of the whites. The future demands a new life, not a complete reversion to the old, 'a new germ . . . from the fusion of the old blood-and-vertebrate consciousness with the white man's present mental-spiritual consciousness'. 'We are creatures of two halves, spiritual and sensual – and each half is as important as the other. Any relation based

199

on the one half . . . *inevitably* brings revulsion and betrayal', Lawrence wrote when he was finishing this novel (?26.i.25).

Like Wordsworth, Ramon believes that 'by the soul/Only, the nations shall be great and free'. It seems to him that politicians and social reformers wash the outside of the egg, to make it look clean, while he wants to get inside, 'right in the middle, to start it growing into a new bird'. He believes in a Catholic Church of the Earth: 'God is one God, but the peoples speak varying languages, and each needs its own prophet to speak with its own tongue'. The people of Mexico need a religion which will relate them to the universe. Ramon is one of God's prophets (xvii); his beliefs appear in hymns and addresses, and the latter are more poetic than the former, echoing the Bible in rhythm and expression (vii, xi, xiii). The Quetzalcoatl myth on which his religion is founded attracted Lawrence for a number of reasons. As god of the wind and rain, breath of life and water of life, Quetzalcoatl could easily be assimilated to a cosmic religion; he helps the snake in man's body to rear its head and reach beyond the sun to the sun of darkness which is the source and final home of life (vii). Furthermore he is a god who is reborn after a long sleep of healing and renewal of strength; Kate is weary to death of a God of one fixed purport. 'Gods should be iridescent, like the rainbow in the storm'; they die with the men who conceive them, but 'the god-stuff roars eternally, like the sea, with too vast a sound to be heard'. 'Even the gods must be born again. We must be born again.' As both bird and serpent, Quetzalcoatl unites sky and earth, the spiritual and the sensual. He therefore represents the Lord of the Two Ways, and is associated with the Morning or Evening Star, set between day and night. How deeply Lawrentian the new religion is may be seen in the ritual at the opening of the Church of Quetzalcoatl (xxi). Ramon's 'Fourfold is man' represents the 'fourfold creative activity' of *Psychoanalysis and the Unconscious*. Yet the vital source (represented by the Morning Star) is one and indivisible:

> For save the Unknown God pours His Spirit over my head and fire into my heart, and sends his power like a fountain of oil into my belly, and His lightning like a hot spring into my loins, I am not. I am nothing. I am a dead gourd.
> And save I take the wine of my spirit and the red of my heart, the strength of my belly and the power of my loins, and mingle them together, and kindle them to the Morning Star, I betray my

body, I betray my soul, I betray my spirit and my God who is Unknown.

It is significant that dancing to jazz by 'the *fifis* and the flappers and the motor-car people from town' breaks against the invisible opposition of the peons in the plaza, before the latter are irresistibly drawn to the native music which precedes the first celebration of Quetzalcoatl's return; and that the subject of the hymn which is sung on this occasion is the passing of Jesus, to make way for the new religion and, in his turn, to sleep long in 'the healing waters'. Christianity had stressed only one way, the spiritual. Quetzalcoatl represents the earth and the sky on which man depends; the serpent at its fiery centre keeps the earth alive and productive, and the bird brings wind and rain. Between earth and sky, man lives like the Morning Star. Ramon tells his listeners that a star can rise in them, between the heart and the loins; it is the manhood of man and the womanhood of woman. Receptive to the influences of snake and bird, they will acquire the courage of lightning and earthquake, the wisdom of snake and eagle, the peace of the serpent and the sun, and the power of the innermost earth and the outermost heaven. At the end of his prayer and testimony, the rain comes with lightning to revive a waste land (xiii). In *Kangaroo* (xvi) Lawrence had tried to explain 'the magic of a leader like Napoleon – his powers of sending out intense vibrations, messages to his men, without the exact intermediation of mental correspondence'. He returns to the subject in *The Plumed Serpent* (xxvi). Kate realizes that there is a 'oneness' of mankind in blood, 'the opposite of the oneness in spirit'. She can now understand the strange union she feels between Ramon and his men, and between Cipriano and his. The godliness of Ramon lies not in his blood or spirit, however, but in a 'mysterious star which unites the vast universal blood with the universal breath of the spirit, and shines between them both'. This implies not only the two-way fulfilment of the self but also an extra, superhuman power that appeals to the whole consciousness of one's fellow-men.

Marriage plays a part in this. The role of Carlota, Ramon's first wife, is primarily Christian, and in a novel of ideas she cannot be judged wholly by normal, human standards. Her dramatic protest when he assumes godhead in the eyes of the public, at the service which inaugurates the Church of Quetzalcoatl, has its human appeal, but all the ritual ceremonies should be regarded on another plane. Carlota prays that

Ramon's life may be taken from him, in order that his soul shall be saved. When she is dying, and he tells her to die utterly, the mode is that of his earlier rejection of her, and is as logical as Aaron's leaving his wife and family. In a wholly human context, his remarks would be abominable; in the more abstract religious conflict which comes to a head they are comparable in kind (if not in degree) to the ostensibly ungrateful rebuff of his parents by Jesus in the temple. In her wifely role, Carlota has lost her spontaneity; her spiritual outlook is set, and her life is motivated mostly by her will. Her pathos and subtle insistence draw her children to her; she resists her husband's views. Her 'charity' is a 'cruel kindness'. There can be no 'star' or 'meeting' between Ramon and her. 'Absurd as it may sound, it is not I who would ravish Carlota. It is she who would ravish me. . . . Letting oneself go, is either ravishing or being ravished. Oh, if we could only abide by our souls, and meet in the abiding place.' It is another instance of victim and victimizer (xviii). Ramon said of Carlota that at best she had only half a soul. 'It takes a man and woman together to make a soul. The soul is the Morning Star, emerging from the two' (xxiv). He finds it with Teresa, who tells Kate that his soul 'comes home' to her, and that 'until you give your soul to a man, and he takes it, your soul is nothing to you'. It is a reciprocal relationship, and it is not wholly spiritual. It presents one aspect of the central tenet of Lawrence's faith which finally becomes Kate's conviction 'that the clue to all living and to all moving-on into new living lay in the vivid blood-relation between man and woman. . . . It was the quick of the whole.'

Kate marries Don Cipriano, who believes that the strength of the army, apart from guns and transport, derives from the earth and from behind the sun; old Indian dancing gives his soldiers 'power over the *living* forces or potencies of the earth'. Under the spell of his 'old, twilit Pan-power', she feels that she is succumbing to a 'demon lover'. At first she is cast for the role of First Woman of Itzpapalotl, as Ramon is First Man of Quetzalcoatl, and Cipriano, First Man of the war god Huitzilopochtli (xvii, xx); then she is named Malintzi (xxii). She is reluctant to become 'a goddess in the Mexican pantheon' but, after marrying Cipriano, agrees to become Malintzi. He is not a *will*, and brings something to marriage which is 'forever virginal'. Her old feminine will for frictional ecstasy ('the beak-like friction of Aphrodite of the foam' which Lawrence condemned as early as *Twilight in Italy* and as late as *Lady Chatterley's Lover*) subsides; it is repulsive to him. Their satisfaction is not conscious but 'dark and untellable'. She lives in his aura, and he in hers; when he is absent, his presence is with her, and hers with him. Theirs is 'a mindless communion of the blood'. The fiery redness which invests him in the lake at sunrise reveals him as one of the Sons of the Morning (cf. the poem 'For the Heroes are Dipped in Scarlet'). As she realizes that her love is like Teresa's for Ramon, she sees a snake, and wonders if it had been disappointed 'at not being able to rise higher in creation: to be able to run on four feet'. Lawrence admires the snake as a 'king' emerging out of chaos (see pp. 110–11), but Kate's reconciliation with it relates to her present state, the blood-communion which gives her a 'new and vast' sense of the universe. The scene which follows is poetical: the pure serenity of lake and sky, the new verdure on the hills and rocks, the red ploughed earth, the bright green sugar cane, and the boat – 'like the boat of Dionysos coming with a message, and the vine sprouting' – make it difficult for Kate to remember 'the dry rigid pallor of the heat, when the whole earth seemed to crepitate viciously with dry malevolence'. The renewal of life in a waste land (another reminder of the influence of Frazer's *The Golden Bough*) harmonizes with Kate's. For Lawrence the Fall is associated with sex-consciousness. Kate has returned to the state of Eve before the Fall; her sympathy goes out to the snake, and the post-lapsarian curse against it is no longer felt.

The fallen Eve-like qualities of Kate (perhaps implied in 'Malintzi', which is similar to the name associated with the woman who betrayed the Mexicans to Cortés) derive from her European upbringing. As she sees Ramon naked to the waist, she knows how Salome felt, looking at the beauty of John the Baptist. She is aware of a richness in Ramon and Cipriano that she does not possess. The 'curse of Eve' is upon her, the curse of the 'itching, prurient, *knowing*, imagining eye', and she wishes they could save her from it (xii). Her vacillation arises from her concept of individuality; she is reluctant to surrender it, although she has learned that the individual 'does not and cannot exist, in the vivid world', only in the world of machines. Jealousy makes her misjudge Teresa completely, and she thinks her capable of 'harem tricks'. She has been brought up to believe in 'the *intrinsic* superiority of the hereditary aristocrat', yet in Mexico she realizes, despite herself, that she and Juana and the *aguador* and the boatman who rowed her on the lake are all of one blood. Ironically her English self makes her wish 'to get back to simple life. To see the buses rolling on the mud in Piccadilly, on Christmas Eve, and the wet pavements crowded with people under the brilliant shops.' Her 'soldier' spirit tells her not to submit to anything; it is this which makes her wrongly assume that Teresa is submissive to Ramon. Recognizing that her will makes her like a cat which seeks to enjoy its own 'isolated individuality', she is horrified at the thought of joining other 'grimalkins' in a London drawing-room. Cipriano has left her free to make her choice, and she chooses to stay. There is a little of the *varium et mutabile semper femina* comedy in this, but principally it stresses the difficulty of shedding the taint of Western civilization.

If some *arrière-pensée* arises over the credibility of *The Plumed Serpent*, it may be rooted in reaction against a religious revolution which is fictionally designed for a writer's own ends. The relevant test is the extent to which the novel succeeds imaginatively in suspending disbelief. To some extent this must depend on how far one can accept Lawrence's ideas; we are told, for example, that the process of change which finally reconciled Kate to Mexico affected not only her spirit but her body and even the constitution of her blood; its 'terrible katabolism and metabolism' changed her to 'another creature'. Most of the wine Lawrence poured into *The Plumed Serpent* is old wine. There is no essential difference between the two-star equilibrium theory of Birkin and the one-star symbolism of Ramon, though the implications of the latter are more fully and consistently revealed. Retrospective analysis suggests rather disparate elements in the composition of the novel, from realism to grandiose mummery. The bull-fight provides one type of spectacle, but it is not as deeply realized as the night-journey by train (v). The attack on Jamiltepec resembles a situation designed for a popular film. Acts of brutality co-exist with the numinous, and Ramon's rejection of Carlota creates a violent contrast to his gentleness of spirit. Rain and the life-breath arrive with miraculous promptitude. By comparison with some of the prose, the hymns are too often uninspiring, sometimes drab in texture; they are fed in, it seems, on the principle of the Men of Quetzalcoatl that 'the thing would drift darkly into the consciousness' by 'slow monotony of repetition'. Yet, read with due regard to emergent values, the novel creates an impression of great co-ordinating strength. The background, hideous or beautiful, is often interesting for its own sake; but, conjointly with the action, the scenes in general acquire an extra-dimensional significance and fascination from symbolic relationship in a daringly mythic theme of epic proportions. E. M. Forster thought *The Plumed Serpent* Lawrence's finest novel.

LADY CHATTERLEY'S LOVER

In his last three novels Lawrence had been preoccupied with the reform of society through politico-spiritual leadership. Gradual realization of the practical absurdity of his aims, and a serious decline in health, encouraged a return to the more fundamental question of human relationships. In a placatory mood, he tells Witter Bynner, with reference to *The Plumed Serpent*, that 'the leader of men is a back number'; it presupposes a 'militant ideal':

> We're sort of sick of all forms of militarism and militantism, and *Miles* is a name no more, for a man . . . the leader-cum-follower relationship is a bore. And the new relationship will be some sort of tenderness, sensitive, between men and men and men and women, and not the one up one down, lead on I follow, *ich dien* sort of business. . . . But still, *in a way*, one has to fight. But not in the O Glory! sort of way. I feel one still has to fight for the phallic reality, as against the non-phallic cerebration unrealities. I suppose the phallic consciousness is part of the whole consciousness which is your aim. To me it's a vital part.

He then mentions an unexpurgated edition of *Lady Chatterley's Lover*, 'this tender and phallic novel, far too good for the public' (13.iii.28); its central aim is the restoration of 'phallic consciousness', something really deeper than 'cerebral sex-consciousness', in fact 'the root of poetry, lived or sung' (15.iii.28).

The first version was written from October 1926 to early March 1927. Frieda's jumbled account (?31.x.26) suggests that Lawrence's main artistic aim was to relate the questions of class against class and soul against body. Typically, Lawrence solved his problems as they arose, and the result was a novel of moderate length instead of the 'long short story' which he originally intended. Published as *The First Lady Chatterley*, it is in most respects rather dull, with few poetic overtones. Characteristically Lawrence soon set to work on its improvement and expansion, finishing this second version in the summer of 1927. So 'improper' was it, he decided to follow Norman Douglas's practice, and have it printed privately in Florence, at two guineas a copy. With this in view he began a final revision, introducing important changes, and completing the work very rapidly by the opening of 1928; the title he had in mind was 'Tenderness'. For the expurgated novel which he hoped his English publishers would accept, he boldly suggested 'John Thomas and Lady Jane' (see p. 58).

The second version contains much that is new, and is half as long again as the first; the introduction and the main action (before Lady Chatterley's departure for the Continent) are expanded to more than double their previous length. Lawrence's principal aim was to give the story greater probability and imaginative cogency. It is much more detailed, introduces more characters for the Wragby Christmas season, evokes more successfully the emptiness of Lady Chatterley's life, and suggests a greater reality in the love that gives new life to her and the gamekeeper Parkin. The theme is reinforced in lyrical passages which fuse human revitalization and joy with natural growth and beauty. Contrastingly, more emphasis is placed on industrial blight: 'Out of the orgy of ugliness and of dismalness and of dreariness, would there, could there ever unfold a flower, a life with beauty in it?' The third version shows incidental pruning and much reorganization. Lawrence's sexual explicitness is even greater than in the second. Whatever his motivation (and one cannot ignore his need for financial gain), the free admission of four-lettered words and the frank discussion of sexual intercourse, from the very outset and sometimes regardless of probability, were the obvious result of his resolve to go ahead with private printing.

The Platonic dichotomy between soul and body which is dominant in the original opening is ultimately reduced to relative insignificance. Clifford is thrilled when he holds Connie's hand. His position is ambivalent, as he recognizes that, unlike thought, the fleshly reality ends with death. He regrets that, as a result of his war injury, he has only one horse to draw the chariot of his soul, and that, with 'the black horse of lust dead in him', he will never reach 'the heights'. His wife wonders why, if she misses immortality on earth, she should fuss about it after death. In the first recension (subsequently referred to as *John Thomas and Lady Jane*, after the title of the Penguin edition. *Lady Chatterley's Lover* is the third version) this motif is modulated into 'the resurrection of the body' in this life (the theme of 'The Man Who Died'), though Clifford enlarges on immortality and mystical experiences, and insists that the black horse of the *Phaedrus* myth is rightly curbed. In *Lady Chatterley's Lover* the discussion is postponed to the climactic period of Connie's love life, and is appropriately related by Clifford to abstract speculations in 'one of the latest scientific-religious books' on the wasting of the earth and its spiritual ascension. Connie thinks the writer a 'wind-machine', one of those people whose minds are 'tacked on to their physical corpses'. The human body, she maintains, was killed by Plato after a 'lovely flicker' of life with the Greeks, and finished off by Jesus; it is now rising from the tomb, and will enjoy a 'lovely life in the lovely universe'.

The principal changes in the opening of the story result from the introduction of new characters. The first of these, Tommy Dukes, speaks for Lawrence, and presents the 'democracy of touch' theme; we have never had 'proper human contact', he says, agreeing with Connie that a civilization will come, when life flows and nobody cares 'terribly about money, or owning things, or bossing other people'. His use of the expression 'I am not yet ascended unto the Father' in discussing the resurrection of the body recalls *Twilight in Italy* and 'Study of Thomas Hardy' (pp. 67, 70). In *Lady Chatterley's Lover* his role is extended. It is the mental life which produces Bolshevism and makes us inhuman; 'once you start the mental life you pluck the apple' and sever the 'organic connexion' with the tree of life. 'Real knowledge comes out of the whole corpus of the consciousness; out of your belly and your penis as much as out of your brain and mind.' This is a more sensible statement than Connie's (in *John Thomas and Lady Jane*), that the penis 'connects us with the stars and the sea and everything', 'touches the planets', and has put the evening stars into her 'inside self'. (For the experience Lawrence had in mind, see p. 146; for the philosophy behind it, see 'A Propos of *Lady Chatterley's Lover*'.) Nevertheless, Dukes is Lawrence's shock-tactician; in his bold intellectualism on the subject of sex he prepares the way for both the story and an unconventional feature in its expression. He believes in 'having a good heart, a chirpy penis, a lively intelligence, and the courage to say "shit!" in front of a lady'. Michaelis, a newcomer in *Lady Chatterley's Lover*, is introduced largely for satirical reasons, but he is given an important part in the preliminary story, ultimately to make Connie realize the 'great nothingness of life' before she meets the gamekeeper Mellors.

In accordance with Lawrence's continued aim to increase the probability of his story, Mellors is very different from the Oliver Parkin of the first two versions. He is less churlish, less politically extreme, and far better educated. He reads, is more refined (he wears pyjamas), and is less physically robust. He had been an army officer in India, can speak well when he wishes, and has 'a natural distinction'. The vernacular returns readily when he is moved: 'Ma lass! . . . I love thee an' th' touch on thee. Dunna argue wi' me! Dunna! Dunna! Dunna! Let's be together.' Not one of the gamekeepers has known real love. The second Parkin suffers from the traumatic experience he had with Bertha Coutts when he was a boy. Mellors' misfortune was to fall in love with cultural and spiritual types, clearly based on Miriam (*SL*) and Helen Corke. All three are repelled by their marital experiences.

The endings of the three novels vary considerably. The first Parkin becomes secretary of a Communist branch in Sheffield. Some amusing working-class family scenes underline the question of class division and the extent to which people are one in their feelings. Lawrence's view is that we are united by 'the stream of desire'; it is that which 'makes a nation a nation'. Yet, though their love is intended to signify a move in this direction, Connie's desire to escape 'the whole leprous contamination' of Wragby, and marry Parkin – 'Anything, to be in contact with life. And if she could possibly be in *contact* with the working people, well and good' – is hardly a convincing note on which to end. The second variant, a meeting of the lovers in Hucknall Church and a walk in the woods towards Felley Mill could have been used more judiciously to give imaginative expression to Lawrence's idea of an eventual return to the 'lusty' days of old England (*WP*.i), when some 'curious blood-connexion held the classes together' (P2.513). In *Lady Chatterley's Lover* the Sheffield scenes are omitted, but the emphasis on the 'democracy of touch' is maintained. Connie tells Mellors that he has the courage of tenderness which will make the future; he believes that it makes men really men and not so 'monkeyish', and that it is especially necessary for the English to 'get into touch with one another'. Duncan Forbes agrees to pose as Connie's lover in order to procure her divorce, but Clifford's resistance makes her tell the truth. His collapse into a state of infantile dependence on Mrs Bolton leads to repulsive physical intimacies, and Lawrence's causal relationship of these with a fierce awakening of steely energy and business acumen in industry reinforces the theme of the necessity for a new life-flow to restore sanity and happiness to western civilization. In a long concluding letter, coloured by allusions to the Etruscan way of life which recall Lawrence's '[Autobiographical Fragment]' (P.817ff.), Mellors insists that the industrial problem will not be solved by money ('getting and spending', in Wordsworth's phrase) but by training the people to live, and live handsomely; they should 'be alive and frisky, and acknowledge the great god Pan'. Although he predicts disaster for the industrial masses, he is confident that nothing can 'blow the crocus out'; his trust is in the forked, Pentecostal flame between him and Connie, and he will abide by it, 'Cliffords and Berthas, colliery companies and governments and the money-mass of people all notwithstanding'. Lawrence leavens his seriousness with some facetiousness. The rank is but the guinea's stamp, and Connie's father, Sir Malcolm Reid, finds that he and Mellors (a 'bloody good poacher') are brothers under their skins. Mellors makes an appointment with Connie outside the Golden Cock in Adam Street, and takes his final bow in a style worthy of Sterne.

Unfortunately Lawrence's sense of humour deserted him when he was fired by zeal as a priest of love or prophet of doom. One can hardly take exception to his intentions in *Lady Chatterley's Lover*: it is in the execution that he shows want of judgment, and in one way or another this is true of each version of the story. He can be romantically absurd and even realistically distasteful. Whatever Swift's horror of physical organs and functions, no normal reader needs to be reminded that either Celia or Connie is humanly unexceptional in this respect; nor will the squeamish become more reasonable by being liberally subjected to four-lettered words. Lawrence's practice runs counter to his belief: 'How does one think when one is thinking passionately . . . ? Not in words at all but in strange surges and cross-currents of emotion which are only half-rendered by words', he wrote in *The First Lady Chatterley*. The most common of the taboo words which he uses in a laudable cause describes, he tells us in *John Thomas and Lady Jane* (xi) 'the cheap and nasty excitation of a moment'. His main defence in 'A Propos of *Lady Chatterley's Lover*' is that we shall 'never free the phallic reality from the "uplift" taint till we give it its own phallic language, and use the obscene words' (P2.514). Yet, however much they are used in relation to love, the degrading associations which they have acquired are too traditional and endemic to be eliminated. Lawrence's attitude towards sex makes their incongruity inoffensive, but the absurdity of their usage does nothing to promote his cause. Aldous Huxley's maturer reflections on the subject are voiced in *The Genius and the Goddess* (1955):

> [Katy] had the instinctive wisdom that taboos the four-lettered words (and *a fortiori* the scientific polysyllables), while tacitly taking for granted the daily and nightly four-letter acts to which they refer. In silence, an act is an act is an act. Verbalized and discussed, it becomes an ethical problem, a *casus belli*, the source of a neurosis. . . . Katy (God bless her!) was neither a Methodist nor a Masochist. She was a goddess, and the silence of goddesses is genuinely golden.

In a letter to Nancy Kelly (21.xi.57) Huxley states that in the dramatized version of the above he did his best to ensure that Katy did and said nothing incompatible with the person on whom she was based. This was Frieda Lawrence.

In *Lady Chatterley's Lover* Lawrence gives greater emphasis to the social aspect of Connie's sexual disillusionment. Her girlish experiences in Germany (based to some extent on Frieda's), stimulated by thrilling 'soul-enlightening discussions' on 'the sex thing', had proved 'a bit of an anti-climax' by comparison with the higher and more wonderful visions of woman's freedom. Her husband's sexual incapacitation as a result of terrible war injuries gives ample probability to her love-affair with Michaelis, but it is her complete disenchantment with him and the society which he and Clifford represent which makes her realize the genuineness of the passion that springs up between her and Mellors. Equally Mellors' sexual disillusionment and consequent disinclination proves the authenticity of his love. For both these 'battered warriors' love awakens tenderly and fully for the first time, all the more keenly for being long denied.

But for symbolical repercussions, Clifford's impotence and dependence on mechanical transport might be regarded as superfluous. He has never been interested in physical fulfilment. The 'sex part' of marriage meant little, even on his honeymoon. He thought that marital intimacy was deeper and more personal; 'sex was merely an accident, or an adjunct, one of the curious obsolete, organic processes which persisted in its own clumsiness, but was not really necessary'. He hopes that Connie can subordinate it; at worst, if lack of sex is disintegrating, that she will 'go out and have a love-affair'. They entertain, but live in ideas and books; he writes clever stories, true to modern psychology but out of touch with life; she lives in a void – even her impressions of the park are 'like the simulacrum of reality'. It is Henry James's 'bitch-goddess' of success which is worshipped, and which brings Michaelis to Wragby. As a writer he is much more successful than Clifford; he is 'even better . . . at making a display of nothingness'. All the great dynamic words such as 'love', 'joy', 'happiness', 'home', 'mother', 'father', 'husband' have become increasingly meaningless to Connie; and a sense of life's futility fills her when the sight of Mellors washing himself, nude to the waist, comes like a vision to her, and the shock reaches her womb.

Individual fulfilment comes from a true relationship in love. Its realization leads to new life-values, and hence to social and industrial regeneration. Such is the faith which inspires *The Rainbow* and *Women in Love*. With a minor qualification, it is the subject of *Lady Chatterley's Lover*, Lawrence combining tenderness with sensual fulfilment as the basis of his 'democracy of touch'. No rainbow of promise appears; the *dies irae* is imminent 'if things go on as they are', but nothing can destroy Mellors' faith that the crocus will continue to bloom. The novel is primarily an allegorical statement of Lawrence's faith in the emergence of a new life and society; and it is in the final version above all that, by skilful re-arrangement of the central story, he imparts imaginative cogency to this theme.

Past and present, a contrast between 'Merrie England' ('Shakespeare's England') and the death of spontaneity in the present, reaches its crescendo in the very centre of the story. Its prelusive notes occur in the wood beyond the park, 'a remnant of the great forest where Robin Hood hunted'. For Clifford it **is** 'really the heart of England', and he declares his intention to keep it intact. As he does so, Connie hears the eleven o'clock hooter of Stacks Gate colliery, but he is 'too used to the sound to notice'. They are a reminder of an alien element; Clifford's chair is another. The war has made him an impotent cripple; he wishes to have a son to ensure that this part of England will be preserved. He is mentally alert, but Connie knows that he has suffered the 'bruise' of a shock which is steadily paralysing his 'affective self'. The next day all his brilliant words seem like dead leaves, 'hosts of fallen leaves of a life that is ineffectual'. The bruise is reflected in the colliers; their threat to strike is not 'a manifestation of energy' but the effect of the 'bruise' sustained deep down in previous industrial strife. 'It would take many years for the living blood of the generations to dissolve' it, 'and it would need a new hope'. All this has its parallel in the 'blow' suffered by the wood, with drastic losses of timber during the war. Yet it is still alive; it retains its mystery, remembering the deer, the archers, and the monks (v). Like the recurrent crocus, it is a symbol of hope in an ultimate future.

The dying movement to Lawrence's theme is the drive Connie takes in central England, 'the England of Robin Hood, where the miners [prowl] with the dismalness of suppressed sporting instincts' when they are not at work (xi). Dismal, blackened Tevershall is 'the utter negation' of natural beauty and gladness, 'the utter death of the human intuitive faculty'. In it she sees a new 'under-world' race, overconscious on the politico-economic side but dead on the spontaneous and intuitive. She feels that 'with such creatures for the industrial masses' there can be no hope, and what she sees represents 'the vast bulk of England'. Castles and stately homes still dominate the rolling country, but they are like ghosts. Fritchley, a perfect old Georgian mansion, is being demolished as Connie passes. 'One England blots out another. . . . And the continuity is not organic, but mechanical'. She sees the colliers trailing from the pits, 'patient and good' in some ways, in others 'non-existent'; 'something that men *should* have was bred and killed out of them'. Mrs Bolton's husband, a sensitive man, had hated the pit. It broke her heart to see him 'as if he'd *wanted* to die'. She feels the pit wanted to kill him; 'they all *want* to separate a woman and a man, if they're together', she maintains.

Significantly the next action is Connie's visit to the keeper's hut, where she sees brown chickens 'running lustily'. The first dandelions are 'making suns'; everywhere leaves and flowers are opening. 'Everywhere the bud-knots and the leap of life!' In this way Lawrence repeatedly links the revival of nature with his theme of human recovery.

The 'fine flower' of Connie's intimacy with Clifford had been 'rather like an orchid, a bulb stuck parasitic on her tree of life' (vii). She is depressed when she goes out in the March wind to see the daffodils by the keeper's cottage; phrases from *Paradise Lost* and Swinburne sweep through her mind, until the sight of the wild flowers makes her think that she is Persephone 'out of hell on a cold morning' (viii). She had forgotten the sight of the keeper's 'thin, white body, like a lonely pistil of an invisible flower'. Now she sees his cottage, 'looking almost rosy, like the flesh underneath a mushroom, its stone warmed in a burst of the sun'. She sits with her back to a pine that sways with life, 'elastic, and powerful, rising up', and watches the daffodils turn golden. Later she is sickened by Clifford's habit of verbalizing everything; to him violets are Juno's eyelids, and windflowers, unravished brides. 'How she hated words, always coming between her and life: they did the ravishing, if anything did: ready-made words and phrases, sucking all the life-sap out of living things.' One day when she comes to the hut she finds two brown hens, sitting on pheasants' eggs, and 'fluffed out so proud and deep in all the heat of the pondering female blood' that she is almost heart-broken to think of herself, 'so forlorn and unused, not a female at all, just a mere thing of terrors'. The love which springs up between her and Mellors is born of tenderness; he is moved by compassion for her as she handles the newly born chicks. Afterwards he walks to the top of a hill from which he sees the bright colliery lights and hears the winding-engines at Stacks Gate. The fault lies 'out there, in those evil electric lights and diabolical rattlings of engines'; there lies 'the vast evil thing' that would soon destroy the wood and the bluebells. He thinks of Connie 'with infinite tenderness':

> Somewhere she was tender, tender with a tenderness of the growing hyacinths, something that has gone out of the celluloid women of today. But he would protect her with his heart for a little while. For a little while, before the insentient iron world and the Mammon of mechanized greed did them both in. . . If only there were men to fight side by side with! But the men were all outside there, glorying in the Thing, triumphing or being trodden down in the rush of mechanized greed or of greedy mechanism.

Next day, when she returns to the wood, Connie can 'almost feel it in her own body, the huge heave of the sap in the massive trees, upwards, up, up to the bud-tips, there to push into little flamey oak-leaves, bronze as blood. It was like a tide running turgid upward, and spreading on the sky.' Passion reaches its perfect consummation, and afterwards she experiences for the first time a yearning adoration, a soft deep rapture. 'She was like a forest, like the dark interlacing of the oak-wood, humming inaudibly with myriad unfolding buds. Meanwhile the birds of desire were asleep in the vast interlaced intricacy of her body.' In this state of physical ecstasy, she has to listen to Clifford reading Racine

213

and stressing the need of 'classic control', while wishing he could be with his technical books, or his pit-manager, or his radio. Connie's sexual experiences have been such that she still has much to learn. It is after her drive in the Midlands that Mellors' haste upsets her psychologically, so that she finds intercourse physically ridiculous ('Even a Maupassant found it a humiliating anti-climax'; cf. 'Making Love to Music', P.161), and resents his use of dialect. Immediately she is sorry, ceases to resist, and reaches a consummation which evokes the finest prose-poetry in all three versions of the novel. She is 'born: a woman'; she is 'still a little afraid', but her hands move down his back, and the touch of him is like 'the sons of god with the daughters of men'. She wonders at the unspeakable beauty of his warm living body where it had previously repelled her, and she even enjoys essaying the dialect herself. As she runs home, the slope is heavingly alive, and all the world seems a dream (xii). After this, their floral decorating of each other's naked parts (xv) is an idyllic disaster, an unintentional John Thomas and Lady Jane burlesque in a poeticizing theme.

It is part of Lawrence's allegory that, under the influence of Mrs Bolton, Clifford becomes more interested in capturing 'the bitch-goddess' by 'brute means of industrial production'. The more dependent on her administrations and the more child-like he becomes, the more he feels he is lord and master of the industrial machine. The scene in which his motor-chair breaks down (xiii) opens with a discussion on this 'boss-ship'. What we need to take up is whips, not swords, he tells Connie. 'Aristocracy is a function, a part of fate. And the masses are a functioning of another part of fate.' The individual hardly matters, and there can be no 'common humanity' between the ruling and working classes. Clifford, in short, is completely opposed to the 'democracy of touch' principle which is the basis of Mellors' faith in a future civilization. Danger signals flash repeatedly. Connie sees the tender beauty of the English spring, but the only remark the bluebells elicit from Clifford is that their fine colour is 'useless for making a painting'. Then, as the chair jolts down the broad riding which is washed over with their blue, Lawrence comments ominously, after Whitman:

> O last of all ships, through the hyacinthian shallows. O pinnace on the last wild waters, sailing in the last voyage of our civilization! Whither, O weird wheeled ship, your slow course steering. . . . O Captain, my Captain, our splendid trip is done! Not yet though!

Soon afterwards, by the well, a mole emerges, 'rowing its pink hands, and waving its blind gimlet of a face, with the tiny nose-tip uplifted'. 'It seems to see with the end of its nose', Connie remarks, and Clifford answers, 'Better than with its eyes!' The mole is an underground worker like the colliers (Lawrence's fauna of the coal-seams). Like Shakespeare's Gloucester they see 'feelingly', and it is no surprise that Clifford thinks 'the unpleasant beast' ought to be killed. On the return journey, his motor breaks down among the hyacinths, and Mellors is called to assist. He starts the engine, but the chair will not budge. Connie sits on a bank, looking at 'the wretched and trampled bluebells', and remembering ironically some of Clifford's expressions: 'Nothing quite so lovely as an English spring', 'I can do my share of ruling', 'What we need to take up now is whips, not swords'. In the end she and Mellors succeed in pushing the machine up hill. There is a kind of conspiracy between them, and she bends suddenly and kisses his hand. The two men are 'as hostile as fire and water'. Connie goes to her room, furious with Clifford. 'Dead fish of a gentleman, with his celluloid soul! . . . She didn't want to be mixed very intimately with him in any sort of feeling. She wanted him not to know anything about herself: and especially, not to know anything about her feeling for the keeper.' The episode may be slight, but it sums up the class-conflict behind industrial failure, and the hope of progress from a 'democracy of touch'. The subject reaches its climax in another love scene, accompanied by thunder (with conventional *dies irae* overtones). Mellors is Lawrence's mouthpiece. If industry and money-making 'go on in this way . . . in algebraical progression . . . then ta-tah! to the human species!' After the first adumbration of an Etruscan-tinged alternative, the thunder ceases, and the scene ends in a bathetic interlude (xv).

Whether the implications of *Lady Chatterley's Lover* are always presented clearly and completely in the novel may be questioned when one reads Lawrence's afterthoughts in 'A Propos of *Lady Chatterley's Lover*'. *Niaiseries* notwithstanding, he undeniably succeeded in his principal aim: to make men and women 'think sex, fully, completely, honestly, and cleanly'. Sanity and wholeness of life can come only 'when our sexual act and our sexual thought are in harmony, and the one does not interfere with the other'. The 'tragic age' and 'the ruins' with which the novel opens refer not just to the calamity of recent war but to the 'dead' and 'meaningless' bodies which three thousand years of idealism have strewn across the stage of life. The question at stake is 'love among the ruins' of the modern world; it is the one which occupies Birkin's mind as he enters London and describes his feelings as 'real death' (*WL*.v). In *Lady Chatterley's Lover* the stress is laid on the 'real tenderness' and 'real sensuality' of love. At various points the story is moulded to enlighten the reader more specifically than ever before on the sexuality which Lawrence condemns: the deliberate, self-seeking, and 'reductive' or debilitating. Nearly all modern sex, he write in 'A Propos' is 'a pure matter of nerves, cold and bloodless'; it may produce 'a sort of ecstasy and a heightening of consciousness' for a time but, 'like the effect of alcohol or drugs', it is 'a process of impoverishment'. Sex which comes naturally from 'warm blood-desire' (and Lawrence links this with the rhythm of the days, the seasons, and the universe) is life-giving, and it is the deepest of communions when consummation for man and woman is reached simultaneously. 'Most folk live their lives through and they never know it', Mellors says. The reason is fear or shame. It is necessary for Connie (as for Ursula, *WL*.xxix) to overcome shame: 'necessary, for ever necessary, to burn out false shames and smelt out the heaviest ore of the body into purity. With the fire of sheer sensuality.' Rather fearful at first, Connie glories in having realized 'her sensual self, naked and unashamed'. 'There was nothing left to disguise or be ashamed of. She shared her ultimate nakedness with a man, another being.' This indicates the kind of liberating effect which the book generates. Read for the right reason, it can do nothing but promote male and female emancipation. To suggest (as some scholars have done) that the passages referred to in *Women in Love* and *Lady Chatterley's Lover* hint at unnatural acts is false to the text and to the whole tenor of Lawrence's copious writings on sex. When it is 'unnatural' he describes it as 'immoral'; and there can be no mistaking his attitude when Anna and Will Brangwen abandon 'the moral position', seeking 'gratification pure and simple'; they show 'no tenderness, no love', but indulge in sensuality which is 'violent and extreme as death', 'a passion of death' (*R*.viii). The 'forked flame' which love has created in Connie and Mellors is the 'cloven flame' of *The Plumed Serpent*. It implies an equilibrium or equality in marriage, and a oneness of spirit which separation cannot extinguish. For Ramon its house is 'the tent of the Holy Ghost'; for Mellors, it is Pentecost.

The best comment on Lawrence's aims and achievement in *Lady*

Chatterley's Lover is to be found in the novel itself (ix). Clifford loves to hear Mrs Bolton's village gossip and scandal. Connie also is fascinated, and then rather ashamed. Yet she realizes that one can listen to most private affairs of other people in a spirit of respect and 'fine, discriminative sympathy'. Lawrence adds:

> It is the way our sympathy flows and recoils that really deter-mines our lives. And here lies the vast importance of the novel, properly handled. It can inform and lead into new places the flow of our sympathetic consciousness, and it can lead our sympathy away in recoil from things gone dead. Therefore, the novel, properly handled, can reveal the most secret places of life: for it is in the *passional* secret places of life, above all, that the tide of sensitive awareness needs to ebb and flow, cleansing and refreshing.

Shorter Stories

Lawrence's first three stories were written for a local Christmas competition (p. 16). Unlike the other two, the winning story, 'A Prelude', was left unrevised. It is simple, rounded, and prettily sentimental, with snowflakes and berried holly, the traditional mummers' play, a carol followed by Giordani's 'Turn once again, heal thou my pain,/Parted from thee my heart is sore', and a happy ending, after the young man whose farming family had been down on its luck had begun to think he had lost his young lady at the mill. The background is clearly sketched with Haggs Farm and Felley Mill in mind. More strange, vivid, and elaborately constructed is 'A Fragment of Stained Glass'. Told by a vicar with archaeological interests, in explanation of a passage in imaginary fifteenth-century records* which described the Devil's face 'flaming red like fire in a basket' and glowering down on the choir, the story is centred in Beauvale Priory, the main character being a mad serf who in his rage has killed a horse, and set fire to the stables in revenge for his punishment. He flees with Martha from the mill (Felley Mill) in a snowstorm, and the love-story reaches its full-blooded climax. Although Lawrence regarded it as 'a bit of a tour de force', he is wonderfully successful in generating a psychological atmosphere of magic from madness and superstition. Many fine touches indicate the serf's delusions, but none more than the description of his attempt to pluck a red flower for Martha, after he has climbed up the face of the 'shadow' and stands on the head of a 'frozen man'. His hand is red and blue, but he cannot grasp any of the 'stuff', which flies in the increasing snow like 'colour of a moth's wing'. Then he feels 'the bright stuff cold' and, being unable to

*The vicar and the reference to Rollestoun's Newthorpe Manor suggest the influence of Baron von Hube's *Griseleia in Snotinghscire* (1901), although the Rollestons were connected principally with Watnall.

pluck any, strikes it with his knife, and finds a gap in the redness. Looking through, he sees white stunted angels gazing up in fear.

'The White Stocking', the third of these stories, was probably extended. It evolved from an incident which happened to Lawrence's mother before her marriage, when she went to a ball at Nottingham Castle, and found she had taken a white stocking in mistake for a handkerchief. The main scene is a Christmas Eve dance at the Castle, but the story (ending happily after all) is one of jealousy which leads to a brutal quarrel, from the deception and bravado of a young wife who does not wish to upset her husband or renounce the attentions of a man to whom she was helplessly drawn at the ball. The narrative is neatly unfolded, and terrible in its probability from first to last. 'Goose Fair', another Nottingham story, is set in a period of depression which Mrs Lawrence remembered. It was written in 1909, two years after the original of 'The White Stocking', and has a slight similarity of construction, Lawrence starting at a point midway in the story and creating suspense. It reaches no effective climax, and has little stylistic genius or depth of character, though Lawrence thought Louisa Burrows would recognize two college students in it. The first story to announce him as a writer of fiction, when it appeared in *The English Review*, it hardly did him justice.

By the summer of 1911 Lawrence had written several stories (25.viii.11). The writing of the early part of *Sons and Lovers* suggested some, the greatest (and probably the first) being 'Odour of Chrysanthemums'. The places in the story are actual, and the tragedy is based on that of Lawrence's Aunt Polly (p. 7); the main scenes are imagined in a cottage not far from where his grandfather lived (postscript, 3.xii.26). To some extent Lawrence owed his inspiration to Synge's 'Riders to the Sea', but it was the lively vigour of the opening description which convinced Ford Madox Hueffer that Lawrence had genius. He makes one see and hear; flames lick the ashy sides of the pit bank like sores, and the colliery winding-machine raps out its little spasms. The dreary forsaken fields and the trapping of a woman between the jolting railway waggons and a hedge seem to prefigure the life and destiny of the woman at the centre of the story. Her husband has not arrived home from the mine, and she assumes he has gone to a public house. She is convinced he will be brought home like a log, and that he will not be able to work the next day. Perhaps the dramatic irony is too obvious for the narrative sequel to excite surprise, but nothing can lessen its emotive power. The husband, staying behind to complete his stint, had been trapped and asphyxiated by a fall. Together his wife and mother mourn his death. He is laid out on the floor of the parlour where the chrysanthemums smell cold and deathly. The wife washes his whole body while his mother's tears flow. Together they dry him His mother remembers him as a boy, and refers to him as 'the lamb, the dear lamb'. His wife realizes for the first time that she has never known him. She felt 'the utter isolation of the human soul', and 'the child within her was a weight apart from her'. This dead man had nothing to do with her children. 'He and she were only channels through which life had flowed. . .' The story echoes to the infinite, with Lawrence's conviction that division in life leads to eternal apartness. An episode, which was hopeless between husband and wife 'long before he died', has closed. Her concern is for her children. She submits to life; but from death, 'her ultimate master', she winces with fear and shame. The conclusion reveals a writer of unusual vision.

The moral poverty of middle-class values is the theme of the more extended 'Daughters of the Vicar' (the 'Two Marriages' of 2.x.11). The conciseness and thrust with which Lawrence presents the effect of socio-economic factors on feeling and personality are remarkable from the outset. The story is a study in contrasts, between the cold unfeeling vicarage family (Louisa excepted) and the working-class Durants, between the daughters Mary and Louisa, and between their marriages. The vicarage is at Brinsley ('Aldecross'), and the Durants' cottage is that of Lawrence's grandparents (see pp. 2, 7). His grandfather is seen in John Durant, whose son (apart from his sailor's career) is just as clearly based on Lawrence's father; the death of the mother recalls that of Lawrence's mother in 1910. Unlike *The White Peacock* the story ends happily, with prospects of an assured marriage and possibly of emigration to Canada. A large family and genteel standards make the Lindleys, who are alien to the colliery district, poor and isolated. Assured of a large income, Mr Massy, a small, physically unattractive curate deputizing temporarily for Mr Lindley, becomes a very eligible husband for Mary, the eldest of the children. He is highly moral and philosophical but has no human feeling. Mary honours him as a Christian, and sacrifices herself in marriage for the sake of being a lady. Louisa is disgusted; how could Mary, her ideal, be spiritually pure when she had sold her body? She detests such calculation, and is determined to marry for love. There is none at home, but she sees it in the Durant family, especially between mother and son. The atmosphere at Christmas, when the Massys return with their two children to the cold, threadbare, gloomy vicarage, contrasts with immediate impressions of the Durant cottage when Louisa visits it for no other reason but to get away from home. It is 'alive and bright'; even in the snow there are spring prospects in the garden. Later, on her deathbed, his mother is anxious that her son, just home from the pit, shall not be neglected. Louisa therefore washes his back as he kneels on the hearthrug. He remains completely inhibited by class-consciousness. It is Louisa's feeling which ultimately break the ice. Mrs Lindley opposes such a vulgar marriage, and the vicar thinks the young couple should live elsewhere for the sake of his reputation. Mr Massy, who has always seemed like an undeveloped child to Louisa, hurries away to attend the baby, an obsession with him like his first. He and his wife recall Mr Casaubon and Dorothea in George Eliot's *Middlemarch*. Lawrence caricatures him a little; already his subject is life and forces in English society which oppose it.

The Croydon stories often show pleasing, colourful observations, but their general tone is artificial. 'Lessford's Rabbits' and 'A Lesson on a Tortoise' suggest that there were times when Lawrence the teacher looked round desperately for something to write about. More unconvincing is 'A Fly in the Ointment', in which he imagines writing to Muriel (Jessie Chambers), after receiving primroses from her. They had made him dreamy and vacant all day at school, and he was oblivious of everything around him when he finished a letter to her late at night, to be confronted by a housebreaker in his landlady's kitchen. 'The Old Adam' has the same Croydon setting, and is undoubtedly based on the jealousy Lawrence aroused in his landlord Mr Jones. The carnal symbolism of the iris recalls a scene in *Sons and Lovers* (xi). Premonitory thunder and lightning reinforce a general impression of fictional contrivance. The story is primarily a fantasy-fulfilment of suppressed feelings. 'The Witch à la Mode' is more subtle, and there is an appropriateness in its cold artificiality, its subject being Lawrence's relationship with Helen Corke. As in *The Trespasser* recurring whiteness stresses the essential neutrality of her friendship; an image links her with Lady Crystabel and the Lady of Shalott. Jessie Chambers can be seen in the Connie of a Yorkshire rectory to whom Coutts is betrothed. After a visit to a pianist friend (Laura MacCartney, to whom Helen Corke introduced Lawrence), he takes Winifred home and embraces her. As he sees her 'swooning on the unnatural ebb of passion', his heart dies with misery and despair. 'This woman gave him anguish and a cutting-short like death: to the other woman he was false.' He catches sight of the pure ivory of the lamp, and his heart flashes with rage. Then he stumbles against the lamp-stand, and sends it spinning. A blue flame licks her dress but, moving his arms down her form, he crushes the blaze. She remains unhurt as he rushes out with burning hands. The symbolism of the climax is expressive; earlier it suggests imitation-Meredith. At the opening the new moon, 'sharp and keen' like 'a knife to be used at the sacrifice', anticipates the 'cutting-short like death' of the close. Yet the conversation on the direction of our lives by fate has no imaginative fusion with the story.

Perhaps the humour of 'Delilah and Mr Bircumshaw' is too near the serious side of married life to be popular. The husband is a mild bully, and his wife becomes 'a little, uncanny machine' when she and her friend engage in ridiculing him. He can cow one woman, but he is afraid of two, and goes off to bed, hoping to inflict 'the penalties of ill-humour on his insolent wife'. Mr Bircumshaw is a bank clerk with 'unspent energy turning sour in his veins'; he is degenerating, and there is nothing at the end of the story to suggest he will change.

'Second Best' is neatly contrived, with an eye to the detail of rural background; for its narrative it relies on a rather unpleasant analogy which creates a kind of symbolism. Not surprisingly, Lawrence did not care for it (19.i.12). The story opposes refined intellectualism and blood-consciousness in love. Frances, a beautiful young woman (in white muslin) has been jilted by a scholarly gentleman. Her sister Anne, 'a wise young body', comforts her and wonders why she is tired. She catches a mole which proves snappy; when it bites her, she kills it with one blow from her sister's walking-cane. Frances also has proved snappy, and something has died in her. They come across Tom Smedley mowing fodder; Frances knows he is ready to accept her. Anne shows him the mole, and he wonders whether Frances would dare to kill one. The next day she does, and presents it to him when he calls in the evening. Her laugh is 'all agitation, and tears, and recklessness of desire'. He is disconcerted, but she takes his arm, and laughs shakily when he invites her to go out with him. Overmastering blood comes up in him; he is carried away by fierce love and tenderness. In a dead voice Frances agrees that they will have to tell her mother, but there is 'a thrill of pleasure in this death'. Clearly Lawrence intended an ambivalence in the title: the story recalls the less happy resolution of a similar conflict in *The White Peacock*. It also points towards the more unpleasant implications of 'Rabbit' in *Women in Love*.

A rarefied quality emanates from 'The Shadow in the Rose Garden'. It is a haunting story of a woman who married below her, and goes with her husband for a seaside holiday, privately to see the garden where she had been courted by the rector's son, an officer who had left the army. She returns to her husband, 'absent, torn, without any being of her own'. He insists on an explanation, and is filled with hate; when her story is concluded, the hate has gone, but shock has reduced their relationship to a state of impersonality. The rectory scenes are memorable; the uncurtained windows are black and soulless, but across the lawn an arch of crimson ramblers with soft sea beyond leads to the rose garden. Transfigured with pain and joy, the wife moves past crimson roses to a terrace, where she sits among white roses. The air is full of pure scent; though her scarlet sunshade is 'a hard blot of colour', she, in her white muslin, is 'no more than a rose', tense and unable to come quite into blossom. She starts cruelly as a shadow crosses her and a figure moves into sight. It is her former lover, and she discovers that he is a lunatic.

Strike conditions when Lawrence returned to Eastwood in February 1912 prompted a number of sketches, the most moving being 'A Sick Collier', the story of a devoted young husband who suffers from a mining accident during the national strike. He hears men outside the window talking of going to the football match in Nottingham; they have just received their strike-pay. He wishes to join them; as he raves and struggles to escape, his wife calls in a neighbour. The delirium subsides, and when he hears that he has been threatening to kill his wife he sobs uncontrollably. His wife knows he meant no harm, but she is afraid neighbours will gossip, and that his compensation will be stopped if 'it gets about as he's out of his mind'. 'Strike-Pay' is in a lighter vein. It begins with an amusing scene as strike-money is handed out by a Union official in the Primitive Methodist Chapel. A group of miners walk to Nottingham to see the football match, and ride on pit ponies in a field between Nuttall and Bulwell as a diversion on the way. One of them finds he has lost his half-sovereign dole, but the other three give him two shillings each, and they go to the match. When he returns home and hands over five-and-sixpence, it is not his wife but his mother-in-law he has to fear. After giving him a piece of his mind, she sails out to her other daughter's, and his wife asks if he would like his dinner warmed up. She is not a meek woman, but he is *her* man, not her mother's.

'Her Turn' may be based on some occurrence the truth of which is a little stranger than fiction. A woman of character shows her husband that, though he is on strike-pay, he must remember her housekeeping money. He restrains his anger; he has a heart, is tender to his doves and tortoise, and writes poetry. 'The Miner at Home' is a more serious satire, and presents a scene familiar to Lawrence from his early years, the mother washing her husband's back as she tries to manage the children. He has been sitting comfortably, smoking his pipe while she does all the work. He mentions a strike threat, and she tells him what she thinks of strikers. The dialogue is spirited. In the end the husband refuses to hold the baby; he is going out for the evening, and she is left weary and vexed, to look after the children as best she can.

'The Christening' is a story of ironies. Hilda, a teacher at the British School and the eldest of the Rowbotham sisters, calls at the baker's to buy cakes, unaware that the baker's man is the father of her unmarried sister's child. She feels responsible for the conduct of her family, and means to 'keep up the prestige of her house in spite of blows'. The child is to be baptized at home (thought to be in Percy Street, Eastwood); there is a special high tea to mark the occasion. The larger irony is with the aged father who prays at great length after the christening, and asks the Lord to be the Father of the child, and take away 'the conceit that our children are ours'. For he had stood between his children and the Lord. They have been 'plants under a stone'; but for him they might have been 'trees in the sunshine'. His mining son returns from work, and makes a great clatter in the kitchen. Catching sight of a paper bag on which is printed 'John Berriman – Bread, Pastries, etc.', he inflates it, bursts it with his fist, and sings 'Pat-a-cake, pat-a-cake, baker's man,/ Bake me a cake as fast as you can;/Prick it and stick it and mark it with P,/And put it i' th'oven for baby an' me.' Hilda wants to know why the mother is upset. The father takes no notice, and 'yet some power, involuntary, like a curse' remains in him, though he is physically a ruin. His will animates the house; his children had never lived, and they remain in awe of him.

In 'A Modern Lover' and 'The Shades of Spring' Lawrence returns to his love of Jessie Chambers, combining the Haggs Farm setting with fiction. The first opens with colourful, highly figurative description, provides an interesting list of the lovers' reading, refers to their 'dreadful strenuousness', and stresses the hope of the lover, on his return from London, that they will begin again – living, not 'speculating and poetising together'. 'It's when you burn a slow fire and save fuel that life's not worth having.' He tells her that she thinks him a wonderful person, as her new admirer regards her, but that he himself is different, and can be just himself with her, however he feels. She insists that he fails to realize that love is different for a woman. The conversation is not always convincing, and the ending is non-committal. 'The Shades of Spring' is mainly fictional, with much natural description. The returning lover is married, and the girl is far more assured than he had known her. It was she, he says, who wanted him to be highly educated, when she tells him that he cast her away on finding he had no further use for her. She is now in love with a gamekeeper. Admittedly the stars are not the same with him, but 'it is one's self that matters'. 'You could make them flash and quiver, and the forget-me-nots came up at me like phosphorescence. . . . But I have them all for myself, now.' He had never understood 'his nun, his Botticelli angel', and feels like William Morris's knight who lay wounded as if dead in the Chapel of Lyonesse. Soon afterwards he overhears Muriel reassuring the jealous keeper, whose anguish is symbolized in a bee-sting. She removes the sting, sucks away the poison, and tells him that the mark her mouth has made is the reddest kiss he will ever have. The story has a sting in its tail: they will be married – but not just yet. A shadow depresses the first lover, but the second is also disappointed. Muriel is not eager for marriage: 'it is most beautiful as it is'.

'Love Among the Haystacks' is woven round an incident which took place when Lawrence assisted the Chambers in the two fields by the vicarage where Baron von Hube lived above Greasley Church (30.vii.08). His Polish origin suggested the lively Polish governess who creates the jealousy on which the fiction is founded. The movements of the stackers are conveyed in varying rhythms, Geoffrey's expressing his feelings; but the finest features of the story are based on scenic memories, in sunshine and twilight, from some of the happiest days in Lawrence's life. The sequel develops amazingly, the innocent events of one night,

amusing on the one hand and admirably charitable on the other, con-
spiring to settle the future marriages of the two men who have always
been shy of women. It is unfortunate that the more serious development
of the story is the more improbable; on this all Lawrence chooses to say
is that 'Geoffrey and Lydia kept faith with one another'.

* * *

'A Chapel among the Mountains' and 'A Hay Hut among the Mountains'
are predominantly of autobiographical interest (see p. 28). Four other
stories arising from Lawrence's elopement with Mrs Weekley are related
to the German army. As the narration suggests, the central story of
'Once' could have been told by Frieda when she and Lawrence were in
the Tyrol; it may derive from her own experience, for 'Anita' is 'an
Answer' to the young officer who draws an armful of roses from under
his cloak and throws them over her as she lies on her bed, just as Frieda
is 'the call' and Lawrence 'the answer' in 'Bei Hennef'. Details in the
setting are obviously fictitious, and there is much altogether that looks
like the literary décor of invention. 'The Mortal Coil' provides a finer
story, from an experience of Frieda's father when he was a young
officer. Lawrence thought it first-class and one of his 'purest creations'
when he made a copy of it (31.x.16). The young officer of the story has
nothing to live for, since he has lost his honour by incurring large
gambling debts; his mistress Marta, the daughter of a tradesman,
cannot understand his lack of resolve. As he sits watching a candle
flame, he realizes it is a 'travelling flood, flowing swiftly from the
source . . . into the darkness'. Marta loves him, and his faith is restored.
A 'golden point of vision' seems to leap out from her eyes as she bids him
farewell in the early morning. Soon afterwards her friend Teresa comes
in, refuels the stove, and joins her in bed to keep warm. The officer finds
it sweet to be marching with his men out of the town into the darkness
of the country, and while his activity lasts during the day he can live.
In the afternoon the sky grows gloomier, and he is more depressed. Near
his house 'the sword of Damocles that had hung over his heart' falls as
he sees a policeman. Two young ladies have been found asphyxiated in
his room, and he is certain that his end has come.

Lawrence had reason to remember the fortifications at Metz (p. 27),
and the experience of the soldier who had no head for heights is excitingly
told in the first part of 'The Thorn in the Flesh'. He is hauled to safety

by a brutal sergeant, who thrusts his head forward and seems to scream at him. The panic-stricken soldier raises his arm involuntarily, and the sergeant reels backwards over the ramparts. The remainder of the story is not nearly as memorable, and the ending is inadequate. The soldier takes refuge with his sweetheart at the house of a baron where she is maidservant. They experience love for the first time, and all is 'whole'. When he is arrested, the baron says 'he's done for' and 'nothing but a fool', and departs in agitation, 'preparing himself for what he could do'.

By contrast the psychological vividness of 'The Prussian Officer' is sustained throughout; Lawrence thought it the best story he had written (?10.vi.13). It is highly imaginary, the starting-point being Frieda's recollections of what she had heard from a corporal friend who told her about bullying in the army, and how he hated it. The original title was 'Honour and Arms'. Lawrence was annoyed when Garnett changed it and used the new title for his first published collection of stories; 'what Prussian officer?' he asked (5.xii.14). His psychological cogency arises from his success in empathizing with both the officer and his victim. The admiration and envy of the one, in conjunction with the growing fear and self-conscious attempt at neutrality of the other, create an inflamed love-hate fixation which leads to terrible sadistic outbreaks despite the officer's good intentions. He cannot suppress his instincts, but the 'intense gratification' he experiences is followed by 'a whole agony of reaction'. When the orderly sees his hand tremble as he receives his coffee, he feels 'everything falling shattered'. It is an index of Lawrence's skill that he makes the brutal murder of the officer seem inevitable and instinctive. Though the orderly's brain becomes fevered to madness, Lawrence's feat in transmitting his sensations is comparable to Stephen Crane's in *The Red Badge of Courage*. Hyperaesthetic effects vary from near to far, from the knocking which announces the tapping of a small bird overhead to the 'wonderlight' of the mountains. 'Half earth, half heaven', they had always held out hope to the suffering orderly; as he lies twisting in a paroxysm, he wishes to leave himself and be identified with them; as he loses consciousness, the mountains, 'so clean and cool', seem to absorb what is lost in him. The cruelty and horror of the story are transcended.

'New Eve and Old Adam' presents a situation which might be more effectively illuminated in the context of a novel. Lawrence was amused by it, although his typist thought it unworthy of him (?14.vii.13). It illustrates the battle 'so many married people fight, without knowing why'. The new Eve seems to love protestations of love; the old Adam is restive because he has lost that 'pride and pleasure in his own physique which the first months of married life had given him'. Each thinks the other self-seeking. She accuses him of assuming that she is a *rib* of himself, without any existence of her own, and his reply is that she *would* never love *him*, and will never be able to love anyone but herself. The best text for Lawrence's dramatic sketch is to be found in Blake's 'The Clod and the Pebble'.

'The Primrose Path' is the last of Lawrence's pre-war stories, and reveals much in the life of his mother's brother Herbert Beardsall, the black sheep of the family. The imaginary journey from Nottingham to Watnall ('Watmore') is a device for presenting him, as taxi-driver, face to face with the bedridden, consumptive, first wife he abandoned when he emigrated to Australia with a sentimental young woman who read Browning. His bullying manner is seen later with the girl who shares his home. A glimpse of it may be seen in 'Rex', where he appears as tenant of a public house (in Sneinton), and the owner of a pup which played such a memorable part in Lawrence's boyhood that he was prompted to write this autobiographical sketch for *The Dial* in 1920, as a companion piece to 'Adolf', after the latter had been rejected by Middleton Murry, as editor of *The Athenaeum*, in 1919.

'The Thimble' was occasioned by the wounding of the Prime Minister's son, Herbert Asquith, early in the war. Lawrence sent the manuscript of the story to his wife Lady Cynthia Asquith for approval, confident that she would find his sketch of her 'better than Sargent or Watts in paint'. The next day (30.x.15) he stressed the theme of resurrection ('whether we dead can rise from the dead and love, and live, in a new life, here'), and said that we should give up everything 'so we may save the hope of a resurrection from the dead, we English, all Europe. What is the whole empire, and kingdom, save the thimble in my story?' Lawrence was trying to say in symbolic narrative what he had said in 'The Crown' (pp. 74–5). The thimble, however, seems more an adjunct than a symbol which fuses imaginatively with the story. The lady had allowed 'accident' to possess her being; it was like an 'overfilming sleep' which had imprinted an image of her husband's disfigurement on her whole consciousness. As he talks about his confrontation with death, the triviality and the dream-psychology vanish; they recognize their interdependence and their power to be reborn. With that the husband throws the thimble out of the window into the street; it was old and aristocratic, representing a dead power and glory. The theme and the occasion encouraged a highly finished composition but, six years later, Lawrence returned to the subject in 'The Ladybird'.

In 'England, My England' Lawrence is frequently heard as a direct commentator. Two episodes stand out: the history of Joyce's crippling for life, and the vivid sensations of her father just before his death on the battlefield in Flanders. The opening presents the Meynell families at Greatham as representatives of old English stock; Greatham ('Crockham') is 'secret, primitive, savage as when the Saxons first came'. Joyce is Sylvia Lucas; her mother, Madeline Meynell, had married Perceval Lucas, and he, as Egbert, is at the centre of Lawrence's satirical analysis of one class of English society. With blue, Viking-like eyes and the agile figure of an English archer, he has no profession; his main interest is folklore. An inheritance of one hundred and fifty pounds a year is fatal; he busies himself, but is amateurish in everything he does. He has plenty of friends in town 'of the same ineffectual sort as himself', but he prefers to ignore the world, and go his way 'like a casual pilgrim down the forsaken sidetracks'. For him his wife, home, and garden are everything. Their children create additional expenses, until the grandfather has to assist them; the whole cost of Joyce's prolonged treatment is borne by him. Snakes in the garden are ominous: she had fallen on a kind of sickle which Egbert had left lying on the grass, and his wife's agony of watching over her in hospital changes her attitude towards him for ever. Winifred becomes the Mater Dolorata, as 'closed as a tomb' to him. The war breaks out. Although he is 'a pure-blooded Englishman' who recoils from mass-feeling (earning Lawrence's admiration in one respect, at least), Egbert enlists. His 'thorough-bred sensibilities' are degraded in 'the ugly intimacy' of camp, and he visits his family at Crockham. Winifred, 'willing to serve the soldier, if not the man', makes 'the grit worse between his teeth'. 'The story is the story of most men and women who are married today – of most men at the War, and wives at home', Lawrence wrote (5.ix.15). W. E. Henley's poem suggests irony of sundry hues in the title.

Lawrence wrote two rather unusual stories in Cornwall at the end of 1916, after completing *Women in Love*. The story of 'Samson and Delilah' would have appealed to Thomas Hardy, but he would have presented it with more humour. In its surprising sequence of unusual events, it is not typical of Lawrence. Perhaps, when he wrote it, he was reminded of reconciliations which followed violent quarrels with Frieda. The husband, who has been bound at Delilah's bidding (after the story in Judges) and thrown out of the inn, finds that the door, which had been locked and barred, is open when he returns. He enters, and finds his wife by the kitchen fire. Having worked as a miner in Montana for nearly sixteen years, after deserting her, he has some admiration for her toughness. They had fought from the first, and 'a bit of a fight for a how-de-do' pleases him. The happy ending is secured by the power of touch, reinforced by the news that the husband has brought home over a thousand pounds. The admixture of comedy at the end contrasts with the romanticism of the second story, 'The Horse Dealer's Daughter', which Lawrence preferred. His brief description (HL.380) shows that its first title was 'The Miracle'. The setting is Eastwood, and the original of the Pervins' home is that of 'The Hollies' (*WP*.III.v). The doctor had been irresistibly fascinated by the girl whose life he restores after rescuing her from the pond where she attempted suicide, but the climax depends on the complete change which takes place in him after he has undressed and dried her, and wrapped her naked in blankets before a fire. On recovering consciousness and learning what has happened, she shuffles forward on her knees, clings to him, and then, looking up with 'flaring, humble eyes of transfiguration', murmurs in strange transport, 'You love me. I know you love me, I know.' He is horrified. To steady himself, he grasps her shoulder, and a flame seems to burn him. As her eyes fill with tears, he can bear no more, and holds her face to his throat; when he kisses her, he knows he has 'crossed over the gulf to her'. Both have entered a new life. The story is movingly told and intrinsically convincing.

'The Blind Man', another story of touch, was planned when Lawrence was staying with the Carswells in the Forest of Dean (p. 41). Isabel Pervin is based on Catherine Carswell, and her cousin Bertie Reid (in professional qualifications), on her husband Donald. The farm, which gives Isabel's husband Maurice, blinded and disfigured in Flanders, a real joy through contacts with life, has the charged atmosphere of the Brangwens' (*R*.ii). After their 'dark, great year of blindness and solitude and unspeakable nearness', Isabel looks forward to maternity, but is anxious about Maurice, who is depressed, irritable, and tired of people and prattle. To her surprise, he welcomes the proposed visit of Bertie Reid. The two men are antipathetic by nature: Bertie is intellectual but Maurice is mentally slow, as if drugged by his strong provincial blood. Behind Lawrence's description of him one can see the image of 'a pillar of blood': he is 'a tower of darkness' to Isabel; when he stands up, his face and neck are surcharged with blood, and the veins stand out on his temples. As long as he can preserve 'immediacy of blood-contact' with the world he is happy. He is anxious to win Bertie's friendship, and requests that he may touch him. After feeling his face, Maurice asks him to touch his eyes and scar. Bertie flinches, but Maurice takes his hand and presses the fingers to his eyes. He is elated, filled with the passion of friendship; and it is from this perhaps that Bertie shrinks most, as Isabel perceives. The story polarizes Lawrence's two planes of consciousness, and poses the question: who is the more blind of the two men, one in his dark world of blood-awareness, the other in an intellectual world of light which bars the way to human contact? No simple answer is forthcoming, for Maurice's awareness is limited, and he deceives himself in the end.

Five other stories seem to have been written at Mountain Cottage, Middleton, Derbyshire. 'You Touched Me' is rather sketchy, and has all the air of a fabricated, conventional plot with a Lawrentian ingredient. The setting is Bromley House (Mellor's Pottery House), Lynncroft, Eastwood; and the crucial turn of events depends less on the power of touch than on the despotism of a father who threatens to disinherit his daughters unless the eldest marries his adopted son Hadrian (who, with the indomitable courage of a rat, seems to foreshadow Henry in 'The Fox'). But for the quirkishness of Matilda's father, his position would be untenable. Her sudden acceptance of him is unmotivated, unless one assumes that the power of touch is magical. Lawrence fails to give the story inherent probability.

Shortly after finishing 'The Blind Man', Lawrence visited his sister Ada at Ripley, leaving the train at Butterley, where he saw the flame-lurid spectacle which invests the opening of 'Fanny and Annie' (?21.xi.18). Other impressions, from his walk into Ripley, enter this rather tragic story of 'second best'. It reaches a climax when Harry, Fanny's first love whom she has returned to marry, is denounced in chapel, at the end of the harvest anthem in which he has sung solo, by the mother of the promiscuous Annie. The narrative loses none of its

231

cogency, even if one ignores the dubious Lawrentian nub that Harry's kisses of long ago had lived in Annie's blood and 'sent roots down into her soul'. Though her soul groans, we are told she is doomed.

'Tickets, Please' is on the same theme, but is more subtle, more true to life, and the most successful of the stories written at Mountain Cottage. After a high-spirited opening which expresses the lively interest Lawrence found in tram journeys on the Nottingham–Ripley line, the emotional changes form a sad decline, particularly for Annie. She is the girl whom John Thomas really loved and, in her bitter disappointment, she is the most vicious of the vengeance-seekers. At the end she is tortured to think what has happened. For she and John Thomas had experienced a rich warm flow in each other's company, and it was she who, in her assurance that he could never leave her, spoilt a happy natural relationship by endeavouring to force it into more intellectual channels. (For the Statutes fair, see p. 7.)

The most curious of the Mountain Cottage stories is 'Wintry Peacock'. It developed from Lawrence's dream of a young blue peacock which fell to the ground after being mauled by two dogs in the air. It kept crying, and a woman came out of a cottage, saying it would be all right (3.vi.18). A *Macbeth* association with the view from Mountain Cottage (?15.xi.18) and the statement 'I wish one could cease to be a human being, and be a demon', which was evoked by the frozen, snow-covered landscape (9.ii.19), are also relevant. Mrs Goyte (named after a Derbyshire river), who learns that her husband (on leave, after being wounded) has been unfaithful, is witch-like. She lives at Tible with her husband's Scottish parents, and he is away in Scotland. She has black features, an ominous frown, and a habit of holding her head 'ducked' between her shoulders. The first view of her and Joey the peacock establishes that they love each other. The next day the narrator finds there has been a heavy snowfall, and the valley (the Via Gellia; cf. 17.iv.25) is 'abstracted as a grove of death'. Down the slope he sees something struggling in the show, and finds Joey almost exhausted. Next day he takes the peacock back to Tible, and learns that with the return of Mrs Goyte's husband there had been a great 'to-do'. It must have been mutual, for he tried to shoot the bird, and it flew off over Griff Low (from Ible across Griffe Grange Valley, above the Via Gellia, west of Matlock). Mrs Goyte's father tells the narrator, 'It's bin heavy weather wi' 'er this last two days. Ay – 'er's bin northeast sin 'er seed you a Wednesday.' Witch hints at this point reinforce the suggestion that the snowstorm has been caused by Mrs Goyte. When her familiar is returned she puts her lips to its beak, and looks more witch-like than ever. The laughter of the two men at the end recalls the laughter of the woman at the beginning, and denotes uncanny influences still at work.

Lawrence wrote a short version of 'The Fox' at Mountain Cottage. Its setting is in Berkshire, like that of 'Monkey Nuts' (cf. ?15.viii.19), which belongs to the period when the Lawrences were living at Hermitage in 1919. Rather a commonplace story, 'Monkey Nuts' shows how a shy young man who had been singled out by a resolute land girl, eventually plucks up courage to withstand her domination, so suddenly and shockingly that she never appears again. His release brings him greater relief than the Armistice cease-fire. A reference to the soldiers who helped to collect the hay appears in the final version of 'The Fox', which was completed in Sicily, where Lawrence added 'a long tail' to the 'bobbed short story' (16.xi.21) which originated from his visit to Violet Monk and her cousin Cecily Lambert (who suggested Nellie March and Jill Banford) at Grimsbury Farm near Hermitage. Lawrence's extension is tedious at times, but his smooth lucidity compares favourably with the cluttered prose of some of his earlier writing. In the first version (which may have occurred to Lawrence at Hermitage, 12.iii.18) Henry's marriage is not delayed, and neither the fox nor Jill Banford is killed. Nellie March, who has accepted a man's responsibility on the farm she shares with Jill, is psychologically upset when Henry arrives. She is mesmerized by him, as she had been by the fox which she was powerless to shoot; for her he is the fox, in appearance and smell. Henry is the predator; he wants not only Nellie but the farm. Under his spell, she dreams of a fox singing both during her sleep and in the daytime. In the dream, the fox's brush burns her mouth; later a 'quick, brushing kiss' from Henry seems 'to burn through her every fibre'. Then, after he has shot the fox and suggested that it will make a lovely fur, she dreams that Jill is dead, and that she can find only a fox-skin to wrap around her in the coffin. When Henry, at army camp, hears that Nellie has changed her mind, and wishes to look after the delicate Jill rather than marry him, he is 'like some creature that is vicious' in his determination to get rid of Banford. He is a Canadian, and completes the felling of the tree with the unerring accuracy of an expert lumberman. Jill, like a willing victim, ignores his warning, and is killed by it, as he hoped. His marriage is not a success: Nellie feels the need to exert herself in love, and Henry resists (in one way, an anticipation of *PS*.xxvi). He hopes that when they go to Canada, she will no longer be 'a man' or 'an independent woman with a man's responsibility'. The ending is more explicit than the earlier one, but the psychological problem arising from Nellie's Lesbianism is too much for Lawrence, and his comments at the end weaken the imaginative impressiveness of the main story.

'The Captain's Doll' has amusing situations, but is unduly prolonged. 'I have just got it high up in the mountains of the Tyrol, and don't quite know how to get it down without breaking its neck', Lawrence wrote (2.xi.21). The second half is based on recollections of a holiday at Thumersbach (p. 45); and the riches of local colour, from the sunny animation of a lakeside resort to heights and glacial horrors, with close-ups of flowers in the way, were more than he could resist. In consequence, the resolution of the story makes progress only at intervals, through little argumentative quarrels. The Countess Hannele and Baroness Mitchka owe something to Frieda and her sister Johanna; the Herr Regierungsrat may be a sketch of the latter's husband, and the Scottish captain (in person), of Donald Carswell. After losing his wife, who lived for adoration, and leaving Hannele, who made a doll of him literally, the captain becomes a changed man. When he returns, and finds his doll reduced to part of an arrangement in a still-life (which he purchases), he tells Hannele, who is engaged to the adoring Herr Regierungsrat (though he makes her feel like a queen 'in exile'):

> *any* woman, today, no matter *how* much she loves her man . . . could start any minute and make a doll of him. And the doll would be her hero; and her hero would be no more than her doll. My wife might have done it. She did do it, in her mind. . . . And her doll was a great deal sillier than the one you made. But it's all the same. If a woman loves you, she'll make a doll out of you. She'll never be satisfied till she's made your doll. And when she's got your doll, that's all she wants.

He is determined that if he marries again, his wife shall honour and obey him. He will love and cherish, but not adore her. In any event, he intends to help a friend in Africa, and write about the moon. Hannele is ready to go to Africa with him, but will not promise to honour and obey him. This Lawrentian comedy was written at a transitional stage between *Aaron's Rod* and *Kangaroo*, and it reverses the typical roles of men and women in Shavian comedy: despite all she professes, the woman is drawn towards the dark gods (cf. p. 192). Hannele's refusal to honour and obey proves to be no more than a teasing prenuptial liberty. She is anxious to burn the picture of the doll and see the captain again; he agrees, and pulls back quickly into the darkness. The symbolism of this conclusive movement is reinforced by early emphasis on the contrast between the captain's sense of insignificance in his wife's presence and Hannele's feeling that all her friends are reduced to insubstantiality on his return.

Lady Cynthia Asquith and the thimble story (pp. 228–9) are adapted to strange effect in 'The Ladybird'. Realistically the narrative is ridiculous; allegorically, it presents the romantic mystique of Lawrence's dark love. The love of Lady Daphne's 'adorable' husband creates a link with 'The Captain's Doll'. It is anathema to Lawrence and Count Dionys: 'white love' had made her nerve-worn; it was 'like moonshine, harmful, the reverse of love'; her eyes were 'like jewels of stone'. When her husband returns from war-service, his eyes burn with 'hard, white, focused light', his face has a 'deathly sub-pallor', and his voice expresses 'strong, cold desire'. He worships her as if she were a goddess, and his face is white with ecstasy until she is sick of his 'adoration-lust'. It is Count Dionys who lures her with his singing in the darkness. True love is dark like the sun; there would be no light but for 'bits of dust and stuff to turn the dark fire into visibility', he tells her. The ladybird on top of the thimble (with a snake coiled round the base) is related to the Egyptian scarab; the Count therefore thinks he is related to the Pharaohs. When blood-consciousness flows round him and Daphne in the darkness, he is 'in flame unconscious, seated erect, like an Egyptian King-god in the statues'. He tells her that she is his by night but not by day, and that she will be his in death. Lawrence refers to Paolo and Francesca, but the Persephone myth is dominant: 'hold her fast, queen of the underworld, himself master of the underworld'. Lawrence's master-principle, one of his prepossessions in the *Aaron's Rod–Kangaroo* period, is extended politically to the unquestioned rule of natural aristocrats. More relevant is the change in Lady Daphne and her husband when the influence of Dionys is felt. Her hard, green-blue eyes begin to express nocturnal stillness and wonder, and her love becomes so virginal that his 'ecstatic, deadly love' is checked. She is 'the wife of the ladybird'. Count Dionys

(Dionysos?) may be 'a little madman', but he is Birkin *redivivus* almost in self-parodic guise.

*   *   *

Although almost contemporary with 'Pan in America' (?12.v.24), 'The Overtone' is a youthful, Swinburnian affirmation, in some of Lawrence's most poetic prose. Past and present are fused principally by images, some of which recall Virginia Woolf. Husband and wife have never lived. She talks altruistically with her friend on the State-endowment of mothers, while he, watching the night's great circle, full of the fire that flickers unquenchably, sits outside reliving the crisis (fictionally prompted by a memory of Louisa Burrows in Leicestershire) from which their mutual inhibitions sprang. The feelings of her host and hostess drift like iridescence upon 'the quick' of the nymph Elsa. As she listens, she stirs her fingers in a bowl of withering rose-leaves, knowing that the husband had never 'bared the sun of himself' to his wife, all of whose flowers had been shed inwards, so that her heart was a heap of 'withered, almost scentless petals that had never given joy to anyone'. To the husband, Pan is dead. The nymph believes that 'Pan is in the darkness, and Christ in the pale light', and that they must go 'day and night, night and day, for ever apart, for ever together'. It is a reconciliation which Lady Daphne could not find in marriage. 'The Overtone' approaches perfection in a kind of fiction which Lawrence attempted too rarely.

By contrast 'None of That' tells the horrible story of an American woman of tremendous will-power, who made the mistake, first of seeking a new husband to match her 'remarkable and epoch-making energy and character' in the wrong country, and then of being captivated by the wrong man. Living for imaginative experience, she stimulated men's minds and thwarted them physically. In Cuesta, the Mexican bull-fighter, she chose a man with neither imagination nor intellect. Being physically attracted but imaginatively balked, she behaved irrationally, giving Cuesta the impression she was playing with him. At the first opportunity, he handed her over to his bull-ring gang; after a nervous collapse, she poisoned herself. The havoc created by dissociation of mind and body in sex is even more the subject of 'The Princess'. Ethel Cane in 'None of That' is betrayed by her imagination; Dollie Urquhart, by her will. Brought up in splendid isolation by her crazy father, she becomes 'impervious as crystal'. Having read Zola and Maupassant, she 'seemed to understand things in a cold light perfectly'. When her father died she came to a dude ranch in New Mexico, assuming that marriage was her goal, though she had no vital interest in men. A vague, unspoken intimacy developed with her Mexican guide Romero, but she could not think of him in marriage. The journey with him into the mountains has symbolical features; it is based on the ascent Lawrence made up San Cristobal Canyon to a razor edge, where he saw, far below in the valley, the blue-green lake around which the climax of the story was imagined. Dollie is determined to look at the secret heart of the mountains, and 'see the wild animals move about in their wild unconsciousness'. Lower down she has glimpses of the fairy-like and paradisal; the summit is corpselike, and she wishes to return. Yet she and her guide go on to their destination, where she is confronted by the 'cold, electric eyes' of a bob-cat, fearless and demonish. At night, in a cabin pervaded by the 'strange squalor of the primitive forest', she wills Romero to take her, ostensibly to warm her. He resents her suggestion that they return the next morning, and imposes his will relentlessly on her, behaving like a madman until he is shot by a rescuer. In violating her, Romero had violated himself. Both had suffered a psychic death. He could not conquer her, but he had roused part of her which she did not wish to realize. The crystal was shattered, and Dollie was found 'not a little mad'.

Earlier in 1924, at Kiowa Ranch, Lawrence had written 'The Woman Who Rode Away' and 'St Mawr'. The former combines impressions of the silver mines he visited with Götzsche near Minas Nuevas, Sonara (on his second journey into Mexico), with those made on an excursion with Mabel Sterne to the ceremonial cave above Arroyo Seco. The significance of the story is spiritual; it is a sustained metaphor expressing renunciation of western values. The ceremonial or ritualistic detail is directed by an Indian myth which appealed to Lawrence's cosmic vision. The gnomic ending derives from the faith which inspires 'New Mexico', that power will desert the white race for one which is more cosmically orientated (P.147). As the story is a kind of allegory, the woman who rode away is generic and anonymous. Her conscious development was arrested on marriage, and her husband had never been real to her, mentally or physically. From her patio she can see only the machinery and refuse tip of a decayed silver mine. The nearest town is inanimate; a dead dog lies among the market-place stalls as if stretched out for ever. Her one desire is to wander into the secret haunts of the mountains, to find a sacred tribe, with descendants of Montezuma and Aztec kings among them. Without warning she rides off; she has no will of her own, and exults when she finds she is subject to Indian control. She is ready to die unto her world, for her life has been a death. She and her escort reach a valley between walls of rock high up in the mountains, where she tells the chief she is weary of the white man's God and wishes to serve the gods of the Indian tribe. She learns that the Indians have lost the sun and the moon to the white race, and that they will be restored when a white woman sacrifices herself to the Indian gods. The woman drifts to this sacrificial consummation. Purification enlarges her sensory awareness until she can distinguish the sound of unfolding flowers and movements far out in the atmosphere. The drumming of the dance helps to destroy the 'quivering nervous consciousness' which is character-istic of her civilization. When winter comes, a sweetened herb drink endows her with a 'passional cosmic consciousness' which enables her to hear the stars like bells in their timeless dance, and the snow twittering and faintly whistling as it falls. With the winter solstice the time comes for her sacrifice, and she is taken to a cave in the mountain side with a shaft of ice hanging from the precipice above. There, when the red sun sinks, casting its light through the shaft to the innermost cave, she is to be sacrificed. The priests look eagerly towards the sun, but the aged cacique looks beyond; his fixed dark eyes express power, 'intensely abstract and remote' but 'deep to the heart of the earth, and the heart of the sun' (cf. p. 263). The moment of rebirth is left anticipated. Only Lawrence's mystical faith could have carried him through to this conclusion.

Behind 'The Overtone', 'The Woman Who Rode Away', and the conclusion of *The Plumed Serpent* is a sense of the deadness of England which Lawrence felt in London (p. 50). The spirit of revulsion rather than of laughter in which 'St Mawr' is written is centred symbolically in hoof-revolt. Dorothy Brett noticed the sheer delight of Lawrence and Frieda's indignation as he read the account of St Mawr's revenge on Rico. The disillusionment of the *déracinée* Lou reflects that of Lawrence, against impressions of the greater reality presented in 'New Mexico' and 'Reflections on the Death of a Porcupine'. For this finale, eked out and illustrated with the history of his ranch, St Mawr and Lewis (left in Texas) are forgotten. The Shropshire section (based on Lawrence's visit to Frederick Carter – 'Cartwright' with his Pan-like face – at Pontes-bury) weakens the narrative by overextension, but insignificance is most tedious in Lewis's boyhood recollections of moon-people and Lou's letters to her mother, which tell us no more than is expected. Such realistic scribbling may have given Lawrence some amusement (as did the dialogue around the jokes on the cup-and-saucer hat and the sympathies of the *belle mère* with the stallion); the difference between this and the unduly protracted ending is that the latter has intrinsic interest and ultimate significance.

Mrs Witt's 'shattering sort of sense' is Lawrence's; she wants to find 'real men', and that is Lawrence's repeated call in his later years. She disapproves of 'social tailoring' (an echo of Carlyle), and finds Lewis more manly than Rico and his set. If there is any absurdity in her proposal of marriage, it is Lawrence's, for Lewis is an example of 'the aristocracy of the invisible powers, the greater influences, nothing to do with human society'. Lou anticipates Lady Chatterley. Like the young chicks in the gamekeeper's hut, the passionate blaze of life-power in St Mawr gives her a vision of another world, and she weeps to think how marriage has failed her; as with Sir Clifford and the bluebells in the park, the question immediately elicited in Rico by the horse relates to colour in painting. Again, when Lou yearns for a 'good life' in a 'far-away wild place', she expresses the view that men and women should 'stay apart till they have learned to be gentle with one another again. Not all this forced passion and destructive philandering.' To her (as in 'The Waste Land') London is an unreal city; she talks to 'handsome young bare-face unrealities, not men at all'. Rico is afraid to let himself go; he might 'erupt like some suddenly wicked horse'. Lou wants a return of wonder in life; she is convinced that men cannot really think when 'the last bit of wild animal dies in them'. Even in the remote country (as in the opening scene of 'The Woman Who Rode Away') 'the dead hand of the war' lies 'like a corpse decomposing'. Whatever Phoenix and Lewis feel about this world, they remain passive; but the stallion St Mawr, whose passion smoulders in resentment at being subjugated, erupts into violent protest at being mismanaged by a rider with no vital awareness. Hearing that Rico is ready to sell the horse and let it be gelded, Lou associates his 'eunuch cruelty' with 'our whole eunuch civilization'. Mrs Witt advises her to let Miss Manby have her husband but not her horse. She should tell her: '*My husband won't need emasculating, and my horse I won't have you meddle with. I'll preserve one last male thing in the museum of the world, if I can.*'

Lawrence gives the horse's 'explosion' greater symbolical import than it can carry imaginatively. Lou sees the dead adder that startled St Mawr, and has 'a vision of evil'. She sees it welling up from 'the core of Asia' and enveloping the whole world, the people like St Mawr thrown backwards and writhing, while the rider, crushed, is still reining them down. No longer its own master, mankind is ridden by a smooth-faced, evil stranger, in a game of betrayal. 'The last of the gods of our era' is 'Judas supreme'. Lawrence sees evil persistent in individuals, society, the press, and in socialism, bolshevism, and resultant fascism. The indictment is colossal. The answer is to fight for 'the one passionate principle of creative being, which recognizes the natural good, and has a sword for the swarms of evil'. Rico is 'one of mankind's myriad conspirators', playing for safety 'whilst willing the minor disintegration of all positive living'. The horse, born to serve nobly, knows that nobility has gone out of men.

Herein lies the justification for the end of 'St Mawr'. Although (like Lawrence on his way to England) Lou realizes 'the glamour of the universe' when she crosses the Gulf of Mexico and contrasts 'the marvellous beauty and fascination of natural wild things' (the porpoises) with 'the horror of man's unnatural life, his heaped-up civilization', she and her mother are disillusioned wherever they go. St Mawr revives on a Texan farm, but they travel on. Lou wishes to recover her soul. Her renovation begins in New Mexico, where she sees the beauty and Darwinian reality of life. Her sympathy for the wild spirit of the place is Lawrence's (cf. 4.vii.24). She recognizes that 'there is no Almighty loving God', and that 'man is only himself when he is fighting on and on' against the sordidness of the lower stages of creation, and the sordidness into which civilization falls 'when it loses its inward vision and its cleaner energy'. Lou dislikes men because 'they're not men enough' (cf. 9.viii.24).

*　　*　　*

Lawrence's annoyance with Murry arose partly from jealousy (pp. 51–2), but mainly from disagreement with his views. It finds expression in his letters (e.g. 7.ii.24, 17.xi.24, 28.i.25, 19.i.26) and more maliciously in short stories. 'The Border Line' is based on Lawrence's visit with Frieda to Baden; it records his impressions even more vividly than 'A Letter from Germany' (P.107–10), with prescient hints of emergent Hitlerism. The 'border line' has various connotations: it is the war-front crossed in the Marne country; it is the boundary between future peace and war; between France and Germany; and between life and death. In Philip, Katherine, and Alan one can see Murry, Frieda, and Lawrence. Alan returns from the dead, and the 'strong, silent kindliness' of his spirit eliminates all Katherine's 'ashy, nervous, horror of the world'. The reddish flush of Strasbourg Cathedral in the night is another border line, indicating that 'the shadowy blood' will 'move erect' once more and blot out the Cross. (In Lawrence's later years the idea often took the form of the triumph of Pan over Christ.) The demarcation line is personal, Philip being 'too much over the wrong side of the border' for Alan, the fighter, the lion. He is a 'subtle equivocator', an 'adjuster of the scales of truth'; he is 'sentimental, on the side of the angels, offering defiance to nobody', a dog, so weak and dependent that, when Alan takes Katherine from him, he dies. The mischievous humour of 'Jimmy and the Desperate Woman' has less to commend it. As the editor of a rather high-brow magazine, the little man who had hoped to nestle, or be nestled, in some woman's bosom, Jimmy (Murry) is 'a Martyred Saint Sebastian with the mind of a Plato' and the face of Pan. He receives a poem from an unhappy miner's wife, visits her when he has to lecture in Sheffield, and invites her and her child to share his home. A teacher before marriage, a writer of verse, and a woman of unrelenting will who knows she has made a mistake, she is like Mrs Lawrence. Jimmy lives in his inner world; the woman he thinks he wants is no more than 'a ghost moving inside his own consciousness'. Her husband gives her *carte blanche* and, though Jimmy back in London does his best to dissuade her, she arrives. He feels her husband's aura about her as he accompanies her to his home, and this goes to his head. The little man has resolved to be king, and the question which comes to the desirous Jimmy is, which of the two will receive the heavier fall, the wife or the husband?

Far more creative genius is found in the mocking fantasy of 'The Last Laugh'. The red-bearded Lorenzo (Lawrence) announces a new world when he sees the new-fallen snow, as he bids farewell to his visitors Marchbanks (Murry) and Miss James (Dorothy Brett) at midnight. To the self-deceptive Marchbanks the snow is only whitewash. As his bowler hat falls off, a street lamp reveals his hooked nose, thick black brows sardonically arched, and a bald spot like a tonsure in his dark curly hair. He is like a satanic priest of a 'faun on the Cross, with all the malice of the complication'. Extraordinary laughter is heard from time to time. Unconsciously Marchbanks joins in, neighing and showing goat-like eyes. A policeman joins the pair. Miss James catches sight of a man's face in the bushes; Marchbanks, who had thought the laughter Somebody calling, goes off in pursuit and is inevitably led to the house of a woman who is 'always expecting Somebody'. The snowstorm increases in intensity, and is accompanied with lightning. It whirls through an empty church, scattering leaves of books and the altar-cloth, and making the organ trill like pan-pipes amid bursts of 'naked low laughter'. There is scent of almond blossom in the air. Next morning 'an absolutely new blue heaven' canopies London. Miss James is still exhilarated, and has lost her deafness; the policeman, the representative of the law, is lamed. She thinks of the face and the laughter. 'He laughs longest who laughs last. He certainly will have the last laugh', she reflects. Her determination to save Marchbanks from himself had been absurd; he took life so seriously, especially his own. 'Soul' was the only thing there had been between him and her (cf. ?26.i.25), and that had gone. He comes in, deep in thought. The policeman discovers that his lame foot is now curiously clubbed, like the paw of an animal. At this point Marchbanks, seeing something which makes him realize he has made a fool of himself, falls dead as if struck by lightning. A faint smell of almond blossom indicates that the triumph of Pan, the new world announced by the satyr-like Lorenzo, is imminent.

'Smile' is Lawrence's last fictional gibe at Murry. The Italian setting is based, according to Merrild, on the memory of Lawrence's visit, at her father's request, to see a Mexican girl on her death-bed. Lawrence imagines Murry's grief over the death of Katherine Mansfield; his face 'would have done for Christ on the Cross, with the thick black eyebrows tilted in the dazed agony'. A faint ironical curl at the corners of his wife's mouth makes Matthew smile, and his smile spreads to the three nuns as he looks at them. Then he turns to his wife with a look of martyrdom. His thoughts are mixed, occasionally Pan-like; and, as he condemns himself for his imperfections, she seems to tell him to smile. At the end Lawrence contrives to leave him looking ridiculous again.

Two satirical stories were prompted by Lawrence's calling on Faith Mackenzie early in 1926, and finding that her husband was away on the Channel island he had rented. Whatever their particular reference, neither can be regarded as venomous; they have sufficient universality to raise them above the personal. 'Two Blue Birds' is a delightful sketch, ending with a dramatic crescendo of artful 'bitchery' against the devoted secretary by the jealous wife who spends so much of her life apart from her husband. The two women (dressed in blue) tear out each other's feathers like the blue-tits which had disturbed the author and his admiring slave. The Lawrentian implications go deeper. How inanimate the married couple are may be seen in the response of the wife to spring flowers, and of the husband to the sun. The importance he attaches to the architecture of the novel is related to her insistence that he is too comfortable to produce great work (see p. 285) and to her suggestion that his secretary writes much that passes as his.

It is clear that the three islands of 'The Man Who Loved Islands' were imagined in the English Channel; as the island author gets his typist with child and deserts her, it is not surprising that Compton Mackenzie threatened a libel suit unless the story were withdrawn from publication. The insular theme derives, however, from Lawrence's recurrent moods of revolt from the civilized world. Whatever appeal the life of isolation had for him, he shows no illusions about it here or in 'The Man Who Was Through with the World'. The first of the islands is the largest, and it is there at night that the islander becomes uneasily aware of the souls of all the dead, the prehistoric blood-ritualists and the pirates. Yet (like Lawrence with his Rananim projects) he plans to make it a Happy Isle, a world of his own; he sets up a farming community, and is greeted as Master. Although the island is fertile, colourful with flowers, and almost frost-free, it transmits the lusts and cruelty of the past; the Master knows he is not loved and, as workers depart and bills come in, he is certain that it is malevolent and treacherous. He sells the island at a great loss, and takes refuge with a few assistants on a smaller island which was leased to him. It is rocky, with no ghosts of any ancient race. He spends most of his time indoors writing, 'not very fast, not very importantly, letting the writing spin softly from him as if it were drowsy gossamer'. The island is smirched by the automatic love between him and his typist. How different it would have been if there had been delicate desire between them, and they could be true (like Mellors and Lady Chatterley) to a 'frail, sensitive, crocus-flame of desire'. Having married and made provision for his wife, he abandons her, to live alone on an islet which he has bought on the outer fringe of the isles; it consists of a few acres of rocks, and is utterly devoid of trees and bushes. He gives up writing, and sits looking at the sea. Then his interest in the seabirds dies, and they desert the island. A boat brings letters which he leaves unopened and hides. The fishermen who bring them are repulsive, as are the sheep which they take away at his request. The whole animal creation is foul to him, and he feels a cruel satisfaction in the thought that soon nothing will be alive in all his regions. His mind is affected, and he is frequently ill. With winter and snow, he looks 'stupidly over the whiteness of his foreign island'. On the verge of death, he is reduced to the state of lifelessness which is reflected around him. Gradually the Utopian isolationist has become not a mere misanthropist but an anti-Lawrentian repudiator of all forms of life. The menace of idealism is carried to its final stage, and should be contrasted with Lawrence's philosophy in *Apocalypse* (see p. 65); it divorces the individual from nature and the community, creates non-fulfilment in love, and restricts him to the abstract inertness of a puny solipsistic world.

One of Lawrence's last stories, 'Things', was suggested by the Brewsters' habit of 'picking up' bric-à-brac in their travels. They are recognizable in the freedom-lovers whose souls climb towards 'the sun of old European culture or old Indian thought', only to find the props supporting their idealistic vines fall one after another, while (unknown to themselves) their 'horizontal' interests make them clutch at 'things'. Exaggeration and fiction are artfully introduced to create a story of delightful comic ironies, impersonal, and without malice. Indirectly it reflects the love of freedom which made Lawrence scorn the impedimenta of possessions.

*   *   *

'Sun' is not a success. Up to a point it is a *Lady Chatterley* story, the wife feeling a blood intimacy with the Mediterranean peasant which makes her wish that her next child could be his and not her husband's. The story is symbolical, the sun entering the woman's body, and relieving her and her child of tensions, until she feels a contempt for human beings. She had been at variance with her shy husband, a business man in America, and the iron had entered her soul; now she is a new person. He arrives unexpectedly, and sees her clothed in the 'golden-rose tan of the sun'. She cannot go back, but she is ready to bear his child. In the original text (published by Harry Crosby) the sun symbolism is clearer; the flower of the wife's womb radiates at the approach of her husband. The ending had been intended (like some of Lawrence's pictures and the later versions of *Lady Chatterley's Lover*) to 'shock people's castrated social spirituality' (27.ii.27). The wider symbolism of the story is to be found in 'Aristocracy' (P2.482).

The difficulty of resolving a symbolical story on sexual love is more obvious in 'Glad Ghosts'. Embodying Lawrence's central beliefs in an unusually gripping narrative, it remains one of his greatest short stories despite some niaiseries in its conclusion. The Lathkills are obvious resurrections of the married pair in 'The Thimble' and 'The Ladybird'; the story presents illustrations of the 'unsunned' people whom the 'Sun' wife regarded as 'graveyard worms'; and plum-blossom as a symbol of rebirth recalls the almond blossom of 'The Last Laugh'. How to quicken 'the unborn body of life hidden within the body of this half-death which we call life' is the kind of war which interests Lawrence's confident proponent Morier. This half-death in a house of ghosts is confirmed by a tomblike atmosphere, cold and suggestions of frost, inaudible pseudo-conversation, and images of snow and glaciers. The unappeased and peregrine ghost of Lucy whom the colonel had never known is eventually soothed, and the family ghost comes to Morier in the dead of night with miraculous results for the two couples who have suffered. But the most remarkable change comes over Lord Lathkill. Like the colonel and his wife, he and Carlotta have been almost ghosts to each other; their children had been born of will and disembodiment, and it is well that they died. His prayer is answered; he is clothed with flesh again, and he speaks for Lawrence on worshipping with the body according to the marriage service, on Jesus who was untouchable, and on the corpselike effect of consciousness on the body (cf. P.569–70).

'The Virgin and the Gipsy' was hurriedly written at the opening of 1926, and its setting in hilly Derbyshire is rendered unidentifiable by many misleading place-names. The opening develops slowly, with some vitriolic sketches of the Weekley family based partly on Barbara's recent gossip; and the fascination the gipsy has for Yvette ensures that the question whether she will disgrace her family at the rectory as her mother had done remains in suspense. Tension is generated with the arrival of subsidiary characters, to be followed by absurd sensationalism. On realistic grounds the story is rarely convincing; symbolically, it achieves little imaginative significance. The flood which appears like 'a wall of lions' may or may not echo 'the peculiarly *dangerous* sort of selfishness, like lions and tigers' of Yvette's mother, though the recurring snow-flower image threatens a similar revolt by the daughter. It comes to nothing; the flood does not carry away Yvette and the gipsy. He saves her, and vanishes. She loves him, but acquiesces in his disappearance, her 'young soul' knowing 'the wisdom of it'. Although he has awakened the early flower of her virginal self, and crystallized her hatred of the rectory, she has many selves which ignore him, and even find him distasteful. One of them is drawn to Major Eastwood, who loves his comforts, and has some of the characteristics of Gerald Crich. He is on his premarital honeymoon with a woman expecting her divorce, and the disgrace of Yvette's associating with them creates the first narrative crisis. Her father, the rector, is convinced of her depravity, and says he will kill her rather than let her go the way of her mother. The girl's 'calm, virgin contempt' is that of 'the free-born for the base-born', and is particularly directed against her grandmother, the 'fungoid' ruler of the home who is like a toad in 'the static inertia of her unsavoury power'. Lawrence wills her death, as Ramon does Carlota's (*PS.*xxi) and with a similar impersonal intent. Neither the evolution of the story nor, at times, the writing suggests critical attention. Leo's smile (unlike the gipsy's penetrating glance) hits Yvette on the outside of the body like a tennis ball; Yvette faints 'appropriately' when she is rescued at the end, and Aunt Cissie weeps 'gallons'.

The reverence with which Lawrence treats his theme in 'The Man Who Died' is expressed in cadences which are often Biblical. There is a parallel between the tied cock and the unnamed Jesus, bandaged and swathed in the tomb, but the escaped cock story (see p. 57) could have been reduced without any symbolical loss. Like the silken green wheat, the red anemones, and the flamelike new leaves of the fig-tree, the bird is but a 'wave-tip' in the tide of 'the swaying ocean of life'. The man who died had been dead in life; he had offered only the corpse of love, even as he had been served with it. His desire to compel had caused his death, but he has left his striving self in the tomb. The teacher and saviour are dead; his business is with his single life. Virginity had been an excess, a kind of greed. He had tried to embrace multitudes, though he had never embraced one person. Now he must be reborn in the body, 'for my reach ends in my finger-tips, and my stride is no longer than the ends of my toes'. After overtaking the two men (on the road to Emmaus) he gets rid of the cock, knowing that its 'aloneness can take on splendour' from the lure of its hens. The priestess of the sequel serves Isis in Search, Isis of 'the subtle lotus, the womb which waits submerged and in bud' for the touch of 'that other inward sun that streams its rays from the loins of the male Osiris'. She thinks that the man who has died is Osiris, and he tells her that he is, if she will heal him. In the ritual healing, the saving from 'death' (not without a touch of *gamin* impudence in 'I am risen'), Lawrence adduces his symbols of the crocus, the plum-blossom, and the sun. 'Suns beyond suns' had dipped the priestess in mysterious fire; her tender desire for the man who had died is like sunshine; and a new sun rises in 'the perfect inner darkness of himself'. She is also the heart of the rose which makes him part of 'the great rose of Space'. The most important expression of this cosmic wholeness recalls 'The Flying Fish' (p. 251), 'the greater day' being contrasted with 'the little day' of little people and unregenerate slaves. The man made whole escapes out to sea from the danger which 'the little life' threatens, promising to return as 'sure as spring' when 'the nightingale calls' from the 'valley-bed' of his healer. He has become like the cock, a wave-tip in the swaying ocean of life.

The remainder of Lawrence's stories are rather occasional and miscel-laneous. 'In Love' is a light, dashed-off comedy on 'lovey-dovey' idiocy, a fictional comment on a common conception of love which has a slight parallel with the theme of 'The Captain's Doll'. The young man is apt to think of his fiancée as if she were a motor-car, and Lawrence is carried away by the idea that she is 'up a tree'. The only question which maintains interest is whether a break between the couple is inevitable. 'Rawdon's Roof' is a slight venture in the Boccaccio style, with no Lawrentian overtones, the main story being that of a man who confirms his boast that no woman shall ever again sleep under his roof but remains ironically ignorant of what goes on in the servants' quarters. 'The Rocking-Horse Winner' is one of those rare stories which is like a parable that speaks for itself and almost defies commentary. Its subject is the will for worldly success which eats the heart out of the mother's life, and drives her anxious boy to frenzy and death. The nursery rocking-horse, intended for enjoyment, becomes a means to an end which can never be satisfied, absorbing, warping, and killing life. The picture of the boy, urging the horse with the energy of madness until he falls exhausted, symbolizes with more complete success than all the Gerald Crich scenes the usurpation and extinction of life by an insistent, worldly-motivated will.

'The Lovely Lady' is a contrived story with symbolism at many points.

Pauline Attenborough seems to have the secret of perennial youth. Its connection with the sun is superficial, for she takes her sun-bath within thick dark yew hedges, and at the critical point of the action their shadows are lengthening. The crucial situation of *Sons and Lovers* has been transplanted to an artificial setting: Pauline has drawn her vitality from the souls of her two sons; Henry is dead, and Robert will be but a 'shell' when she is dead. Cecilia loves him, and finds her life as negative as his, as a result of his mother's possessive spirit. The rain-pipe is the channel by which she hears revelations which enable her to deliver a quick mortal riposte. Pauline's will-power had been selfish and malevolent; emblematically she appears in 'a dress of black lace over ivory colour' and, when she is dying, has all her mirrors taken away. She had a collector's passion for beautiful and exotic things, and her anti-life interests are reflected after her death in the bequest of most of her wealth, with the nucleus of her valuable antiques, to 'The Pauline Attenborough Museum'.

In 'The Blue Moccasins' emotions generated by a call-up result in the marriage of a young man to a woman socially superior and more than twenty years his senior. After the war his married life becomes increasingly negative, and he finds happiness in the company of a war widow of his own age. There can be no doubt where Lawrence's sympathies lie. With the Christmas Eve theatricals he reaches a fascinating climax in what has all the appearance of an entertaining story. As in 'The Lovely Lady', *Lady Chatterley's Lover*, and other late stories, art or collecting *objets d'art* is associated with physical inanition; Lawrence's distinction is between the quick and the dead. How heavily it was intended to weigh against the elderly lady of this unfinished story is conjectural. In 'Mother and Daughter' the satire is unqualified. The two stories have much in common. One mother is ready to 'put the lid on' her sons' marriages, the other on her daughter's. Both are dehumanizing Circes who are finally defeated. Apart from its Bloomsbury setting, 'Mother and Daughter' has nothing really new in it; it is a selection of familiar Lawrentian ingredients, heavily spiced with the mother's sarcasm and her author's satire. Artificial, evidently composed in the head, Lawrence's last story prompts the question how much as a writer, much travelled but, by and large, restricted to a narrow life, he had lost and gained since he wrote 'Odour of Chrysanthemums' and 'Daughters of the Vicar' in 1911.

Other Writings

FRAGMENTS AND AN INTRODUCTION

There is nothing in *Mr Noon* to suggest that it is the Robert Burns novel which Lawrence projected in December 1912, though its 'spooning' was probably sufficient to disqualify it for the serialization he had contemplated (4.iv.21). If one wishes to find Lawrence relaxed, enjoying himself at length, and taking nothing human seriously, not even love, this fragment can be recommended for light, casual reading. It is a literary spree, at times in a manner almost reminiscent of Laurence Sterne; Lawrence thought it 'very comical'. The story is trivialized; the narrative is tenuous at times; the 'dear reader' humour is overdone: yet verve and wit continually well up, so much so that the non-publishing of the additional sections which have been discovered is regrettable. The subject was probably suggested by the vivacious style of the early chapters of *The Lost Girl*, in association with memories of Eastwood, for Lawrence began *Mr Noon* only a few days after completing that novel, and included Alvina Houghton in a memorable chapel scene. Most of it is treated episodically. The hero is based on George Neville (though Gilbert Noon was a contemporary student with Lawrence at the Ilkeston pupil-teacher centre), and one or two stories which Lawrence heard from the Hopkins are included. Lewis and Patty Goddard are William and Sallie Hopkin, and it was they who were caught in Eastwood Hall park as described in 'Aphrodite and the Cow'; the farcical greenhouse crisis occurred at New Eastwood, not far from the canal. The Eakrast scenes were created from Lawrence's visit (on a bicycle) to see Kitty Holderness and her father (p. 24) at Eakring.

Seriousness would detract from this high-spirited story, and twice

Lawrence narrowly evades an excess of it in 'Aphrodite and the Cow'·
The contemplation of star-shaped cracks at the end of trunk sections in a
woodyard threatens a lecture on histology and morphology; it gives
Lawrence the opportunity to present scientific explanations in a sceptical
light and to stress the element of individuality which is 'not attributable
to any cause'. Patty Goddard's efforts to rouse a more serious attitude
towards women and marriage makes Mr Noon self-consciously aware of
a new Aphrodite emerging from 'the stiff dark sea of middle-aged
matronliness, an Aphrodite drenched with knowledge'. She feels that
he is looking at her with 'strange, full eyes, seeing her in her unguessed
ivory-soft nudity . . . and desiring her with a profound desire . . . like a
deep, far-off bell booming, or a sea coming up'. Further embarrassment
on this score is driven out by terror of the charging cow. When she is
escorted home, she wishes above all things to join her husband.

Lawrence makes great play with the imagery of idiomatic English.
The pretty kettle of fish which was being prepared for Mr Noon when
he was summoned before a meeting *in camera* of his Education Com-
mittee proves to be 'all lobsters but one'. Patty's talk on a State Endow-
ment of Motherhood (recalled in 'The Overtone') knocks the wind out of
Mr Noon's sails as he sits at her tea-table 'like a water-logged hulk'. Was
he to remain there 'like a leaky wreck foundering? Thank goodness his
legs had taken the matter into their own hands – pardon the Irishism –
and had jerked him on his feet.' With 'morning at seven' and breakfast
bacon recalling one of Thomas Hood's puns ('why shouldn't she, as well
as some Earl's daughter, enrich the dip of her bacon with Browning?')
we reach the nadir of Lawrence's wit in this free-and-easy, bright-and-
breezy holiday scribble. When the hero joins Emmie and her intended
at Eakrast, the flow of conversation is frozen; the eternal triangle becomes
obtuse-angled, and Lawrence adjures the *Deus ex machina* to 'get up
steam and come to our assistance', promising (the cow in this volume
having 'jumped over the moon') a second volume in which 'the dish,
dear reader, shall run away with the spoon. Scandalous the elopement,
and a *decree nisi* for the fork.'

If this, in mood at least, is at one end of Lawrence's fictional scale,
'The Flying Fish' is at the other. It was penned by Frieda at Lawrence's
dictation when he was recovering from his illness in Mexico (p. 53). At
Gsteig-bei-Gstaad he read it to the Brewsters, telling them that the final
section was intended to be about 'regenerate man'. He had an intuition

250

that he would never finish it; it was written 'so near the borderline of death' that he had never been able 'to carry it through, in the cold light of day'. With the vision of the sea-creatures in the Gulf of Mexico, inspired by recollections of *Moby Dick* as well as of the voyage from Vera Cruz to Havana on his return to London at the end of 1923 (for the reference in 'St Mawr' see p. 240), Lawrence's prose reaches one of its highest levels of purity and magic. Such at times is the effect of verbal translucency within varying rhythms that a dreamlike spell of images in motion is created where conscious awareness of words hardly exists.

The narrative-descriptive backbone of the fragment is autobiographical. Although Daybrook is in Derbyshire, the name came from the village outside Nottingham which Lawrence knew from his visits to the Chambers after they had left Haggs Farm. It is chosen for its symbolical import, Lawrence's subject being the attainment of 'the Greater Day', a life which is true and full. As Gethin Day, he sees it in the eyes of the Mexicans; but something in their impassivity, their 'dying back into the Greater Day', repels him, and he wishes to return home, chiefly because his sister Lydia (named after Lawrence's mother) is dead or dying, and his family tradition runs, 'No Day in Daybrook; for the Vale a bad outlook'. In his *Book of Days* (the title recalls both Daybrook and the Chambers, after *The Book of Days, A Miscellany of Popular Antiquities*, published by W. & R. Chambers, London and Edinburgh) his ancestor had described Daybrook as an ark, and added, 'While Day there be in Daybrook, the floods shall not cover the Vale nor shall they ride over England completely.' Their significance is similar to that of the flood in *The Rainbow*, as is clear from another passage, where an allusion to the 'Sons of God' is unmistakable: 'little men will shudder and die out' while 'tall men remain alone in the land, moving deeper in the Greater Day . . . Even as the flying fish, when he leaves the air and recovereth his element in the depth, plunges and invisibly rejoices.' The weather-vane at Daybrook is a flying fish.

In saying that Gethin Day wished to return home, where he would 'dare face the sun behind the sun, and come into his own in the Greater Day', Lawrence assumes the cosmic imagery of *The Plumed Serpent*, which he had just finished (see p. 198). The *Book of Days* shows that the Greater Day includes death: 'Thou art a fish of the timeless Ocean, and must needs fall back. . . . Cease then the struggle of thy flight, and fall back into the deep element where death is and is not, and life is not a fleeing away.' The 'timeless Ocean' is given greater clarification in 'The Proper Study', which is the relationship of man to the 'Oceanic God', 'the Father, not the Son, of all our beginnings'. Then, Lawrence concludes, 'you realize the new relation of man. Men like fishes lifted on a great wave of the God of the End, swimming together, and apart, in a new medium. A new relation, in a new whole' (P.722–3).

On caring and knowing (represented by 'the Son') and the full life, the *Book of Days* runs:

> Thou hast a sun in thee, and it is not timed. Therefore wait . . . and be at peace with thine own sun. . . And if a nightingale would not sing, his song unsung in him would slay him . . . unsung songs are the Erinyes, the impure Furies of vengeance. . . . Take no care, for what thou knowest is ever less than what thou art. The full fire even of thine own sun in thine own body, thou canst never know.

Gethin finds his ancestor's words more real to him than his surroundings. At Vera Cruz there is a strike; it is a point where the wild primeval 'day' of the natives meets the white man's 'day', and the result is 'a port of nullity, nihilism concrete and actual, calling itself the city of the True Cross'.

'The little day' is seen also at Havana. 'See Naples and die', comments Lawrence. 'Go seeing any place, and you'll be half dead of exhaustion and tedium by dinner time.' The Atlantic is 'like a cemetery'. All this is in contrast to the Greater Day which is experienced in the Gulf of Mexico, with the flying fish and the porpoises. Gethin is spell-bound as he watches their exhilarating movements, the sheer joy of life which men have lost or never accomplished. 'What civilization will bring us to such a pitch of swift laughing togetherness, as these fish have reached?' Whether, after the evanescence of his initial inspiration, Lawrence could ever have brought this religious novel to a successful conclusion is doubtful. His notes seem to confirm his doubt; they suggest an intermediate stage of fantastic invention (see the Penguin edition of D. H. Lawrence, *'The Princess' and Other Stories*, 1971, p. 9). His dilemma was more like that of Coleridge over 'Kubla Khan' than his own over 'The Blue Moccasins'. He comes back to the subject in 'The Man Who Died' but, successful though that story is, its range does not extend to the whole of 'the Greater Day'.

One picture of it is found in the untitled fragment which describes

the imaginary changes which Lawrence found in Eastwood after a Rip
Van Winkle sleep of a thousand years. His millennium is Etruscan
rather than English, and it assumes a change of climate which is more
desirable than probable. '[Autobiographical Fragment]', as it has been
labelled, begins rather like an essay intended for *Assorted Articles*, its
subject being changes in the generations, to the tune 'We are such
stuff as our grandmothers' dreams were made on'. In the general
analysis, we can see how the failure of Lawrence's mother to make her
husband conform found recompense in elevating her children. The
miners of Lawrence's generation have, as a result of such forces, become
'decent' and submissive, 'with smart daughters and bossy wives and
cigarette-smoking lads of their own'. In the economic depression they are
'spectral' and self-effacing. This is the main feature in the background
to the dream of the sequel. Lawrence then looks at the changes in the
scene, especially at Moorgreen colliery, as he takes (in imagination) his
familiar walk to a quarry, where he curls up in a tiny cave and falls
asleep. When he wakens he does not know whether he has slept a
minute or an eternity. We are in the world of Utopian fiction.

The colliery, the railway lines, and the hedgerow enclosures have
all gone, yet the land is tended. Oxen are employed for hauling. Everyone speaks in the vernacular. In the late afternoon light, the town on
the top of the hill appears yellow, its curved walls rising amid orchards,
and looking 'soft and majestical'. The imaginary Lawrence knows that
it had been his birthplace, 'the ugly colliery townlet of dirty red brick'.
In the evening he walks past where the Wesleyan and Congregational
chapels had stood: the former site is 'all softly lighted, golden-coloured
porticoes, with people passing in green or blue or grey-and-scarlet cloaks';
the latter is a circular space with a central tower like a lighthouse,
rosy-coloured in the lamplight, supporting a big ball of light away in the
sky. In the sun many people walk naked, the young women rosy-tanned,
with fringed girdles round their hips, their folded smocks in bundles
on their heads. The men are ruddy and bare-headed, many with trimmed
beards, some clean-shaven. All radiate life and, though new life comes
to the awakened sleeper, he envies the wholeness of the inhabitants –
'body and mind and spirit, without split'. As the sun sets, they gather
in the square; music and dancing begin, and it sweeps into rhythmic
unison, onlookers accompanying with song under the vaulted porticoes.
All happens by instinct 'like the wheeling and flashing of a shoal of

fish or of a flock of birds dipping and spreading in the sky'. In wishing to be 'a drop in that wave of life' Lawrence unites the fulfilment of 'The Man Who Died' with the Greater Day of 'The Flying Fish'. Life is communal and free. All is instinctive cleanliness and comeliness. When, after learning that he has slept a thousand years, Lawrence asks how much longer he has to live, he is told that 'life is not a clock'. As it is written in the *Book of Days*, 'Thou hast a sun in thee, and it is not timed.' '[Autobiographical Fragment]' is primarily an attempt to present Lawrence's idea of regenerate man; incidentally it is an indictment of the aesthetic poverty of England, the 'dry, brittle, terrible corruption spreading over the face of the land', as it is seen at the end of *The Rainbow*.

* * *

Lawrence knew Maurice Magnus, the American-born, illegitimate grandson of a German Kaiser, from November 1919, when he met him with Norman Douglas in Florence, to May 1920, when he left him in Malta. He was a fervent Roman Catholic convert, living like a first-class citizen, though continually in debt and fleeing from justice. Lawrence's principal aim in writing an introduction to his *Memoirs of the Foreign Legion* (P2.303ff.) was the repayment of Magnus's debts to the two Maltese who had assisted him before his suicide. How Lawrence became responsible for the publication of Magnus's work in 1924 is best told by Lawrence himself in a letter to *The New Statesman* (P.806–7), in reply to complaints and accusations by Norman Douglas. Lawrence's determination to record the whole truth seems as evident in this as in his introduction. Written in 1922, about two years after the events of its most memorable episode, it illustrates abundantly his wonderful faculty of graphic recall. It is a novelist's introduction, with much dialogue and vivid narrative description, and almost a masterpiece. Altogether it is superior to a great deal in Lawrence's novels, with the tragically insidious Magnus emerging as one of his most real characters.

How Lawrence's generosity repeatedly 'saved the life' of this confirmed misogynist (Mr May in *The Lost Girl*); how he had to listen to the profuse complaints of the insistent Sicilian creditor Melenga; how Magnus boarded the ship for Malta like the grandest gentleman on earth, and went immediately into hiding to escape his porter and the carabinieri: these, and many other details that hold the reader, have less significance than features in the account of Lawrence's two-day visit to Monte Cassino, where Magnus had sought refuge. Lawrence remembers looking up at the blue, big-faced old clock on the campanile in the piazza of Capri as he set off one dark January morning; he imagines colourful Renaissance life in the Bramante courtyard at Monte Cassino; he recalls the varicoloured marbles of the church, as he walked round in Magnus's 'millionairish' big black overcoat, Magnus 'bowing waxily down' till his knee touched the pavement; recalls too the examination of 'queer fat babies' among the carvings of the choir stalls, and the glittering mosaics of the illuminated crypt. It is with Lawrence's thoughts and feelings, however, that the narrative reaches a higher plane. He felt that he was in the old world of the Middle Ages, especially when he saw how humble the peasants were kept. To Magnus this was as it should be, but Lawrence could not accept his superiority, and preferred one old peasant who caught his attention; he had a strong 'blood-presence' and lacked Magnus's complacency, glib talk, and conceit. Lawrence was certain that the 'leading-classes' with their education and culture were parasites, sapping the tree of life, which 'still remains in the lower classes'; (hence the retention of the vernacular in his Utopian Eastwood). Magnus hoped to be a monk, but Lawrence thought him too worldly. He himself could not retreat; looking down to the plain, he realized what a barren world it was with its democracy, industrialism, socialism, and its Communist and Fascist flags; but he knew that one had to 'go through with the life down there', and 'get somewhere beyond it'.

Unlike Malta, 'stark as a corpse', Sicily with its Greek associations rouses Lawrence to lyricism. From Fontana Vecchia he sees Calabria like a changing opal across the bright blue straits, the sun rising with 'a splendour like trumpets' every morning, as he rejoices in this 'day-dawn, life-dawn, the dawn which is Greece, which is me'. The 'peaky, pointed, bunched effect of many-tipped Sicily in the north' is contrasted with the sinuous sky-line along the south coast beyond the beautiful round harbour at Syracuse, 'where the Athenian ships came'. He recalls a journey from Catania to Syracuse, winding round the blueness of the sea in spring (before 'the serpent' Magnus arrived), with purple anemones in the fields and 'Adonis-blood red on the little ledges', the tall pink asphodel dying, and 'the yellow asphodel like a lily showing her silk'. 'Lovely, lovely Sicily, the dawn-place, Europe's dawn, with Odysseus pushing his ship out of the shadows into the blue. Whatever had died for me, Sicily had not then died: dawn-lovely Sicily, and the Ionian Sea.'

Though he regarded Magnus as a 'little loving vampire', one of the many 'kiss-giving Judases' who traded on his power to arouse affection and even tenderness (one who should have died sooner), Lawrence admired him for the way in which, 'like a good rat', he was determined not to be trapped. He showed it in the French Legion, and Lawrence liked 'the sharp and quick way he made use of every one of his opportunities to get out of that beastly army'. On the subject of war Lawrence loses self-control. We must face up to humanity's criminal tendency, he says. Knowledge is like vaccination; it prevents 'the continuing of ghastly moral disease'. Because the 'scamp' and 'hypocrite' Magnus resisted war, Lawrence is 'with him through eternity'. The thought of the foulness of war whips him into megalomaniac raving. As long as he is a man, 'such a war shall never occur again'. Diabolic mechanisms are man's, therefore his; and he smashes them 'into oblivion'. 'Men have conjured them up. I, a man, will conjure them down again. Won't I? – but I will! I am not one man, I am many, I am most.' For once he is *Vox Populi*. The idea is unexceptionable; it is the manner which is ludicrous, the one absurdity in a work of considerable genius.

Public appearances were uppermost in Magnus's mind to the very end: 'I want to be buried first-class, my wife will pay', he wrote just before his suicide. Their marriage had broken down; perhaps she despised him, but she paid.

TRAVEL

Personal and psychological reasons for Lawrence's unresting doom after he left England in 1912 are not hard to find; during the war period his unrest was maddeningly aggravated by a sense of persecution and disgust which drove him like a goad. Behind the positive movements in his 'savage pilgrimage' there was always a 'yearning to land on the coasts of illusion' (P.343). He was happy in Sicily, but the search for 'inner realities' made him travel east. Ill-health compelled him to give up New Mexico, where he found much happiness on the ranch in the milder seasons. Undoubtedly novelty of life and scene was a gratification from the very start of his odyssey (cf. 17.i.13); it was also a literary stimulus, as his letters and works abundantly testify (cf. *LG*.xiv–xvi, *Kangaroo*, and the protracted but magnificent Tyrolean climax of 'The Captain's Doll'). Lawrence's visual response was swift and clear, and he could revive impressions with extraordinary facility in his creative writing. 'What with Rockies and Indians and deserts . . . *you ought to find something to paint and I to write*', he told Jan Juta when he thought of leaving Sicily for Taos (9.i.22). In a letter to Catherine Carswell from Taos (29.ix.22) he stated that seeing the world excited only 'the outside' of him, adding very significantly, 'It is all a form of running away from oneself and the great problems: all this wild west and the strange Australia.' Eventually he found it a relief to return to the Mediterranean, 'and gradually let the tight coils inside oneself come slack'. There was much more life in 'a deep insouciance, which really is the clue to faith' than in the 'frenzied, keyed-up care' which was characteristic of western civilization, and found at its most intense in America (P.118).

Novels such as *Aaron's Rod* (cf. P.60–4) and *The Plumed Serpent* are rich in travel impressions; a visit to Ceylon evoked the most ambitious descriptive poem in *Birds, Beasts and Flowers;* early impressions in Europe (P.71–86) and later ones (P.45–58, 107–10, 117–32) are the subject of descriptive essays; likewise, Indian dances and Taos (P.92–103), the exasperating malevolence of Mexico (P.104–6), and the merciless magnificence of New Mexico (P.141–7). Four of his works are commonly regarded as travel books. Of these, only one belongs strictly to that genre; two consist of sketches, and one is a guidebook of special quality and distinction.

Twilight in Italy is rather a hybrid, including Lawrence's first outlines of his basic philosophy. The sketches were written from the end of 1912, after Lawrence had settled at Gargnano, to October 1913, and revised in 1915 for publication in book form. The first essay, a revision of 'Christs in the Tirol' (P.82–6), discusses variations Lawrence noticed in crucifixes from Bavaria across the Alps, with special attention to some half-dozen. Only high up did they express 'the old beauty and religion'. Below the Brenner one was foppish; others were sentimental or sensationally gory. Lawrence's essay is reverential; his sympathy is for the Christ who resists suffering and finds no solution to his soul's anxiety in death. The crucifix reflects the Bavarian peasant, mindless, mystically sensuous in his physical experience, with the eternal negativeness or radiance of 'not-being' in the snows above him. Hence his beauty and completeness for Lawrence; for him there is 'no becoming and no passing away. Everything *is*, now and for ever.'

The first of the Gargnano scenes is a poetical sermon by the priest of love. After meeting the aged spinner high above the lake, and discovering that she lives unselfconsciously in her own world, Lawrence climbs higher, gazing at the rocks and cypress spires high up in the sunlight, then at the 'mist of grey-green olives fuming down to the lake-side'. Presently he sees below him two monks who seem to slide between the 'naked, bony vines' of their garden. Snow on the mountains beyond them takes on a rosy glow; above it the rising moon gradually makes day and night one. The little old woman had gone; she lived for the sunshine, and knew nothing of 'the unknown, through the senses', under 'a superb moon'. The monks continued their walk in a neutral shadow. Neither 'the completeness of night' nor 'the flare of day' reached them. 'Neither the blood nor the spirit spoke in them, only the law. . .'. Where then is 'the supreme ecstasy', uniting day and night, soul and body, under the moon? Where is 'the meeting-point', 'day hovering in the embrace of the coming night' like Persephone in the arms of Pluto?

The next two essays, 'The Lemon Gardens' and 'The Theatre', have Gargnano settings. The former is little more than a pretext for two instalments of philosophy (pp. 66–7), followed by an attack on English industrialism. Fortunately the human interest of 'The Theatre' outweighs the philosophy. Subjective no doubt but alive, it gives us a pictorial analysis of a community. Lawrence concludes that it is matriarchy which makes the young men emigrate to America. He sympathizes fully with the leading character in the local production of Ibsen's *Ghosts* whose spirit cries out helplessly 'through the insistent, inflammable flesh' in a way which is alien to the 'mental and perverted' approach to sex in Scandinavian writers. The rhetoric of D'Annunzio, 'bosh' though it is, controls 'the current of the blood' and makes him popular. Lawrence's reaction to the suffering heroine of the stage is admirably revelatory though admittedly ambivalent. He is revolted by Hamlet's sense of corruption in the flesh; and the question 'To be, or not to be' leads to a discussion of human fulfilment and a convenient historico-philosophical interpretation of the play in a context extending back to Orestes and from the Middle Ages to the twentieth century.

As winter passes, the sunshine is like iced wine; flowers appear, and bright colours change on Lake Garda and the snow-covered heights.

With spring, we move to San Gaudenzio (p. 30). The first main subject is the family with whom the Lawrences stayed in the farm on the headland overlooking the lake, particularly old Paolo, who had been driven by his mercenary wife Maria to the goldmines of America for the sake of her children. The elder son would go too, for the old order of Paolo (who had an instinctive reverence for gentlemen, thinking they belonged to 'the aristocracy of the spirit') is changing, and San Gaudenzio is no longer prosperous. 'The Dance' testifies to Maria's cupidity and to the malicious humour of the local peasants under the influence of wine; (for the wild wood-cutter with the wooden leg, see 5.iv.13). Lawrence's conclusion that Il Duro, the expert vine-grafter who had made his money in America and had 'seen too much' to marry, was a single, isolated being like Pan is less convincing than his sketch of John, who had given up his training as a civil engineer when his widower father, a courtly, handsome innkeeper, had wanted him to look after his shop. He had then emigrated to America, where, after almost killing a man for calling him a 'damn Dago', he had become a foreman in a store. When Lawrence first saw him, he was long-haired and shabby in his American clothes, playing in the village band. He had returned to do military service, rather than be debarred from seeing his father, and was going back to America, perhaps for four or five years, leaving his wife and child.

'Italians in Exile' describes the first part of Lawrence's second walking tour through the Alps (p. 31), with particular reference to a group he met rehearsing a play near Lake Zurich. They were members of a colony of Italian families who worked at a silk factory. On the stage the party seemed like magic in a barren country. They were passionately fond of Italy, but would never go back. Lawrence thought it strange that, when northern Europe was 'turning back on its own Christianity', the Italians should be ready to suffer 'a death in the flesh' for the sake of riches and greater freedom. His return to Italy is continued in the final sketch. It has a general and biographical interest, but little of special significance. An Englishman, with snow-burned face, driven by his will into 'cruel self-torture of fatigue', seems, in conjunction with mountain-tops 'like death' with 'transcendent snow', a forestalment of Gerald Crich. Lawrence's 'joy of progression' southwards and his sense of Pan on the southern Alpine slopes are diminished by modern developments such as tourism, villas, cubical houses, mechanization, navvy-work, and a terrifying disintegration of the old stability. The main idea in the title of this rather uneven collection is posed pictorially in the concluding pages of 'The Spinner and the Monks'.

Sea and Sardinia was written within six weeks of Lawrence's return from his excursion to the island with Frieda in January 1921. She thought he had described 'every minute' of it 'with extraordinary accuracy'. He relied entirely on memory, and the work bears wonderful testimony to his sharp powers of observation and recall. Few writers have transcribed life more vividly and dramatically. Undoubtedly Lawrence's enthusiasm flagged towards the end of his island journey, but that was due to tiredness, the monotony of a long bus journey, and the declining interest of the countryside. The book is often more enjoyable than were the experiences it narrates; there are few pages in it which are not sparkling or dynamic. The vital immediacy of its impact is strengthened, particularly in the first half, by the predominance of narrative in the present tense and often in a staccato style. Further differentiation from travel-writers like Kinglake comes from Lawrence's confident recourse to racy idiom: kitchen filth swilkers back and forth along the ship's side; an old woman who has vacated a seat she does not need on the train chunters her head off when it is taken; and a 'sludge-queen' waitress at an inn planks down lumps of bread on a dirty cloth. Visual personification imparts some lively detail: the steamer smokes her cigarette, and a big boat turns her posterior to the quay; hills at dawn prick up their ears on the skyline, and railway engines stroll about sidelines, snuffing at trucks.

Sudden impulse prompted this trip. Free from 'the hemmed-in life' and 'the horror of human tension' which has been a 'long-drawn-out agony' among 'resistant people on land', Lawrence wishes he could 'sail for ever, on a small, quiet, lonely ship, from land to land and isle to isle', sauntering through the spaces of 'this lovely world'. The openness of Sardinia is like liberty itself, after the peaky confines of Sicily. At Mandas he was reminded of Cornwall and the Derbyshire uplands; it was Celtic country, 'far more moving, disturbing, than the glamour of Italy and Greece'. On the road to Nuoro, seeing frost among 'the tangled, still savage bushes', he was thrilled again; Italy had given him a knowledge of the past, but all was not *connu*. Life is not only 'a process of rediscovering backwards' but a move forwards; there are 'unknown, unworked lands where the salt has not lost its savour'.

Colour excites him, even in fruit and vegetable markets. On the ship at Palermo he watches pale gold clouds and turquoise sky over Monte

Pellegrino, and yellow carts on the quayside, drawn by mules 'nodding their high weird plumes of scarlet'. In Cagliari the red of the full-petticoated peasant woman 'goes flash-flash-flash, like a bird showing its colours'. For colourful detail nothing surpasses the description of the Sunday procession at Tonara; Lawrence regards the women closely, noticing the studs of gold filigree which fasten 'the full-bosomed white shirts' at the throat, and great white sleeves billowing from scarlet, purplish-and-green-edged boleros. Yet 'all the strange magic of Sardinia' is in the sight of a solitary peasant in his black and white costume, like a magpie on the landscape. Lawrence sees naked trees he would like to paint: poplars of a 'ghostly, almost phosphorescent luminousness' in the shadow of a valley, and 'the gleaming mauve-silver fig', coldly incandescent, 'tangled, like some sensitive creature emerged from the rock'. As he writes, the recollection of almond trees poising sky-rosy on the sun-pale land near Orosei has the pure glamour of a lost pearl.

There were amusing incidents. Few can forget the wife who wandered too far at a station, and was last seen raising her arms to heaven, then bringing them down in utter despair on her head as her train drove off with her fat, furious husband; or the man who, after trying to travel free on the bus with two black squealing piglets, was speechless with rage and flung them like two bottles over the saddle of an attendant ass. The driver, whose seriousness earns him the sobriquet of Hamlet or Rochester, takes vindictive delight in making someone who has kept him waiting think he has lost his bus. Lawrence is full of admiration for his driving, but not that of his inexpert assistant, who entertains the hope that Lawrence would employ him as his chauffeur in England. On the whole however, close contact with humanity was not pleasing. Rarely were accommodation and food satisfactory. Those who served on the ship to Sardinia were 'voracious blowflies'; and so it was at Sorgono, nestling high up among wooded slopes ironically reminiscent of Hardy's country. One walk, while he and Frieda waited for dinner, took them without warning into the 'public lavatory' of a lane. The finishing touch comes with the long wait in the dungeon of a room, seeing a kid roasted expertly until it is done to a turn, then, after further delay, being served with cold portions, mainly of bone. No wonder they envied the soldiers on the boat for Italy their plentiful portions of roast fowl, kid, legs of lamb, and bread, with wine.

In Sardinia it had been reassuring to find manly peasants, though it was a reminder that the race of men was extinct in Europe, with its 'Christ-like heroes', 'woman-worshipping Don Juans, and rabid equality-mongrels'. Lawrence was glad that tenderness did not seem to be a Sardinian quality, preferring the 'old salty way of love' to sentiment and 'the maccaroni slithery-slobbery mess of modern adorations'. At Nuoro it had been a blessed relief to find really well-bred people who did not show off, and knew a man 'stands alone' despite all attributes; equally, a relief to see life as it really is, without affectation and 'sights', even Peruginos. In contact with more worldly citizens, Lawrence was continually irritated – with talk of liras buzzing round his ears 'like venomous mosquitoes', barbed remarks on an exchange rate in England's favour, and talk on post-war Europe which convinced him that, deep down, the envious Italians were full of hatred towards Britain. The sight of the towering Sicilian coast, with its old Grecian magic, raised his spirits; he was glad to get off the ship at Palermo. With the marionette show, and the old witch who, like snow-capped Etna, has occupied man's soul and estranged it from his body, he was his old self. The audience hated her, and Lawrence loved their 'generous, hot southern blood, so subtle and spontaneous, that asks for blood contact, not for mental communion or spirit sympathy'.

The last brief sketch in *Mornings in Mexico* is a recollection of Lawrence's ranch which was written at Spotorno on the evening of St Catherine's Day, 1925, in an attempt to round off a bifurcated assemblage of Mexican and New Mexican subjects. The first four are related, and were written at Oaxaca in December 1924. The three which follow are on ritualistic Indian dances, the first providing a general introduction to the corn dance which Lawrence saw at San Domingo in March 1924, and to the Hopi snake dance which he may have seen the following August.

Few readers will find 'Corasmin and the Parrots' as diverting as Lawrence seems to have done when he wrote it. He indulges the fancy that an explosion theory accounts for new species and mutations better than the theory of evolution, finding support in the Aztec succession of Suns (worlds created and destroyed), and applying it to the parrots and the dog Corasmin, to monkeys and men, and to the communication barrier between himself and his young Indian servant Rosalino. The walk from Oaxaca to Huayápam presents prospects of Mexican country and interesting glimpses of village life; Rosalino may be a 'dumb-bell', but he is shrewder than Lawrence in judging the Mexicans. A brief analysis of the Indian conception of the 'white monkey' race leads in 'The Mozo' to an account of Rosalino's habits. The Aztec goddess of love brought forth an obsidian knife; the image is applied to young Mexican men with their taut, keen bodies and black flinty eyes, and to Rosalino when a 'reptilian' gloom envelops him after his visit to Huayá-pam; nostalgia inspired by the Indian hill-village had intensified the conflict within him which began when, on receiving his photograph from Frieda, his mother had asked him to return home. Marketing makes him feel happier, and ultimately he wishes to stay, even to go to England, with the Lawrences. He is afraid that he will be caught and ill-treated by soldiers of one party or another, as had happened to him in the last revolution. 'Market Day' has interesting bargaining scenes, but its theme is the need for contact which motivates the 'centripetal flow' of Indians from the country. The market is the centre where life concentrates, and the intimacy it renews is more important than sale or purchase.

To understand Indian dances, Lawrence tells us to dispense with the kind of consciousness with which we look on stage productions as if we were 'little gods in a democratic heaven'. Indian song and dance are not individual but tribal, an experience of the blood-stream, the spirit seeking identification with the life-forces of sky and earth. There is no god in Indian religion; creation is for ever flowing; all is godly. Virtue lies in the heroic response to this creative wonder. 'Dance of the Sprouting Corn' illustrates this magnificently; Lawrence's art is more conscious, and his prose more rhythmic, here than anywhere else in this volume. His first description of the Hopi snake dance (CL.802–4) is a satirical *jeu d'esprit* on the American sight-seer; how far it differs from the views of the Lawrence who wrote *The Plumed Serpent* can be seen in *Mornings in Mexico*. The snakes of the dance return to the earth (which has its own dark sun) with man's 'messages of tenderness, of request, and of power', which are then transmitted to 'the dark heart of the first of suns'. Only from this come 'the rays that make men strong and glad', 'gods who can range between the known and the unknown'. The old animistic ideas inspiring Indian ritualistic dance were akin to Lawrence's own cosmic vision.

Etruscan Places was planned as a book of twelve sketches, only six of which were completed (10.x.27). Ill-health made it impossible for

Lawrence to visit all the sites he wished to see, and the book was published posthumously (1932). He first thought of it in April 1926, having been attracted to 'Etruscan things' in the museum at Perugia. One of his principal reasons for moving to Villa Mirenda, Scandicci, was to be better situated for travelling in pursuance of his research, but it was not until April 1927 that he was able to visit Cerveteri, Tarquinia, Vulci, and Volterra, in the company of Earl Brewster. It was the danger of malaria which made him choose this season (and resist the temptation to live in the foothills near Vulci). Lawrence's affinity with the Etruscan spirit, together with his knowledge of the subject from visits to Italian museums and from English and Italian writers (particularly George Dennis and Pericle Ducati) enabled him to form his impressions rapidly. The essays were completed before the end of June.

Much space is devoted to descriptive accounts of the visits to the sites, and those to Vulci and Volterra are impressive; but the vivacity of *Sea and Sardinia* has gone, and the personal element is less to the fore. The appeal of wild flowers, especially the asphodel, cannot be withstood. Lawrence artfully associates with the scene before him evocations of the Etruscan past (sometimes, one suspects, more in terms of their art than of reality); and it is his obsession with blood-consciousness which explains the beauty of proportion in the underground chambers at Cerveteri, and the 'vivid, warm faces' of some of the local peasants. The painted legend '*Mussolini ha sempre ragione*' amuses him. 'Some are born infallible, some achieve infallibility, and some have it thrust upon them', he comments, adding that it is not for him to interfere in foreign affairs: 'Let those rule who can rule.' He is no museum-lover, is obviously disappointed to find Vulci 'tomb-rifled', and thinks that, if there must be museums, they should be small and local. What one wants is contact with the past; the Etruscans are not 'a theory or a thesis' but an experience. For Lawrence systematization of knowledge tends to destroy the 'vital touch'.

The painted tombs of Tarquinia evoke his most lyrical descriptions. The walls of the Tomb of Leopards are 'a dance of real delight', the art of which, like that of Lawrence's prose, is lost in the communion. 'You cannot think of art, but only of life itself, as if this were the very life of the Etruscans . . . dancing and fluting along through the little olive-trees, out in the fresh day.' He finds a real sense of touch, 'one of the rarest qualities, in life as well as in art', in the Etruscan figures. Painting after painting expresses a vitality, a 'natural flowering of life' which reflects the Etruscan religion. The whole cosmos was alive; it had its great soul or *anima*. 'The active religious idea' behind 'all the great old civilizations' was that man could absorb life from the cosmos until he blazed like a god. For this reason the old kings and the Etruscan Lucomones are clothed in scarlet. They are 'the vermilion clue to the mystery and the delight of death and life', the 'life-bringers and the death-guides'. The Etruscan people gained a sense of these mysteries from ritual and such symbols as the tombs display. Balancing the inner fire of the earth, for example, was the sea, out of which all things emerge and into which they return. The dolphin, 'which gives up the sea's rainbows only when he dies', leaps suddenly in and out of it (cf. the poems 'They Say the Sea is Loveless' and 'Whales Weep Not!'). Beyond the sea and the ultimate fire lay that 'oneness' which only the Lucomones knew. It was because the fish was the *anima* of the sea that it came to represent Jesus, especially in Italy, where the people still thought in Etruscan symbols. The continual repetition of lion against deer represents 'the polarized activity of the divine cosmos', the process of destruction and creation which Lawrence accepted as a principle of life.

He thought that the 'strange potency and beauty' of Etruscan art was due to its symbolical profundity. It demonstrates the non-anthropomorphic quality of all those natural forces 'which go to the building up and the destroying of the soul'. The 'undivided Godhead' is symbolized in the *mundum*, the plasm-cell with its nucleus, so different from the Christian conception of the Word; it remains 'alive and unbroken to the end, the eternal quick of all things', the source of nature which changes through division and subdivision. The Etruscans lived by the 'subjective control' of these great natural powers; they fell before the 'objective power' of the Romans. With the supervention of Greek and Roman thought came 'the idea of a gloomy Hades, a hell and purgatory. To the peoples of the great natural religions the after-life was a continuing of the wonder-journey of life.' How far the Etruscan religion harmonized with Lawrence's may best be seen in some of his last great poems.

THE PLAYS

So prolific was Lawrence's writing (novels, short stories, poetry, letters) during his period of post-collegiate teaching that his attention to drama

265

is often overlooked. His mimetic talent was exceptional, and his interest in the theatre and play-reading is noted in Jessie Chambers' memoirs. By September 1911 he had composed three lengthy plays; they had been sent to Ford Madox Hueffer, who had mislaid two of them. All were returned the following spring (at the time of the General Strike) with a note from Mrs Hueffer that they might have 'taken quite well', collieries being 'in the air', but perhaps it was not too late to get them published 'with the aid of Mr Garnett'. Form would never be Lawrence's strong point, she commented with prophetic insight. Lawrence did not quite agree, and thought the plays very interesting (5.iv.12). After sending more plays to Garnett, he wrote (1.ii.13):

> I believe that, just as an audience was found in Russia for Tchehov, so an audience might be found in England for some of my stuff, if there were a man to whip 'em in. It's the producer that is lacking, not the audience. I am sure we are sick of the rather bony, bloodless drama we get nowadays – it is time for a reaction against Shaw and Galsworthy and Barker and Irishy (except Synge) people – the rule and measure mathematical folk . . . I don't want to write like Galsworthy nor Ibsen, nor Strindberg . . . We have to hate our immediate predecessors, to get free from their authority.

Garnett too was critical of Lawrence's formal shortcomings, for Lawrence had requested the return of his plays in the hope of 're-casting and re-forming them' (14.xi.12). Soon he had a new play; 'no doubt,' he told Garnett (12.i.13), 'like most of my stuff, it wants weeding out a bit . . . I enjoy so much writing my plays – they come so quick and exciting from the pen – that you mustn't growl at me if you think them waste of time. At any rate, they'll be stuff for shaping later on, when I'm more of a workman.' Both Hueffer and Edward Garnett were impressed by *The Widowing of Mrs Holroyd*.

Lawrence revised his plays, but he was less interested in stage effects and conventional plot strategy than in the development of lifelike scenes. His unusual facility for dialogue was both an asset and a danger. Sometimes he generates little dramatic tension, while situations hardly develop; his sense of proportion can be deficient through keeping too close to life. This may be seen even in *A Collier's Friday Night*, his first play and one of his best. It is doubtful whether he sketched it when he was twenty-one, as his manuscript note states; it suggests a later period of college life, and the reference to Swinburne's death (April 1909) points to subsequent revision. Allusions to Louie Burrows are varied, but the central situation is that of *Sons and Lovers* (viii), where Beatrice Wyld and the miner Barker re-appear, and the incidents of the play are given heightened contrasts, greater tension, and a more tragic cast. The father, like Morel, comes home to wash and change before his 'butty' share-out takes place; the burning of the bread follows, leading to a climax of jealousy between the parents, and mother and son, when the men return, the father from an evening at the pub, and the son from escorting Maggie Pearson on her way home. Like Miriam, she is based on Jessie Chambers; her ruddy complexion seems to merge at the end with the crushed rose which Ernest associates with 'two hearts caught up in a game/Of shuttlecock'. The bread-making which links the scenes signifies a mother's way of life from which Ernest yearns for some freedom; if he likes apples, does it mean he doesn't like bread, he asks her. Surface hints of the swirling undercurrents of jealousy and spite which affect all the characters except Maggie appear in little things. The father's behaviour is aggravated by his family's superiority and disregard. He may be tired, but the mother's thoughts run on Ernest, 'trailing from college to a house like this, tired out with study and all this journey'. He addresses his mother as Mütterchen, Mater, Mütter, and Matoushka, and talks of college lectures while his splenetic father is intent on his ablutions. Later he reads Baudelaire's 'Le Balcon' to Maggie, but less brutally than Paul does to Miriam. Despite a climax of jealous conflicts, the play is closer to life than the novel, where tensions flare up with dramatic swiftness and ugly, violent threats. There is a 'dangerous gentleness' in the tones of the mother and son as they bid each other goodnight, and the last impression by candlelight is of a little woman who is 'bowed and pathetic'.

The Widowing of Mrs Holroyd has the same origin and setting as 'Odour of Chrysanthemums' (p. 219). It was first written in 1911, revised about two years later (8.ix.13), and again at Fiascherino (P.233). Lawrence disliked the early version at two points, first where the wife and her admirer expressed their love in the room where the husband lay drunk, and finally as they wrangled across his dead body. The two characters gain in dignity from the changes he introduced. The play is tauter in texture, and has greater tension and action than *A Collier's Friday Night*. G. B. Shaw attended Esmé Percy's production of it in 1926, and wished he could equal its dialogue. The subject never becomes melodramatic: Blackmore cannot hate Mr Holroyd altogether; the mother-in-law is critical of Mrs Holroyd, but admits that her son has been 'a handful of trouble'; and gradually it emerges that the love of neither wife nor husband for the other is spent. Mrs Holroyd's dilemma is presented through her children: the boy wishes his father would drop down the pit-shaft; the girl thinks the house might be more peaceful if her mother were nice to him; and Mrs Holroyd wonders whether they should go to another country to avoid him. It is a dream, a temptation from Blackmore, who appears 'like the Evil One out of the darkness' when the play opens. Neither this nor the rats impart any symbolical meaning to the work as a whole. The temptation becomes an irrelevance in the grief that follows the husband's death, which Mrs Holroyd interprets as a judgment for a disloyalty she knows he has felt. She can now see that she has never loved him enough, though he had not tried to love as she had done. This had been their fate; her widowing had begun before his death. At the end she and her mother-in-law are one in grief. The play, which undoubtedly owes something to the parental discords Lawrence knew at home, is realistic at a highly charged, sometimes explosive level, but it is less moving than 'Odour of Chrysanthemums', with its dramatic irony, poetical overtones, and final vision. It leaves one with a suggestion of incompleteness, a feeling that Lawrence had not quite achieved the tragic climax or conclusion which the subject deserves. He seems to have agreed with the critics when the play was produced, wishing to 're-model the end' for any new production. 'Probably they're quite right when they say that the last act is too much taken up with washing the dead, instead of getting on a bit with life. I bet that would be my present opinion', he wrote (19.xii.26).

It now seems clear that *The Daughter-in-Law* was written wholly by Lawrence. An early version of it could have been the third of the colliery plays submitted to Hueffer. (The setting is Moorgreen; for the reference to redcoats during the strike and Watnall pit-top on fire, see p. 5.) Certainly it consorts well with *A Collier's Friday Night* and *The Widowing of Mrs Holroyd*. The conflict it resolves combines the central issues of both, the hold of a possessive mother on her son, and the early discords of a marriage which seems doomed to founder on social discrepancies. The daughter-in-law fights the battle on both fronts, and wins; she ensures that the tragedy which overtook Lawrence's parents, Mrs Holroyd, and Paul in *Sons and Lovers*, is not repeated.

Lawrence relies on dialect even more than in the other two plays, and to good effect. The news that Bertha Purdy is with child by Luther may take a disproportionate amount of time to reach successively Mrs Gascoigne, her son Luther, and his wife Minnie, six weeks after their marriage, but, with the strike, it brings the central issue to a head. Much is made of payment at almost every turn, and Luther comments bitterly that he must pay for six weeks of married life with Minnie. To shelter her, his brother Joe, honest and outspoken, would readily recompense the Purdys himself; so would Minnie. He is prevented by his domineering mother, who is only too glad to take her daughter-in-law down a peg or two; Minnie, who can adjust herself to realities, is defeated by the pride of a husband who resents her criticism. She wants him to be decisive and manly, and, in her spick and span house, sees less of the tame rabbit in him when, after arriving home unexpectedly late, he has his meal in all his 'pit-dirt'. Joe's deliberate breaking of one of her plates hints that there is more in life than material possessions; and in the end Minnie creates the greatest surprise of all by getting rid of her money, partly (like the wife in 'Her Turn') to make her husband face the reality of home economics during a strike, primarily to remove the social barrier between them. She and her mother-in-law are women of strong character. Mrs Gascoigne uses trenchant local idiom to subdue her sons, and is just as freely spoken with Minnie. Minnie stands up to her; she would rather have a husband who knocked her about than one who was good because he belonged to his mother. It is because she and Luther are hurt that they wound each other in a war of words, in which Joe is preferable to one and Bertha to the other. Like Mrs Holroyd, Mrs Gascoigne believes that men incur accidents to spite their women; being possessive, she is certain they will bring 'the house down crash' on a woman's head. Minnie is confident that it depends on how and what the woman builds. When Luther returns injured from a night encounter with strike blacklegs, he is ready for the reconciliation she desires. It is sudden; perhaps more should have been made of it. It brings the release which each has long been seeking, and an implicit recognition that nothing matters but their mutual relationship.

After these three plays, *The Married Man* seems a rather absurd artificial comedy in which Lawrence shows little genius. Although the opening pages of the manuscript are missing and what remains of the first act is very brief, it is not the content of the play but its aim which is baffling. Probably an improvization on the philandering proclivities of George Neville (8.iii.12), it leaves a general impression of late-adolescent and almost characterless sketchiness. A moral remark on the need for a married man, if he fall in love with another woman, to disclose the truth to her, and, if there is any strain, to his wife, seems too serious for this flirting sally.

The Merry-Go-Round is much more entertaining. Writing defensively to Garnett (14.xi.12), Lawrence described it as an impromptu, but, though the *brio* of movement and expression testify to zestful inspiration, the ingenuity of its construction, and the individuality and variety of its characters, suggest that this full-length drama was not only absorbing but the product of careful planning. Although the parish nurse is the central figure, it was, one suspects, the memory of Rodolph Baron von Hube which originated the play. 'Greenway' for Greasley suggests familiarity with the Baron's *Griseleia* (where the parish name is derived from grassland in a forest opening); 'Northrop' is Newthorpe. Marriage is the question for old and young, and lovers' nocturnal meetings convince Baron Rudolf von Ruge, a soldier of Christ, that his is 'a parish of sin'. The ubiquitous parish nurse is the one most sought in marriage, and money enters the reckoning of several characters, particularly with reference to the death and will of Mrs Hemstock. Mothering of grown-up sons becomes a subject of fun. Although Mrs Hemstock had encouraged Harry to go out with Rachel Wilcox, in the hope that he would grow up, he remains a 'soft 'un', as soft as the goose which is appropriately his companion at home. The nurse as a marriage prospect is a mother figure. Mrs Hemstock wishes her to marry Harry, who prefers her to Rachel, the thought of whom makes him 'heave wi' sickness'. Dr Foules, another mother-dominated figure, partial to literary tags, still hankers after the nurse, though he had given her up eight years earlier in deference to his mother. Judgments are emotionally subjective. To Mrs Hemstock, who, though bedridden and dying, has a lively stock of figurative idiomatic English, Rachel Wilcox is 'a cat foriver slidin', rubbin' 'erself' against her Harry. When Rachel is sought in marriage by the mercenary baker, who has large debts to pay, she is described by the jealous Susy as one who would 'fuss round a pair of breeches on a clothesline, rather than have no man'. Mrs Hemstock dies; there is a strike; Harry, as a reward for rescuing the influential Baron, gains employment as a miner, and almost inevitably is seen having his back washed at the end of his first day's work. Yet no serious note from the outer world is allowed to prevail. We move smoothly from scene to scene, indoors and out. The merry-go-round of imagined marriage permutations, conjured up by hope, jealousy, design, or force of circumstances, continues to the end. Rachel's father and Harry fail to win the nurse; after his mother's death, Harry falls an easy prey to Rachel. Misunderstanding leads to the announcement of wrong marriage banns, and the opposition of the Baron and Baroness to their rectification. For most it is 'As You Like It'; for Mr Wilcox, 'As You Lump It'. We are in a delightful, rather crazy world, fantastically farcical when the Baron and his wife intervene. It is not the same as Dylan Thomas's *Under Milk Wood* yet, like it, it generates its own artistic probability. It is close to life and yet removed from it. One can imagine it as another midsummer night's dream or even as comic opera.

The Fight for Barbara has its setting in Villa Igéa, Gargnano, where it was written in three days as 'a sort of interlude to *Paul Morel*', much of it being 'word for word true' (30.x.12). Though the main events are imaginary, the central situation is clearly that of the Lawrences at the time of writing, with threats of murder and suicide arriving by post from Professor Weekley while he refused to divorce Frieda (cf. 5.xii.12). Anxieties, recriminations, jealousy, and Weekley's missives account for the word-for-word veracity of 'much of it'. Looking at his position with what detachment he could, Lawrence may have seen comedy in it, and found some therapy in writing the play, but that is hardly the tone it conveys. It opens with light comedy, the milk girl's visit eliciting a flicker of jealousy which is offset a little later when the young butcher calls. The account of the first night of Frederick's honeymoon (based closely on that of Frieda and Ernest Weekley at Lucerne) is amusing; his interview with Barbara has touches of melodramatic absurdity, but it creates the most dramatic scene in a play where jealousy continually wells to the surface and is sometimes torturing. The result of the fight for Barbara remains uncertain to the very end; when she insists on leaving to see Frederick again, it seems lost. Wesson meets her with physical resistance, and 'flings her with a smash on to the couch'. Here and earlier in a milder form, the title has literal overtones. The passionate reconciliation which follows is hardly an unqualified assurance for the future. The play is rather slight, and Garnett's failure to be impressed by it (19.xi.12) cannot be wholly surprising.

Contrasting plays such as *The Widowing of Mrs Holroyd* and *The Merry-Go-Round* illustrate gifts which Lawrence might have fostered had these plays been successfully staged before the First World War. His next play, *Touch and Go*, a development from his unpublished *Women in Love* (xvii) was not written until 1919. Gerald Barlow is a more sympathetic presentation of Gerald Crich; Oliver Turton echoes Birkin; and Anabel Wrath is a more mature Gudrun. Like Gudrun, she helps Winifred in her studio, a sanctum from which, whatever her father thinks, life is not excluded. We hear much of the collieries, past and present, and of Anabel's progression from a cold Norwegian love to something more hopeful that makes her return to Gerald. Oliver has brought Winifred a marble gift of a goat seized by a wolf. With Anabel's emphasis on 'the inexpressible poise of the living thing, that makes it so different from a dead thing' and constitutes its 'soul', it takes us back to 'The Reality of Peace', where the equipoise of the lion and the lamb, or of hate and love, creates a perfect conjunction. 'It is not of love that we are fulfilled, but of love in such intimate equipoise with hate that the transcendence takes place.' Gerald has yet to resolve 'the two halves' of himself, and the same principle applies to all the contending forces involved in the strike. The issues it presents are just as alive today as they were in Lawrence's time. Lilley House, at the centre of conflicting interests, is a heartbreak house. The extremes are found in Gerald's parents, his mother being militant towards the workers, his father a true Christian. Mr Barlow has seen the dehumanization of the miners and the emergence of two opposite camps. Oliver Turton sees the root of the trouble in the system, everyone wanting to be rich. Both he and Gerald think the working man rather like the employer, neither showing '*life* intelligence'. Job Arthur Freer, a mealy-mouthed leader of the miners (mentioned in *AR*.i), is described by Turton as 'the modern Judas' who lives for the moment when he can kiss Gerald in the Garden of Olives; and it is in the park scene* which follows that his lust to destroy the rich (the 'vermin') is given full vent.

This scene takes us closer to the market-place where the play begins and ends. Socialist Willie Houghton accuses the miners of being slaves,

*Lilley Close is Lamb Close; the park is that of Eastwood Hall, once the home of the Walkers of Barber, Walker & Co., the local colliery owners. Willie Houghton is the Socialist Willie Hopkin.

of refusing to think and be 'men'. At the end he accuses Freer of wanting to replace one set of masters by a worse. Gerald is violently manhandled by the strikers while Freer tries to conduct an inquisition, and he is in danger of being trampled when Anabel shrieks that it is enough: 'he's a man as you are'. The moral, put forward by Turton, and supported by Houghton and Gerald, is that the truth does not belong to one faction, that 'bullying' is not the answer, and that it would be better to stop and 'set up a new state of things'. Lawrence's simple way of stating a truth runs the danger of being ignored at all times. In the preface which he wrote (P2.289–93), thinking his play was to be the first in a series published for the People's Theatre (organized by Douglas Goldring), Lawrence argued that 'great numbers of decent people are squeezed' between the upper and nether millstones of Capital and Labour, and that 'the proletariat isn't poor'. We want 'men who are somebody, not men who are something'; we are sick of people who are 'bits', representatives of this party or that. For people who are 'bits', the struggle between Labour and Capital is a disaster; for men who are still men, it is a tragedy. It is as if one party would scuttle the ship to sink the other. If, on the other hand, we had the *life* intelligence which both Oliver and Gerald look for, we should aim at a new order, emerging through 'death' to 'a new freedom, a new life'. The positive accent of the play is on freedom and against 'bullying' from first to last.

The fragment *Altitude* is a skit on Mabel Luhan, Clarence Thompson (a screen writer introduced to Mabel by Alice Sprague), and Willard ('Spud') Johnson; Ida Rauh and Tony Luhan also appear. Whether *Noah's Flood* was written in New Mexico is uncertain. It hardly gets under way, ending with the entrance of Noah, after men decide that they can destroy the power of the demi-gods (the 'sons of God', represented by Noah, Shem, Ham, and Japheth) by seizing the gift of fire. One talks in a Lawrentian way on the source of cosmic energy; men do not respond to it as do the creatures, and are 'stale, and inclining towards deadness' in consequence. Japheth's advice is that man should learn to ask until no secrets remain, but the men know better. With control of fire, they will have dominion over the universe. 'Even the stars shall bow humbly, and yield us their reply, and the sun shall no more have a will of his own.' It is unfortunate that Lawrence was unable to continue a subject which meant so much to him: 'When you come to think of it, Noah matters more than the deluge, and the ark is more than all the

world washed out' (P.733). The thought is the same as that of emerging
from death in the preface to *Touch and Go*.

David, Lawrence's last play and his most ambitious, was written
expressly for the theatre (1.vii.25) and in the hope that Ida Rauh would
play the part of Michal. It was not performed, however, until May 1927,
in London. Lawrence had supplied music, knowing that its success
depended on conveying 'primitive religious passion' (16.x.26). Illness
and delays in production exasperated him until he could no longer think
of travelling from Italy to see it. Adverse reviews angered him (28.v.27).
In sixteen scenes which embody a chronicle of epic effect, the play
presents major episodes in the story of David's rise and Saul's treacherous
attempts to destroy him. Lawrence employs invention, but follows the
Biblical accounts closely, even in style. Once again he shows his facility
for Biblical rhythms and imagery of a Hebraic cast. It is a drama of
elevated prose rather than of poetry, but an image can suffuse a passage
with poetic light, when Jonathan, for example, feeling that David
stands apart because the Lord has entered his soul, assumes that father
or mother or friend means nothing to him, and is answered 'They are
the same. But when the Lord is there, all the branches are hidden
in blossom.' The Lord seems to be partially Red Indian in origin; he is
the Whirlwind, whose source is 'behind the sun'. When a man's will
and the Whirlwind are one, 'all is well'; but 'when the will of man is
against the Whirlwind, all is ill' (v). Saul's sin arises from following his
own bidding and 'the voice of his people'; there is no forgiveness. Once he
was 'a burning bush, afire with God. Alas, that he saw his own image
mirrored in the faces of men!' So, incidentally, Lawrence casts a stone at
democracy (*vox Dei*) in the context of his faith that cosmic wisdom is the
prerogative of the few. 'Cursed be the man that trusteth in man, and
maketh flesh his arm, and whose heart departeth from the Lord', wrote
Jeremiah. This kind of self-sufficiency or hubris is represented by
David's brother Eliab (iii). 'Henceforward thou art not thine own. The
Lord is upon thee, and thou art His', Samuel tells David as he anoints
him. Samuel's Lord has a Lawrentian bias in favour of individual
development: 'each man's Lord is his own, though God be but one' (xv).
(David's fox-red beard seems to be a hint of some identification between
the author and his hero namesake; cf. 'The Red Wolf'.)

Among predominant rhythms, some stand out for their special effects:
primitive exultation with the defeat of the Amalekites at the opening;

the repetition of rhymed staccato lines in chant-like dialogue, with prolonged alleluias at intervals, after the slaying of Goliath (which is excitingly dramatized) and after David's defeat of the Philistines (ix); and the singing of David's psalm before Saul's gloomy look into the future, far beyond his own disastrous end to the defeat of David's God and a glimpse of the modern godless era when men inherit the earth. Saul, possessed of evil spirits, rejoices in the prospect (xi). They make him repeatedly false and treacherous to David, who, in a highly dramatic scene at his house in Gilgal, escapes with the help of Jonathan and Michal. It is only when Saul comes to the hill of Samuel and the prophets and, unlike one of his soldiers, finds no responsive flame from the Lord, that he becomes resigned to his fate. The play does not end with David's triumph, however; he still has to flee, and Jonathan, who will not strain against God as his father has done, is his guardian. One with him in spirit, he had given David his robes and weapons of war to make him appear as 'the King's son and the eagle of the Lord, in the eyes of the people'. For Lawrence life is a continual conflict of old and new. Jonathan knows that he is doomed to die in battle with his father; and with him the 'man-for-man love' also dies (*St.Am*.xii). He also knows David's limitations, and looks beyond the new day of his reign, convinced that the time will come when 'the blood gets back its flame'. The play ends undramatically with this affirmation of Lawrence's faith.

LITERARY CRITICISM

Disinterested criticism is rare in Lawrence; and few would have it otherwise, for his interpretations and judgments are most alive when they express his own views. Nowhere are they more remarkable and false than in his 'Study of Thomas Hardy', an early work in which Lawrence elaborated his philosophy of life with supreme assurance. At first he intended a 'little book' on Hardy; in six weeks he had read him again, with the aid of Lascelles Abercrombie's *Thomas Hardy* (1912), and started a book that would be 'about anything but Thomas Hardy' (15, 17.vii.14, 5.ix.14). Much of his reading must have been as hasty as his writing; twice he announces important intentions which are never fulfilled. Not one of the analyses of Hardy's first six novels (the rest are overlooked) is wholly acceptable; it is Lawrence, for example, who starts the irrelevant and specious conclusion that Dick Dewy will have a bad time in marriage. He is inaccurate, making Manston a murderer, Eustacia of Italian descent, and Tess and Alec kinsfolk. With *The Return of the Native* he gets under way. Lawrence's Egdon Heath is not Hardy's; it is a fecund source of eternal life, black and powerful, heaving with 'raw instinct'. Clym was born 'out of passionate Egdon to live as a passionate being'. The man who decided to teach is an abstraction; the heath-dwellers were not interested in enrichment, and they had enough instinctive wisdom to teach him. Lawrence would have us believe that the woodlands and the 'unfathomed stars' provide a similar background in *The Woodlanders* and *Two on a Tower*. It does not occur to him that Hardy's 'primal morality' is more comprehensive than his own; more than three years later (in two letters, 12.iii.18) he writes of *The Woodlanders* country as if it were idyllic. For the individualistic Lawrence, everyone needs to follow his passional self. The force of chance, or circumstance and heredity, which weighed so heavily with Hardy, is ignored. Lawrence insists that there is 'nothing more metaphysical' in his tragedy than man's conflict with the community and convention; nothing metaphysical, in short. He assumes that nature provides the greater morality, and that there is nothing in Clym or Tess, or their circumstances, which makes them act as they do or fail to do. He also assumes that, in great tragedy, heroes such as Oedipus and Macbeth are strong because they defy the conventional morality of their society (iii).

How misleading Lawrence's abstract reasoning can be is further illustrated when he returns to his subject (v). He reduces *Desperate Remedies* to a morality play, and then lists the characters in Hardy who are Lawrentian aristocrats, representing 'the glory of mankind'; among them are Manston, Lord Luxellian, Troy, Wildeve, de Stancy, Lucetta, Fitzpiers, Alec d'Urberville, and (we see later) Arabella. His contention is that Hardy, 'starting with bourgeois morality', turns 'all exceptional or strong individual traits' into 'weaknesses or wicked faults'. Not for a moment does he allow that Hardy was in conflict with Victorian morality, or that his most passionate 'criticism of life' was rooted in Hellenic, Swinburnian sympathies. It is worth noting that Lawrence would have the Manstons and Alecs triumph in his 'heroic age'. He returns to Oedipus and the rest, as if the circumstances of Jude and Tess are comparable to those of the great in myth and legend. Lawrence always takes refuge in 'eternal, immutable laws', as if they had no reference to Hardy's world. It is part of Hardy's greatness that they have, and that his laws are scientific, while Lawrence's are arbitrary, mythical, and sometimes absurdly subjective. For one who made abstract deduction his *bête noire*, Lawrence's chop-logic is amazing; disregarding the evidence repeatedly, he categorizes and equates Hardy's characters as if he were engaged in an intellectual exercise played according to his own rules for his own Q.E.D. conclusions.

This is illustrated again when he returns to Hardy in a section (ix) where the predominant assumption is that spirit/intellect is male and flesh female (as if individuals in life or fiction can be adequately discussed in this way). Hardy makes a poor metaphysician, Lawrence repeats; and the Wessex novels are 'sheer rubbish' in parts. Arguing that Alec and Tess were naturally akin, and that she did not hate him, he rules out personal choice, and assumes nothing but Male Principle and Female Principle. He re-creates Arabella, and makes it clear that Hardy did not know much about her. In discussing Jude and 'his purpose in becoming a Don' (*sic*), Lawrence is thinking more of himself and Frieda *vis-à-vis* Professor Weekley. Jude is taken out of the novel: he lost nothing by his marriage to Arabella, and he wished to live 'only in his mentality'. Knowing the type from Helen Corke, Lawrence is on much surer ground with Sue. An exceptional (if not improbable) character, she fits his schematization extremely well, and he had obviously read *Jude* with unusual interest. His worst fault is to declare that she made no mistake in marrying Phillotson. It illustrates Lawrence's habit of finding in literature what he wanted to serve his own ends.

The same generalization applies to *Studies in Classic American Literature*. Taken for what it is (and not too seriously), it affords some delightful, impudent reading; it is not quite a masterpiece, but it is a work *per se*. Lawrence tells us that by the end of September 1919 he had been preparing it for five years (cf. ?30.v.16). From 1917 to the winter of 1922–3 he wrote and modified it considerably, jettisoning most of his heavy 'philosophical' load, becoming increasingly anti-American, and adopting the devil-may-care style of a freebooter. He found more truth in 'classic' American authors than in modern, but they needed to be divested of their 'democratic and idealistic clothes' for its revelation. 'The proper function of a critic is to save the tale from the artist who created it.' Once laid bare, art 'will tell you the truth of his day', and this is 'all that matters'. 'Away with eternal truth. Truth lives from day to day', Lawrence proclaims, forgetting (it seems) the 'eternal, immutable laws' by which he had judged Hardy. He scoffs at the American idea of democracy, insisting that to be truly free people must have a positive purpose, in response to their deepest individual selves (i). The 'dummy standards' of Benjamin Franklin's ideal man are unacceptable because man has many selves; his virtues would make men automata. Lawrence then gives his own creed (p. 90), and asks how one can be free without serving many gods; he is sick of serving his fellow-men, and must find his own soul (ii).

It was Crèvecoeur who, with Chateaubriand and others, spread the romantic idea of the noble North American savage. Franklin was the practical American prototype; Crèvecoeur, the emotional, presenting nature sweet and pure. Yet the artist may be seen beneath the idealizer; Crèvecoeur shows glimpses of Darwinian reality and 'blood-knowledge'; and, although his intellectual self maintains his duplicity, deep down he wishes to know the dark, sensual life of the Red Indians. No reconciliation is possible between them and the whites, Lawrence asserts; when their last nuclei disintegrate, the full force of their unappeased ghosts will be felt. He had read Fenimore Cooper's novels with enthusiasm, but knows that his presentation of the Indians is a wish-fulfilment. His 'white novels' reveal Americans, not as true human beings, accepting natural inequalities, but pinned down by fixed ideas such as egalitarianism. Cooper wished to be regarded as a gentleman and a great American author in Europe, but his heart was with Natty Bumppo, the hero of the five leatherstocking novels. In the 'immortal friendship' of Natty and Chingachgook, Lawrence sees the American of the future. It is not a question of equals or unequals, but of integrity, and Natty preserves his by turning his back on white society. In him Lawrence finds 'the very intrinsic-most American', and adds portentously that 'something will be happening' when he breaks from his 'static isolation'.

Edgar Allan Poe's stories, 'Ligeia', 'Eleonora', and 'The Fall of the House of Usher' in particular, are interpreted to show the killing power of spiritual, nervous love. 'An adventurer into vaults and cellars and horrible underground passages of the human soul', he records the disease of the 'old white psyche'. In trying to make it attractive, he employs the falseness of art. The American must destroy 'the whole corpus of the white psyche', Lawrence insists. For him Hawthorne's *The Scarlet*

Letter, as a revelation of the human spirit 'fixed in a lie', is both a satire and one of the greatest allegories in literature. The Fall occurred when sex entered man's consciousness and became his cross. America retains its belief in the spirit to all appearances, and 'inwardly gives not a fig for it'. Dimmesdale is seduced gloatingly; his spiritual love is false. Hester Prynne is 'the *knowing* Ligeia risen diabolic from the grave. Having her own back.' With invectives against women saviours, Lawrence declares that woman will destroy man unless he 'believes in himself and his gods'. If he becomes 'a spiritual fornicator and liar' like Dimmesdale, she must retaliate against her betrayer. Sin is not 'the breaking of divine commandments' but of 'one's own integrity'. The Pearls of the modern world, assuming that there is no Father to sin against, forget that the Holy Ghost within one does not forgive. Turning to *The Blithedale Romance* and its picture of the Brook Farm experiment, Lawrence argues that, because hard work cannot be idealized (a doubtful premiss), the idealists 'left off brookfarming, and took to bookfarming'. Spiritualism and psychic tricks spell disintegration: 'When men want to be supernatural, be sure that something has gone wrong in their natural stuff. More so, even, with a woman', Lawrence adds.

Male chauvinism emerges, but Lawrence reveals himself in a more objectionable light on Dana. His quotations from *Two Years Before the Mast* are impressive, and his application to life of the ship's 'winged centrality' in perfect equipoise with the elements is felicitous. He is specious on a number of authors, including Hardy and Dana, concluding from the dull respectability of the latter's life after his two years at sea that 'knowing' (which he equates with experience) is 'the slow death of being'. Lawrence's mental consciousness makes him blind to 'being', and his sadism is apparent when he defends the flogging of Sam as natural 'polarization' or 'human coition'. The 'I say so' with which he concludes his pronouncement proclaims his bullying conceit. It follows an explanatory passage of jargon on ganglia and the 'vital' electric circuit, which serves to remind the reader how much he was spared when Lawrence jettisoned 'The Two Principles' (pp. 81–2). In Melville he recognizes 'the greatest seer and poet of the sea', a blue-eyed Viking who turned away from life 'to the abstract, to the elements'. His *Typee* (which elicits Lawrence's comment that cannibalism is more valid than the Christian sacrament) reveals a Pacific paradise, but he could not stay there, any more than Lawrence could. All his life, however, Melville was pinned down and tortured by the idealism of 'perfect relationship, possible perfect love', a desire which for Lawrence is 'just a vicious, unmanly craving'. The chapter on *Moby Dick*, 'the greatest book of the sea ever written', consists largely of well-known extracts. When 'he ceases to be American' *au grand sérieux* and gives his 'sheer apprehension of the world', Melville (like Dana) is wonderful; he registers it 'like a marvellous wireless-station'. For Lawrence the *Pequod* with its maniac captain, its eminently practical mates, and its crew of mixed races and creeds, is America. It pursues the warm-blooded Moby Dick, and its sinking signals 'the doom of our white day', the doom that 'is in America', the triumph of blood-consciousness over 'parasitic mental or ideal consciousness'.

Lawrence's disregard for literary criticism may be seen in his concluding essay on Whitman. It is easy to ridicule an author by facetious comments on snippets, and this Lawrence does. If Whitman 'drove an automobile with a very fierce headlight along the track of a fixed idea', Lawrence with a few fixed ideas drove his with fiercer headlights. Whitman's Identity theme is overdone, and it is his 'open road' philosophy, with important Lawrentian qualifications, which points the way ahead. Though 'fearfully mistaken', he is 'the great leader', an American Moses who gives us 'Pisgah sights'. Art is moral, Lawrence affirms, but its morality is not that of Whitman's predecessors; it is a passionate morality which 'changes the blood, rather than the mind'. There is only the open road, with no known direction; what matters is that the soul should remain true to herself. Whitman's mistake was the idealistic extension of love to all and sundry. The soul must discriminate; it recognizes different shades of love and hatred on the open road, and its sympathy is shown accordingly in love or hatred. True democracy is 'a recognition of souls' and 'a gladder worship of great and greater souls'; the only riches are the great souls. Lawrence uses American literature to preach his own gospel.

He has remarkably little to say in favour of 'classic' Russian writers and their general exaltation of 'quite commonplace people'. Although strongly opposed to his Christian socialism, he recognized the artist in the Tolstoy who 'worshipped . . . every manifestation of pure, spontaneous, passionate life'. Lawrence's study of Hardy proves his impatience with any author who believed that the moral code could play a retributive role in life; Tolstoy's greatest sin was to make 'the later Vronsky abject and pitiable' from envy of 'the reckless passionate male' (P.227, 246–7, P2.417, 423–4). He admired Dostoevsky greatly at first (?8.iv.15) but, on discovering that all his characters were 'fallen angels', became bored with them. His notes to Murry are of special interest (17.ii.16); once again, it can be seen that Lawrence's anti-Christianity was the principal reason for his condemnation, though there can be little doubt that Murry's defence of Dostoevsky increased his distaste (cf. ?15.xii.16; Murry had sent Lawrence his book on Dostoevsky the previous September). Dostoevsky's art shows that he is 'a little horror', 'posing as a sort of Jesus' (*St.Am.*i). Yet late in his life Lawrence found 'the final and unanswerable criticism of Christ' in 'The Grand Inquisitor'; it confirmed his belief that wisdom belongs only to 'the specially gifted few' (P.283–91). Turgenev appeared an old maid in *A Sportsman's Sketches*, and a 'come-down' after *The Deerslayer*. All three Russian writers (and Maupassant and Flaubert) were '*obvious* and coarse' compared with Fenimore Cooper and Hardy, and Lawrence rated 'English art, at its best . . . by far the subtlest and loveliest and most perfect in the world' (27.xi.16). He found Tchehov depressing (P.223).

Lawrence's interest in Russian literature continued largely through his friend Koteliansky's translations, some of which he revised. Shestov's *All Things Are Possible* (P.215–17) revealed the emergence of a Russia which will 'certainly inherit the future'. 'Inoculated with the virus of European culture and ethic', the Russians had inevitably suffered from spiritual division and conflict. Shestov is seen 'tweaking the nose of European idealism' and expressing a view of life comparable to Lawrence's at the end of his essay on Whitman. The review of Rozanov's *Solitaria* (P.367–71) is more antipathetic to Dostoevsky than Lawrence's later introduction to Koteliansky's translation of 'The Grand Inquisitor'. Rozanov has a lust-ascetism complex or Dostoevskian duality, and his attack on Christianity reveals a genuine pagan or 'phallic' vision. The first Russian who had ever 'said anything' to Lawrence, he is described as 'the living and resurrected pagan' (probably with 'The Man Who Died' in mind). In *Fallen Leaves* (P.388–92) Lawrence finds 'the last word of the Russian, before the great *débâcle*'. Rozanov realizes his nullity, the stoniness that makes him a monster, and the 'dreaminess' that makes him capable of anything or nothing. The book shows the struggle to gain his positive self. If he does not 'put the fear of God into us, he puts a real fear of destiny, or of doom'. Such reviews illustrate

Lawrence's great potentiality as a moral critic. His essay on Dahlberg's *Bottom Dogs* (P.267–73) is even more impressive. Most of it is a penetrating socio-psychological analysis of the American background which suggests the direction of modern literature and life. In 'psychic disintegration' this novel goes many stages beyond Aldous Huxley's *Point Counter Point*, revealing the state to which 'the trend of consciousness' is taking all of us, especially the young. Lawrence hopes that it is the *ne plus ultra*. He attributes the 'repulsiveness of human flesh' in Huxley, Gide, and Joyce to 'the collapse of the physical sympathetic flow' in western civilization, and finds sexual morbidity in *Hamlet* and English literature from Chaucer onwards (P.551–2). Joyce is not only distasteful but boring, with minute analyses of individual feelings and experience; the long drawn out absurdity of self-consciousness in *Ulysses* suggests 'the death-bed of the serious novel' (P.517–18; cf. 15.viii.28).

Lawrence's introductions to two volumes of his Verga translations make interesting reading. The *Cavalleria Rusticana* collection of stories marks a turning-point in Verga's literary career, and a recoil from the *beau monde* of Italy, with genuine sympathy for Sicilian peasant life. Verga's preoccupation with form and his omission of 'transition passages' lead Lawrence into comments on formlessness and 'the curious swoops and circles' of emotional thinking which can be applied to his own work (P.248–50). The first of the two introductions to *Mastro-don Gesualdo* (P.223–31, P2.279–88) was discarded; it is less inclusive, but it contains all Lawrence's major observations. Finding *I Malavoglia* too much subject to the pity-the-poor attitude of its period, he discusses the depression of tragedy when it is borne by ordinary people who are not commensurate with the artist's tragic vision. There is a change in *Mastro-don Gesualdo*. The hero's splendid dauntlessness has a Grecian quality, and none of the soul-twisting and introspection which Lawrence associates with Russian fiction. It is a book which will appeal to anyone with a 'physical feeling for life'; it lives by virtue of its vividness and the 'powerful pulsing of its life-portrayal'.

Some of Lawrence's most sustained literary criticism is found in his 'John Galsworthy' (P.539–50). Distinguishing between social and human beings (the latter in touch with the universe), he asserts that it is the collapse of 'natural innocent pride' which makes people fearful and anxious to insure themselves by amassing money and property. He does not find a single human being in the whole gamut of Galsworthy's

characters. Galsworthy lacked the courage to continue satirically as he
began. The only anti-Forsytism he offers is passion in a parasitic class.
It is faked and sentimental, a 'doggish amorousness' which he would have
done better to satirize. Instead, he glorifies the *anti*, the typical modern
'social being' who is worse than the Forsytes he rebels against. The essay
opens with Lawrence's views on literary criticism. It can never be a
science, for it is far too personal, and it is 'concerned with values that
science ignores'. He dismisses discussion of style and form as 'critical
twiddle-twaddle', and condemns pseudo-scientific classification and
analysis. 'We judge a work of art by its effect on our sincere and vital
emotion, and nothing else'; and he clarifies this best when he writes: 'A
critic must be emotionally alive in every fibre, intellectually capable and
skilful in essential logic, and then morally very honest.' The importance
Lawrence attaches to moral integrity makes him admire Sainte-Beuve
and distrust Macaulay.

Lawrence's faith in life made him impatient not only with Tchehov but
with tragedy in general. In apparent disregard of the uplifting and positive
values of tragic protest, he preferred the literature of critical affirmation.
'For man always becomes what he passionately thinks he is; since he is
capable of becoming almost anything', he declared (P2.281). He hated
Bennett's resignation in *Anna of the Five Towns*, and thought that
'tragedy ought really to be a great kick at misery' (6.x.12). Conrad,
whose stories he could admire, made him furious; for 'being so sad and
for giving in' he was unforgivable (30.x.12). In his later years Lawrence
shook off the depression induced by thoughts of 'the great tragedy of our
material-mechanical civilization'; he alludes to it and to its acceptance
by the public at the opening of *Lady Chatterley's Lover*, but his novel is
a vigorous protest against 'crushing out the natural human life'. His
attitude to tragedy had not changed; it looked 'like man in love with
his own defeat' (CP.508).

Two of his reviews discuss the novel in form and substance. Unlike
Tono-Bungay, Wells's *The World of William Clissold* is not a novel
'because it contains none of the passionate and emotional reactions which
are at the very root of all thought'; it is 'all words, words, words, about
Socialism and Karl Marx, bankers and cave-men, money and the superman. One would welcome any old scarecrow of a character on this
dreary, flinty hillside of abstract words' (P.346–50). Lawrence regards
Thomas Mann as a disciple of Flaubert in his devotion to art. Writers

such as Shakespeare and Goethe had to 'give themselves to life as well as to art', and Lawrence concludes that 'craving for form is the outcome, not of artistic conscience, but of a certain attitude to life'. He asks if one can fix 'the definite line of a book' any more than one can fix 'any definite line of action for a human being'. One cannot equate the human being in life with a character in fiction, but it is the trend of Lawrence's thought that matters. He sees in both Flaubert and Mann an anti-vitalism which deadens the rhythm of their work (P.308–13), and is convinced (as he states with reference to some of Verga's short stories) that the writer of fiction needs an 'apparent formlessness', since 'definite form is mechanical'.

In *Lady Chatterley's Lover* Lawrence defines the 'vast importance of the novel, properly handled' as a life-giving medium (see p. 217); and in 'Why the Novel Matters' he expresses his conviction that the novel can do more to make the 'whole man' more sensitively aware of life than can any other medium, even poetry (P.535). Life, he argues in 'Morality and the Novel', consists in achieving 'a pure relationship between ourselves and the living universe about us', and 'the highest example of subtle inter-relatedness' achieved by man is to be found in the novel. 'Everything is true in its own time, place, circumstance, and untrue out of its own place, time, circumstance.' The morality is in the 'true and vivid relationships' (P.528, 530). Further light is thrown on this in 'The Novel', where he states that the hero of every great novel is not any of the characters but 'some unnamed and nameless flame behind them all'. 'We have to choose between the quick and the dead. The quick is God-flame, in everything'; and 'the quickness of the quick' lies in the 'fluid, changing . . . relatedness' of all, people and 'things'. The novel must be quick; interrelated in all its parts, vitally, organically; honourable, in the sense that the novelist must be true to the flame that leaps within him (P2.419–20, 422–3, 425). The same essay clarifies Lawrence's meaning in 'Morality and the Novel', when he declares that 'immorality' does not as a rule arise because the novelist has a dominant idea or purpose but when he 'puts his thumb in the scale [of the inter-relatedness], to pull down the balance to his own predilection'. This implies a 'didactic purpose' which is contrary to his 'passional inspiration' or 'art-speech' (P2.416–17, *St.Am.*i).

Postscript

The weakness in form which is apparent in most of Lawrence's major works reflects his individuality. Anything contrary to his spontaneous self was inimical to life. Form was mechanical; he saw its deadening effect in Flaubert and Thomas Mann. In response to his passional creative self, he preferred to rewrite rather than plan fastidiously or subject his work to intensive critical revision. The cult of spontaneity has obvious dangers; it can create illusions of grandeur and liveliness even in lapses and *longueurs*, and the self-congratulation engendered in Lawrence by his latest writing is amply testified in his letters. Disproportion, turgidity, repetitiousness, and lack of precision at critical points will be found in his greatest novels, *The Rainbow* and *Women in Love*. When imaginative inspiration dies, impatience leads to the didactic authorial self-expression of *Aaron's Rod* and *Kangaroo*. Lawrence's problem was to subordinate his metaphysic to art rather than the reverse. He did not care for 'neat works of art', believing that an author should present the 'scrimmage' of life rather than an isolated stage-spectacle (22.i.25). 'Art for my sake' meant writing when he wanted to write, a readiness to re-create rather than 'trim and garnish', and to write what he enjoyed irrespective of the reader (24.xii.12, 12 and 17.i.13). Auden concluded that 'the spirit has failed to make itself a body fit to live in' in many of Lawrence's poems. Immediacy of experience is often weakened by diffuseness, and they rarely approach perfection of form.

A second factor which must be taken into account in the evaluation of Lawrence as a writer is his loss of interest in people (p. 182) and the outer world (24.v.16). He admitted that travel was a form of escape; it provided some stimulating backgrounds, but only in New Mexico did it deepen his experience. Isolation in Australia aggravated his anti-social, anti-Whitman prejudices, to create a monster in Kangaroo. From the imaginative reality of the best in his earlier fiction he moves towards abstraction, his principal characters representing forces, those undercurrents of life which made him impatient with people *ad nauseam* in E. M. Forster (23.vii.24). He knew from experience the danger of 'the man who loved islands', as is seen in Birkin and his island misanthropy (*WL*.xi). Lawrence has a humanitarian goal, but it is long-term and general, while he remains combative and rather self-centred, showing little sympathy for the individual, and regarding a tragic attitude towards life as unmanly. Though *Lady Chatterley's Lover* marks a revival of 'old blood-affinity' with his fellow-men, the depersonalizing trend is still evident, and this was inevitable for one whose bourgeois antipathies and divorce from his own class (P2.595-6) combined to frustrate his 'primeval societal instinct' (p. 89).

A short story such as 'Tickets, Please' illustrates the human interest excited by a return to the Midlands, but most of the later stories arise from old ideas in new settings, the best gaining appeal from poetic overtones or the symbolical life of coadunating image and situation. Despite its excesses, Lawrence's imaginative power was at its most intense and fecund in the years immediately following his marriage. Its most original feature lies in scenes and actions which are predominantly figurative, expressing feeling, intention, or states of being, and often developed with brilliant virtuosity. Such are the moon scenes between Anna and Will, and Ursula and Skrebensky; the surrealistic effects of the horses confronting Ursula; palustral vegetative images before Gudrun notices Gerald Crich's approach; Birkin's attempt to destroy the millpond reflection of the moon; the darkness beyond knowledge which he attains with Ursula (*WL*.xxiii); and the contrasting death of Gerald by 'process of frost-knowledge, death by perfect cold' (xix) in the great cul-de-sac of snow among the Tyrolean Alps.

Lawrence did not acquire a generally assured style – easy, intimate, idiomatic, but above all lucid and economical – until after the war of 1914-18. Previous creative pressures had often resulted in hypertrophy, repetitious sometimes to the point of tautology. Repetition may exert an emotional hold through cyclic, incantatory rhythms (P.249-50); or it may produce effective emphasis. 'The only answer is that it is natural to the author: and that every natural crisis in emotion or passion or understanding comes from this pulsing, frictional to-and-fro, which works up to a culmination' (P2.276). It is often characteristic of a plethoric style which is hardly justifiable. A passage devoted principally to a 'fecund' climactic kiss is the subject of three pages (*R*.xv). Having rich sensual, mindless overtones, it takes place in 'massive' Lawrentian darkness, the image of which recurs more than thirty times, often in close succession. A preliminary sentence tells us that the night which had 'seemed to come to pass' was 'turgid, teeming, heavy with fecundity in which every molecule of matter grew big with increase, secretly urgent with fecund desire'. Inflated writing of this kind can cloud meaning. Perplexity or misunderstanding can arise also when, at the other extreme, Lawrence uses the 'vicious, old-adamish' style to preserve 'the edge of his awareness' as a creative writer (P.373). Cicio's sexual assassination of Alvina is strikingly clear, but the hyperbole of Skrebensky's destruction by a girl's kiss will remain conjecturally vague for most readers. Lawrence's expression is frequently exaggerated, and sometimes violent.

Although sexual perversion exists in the interpretation of some of his critics far more than in Lawrence, misreading on this issue is largely his fault. The whole tenor of his work confirms his religious belief in natural sex-fulfilment and his loathing of sexuality or sex-exploitation, the prostitution of the body to the mind (P.573). The abuse of the body, in sex, drugs, or drink, filled him with a repulsion reminiscent of Swift's against natural bodily functions (P.771). His loathing of perversion is seen in 'I Know a Noble Englishman' (CP.965–7) and in *Fantasia* (x). Will Brangwen's unnaturalness develops from sex-in-the-head. If Lawrence's condemnation is not clear, it is because he does not distinguish sufficiently between fictional subjectivism and authorial comment (*R*.viii). Insistence on the need to remove false shame in marriage explains words such as 'bestial' and 'shameful' where 'shameless' could be expected (*W*.xxix). Annable's 'Be a good animal' may seem crude; it implies an abhorrence of the unnatural. Mellors' disgust with Bertha Coutts's allegations conveys a dignity which effectively places her beneath contempt; like Lawrence he stands for the Pentecostal flame, Coutts and other evils notwithstanding.

The charge of Fascism which Bertrand Russell levelled against Lawrence is absurd, yet Lawrence's opposition to Communism, socialism, and the bullying greed of trade unionism makes its renewal inevitable. He was repelled by any form of subservience: marital and social (*Aaron's Rod*) or party-political (*Kangaroo*). (Lawrence's failure to attain a state of 'star-equilibrium' with Frieda led to notable 'male-chauvinist' outbursts in the early 1920s.) He was convinced that most people are unable to think for themselves, and that democracy produces a 'cabbage' state (P2.384–8); maddened by war, and critically blinded by the imagery of ideas, he could write on this subject with shocking intemperance (P.683–7). Nevertheless, his perception of weakness and corruption in our modern society is remarkable: for example, Tom Brangwen of Wiggiston, content to live comfortably and, with 'the instinct of growing inertia', to 'let the machinery carry him' (R.xii), is the prototype of thousands created at all levels of employment by expanding bureaucratic units. Lawrence believed that the State should provide the means to live, thereby enabling the individual, released from money-craving, to develop his unique self; that this 'singling out' comes from fulfilment in marriage; and that such fulfilment will restore 'flesh-and-blood' kinship between the classes. It is assumed that the achievement of this kind of manhood and womanhood will lead to maturity in all other adult relationships, and to the amelioration of society as a whole. 'Now we know one another only as ideal or social or political entities', and are intuitively 'dead to one another' (P.556). The only way to solve the industrial problem is to train people in the art of living (LC.xix). Lawrence never pauses to consider how his rulers, the natural 'aristocrats' (CP.650), are to be chosen; and at one point ventures to believe that education might make everyone an aristocrat (p. 118). Yet his vision is grounded on one general reality: he knows that human nature makes any millennium impossible. There can be 'no fixed direction', only a continual dialectical process of growth from decay; as Lawrence insists at the end of 'St Mawr', 'man is only himself when he is fighting on and on'.

Lawrence's spirit recalls Shelley's: 'tameless, and swift, and proud'. Before he eloped with Frieda Weekley, he told her that every man must take his own and go his way regardless of system and State; he was greater than the State. 'There is no need to break laws. The only need is to be a law unto one's self.' 'And if sufficient people came out of the walled defences and pitched in the open, then very soon the walled city would be a mere dependant on the free tents of the wilderness', he added. This explains his criticism of Hardy, and the unpractical idealism on which it is based. It suggests anarchy, differing from Godwin's (as Wordsworth saw it) in being based on the passional self rather than on the light of reason. Many of Lawrence's views were expressed impulsively, and were subject to change. A deeper, counterbalancing judgment will be found in a much later statement (*St.Am.*i):

> Men are free when they are obeying some deep, inward voice of religious belief. Obeying from within. Men are free when they belong to a living, organic, *believing* community, active in fulfilling some unfulfilled, perhaps unrealized purpose. . . . Men are not free when they are doing just what they like. The moment you can do just what you like, there is nothing you care about doing. Men are only free when they are doing what the deepest self likes.

Lawrence seems never to have resolved this issue satisfactorily. For him individual fulfilment or 'the glad absolution of the rose' is the equipoise of the lion and the lamb (P.693). With Heraclitus he believes that 'in the tension of opposites all things have their being' (CP.348). In the words of 'Manifesto', 'we shall love, we shall hate,/but it will be like music'. If a man really wishes to make war, he should not be withstood, for passional killing is not evil (CP.715, HP.98). Our spontaneous wishes are our intimations of immortality (16.vii.16).

Such beliefs had their origin in Lawrence's inner conflicts, and provided self-vindication for outbreaks of hatred and aggressiveness, in literature and life. His rages against the world and his wife find their counterpart in the inhumanity of his letter to Katherine Mansfield (p. 44), his rabid abuse of Murry, the treatment of Lady Ottoline Morrell in *Women in Love*, and of his Turin host and hostess in *Aaron's Rod*. Richard Aldington had good reason to note how most of those who befriended Lawrence in London became the subject of his moral satire. People he knew provided convenient copy, and there were many whom he chose to present falsely for fictional ends besides Jessie Chambers in *Sons and Lovers*, the Lucases in 'England, My England', and Violet Monk and Cecily Lambert in 'The Fox'. This proclivity suggests not only a wilful meanness but a creative shortcoming. Only a spiteful anti-bourgeois humour can explain the naming of his famed *déclassée* heroine after Constance Chatterley (daughter of the secretary and estate agent for Barber, Walker & Co), who lived at The Hollies, Eastwood, and travelled daily to school in Nottingham on the same train as Lawrence. The naming of the hero in *Mr Noon* had a similar origin (p. 249). Personal pique was undoubtedly a factor in the presentation of Will Brangwen in *The Rainbow* and *Women in Love*. Lawrence's awareness of the victim–victimizer complex (an important feature of *The Plumed Serpent*) grew from the reactions of his own passional self.

For Lawrence 'humility' was a cant word (P.573); his lack of that virtue is nowhere more apparent than in his attitude to science. Ridiculing astronomy, he states that his habit was to test beliefs on his body and 'intuitional consciousness'; 'when I get a response there, then I accept'. The mind can assert anything, he claimed; scientists were 'cocksure', 'too egoistic and ranting to be *intuitively, instinctively* sure' (P.575). In creating his own cosmography and physio-psychology, it never occurred to him that he was guilty of failings he attributed to the scientists. Starting with intuitions, he developed his own views through symbolical association, a kind of poetic logic without which much in his theorizing and fiction would be dull. One of the conclusions reached by this 'solar plexus' method of affirmation (HL.p.xv) is that marriage is no marriage unless, in addition to being 'basically and permanently phallic', it is 'linked up with the sun and the earth, the moon and the fixed stars and the planets, in the rhythm of days, in the rhythm of months, in the rhythm of quarters, of years, of decades and of centuries' (P2.505).

Lawrence's main criticism of modern industrial civilization is that it stunts individuality. He saw the educational need for more emphasis on practical skills, and the development of tactile sensitivity in art and crafts. He felt that America teemed with mechanical inventions because nobody 'ever wants to *do* anything' (*St.Am.*iii). At the end of his life he found much to admire in a statement by Eric Gill on working voluntarily in one's spare time: 'happily doing one's best at the job in hand, and being livingly absorbed in . . . the creative spirit, which is God' (P.395).

The deadening effect of industry and automation is seen not only in people's lives but in their environment. 'The real tragedy of England', Lawrence wrote, 'is the tragedy of ugliness. The country is so lovely: the man-made England is so vile' (P.137). His anti-Galilean, anti-intellectual campaign may already appear overdone and outdated. It implies a desire for spontaneous living, which modern civilization seems to stifle, both in work and leisure. Ugliness of surroundings reflects a diminished life-force; its effect on Lawrence is graphically expressed in *Lady Chatterley's Lover* (xi) and contrasted with the Etruscan love of life (xix). Ultimately the heroine of *The Plumed Serpent* is convinced that 'the clue to all living and to all moving-on into new living', the 'quick of the whole', lies in 'the vivid blood-relation between man and woman' (xxv). Heaven lies about us, not in infancy but 'in the consummation of manhood, if we are men' (P.685). The positive force of Lawrence's gospel depends precariously upon this qualifying premise. Regeneration requires human wholeness or integrity, 'like a whole fruit, body and mind and spirit, without split'. Man is not the master of his fate; he must respond to the unknown, the Holy Ghost (P.696–8). 'The only thing that ever avails is the living adventurous spark in the souls of men', and this Lawrence had to an amazing degree. It is communicated in much of his writing, and is the source of his moral and imaginative vigour. He fought, as he implies at the end of *Assorted Articles*, for 'a new conception of life and God'. 'But you have to fight even to plant seed. To plant seed you've got to kill a great deal of weeds and break much ground.'

It must be admitted that sex was an obsession with Lawrence, and that some of his egocentric beliefs, especially the cosmological, were absurd. Yet he had an exceptional awareness of the 'ghoulish' or life-reductive influences affecting both the individual and the community in western civilization. 'Fata volentem ducunt, nolentem trahunt'; most of us are probably too involved to recognize or accept the validity of his strictures. Few, however, would dispute his merits and distinction as a writer. Lawrence's creative vitality is most evident from 1912 to 1916, but it breaks out continually in his later works, and nowhere more artistically than in some of his shorter stories. Its distinguishing feature is the extension of metaphor to scene and action which communicate attitudes and feelings, life forces and anti-life forces. So Lawrence conveys his criticism and values imaginatively, and the picture may assume symbolical import in retrospect. Examples in the novels have already been given. Pictorial fusion of idea and image is splendidly exemplified in a Gargnano scene (p. 258). The wood and bluebell question (pp. 145–6) illustrates it in embryonic form; the garden scene which follows shows it fully operative on a minor scale. Metaphorical action is crucial to 'St Mawr' and 'The Captain's Doll'; with ampler reference to background, it becomes the major element in 'The Princess' and 'The Woman Who Rode Away'. In 'The Rocking-Horse Winner' it is virtually the story itself. Other writers have employed this technique, but none more strikingly or effectively.

Appendixes

THE MOON AND THE ROSE

The heroine of 'The Ladybird' is adored. She sits in front of her mirror, regarding the face that has appeared in numerous society magazines; and one recalls the Lady of Shalott or Lady Crystabel type of love which Lawrence condemns in his first two novels. Count Dionys describes her eyes as 'jewels of stone', her beauty as a 'whited sepulchre' or 'white plucked lily' (that is, 'half-dead', as stated in the two pages of the manuscript that have been inadvertently omitted. See *The Review of English Studies*, 1973, pp. 191–2), and her 'white love' as 'moonshine, harmful, the reverse of love'. Lettie in *The White Peacock* is false to her natural self and George Saxton; she marries for socio-cultural reasons, and appears white by moonlight at the climax of her triumph and pavonian splendour. In three poems (p. 96) a white moon is the symbol of spiritual, passionless love with reference to Jessie Chambers, 'the first white love' of Lawrence's youth. Comparison of 'And Jude the Obscure and his Beloved' (CP.888–9) with 'Passing Visit to Helen' shows that Lawrence regarded Helen Corke as a Sue Bridehead (mentally an Aphrodite-worshipper, physically moonlit and cold, P.502, 505). 'Coldness in Love', imagined as Helen's recollection, is a dramatic monologue in which she appears 'cold, like the shell of the moon'. In *The Trespasser* (based on her diary of a holiday with the violin-teacher whose love for her evoked only a sympathetic response) the predominant colour in her presentation is white, and she is associated with the moon (*T*.i, ii). Siegmund sees sympathy in 'the silver of tears among the moonlit ivory of her face', and catches sight of the sea in 'white transport' beneath the moon. When their holiday nears its end, he watches the rising moon spill its liquor in ruddy splashes on the waves; thinking of the life he has spilled, he looks at Helena, and finds her face as 'white and shining as the empty moon' (*T*.v, xvi).

The implied distinction between the sun as a source of human vitality and the moon as a dead satellite is taken up incidentally in 'Introduction to Pictures' (*P*.768–70). The mental consciousness reflects the spontaneous self, 'the great primary consciousness of the old Adam', as the moon reflects the sun. In conflict with this natural self, consciousness makes one a 'pale Galilean *simulacrum*', and love becomes 'a dead shell of an idea'. Self-consciousness in opposition to the spontaneous self is paralleled in Lawrence's cosmology, the moon counteracting the gravitational influence of the sun to create, as it were, 'the pole' of our 'terrestrial *volition*' (*Fan*.xiii, xiv). Lawrence's moon can therefore imply not only coldness and restraint but also will and self-assertion.

Frequently he associates the 'great primary consciousness', or blood-consciousness, with darkness. When Miriam sacrifices herself to him, Paul says he likes the darkness and wishes it were 'thicker – good, thick darkness'. For this he seeks Clara Dawes; his resolution to renounce Miriam coincides with the sinking of the moon behind a black sycamore as darkness gathers (*SL*.xi; cf. xiii). Neither love succeeds, in consequence of Paul's spiritual bondage to his mother. (For the white moonlight and lilies setting of its prenatal inception, see p. 142.)

The moon symbol has two values. It is a benign power uniting darkness and light in ecstasy of body and soul ('the yielding up of the senses and the possession of the unknown, through the senses, which happens under a superb moon', p. 258; cf. the poem 'Reminder'). Such ecstasy is spontaneous and unwilled. It is that of Anna in the harvest scene (*R*.iv), responding to the unconscious; she feels her bosom 'heaving and panting with moonlight' which makes her 'drift and ebb like a wave'. The moon-link may have been suggested by Greiffenhagen's 'An Idyll'.

The moon is malign in association with the will, whether it opposes natural love from coldness or for ideal reasons, or in conscious pursuit of sexual gratification. With the latter connotation, Lawrence associates it with Aphrodite, white cold fire, sea phosphorescence, the cat, and electric sensation (*TI*. 'The Lemon Gardens'). Such imagery is applied to Will Brangwen from the first (*R*.iv). He deliberately breaks the moonlight harvesting rhythm; his will drums persistently, and conscious desire makes him harder and colder in his resolve to marry Anna. It is as if his soul has turned into hard crystal. In stating that Anna accepts him 'out of her unconsciousness', Lawrence implies her 'possession of the unknown, through the senses'. Will is victimized and degraded by mental sex, and Anna sinks to his level. Their marriage becomes 'a sensuality violent and extreme as death'.

The adolescent love of Ursula and Skrebensky is willed. She responds to the moon, but wishes to be alone. He persists; she remains 'hard as salt, and deadly' until she destroys him in a kiss 'cold as the moon and burning as a fierce salt' (*R*.xi). When he returns from Africa, their love revives, and they are 'one dark fecundity'. Eventually she tires of his 'fixity', his will; he no longer leads her into 'the unknown; there is no 'reverence of love' between them. By the sea, the salt passion of which had roused an urge for new life and fulfilment in her (cf. P2.403), she knows he is not fit for her. Suddenly, in glaring white moonlight, she seizes him as if she has 'the strength of destruction', and entices him with a harpy's kiss. Their passion is completely destructive, and they become like 'two dead people' who dare not recognize one another (xv). All spontaneous love for Skrebensky has come to an end; there is now, in Lawrence's words, 'no moon' for Ursula, 'no sea'.

The moon image in *Women in Love* has different implications. Birkin rejects Hermione because her enthusiasm for passion and 'animal instincts' is 'the worst and last form of intellectualism'. She wants to enjoy them consciously; it is the 'Lady of Shalott business' (iii). He believes in the 'singling away into purity and clear being' through sexual passion, the 'manly being taken into the being of the man', the womanly into the woman, and 'the admixture of sex' being surpassed, 'leaving two single beings constellated together like two stars' (xvi). Though her idea of love is still too possessive and conventional, Ursula yearns for 'pure love'. As she approaches the mill-pond, the moon seems to mock her with its 'white and deathly smile', but she wants 'another night, not this moon-brilliant hardness'. For Birkin its reflection in the pond (xix) symbolizes the accursed Cybele, once identified with the Magna Mater. Woman's desire to be dominant, 'the Great Mother of everything', had infuriated him during his illness; he wants Ursula to drop her 'assertive *will*'. He casts stones to destroy the white reflection; white fragmentation in the scattered water assumes hostile forms such as cuttle-fish and fire, which battles with the dark waves that keep streaming in. Eventually the 'white-burning centre' of the moon vanishes from the water, and only darkened confusion is left, but flakes of scattered light appear like rose petals, and gradually the reflected moon re-forms like a ragged rose, trying to be 'whole and composed, at peace'. Both the rose and the darkness point to ultimate fulfilment in marriage; the heart of the developing rose contrasts with the dead husks of flowers that Birkin had thrown on the water, saying 'There wouldn't have to be any truth, if there weren't any lies'.

Soon after completing *Women in Love*, Lawrence clarified the rose image in his essay 'Love'. Stressing the spiritual as well as the physical, he states that sensual passion is 'the only fire that will purify us into singleness'. The rose is a state of transcendence when lovers achieve 'perfect singleness', and are transported into 'one surpassing heaven' of 'pure communion' and equilibrium (P.153–5). 'Flesh and blood and bone, and mind and soul and spirit' are 'one rose of unison' in the timelessness of pure being (P.680). This sensual-transcendental theory informs the poem 'I am Like a Rose', which Lawrence wrote early in his married life. In 'Rose of All the World' his ideas are tentative. The two-in-one relationship is implied; the question (in the rose or its seed, the 'sharp begetting, or the child begot') is whether love is enough in itself or whether it exists to give purpose to life. The 'rose of the world' image in 'Love' relates to the preservation of individuality in 'brotherly love' (P.155–6).

The last of a succession of images on the same subject, the rose is an emblem of a more fully defined consummation than the 'superb moon' or the 'superb bridge' of *Twilight in Italy*. Each of these represents the Holy Ghost proceeding from Lawrence's Father and Son, the senses and spirit, in unison. The crown which is 'the *raison d'être*' of the lion and the unicorn has the same significance, and at one point (P2.373) merges into the rainbow, 'the iridescence which is darkness at once and light'. From this, and Birkin's reflections on starry singleness in marriage, it can be assumed that the hope symbolized in the key image at the end of *The Rainbow* implies the emergence of a spiritual life of the senses after a 'flood' of sexuality and corruption. It portends Lawrence's Resurrection on earth, when men become 'perfect in body and spirit, whole and glad in the flesh' (end of *R*.x), a subject he returns to most explicitly in 'The Man Who Died'.

PEOPLE AND PLACES IN THE NOVELS

Names were often taken from families and places Lawrence knew, especially in the Eastwood area, e.g. Bricknell, Constance Chatterley, Annable's Gorse near Watnall colliery, and Leivers' Hill to the north.

Resemblances between actual people and the fictional characters can easily be exaggerated; it is difficult to see, for example, what important bearing Murry and Katherine Mansfield could have had on Gerald Crich and Gudrun Brangwen. The – sign implies some degree of derivation.

Other identifications have been made incidentally in the chapter on the shorter stories.

THE WHITE PEACOCK.   *Some of the Chambers family, the parents, Alan (George Saxton), and Jessie (Emily) have been transferred to Felley (Strelley) Mill, with the horse Flower and the white bull-terrier Trip. Mrs Lawrence and D. H. Lawrence have been elevated to genteel estate, their home (Woodside) being imagined on the High Park Wood side of Moorgreen Reservoir (Nethermere); the suggested resemblance between Ada Lawrence and Lettie is improbable in most respects. 'Beardsall' was Mrs Lawrence's maiden name; 'Saxton', the name of Lawrence's Aunt Emma (p. 7). Alice Gall is Alice Hall 'produced faithfully from life' (30.vii.08); after reading the novel, her husband threatened legal action.*

The Abbey: *Beauvale Priory*. Cossethay: *Cossall*. Eberwich: *Eastwood* (*the schools, the Ram Inn; see map, p. 3, for* 'The Hollies'). Greymede: *Greasley* (*including Moorgreen*). The Hall: *Annesley Hall*. Highclose: *Lamb Close*. Newerton: *Newthorpe*. Old Brayford: *West Bridgford*. Selsby: *Underwood*. Westwold: *Westwood*.
Basford, Bingham, Cinderhill, Colwick, Nottingham (*the Spread Eagle, Theatre Royal, Victoria Hotel*), *Papplewick, Watnall*.

THE TRESPASSER.   Allport – *R. H. Aylwin* (*Croydon teacher*). Cecil Byrne – *D. H. Lawrence*. Holiday – *E. Humphreys* (*Croydon teacher*). Louisa – *Agnes Mason* (*Croydon teacher*). Siegmund MacNair – *H. B. MacCartney.* MacWhirter – *A. W. McLeod* (*Croydon teacher*). Olive – *Violet Babbage* (*Croydon teacher*). Helena Verden – *Helen Corke.*

All places are actual.

SONS AND LOVERS. Morels – *Lawrences:* William – *William Ernest;* Annie – *Ada;* Paul – *David* (D.H.). Leivers – *Chambers:* Agatha – *May;* Edgar – *Alan;* Maurice – *Hubert;* Miriam – *Jessie.* Clara Dawes – *Mrs Dax* (?). Newton – *George Neville.* Louisa L. D. Western – *Gypsy Dennis.* Beatrice Wyld – *Alice Hall.*

Beggarlee, Bretty: *Brinsley* (*colliery*). Bestwood: *Eastwood* (the Bottoms: *the Breach; Greenhill Lane; The Miners' Arms;* The Moon and Stars, the Three Spots: *the Three Tuns; the Nelson; the New Inn* (*Brinsley*); *the Palmerston Arms; the Prince of Wales* (*Brinsley*); Scargill Street: *Walker Street*). Broughton: *Sutton Bonington* (*10 m. SSW of Nottingham*). Herod's Farm: *Coneygrey Farm.* Keston: *Kimberley.* Minton: *Moorgreen* (*colliery*). Minton Church: *Greasley Church, by Castle Farm.* Nether Green: *Moorgreen.* Nethermere: *Moorgreen Reservoir.* Nuttall: *Watnall.* Pentrich Hill: *Alma Hill.* Selby: *Underwood.* Sethley Bridge, Shepstone: *Langley Mill.* Spinney Park: *High* (*Wood*) *Park* (*colliery*). Strelley Mill: *Felley Mill.* Tinder Hill: *Cinderhill.* Willey Farm: *Haggs Farm.* Woodlinton: *Woodside* (*Cotmanhay*)?

Alfreton, Ambergate, Annesley, Blackpool, Bulwell, Clifton, Clifton Grove, Colwick, Crich, Crossleigh Bank(s) Farm, Daybrook, Derby, Heanor, the Hemlock Stone (*New Stapleford*), *Hucknall Torkard, Ilkeston, Lambley, Lincoln, Mablethorpe, Mapperley Plains, Marlpool, Nottingham* (Jordan & Co: *J. H. Haywood's; Bluebell Hill; Sneinton*), *Reckoning House Farm, Ripley, Sheffield, Skegness, Southwell, Sutton* (*-on-Sea*), *Theddlethorpe, Whatstandwell, Wilford, Wingfield Manor.*

THE RAINBOW. Ursula Brangwen – *Louisa Burrows, Frieda Lawrence* (*29.i.14*). Will Brangwen – *Alfred Burrows of Church Cottage, Cossall; church organist and teacher of woodcarving; father of Louisa.* Mr Harby – *based probably on a teacher Lawrence or one of his friends*

297

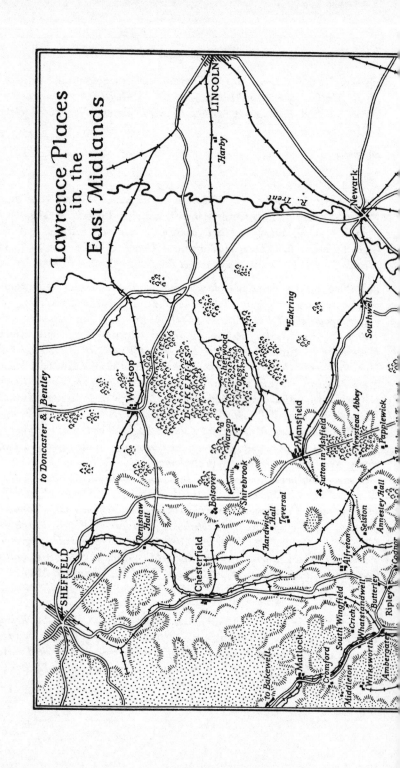

Lawrence Places
in the
East Midlands

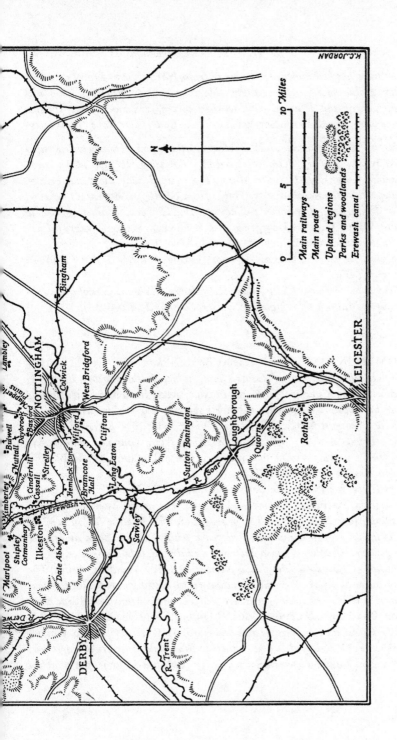

K.C.JORDAN

N

0   5   10 Miles

Main railways
Main roads
Upland regions
Parks and woodlands
Erewash canal

LEICESTER

Birtgham

NOTTINGHAM

Colwick

West Bridgford

Lambley

Mapperley Plains

Basford

Bulwell

Nuttall Daybrook

Kimberley

Cinderhill

Strelley

Hemlock Stone

Wilford

Clifton

Sutton Bonington

Loughborough

Quorn

Rothley

R. Soar

Bramcote Hall

Long Eaton

R. Erewash

Ilkeston

Cossall

Cotmanhay

Shipley

Marlpool

R. Derwent

Dale Abbey

Sawley

R. Trent

DERBY

may have worked under; the name is from Harby (near Lincoln), where Kitty Holderness (p. 24) taught. He is not T.A. Beacroft, who was principal of the Ilkeston pupil-teacher centre, and not of an Ilkeston elementary school. Baron Skrebensky – *Rev. Rudolf von Hube of Greasley.*

Belcote Hall: *Bramcote Hall.* Beldover – *Eastwood, transferred possibly to a region east of Bolsover.* Briswell: *Greasley, though placed near Lincoln.* Cossethay: *Cossall; Marsh Farm stood near the canal bridge, as located in the novel.* Shelly (Hall), *from Strelley.* Wiggiston: *Bentley, near Doncaster; first main colliery sinking (Barber, Walker & Co) in 1906.* Willey Green: *Moorgreen* (see Beldover). Willey Water: *Moorgreen Reservoir* (see Beldover). *For the names* 'Beldover', 'Lethley', and 'Hainor', *see p. 159*; Hainor: *Heanor;* Lethley (cf. *SL.* Sethley Bridge): *Langley Mill.*

Ambergate, Arundel Castle, Bakewell, Derby, Ilkeston, Lincoln, Loughborough, Matlock, Nottingham, Sawley, Southwell, Wirksworth.

WOMEN IN LOVE.   Rupert Birkin – *Lawrence.* Gerald Crich – *Thomas Philip Barber of Lamb Close; he accidentally killed a brother, and his young sister was drowned in Moorgreen Reservoir, after falling from her father's houseboat; a doctor's son was drowned in his attempt to save her (August 1892), Middleton Murry.* Gudrun – *Katherine Mansfield, Frieda's sister Johanna (the name from Gutrine, who excites Siegfried's passion with a love-potion in* Götterdämmerung). Halliday – *Philip Heseltine (13.i.16, 15.ii.16, 10.xi.21).* Loerke – *Loki, a Norse god of evil; see 9.x.16 (on Gertler's 'The Merry-Go-Round') and 5.xii.16.* Sir Joshua Mattheson – *Bertrand Russell.* Hermione Roddice – *Lady Ottoline Morrell (23.iv.15); her provoked violence against Birkin is based on Frieda's sudden assault on Lawrence with a dinner plate at Higher Tregerthen.* Ursula – *Louisa Burrows initially, Frieda Lawrence.*

Beldover – *Eastwood (the Lord Nelson); see* The Rainbow *above. The clock-tower is at Ripley; the tramline from Nottingham to Ripley was opened in 1914. The colliery railway bridge is on the Mansfield Road, Eastwood.* Breadalby – *Willesley Castle, Cromford, above the Derwent (cf. 20.ii. 17, 17.iv.25); the company is based on some of the Garsington circle.* Pompadour Café: *Café Royal; when Katherine Mansfield heard two people who had known Lawrence jeering at his newly published* Amores, *she snatched*

the book from them and walked out of the café with it. Selby: *Underwood.*
Shortlands, Highclose (xvii; cf. *WP*): *Lamb Close.* Willey Green:
Moorgreen and Greasley. Willey Water: *Moorgreen Reservoir* (the
mill-farm: *Felley Mill*). Winthorpe: *Newthorpe.* Whatmore: *Watnall*
(King's Head: *Queen's Head*).
Southwell (Minster, Saracen's Head).

THE LOST GIRL.   Miss Frost – *Miss Wright, who supervised
Cullen's household, taught Lawrence's sisters music, and sometimes helped
him with his French (when he was a pupil at Nottingham High School).*
Alvina Houghton -- *Florence Cullen; she became a nurse, and played the
piano at her father's cinema in Langley Mill.* James Houghton – *George
Henry Cullen of London House, Eastwood.* Mr May – *Maurice Magnus
(pp. 42–4), named after a neighbour of the Lawrences (p. 6).* Pancrazio –
Orazio Cervi (p. 42). Miss Pinnegar – *Miss Pidsley, chief assistant in
London House.*

Bagthorpe: *New Eastwood, near Newthorpe Station; Lawrence named the
brickfield 'Klondyke' after one which had existed below Walker Street,
Eastwood.* Hathersedge: *Heanor.* Knarborough: *Nottingham (knar =
knot in wood).* Lumley: *Langley Mill.* Pescocalascio: *Picinisco (16.xii.19).*
Rapton: *Ripley.* Selverhay: *Selston (?). Bulwell Station is deliberately
misleading.* Woodhouse: *Eastwood (Congregational Chapel;* Manchester
House: *London House; Miners' Arms;* Moon and Stars: *Sun Inn,*
mentioned (x); *Throttle-Ha'penny; Wellington Street).*
*Alfreton, Doncaster, Lancaster, Leeds, London (Battersea, Islington),
Mansfield, Scarborough, Sheffield.*

AARON'S ROD.   James Argyle – *Norman Douglas.* Jim Bricknell – *Capt. J. R. White, named after the Brentnalls of Cocker House
(see below).* Clariss Browning – *Brigit Patmore.* Algy Constable – *Reggie
Turner.* Julia Cunningham – *Hilda Aldington (p. 39).* Robert Cunningham – *Richard Aldington.* Josephine Ford – *Dorothy Yorke.* Sir William
and Lady Franks – *Sir William and Lady Becker (18.xi.19).* Lady
Artemis Hooper – *Lady Diana Cooper.* Rawdon Lilly and his wife
Tanny – *D. H. Lawrence and Frieda; Lawrence nursed Middleton*

Murry at Greatham in February 1915 as Lilly did Aaron. Cyril Scott – *Cecil Gray.* Dr Sherardy – *Dr Russell, a Parsee Eastwood doctor.* Aaron Sisson – *D. H. Lawrence, also (as flautist) Thomas Cooper (p. 12).* Struthers – *Augustus John.*

Beldover: *Eastwood (Aaron's house: the Lawrences' in Lynncroft; Bestwood Colliery: Moorgreen; Shottle House: Cocker House at the end of Cockerhouse Road;* the Royal Oak: *the Thorn Tree, Mansfield Road).* Hampshire cottage: *at Hermitage, Berkshire, where the 'punch in the wind' took place during White's visit.*
London (Covent Garden), Florence, Milan, Novara (Lawrence stayed with the Beckers in Turin).

KANGAROO.   The American wife – *Hilda Doolittle, wife of Richard Aldington.* John Thomas Buryan – *W. H. Hocking (p. 39).* Ben Cooley ('Kangaroo') – *Sir John Monash (Australian), S. S. Koteliansky (Lawrence denied this), Dr Eder (according to Frieda).* Monsell – *Robert Mountsier (Lawrence's American literary agent).* Mrs Redburn – *Dollie Radford.* James Sharpe – *Cecil Gray.* Richard Lovat Somers and his wife Harriet – *Lawrence and Frieda.* Willie Struthers – *William Hopkin (appearance of James Holman, a Labour Party leader in Australia).*

Mullumbimby: *Thirroul. Sydney.* Wolloona: *Wollongong. (England) Bodmin, Derby,* cottage in Derbyshire: *Mountain Cottage (p. 40),* cottage in Oxfordshire: *at Hermitage (Berkshire),* Trevatham Cottage: *at Higher Tregerthen (p. 37).*

THE PLUMED SERPENT.   *Suggestions for* Ramon *and* Cipriano *came no doubt from Mexican leaders, but pre-eminently they express Lawrence's views in terms of Mexican mythology.* Juana – *Isabel, the Lawrences' domestic servant at Chapala.* Kate Leslie – *D. H. Lawrence, sometimes Frieda.* Mrs Norris – *Mrs Zelia Nuttall (p. 195).* Owen Rhys – *Witter Bynner.* Bud Villiers – *Willard Johnson.*

Ixtlahuacán: *Ocotlán. Mexico City* (Hotel San Remo: *Hotel Monte Carlo, where the Lawrences stayed).* Orilla: *El Fuerte.* Sayula: *Chapala; Bynner identifies* Jamiltepec *with the villa El Manglar at Chapala.*

LADY CHATTERLEY'S LOVER. Constance Chatterley (*see p. 289*). Duncan Forbes – *Duncan Grant* (*27.i.15; cf. P.565*), *named after an Eastwood doctor, son-in-law of Thomas Barber of Lamb Close.*

From all three versions it is clear that Wragby Hall *is north of Chesterfield and not far from Sheffield. Its general description and some important detail (third floor in central portion of the house, park, adjacent bridge, colliery) suggest Renishaw Hall, home of the Sitwells whose parents Lawrence met in Italy; see p. 56. Lawrence does his best to mystify. He mentions Chesterfield, but* Uthwaite *with its twisted spire is Chesterfield. Bolsover is mentioned. The first version shows that* Chadwick Hall *and* Warsop Castle *are Hardwick Hall and Bolsover Castle.* Te(v)ershall *is no particular place; the name comes from Teversal, west of Mansfield. Lawrence includes inns (the* Miners' Arms, *the* Nelson, *the* Sun, *the* Three Tuns, *the* Wellington) *and the Congregational Chapel from Eastwood, and refers to* Engine Row *and* High Park (*from Engine Lane and High Park colliery near Eastwood*). *Other places which serve to create topographical confusion are Fritchley near Crich (see p. 13) and Shipley, north of Ilkeston.* Old Heanor *was suggested by Heanor near Eastwood. Mansfield, Sheffield, etc. London, Paris, Venice.*

SELECT BIBLIOGRAPHY

Works

No standard texts are available. All the works are published by Heinemann. Much of the fiction is published in American paperbacks; the Penguin editions provide the fiction and other major works, with selections from the poems, plays, letters, and more miscellaneous writings. *Phoenix* and *Phoenix II* are two large collections of miscellaneous prose (Heinemann).

Letters

J. T. Boulton (ed.), *Lawrence in Love*, Nottingham, 1968; Carbondale, Ill., 1969. Letters to Louisa Burrows.

Aldous Huxley (ed.), *The Letters of D. H. Lawrence*, London, 1932.

H. T. Moore (ed.), *The Collected Letters of D. H. Lawrence* (2 vols.), London and New York, 1962. With notes on who's who in the letters, and Aldous Huxley's introduction to his selection.

The complete collection of Lawrence's letters, in seven volumes under the general editorship of Professor J. T. Boulton, is due for publication from 1978 onwards by the Cambridge University Press.

Bibliography

A. E. Dyson (ed.), *The English Novel: Select Bibliographical Guides*, Oxford, 1974. A descriptive chapter with classified lists by Mark Spilka.

Warren Roberts, *A Bibliography of D. H. Lawrence*, London, 1963. The standard work for Lawrence's works, articles, translations, etc.

Biography

H. T. Moore, *The Priest of Love*, London, 1974. A revision of *The Intelligent Heart*.

Edward Nehls, *D. H. Lawrence, A Composite Biography* (3 vols: 1885–1919, 1919–25, 1925–30), Madison, Wis., 1957, 1958, 1959. A kaleidoscopic narrative of great interest from memoirs, letters, etc., with notes.

Ancillary Works:

Dorothy Brett, *Lawrence and Brett, A Friendship*, Philadelphia, 1933.

Jessie Chambers (pseudonym E.T., from the title of her novel *Eunice Temple*, which she destroyed), *D. H. Lawrence, A Personal Record*, 2nd edition, ed. J. D. Chambers, London and New York, 1965. Important testimony.

Helen Corke, *In Our Infancy*, Cambridge, 1975. Includes the diary Lawrence used for *The Trespasser*.

Ada Lawrence and G. Stuart Gelder, *Early Life of D. H. Lawrence*, London, 1932. Ada's memoir is valuable.

Frieda Lawrence, *Not I, But the Wind*, New York, 1934; London, 1935. Some chronological inaccuracies.

Knud Merrild, *With Lawrence in New Mexico*, London, 1964. First published as *A Poet and Two Painters*, London, 1938.

Appendixes

General

H. T. Moore (ed.), *A. D. H. Lawrence Miscellany*, Carbondale, Ill., 1959; London, 1961.

Stephen Spender (ed.), *D. H. Lawrence: Novelist, Poet, Prophet*, London, 1973.

Critical Studies

The list is limited in the interests of the reader, but inclusions have been made to cover all the major areas of Lawrence's work. More specialized are L. D. Clark, *Dark Night of the Body*, Austin, Tex., 1964, which gives the Mexican background of *The Plumed Serpent*, and E. W. Tedlock (ed.), *D. H. Lawrence and 'Sons and Lovers'*, New York, 1965; London, 1966.

Principal Recommendations:

David Cavitch, *D. H. Lawrence and the New World*, New York, 1969.

H. M. Daleski, *The Forked Flame*, London and Evanston, Ill., 1965.

Sandra M. Gilbert, *Acts of Attention, The Poems of D. H. Lawrence*, Ithaca and London, 1972.

David J. Gordon, *D. H. Lawrence as a Literary Critic*, New Haven and London, 1966.

Graham Hough, *The Dark Sun*, London, 1956; New York, 1957.

F. R. Leavis, *D. H. Lawrence: Novelist*, London, 1955; New York, 1956.

Julian Moynahan, *The Deed of Life. The Novels and Tales of D. H. Lawrence*, Princeton and Oxford, 1963.

Keith Sagar, *The Art of D. H. Lawrence*, Cambridge, 1966.

Sylvia Sklar, *The Plays of D. H. Lawrence*, New York and London, 1975.

Mark Spilka, *The Love Ethic of D. H. Lawrence*, Bloomington, Ind., 1955; London, 1957.

E. W. Tedlock, *D. H. Lawrence, Artist and Rebel*, Albuquerque, N. Mex., 1963.

Eliseo Vivas, *D. H. Lawrence, The Failure and Triumph of Art*, Evanston, Ill., 1960; London, 1961.

LAWRENCE FILMS

Relevant information is not readily available, and the following notes provide only a fragmentary record.

Lawrence repeatedly emphasized the unreality of popular films, and would have been horrified at the 'sexploitation' which characterizes the filming of some of his works (cf. P.171). Much of *The Literature/Film Quarterly*, January 1973, Salisbury State College, Maryland, is devoted to Lawrence's views on the subject and to critical articles on films of three of his novels and three of his shorter stories. They are Anthony Pelissier's *The Rocking-Horse Winner* (1949), Marc Allégret's *L'Amant de Lady Chatterley* (1955), *Sons and Lovers* (adapted by Jerry Wald and directed by Jack Cardiff, 1960), Mark Rydell's *The Fox* (1968), *Women in Love* (adapted by Larry Kramer and directed by Ken Russell), and Christopher Miles's *The Virgin and the Gypsy* (1970). The last two are in colour. *L'Amant de Lady Chatterley* is a simplified and emasculated version of the main story; *Women in Love* is more true to Lawrence's ideas than to the novel itself; *Sons and Lovers*, though much contracted, is more faithful to the original.

Subsequent listings of these six films give:

The Rocking-Horse Winner   Two Cities Films   1949
Lady Chatterley's Lover   Columbia   1956
Sons and Lovers   Twentieth Century Fox   1960
The Fox   Warner   1968
Women in Love   United Artists   1969
The Virgin and the Gypsy   London Screenplays   1971

Six productions of Lawrence stories, all by Granada, were broadcast on the ITV network in 1967: *Strike-Pay*, *Blue Moccasins*, *Mother and Daughter* (6, 13, 20 June); *The Prussian Officer*, *The Thorn in the Flesh*, and *None of That* (16, 23, 30 October). On 10 August 1977 *The Rocking-Horse Winner* (adapted by Julian Bond and directed by Peter Medak for Harlech Television) was produced on the same channels.

Three films on Lawrence have been traced in BBC programmes:
11.7.60   Production by John Morgan. No details available.
5.1.64   'Death of My Mother', by David Jones.
8.7.69   'D. H. Lawrence in Taos', by Peter Davis. This documentary was filmed at Taos, and describes the impact Lawrence and his circle made there from 1922 to 1925.

Index

Index

Index

Flecker, James Elroy 114
Florence 42, 44, 45, 55, 56, 58, 60, 110, 186, 188
Fontana Vecchia (Sicily) 43, 44, 108, 255
Ford, Ford Madox *see* Hueffer
Forster, E. M. 34–5, 205, 286
Franklin, Benjamin 278
Frazer, Sir James 203
Freud, Sigmund 26, 29, 81, 82, 88, 89

Galsworthy, John 17, 23, 152, 266, 282–3
Gargnano 29–30, 66, 67, 257, 258, 271
Garnett, Constance 31, 32
Garnett, David 28–9, 35
Garnett, Edward 24, 25, 27, 30, 31, 33, 140, 141, 149, 227, 266
Garsington Manor 34, 36
Gertler, Mark 33, 51, 62, 300
Gibson, W. W. 32
Gide, André 282
Gill, Eric 290
Goldring, Douglas 273
Gótzsche, Kai 47–8, 49, 50, 112, 237
Gray, Cecil 39, 40, 302
Greasley 18, 25, 95, 225, 270, 296, 297, 300, 301
Greatham 34, 229, 302
Greiffenhagen, Maurice 24, 30, 128, 293
Gross, Dr Otto 26
Gsteig-bei-Gstaad 58–9, 250
Guadalajara 49, 50

Haggs Farm 10, 11, 14, 18, 56, 95, 218, 225, 297
Hall, Alice 12, 18, 19, 296, 297
Hampstead 27, 36, 39
Hardy, Thomas 17, 129, 130, 149,

153, 162, 194, 229, 261, 279, 280, 281; Sue Bridehead 98, 292; *The Woodlanders* 40, 276 *see also* Study of Thomas Hardy (pp. 313–14)
Hawk, Rachel 53
Hawthorne, Nathaniel 89, 278–9
Haywood, J. H. 11, 297
Hermitage 39, 40, 41, 42, 233, 302
Heseltine, Philip 37, 39, 45, 300
Hobson, Harold 29, 30
Hocking, W. H. 39, 40, 302
Holderness, George 12, 24
Holt, Agnes 20
Hopkin, Sallie 18, 21, 28, 30, 31, 41, 149, 249
Hopkin, William x, 18, 21, 22, 31, 41, 56, 249, 272n., 302
Hube, the Rev. Rodolph von 218n., 225, 270, 300
Hueffer, Ford Madox 20, 219, 266
Huxley, Aldous and his wife Maria 56, 58, 60, 63, 210, 303; *Point Counter Point* 59, 115, 282
Huxley, Julian and his wife Juliette 58

Ibsen, Henrik 17, 67, 258, 266
Icking 27, 28
Ilkeston 12, 13, 14, 249, 297, 300
Irschenhausen 30, 31, 57

Jaffe, Dr Else 26, 30, 49, 57, 62, 177
Jane Eyre 14, 128, 138
Jennings, Blanche 18, 20, 24
John, Augustus 302
Johnson, Willard 49, 51, 195, 273, 302
Jones, J. W. 20, 24
Joyce, James 282
Juta, Jan 44, 45, 257

309

Index

LAWRENCE, DAVID HERBERT

General:

his 'aristocracy' 67, 71, 75, 76, 78, 91, 117–18, 120, 235, 239, 274, 276, 280, 288
on education 77–80, 85–6, 91–2
Egypt 72, 82, 153, 174, 176, 235
England e.g. 56, 134, 151, 166, 174–5, 177, 203–4, 211–12, 213, 229, 239–40, 253–4, 290
films 118, 179, 188, 306
his 'great religion' 65–71, 72–5, 76–7, 82, 90–2, 105–6, 110–11, 153–4, 161, 191–2, 199–200, 251–2, 263, 264–5, 295
individuality 76, 79, 80–1, 187, 192, 196, 278, 288–9, 290–1
mechanization 67, 69, 115–16, 120, 121–2, 123, 157, 170–1, 197–8, 208–9, 211–12, 214, 256, 283, 290
money 65, 69, 91, 116, 117, 209, 288
the moon 87–8, 92, 122, 124–5, 137, 154, 168–9, 258, 292–5
his paintings 56–61 passim
his prose 75, 76, 84, 115, 151, 172, 176, 183, 233, 246, 264, 274–5, 286–7
reading in his early years 14–15, 16, 17, 23
scenic metaphor e.g. 133–4, 137–8, 142, 145–6, 154, 156–7, 157–8, 168–9, 222–3, 239–40, 247, 258, 286, 291, 293–5
science 81, 87–8, 250, 290
sex-in-the-head 73–4, 79, 82–3, 86–7, 89, 107–8, 168–9, 171, 172, 203, 205, 235, 236–7, 287, 292–4
the sun 81, 87–8, 90–1, 97, 109, 117, 125, 195, 200, 243, 244, 245, 247, 251, 293
tragedy 283
work 69, 80, 118, 178, 290

His Works:

MISCELLANEOUS PROSE

Adolf 6, 42, 228; A Propos of *Lady Chatterley's Lover* 61, 66, 207, 209, 215; *Apocalypse* 61–2, 65, 91–2; Aristocracy 91, 104, 245; *Assorted Articles* 59, 115, 148 ('The State of Funk'), 291; [Autobiographical Fragment] 91, 209, 252–4, 255; Christs in the Tirol 257; The Crown 36, 72–5, 110; Democracy 80–1; Education of the People 41, 77–80; *Etruscan Places* 57, 91, 263–5; *Fantasia of the Unconscious* 44–5, 51, 84–8, 132, 199; Flowering Tuscany 57; The Flying Fish 53, 247, 250–2; Indians and an Englishman 47; Introduction to *Memoirs of a Foreign Legion* 45, 154–6; Introduction to Pictures 293; John Galsworthy 282–3; A Letter from Germany 51, 240; Love 295; Making Love to Music 214; Morality and the Novel 284; *Mornings in Mexico* 53, 262–3; *Movements in European History* 40, 41, 54; *Mr Noon* 43, 249–50; New Mexico 237, 238; The Nightingale 57; The Novel 284; On Coming Home 51; Pan in America 52, 236; Pornography and Obscenity 61; The Proper Study 110, 252; *Psychoanalysis and the Unconscious* 45, 82–4, 200; The Real Thing 92, 117; The Reality of Peace 39, 75–7, 105, 272; Reflections on the Death of a Porcupine 54, 91, 238; Rex 6; *Sea and Sardinia* 260–2; *Studies in Classic American Literature* 40, 49, 81, 89–90, 96, 111, 182, 277–80; Study of

313

Index

Come Sorrow 97; Corot 100; Correspondence in After Years 119; Craving for Spring 105; The Cross 120; Departure 123; Difficult Death 126; Discipline 20, 95; A Doe at Evening 104; Dog-Tired 95; The Drained Cup 101; Dreams Old and Nascent 20, 95, 101–2; Elegy 99, 102; The End 23, 99; End of Another Home Holiday 98–9; Endless Anxiety 99; Everlasting Flowers 99; Evil is Homeless 123; Excursion Train 98; False Democracy and Real 120; Fellow-Men 119; For the Heroes are Dipped in Scarlet 122, 203; Frohnleichnam 103; Full Life 119; Giorno dei Morti 104; Gipsy 99; Gladness of Death 120; Glory of Darkness 61; God is Born 121; The Greeks are Coming! 121; Guelder Roses 109, 131; The Hands of the Betrothed 97; The Houseless Dead 125; Hymn to Priapus 96, 102; I am Like a Rose 104, 295; I Know a Noble Englishman 287; Image-Making Love 119; Impulse 120; In Trouble and Shame 99; Initiation Degrees 120; Intimates 119; Invocation to the Moon 124–5; Kisses in the Train 97; Kissing and Horrid Strife 123; Last Words to Miriam 96; Letter from Town: On a Grey Morning in March 95; Letter from Town: The Almond-Tree 95; Lightning 95; Lilies in the Fire 97; *Look! We Have Come Through!* 38, 102–6; Lotus and Frost 97; Love on the Farm 94–5, 128; *Love Poems and Others* 30; A Love Song 97; Lucifer 125; The Man of Tyre 123; Manifesto 105, 176, 289;

Maximus 122; Meeting Among the Mountains 104; Michael Angelo 100; Middle of the World 121–2; Monologue of a Mother 98; Multitudes 120; Mystery 97; *New Poems* 102, 103; *Nettles* 61, 62, 118–19; New Heaven and Earth 105, 169, 176; Non-Existence 119; On That Day 99; On the March 101; One Woman to All Women 105; Only Man 120, 121; A Pang of Reminiscence 96; *Pansies* 60, 61, 115–18; Passing Visit to Helen 98, 292; Pax 122, 124; Piano 99; Phoenix 124; Rabbit Snared in the Night 110, 168; Red 97; Red Moon-Rise 100; The Red Wolf 113, 274; Release 98; Reminder 96, 99, 293; Renascence 94, 95; Reproach 98; Repulsed 97; Return 97; River Roses 104; Rose of All the World 104, 295; Scent of Irises 96; The Shadow of Death 99; Shadows 124; She Looks Back 103; She Said as Well to Me 104; The Ship of Death 125–126; Sigh No More 95; The Sight of God 119; Silence 124; Snap-Dragon 16, 96–7; A Snowy Day in School 100; So Let me Live 120; Song of a Man Who Has Come Through 68, 104, 105–6; Song of a Man Who is Loved 104; Sorrow 99; Spirits Summoned West 99, 109; A Spiritual Woman 98; Spring Morning 104–5; Submergence 99; Sunday Afternoon in Italy 104; Suspense 99; Tease 97; These Clever Women 98; They Say the Sea is Loveless 123, 265; Troth with the Dead 99; Two Ways of Living and Dying 120; Two Wives 101; Twofold 97;

Alister Ross